# Life, Liberty, and the Pursuit of Money

Lizzie - I was nearby when you first smiled. I was there when you started to play the clapping game which you took very seriously. I expect to be there when you graduate from high school and all the fun times in between. I hope you inherit your mom's athletic ability and that of your grandmother and great-grandmother perhaps mine too (though I was a terrible golfer).

Love your mom and dad as they love you — be friends to all — help others when you can — enjoy life — have fun + hold true to your faith. I will always be watching.

Love forever — Grandpa ( G'Pa )

+

May all who read this book gain in wisdom and knowledge through the inspiration of the Holy Spirit.

David Barrett

Easter: March 27, 2016

# Life, Liberty, and the Pursuit of Money

GOD'S MONEY

---

A Heuristic Thesis on Political Economy and Modernity

*David Barrett*

Copyright © 2015 David Barrett
All rights reserved.

ISBN-13: 9781518752902
ISBN-10: 151875290X
Library of Congress Control Number: 2015917751
**CreateSpace, Subsidiary of Amazon,
North Charleston, South Carolina**

*To Barbara…now and forever…this life and the next…all my love.*

*For an eternity of wonderful memories…my mom and dad, grandparents, brothers, and loving children: David Jr., Sharon, Laura, Tim, and Anne, and their spouses, Tracy, Steve, Russell, Connie and Ollie…and the best grandkids: Parker, Owen, Billy, Alex, Benjamin, Declan, Caitlyn, Andrew, Tucker, and Elizabeth. Endless love and kisses to all.*

*And for so many family, friends, and associates who gave me their love, time, and energy while providing the mentoring and inspiration that allowed me to write this book…cousins, uncles, and close friends… J. & H. Nesbitt, J. & P. Nesbitt, J. & D. Schermerhorn, L. & P. Lessing, D. Lessing, D. & J. Toomey, P. Reavey, W. Hohman, SJ, A. Riehl, R. Emerich, T. & J. McHugh, G. E. Barnett, D. Hornor, J. Fleiss, J. Larkin, D. K. Pfeffer, C. B. McGovern, F. R. Saul, J. Allen, A. Titus, R. Metzner, I. Gelfand, P. Geraghty, J. & W. Delz, J. & R. Anner, and countless others, making the list legion and unforgettable.*

> "And she began: 'All things whate'er they be
> Have order among themselves, and this is form,
> That makes the universe resemble God.'"
> —*The Divine Comedy*, Dante

> "Only fools attempt to predict the future.
> Genius unites the past and the present in wisdom."
> —David Barrett

# Contents

| | | |
|---|---|---|
| | Preface | xi |
| | Introduction: What in the World Is Driving the Money Mania; or, From the Garden of Paradise, How Did We Ever Get Here? | xiii |
| Chapter 1 | The Sad and Sordid History of Money—Interlaced with Brief Moments of Enlightenment | 1 |
| Chapter 2 | The Collapse of Empire | 8 |
| Chapter 3 | From the Dark to the Middle Ages | 13 |
| Chapter 4 | Henry VIII, King of England and Ireland, 1509–1547 | 28 |
| Chapter 5 | Money and Banking | 35 |
| Chapter 6 | Empires in Crisis | 63 |
| Chapter 7 | The Other Side of the Atlantic | 110 |
| Chapter 8 | The Debt Is Paid—A New Nation Begins Its Journey | 141 |
| Chapter 9 | The War of 1812—The Republic Staggers: Will It Survive? | 149 |
| Chapter 10 | The Matter of a Central Bank | 161 |
| Chapter 11 | War: Biddle versus Jackson | 163 |
| Chapter 12 | Manifest Destiny | 170 |
| Chapter 13 | Nineteenth-Century State Banking | 176 |
| Chapter 14 | Lincoln, the War, and Finance | 180 |
| Chapter 15 | Europe—1860 and Beyond | 192 |
| Chapter 16 | Gold and Wealth | 207 |
| Chapter 17 | The Extended Depression | 217 |

| | | |
|---|---|---|
| Chapter 18 | The Twentieth Century | 231 |
| Chapter 19 | The Price of Currency | 240 |
| Chapter 20 | Depression Overwhelms the United States | 247 |
| Chapter 21 | Before the Depression, the Roaring Twenties—A Great Misnomer | 257 |
| Chapter 22 | The Horrible Thirties | 262 |
| Chapter 23 | The Roosevelt Era—A Lifeline Stretching to Modernity | 276 |
| Chapter 24 | A New World | 291 |
| Chapter 25 | A Standard for All Time | 308 |
| Chapter 26 | Pearl Harbor and Beyond | 314 |
| Chapter 27 | Roosevelt to Truman | 328 |
| Chapter 28 | The Critical Year, 1948 | 343 |
| Chapter 29 | The Marshall Plan | 356 |
| Chapter 30 | The Deutsche Mark | 366 |
| Chapter 31 | The Real Rate of Return | 385 |
| Chapter 32 | Andrew Jackson Incarnate, Ronald Reagan (1980–1988) | 411 |
| Chapter 33 | OPEC and China | 419 |
| Chapter 34 | Reform | 428 |
| | Addendum: A View of the Concepts | 439 |
| | Selected Bibliography | 481 |
| | Notes | 485 |
| | Index | 495 |

# Preface

YES, THIS IS A BOOK about money, but not just another rendition. What will the reader gain from reading this thesis? Is it really worth your time?

The lessons of the past few years have sadly taught us more than we ever cared to know or thought we would ever have to know about the money subject. It is hard to imagine that there is more.

Oh, but there is—a lot more. Will it matter to you? After this reading you will be in a far better position to judge.

You already know a great deal about money. After all, you deal with it every day, but the reality is that you and vast numbers of intelligent, knowledgeable people know so little.

In a very real sense, this is understandable. Life keeps us busy. Few of us have time for the extraneous, that is, what we assume to be irrelevant.

That has been the case throughout history. It is the critical reason we are in so much trouble.

All of this can be nicely summed up in one word—*confusion*. Money confusion abounds.

The commercial world and most individuals carry on their financial affairs in a continuing state of confusion—frequently despair, seldom with equanimity, in search of the undefined.

Inevitably this leads us into an abyss, a giant black hole, from which there is no apparent escape. We thrash, we blame, we cry, and finally we face disappointment.

It is all, well, so unfair.

Rest assured, I do not lecture or preach in this essay.

I relate the facts of history intertwined with the money concept. History is the oracle of life. History teaches. It is the fount that advises all. We learn from it. It shows us where the world has been and where it is today and is likely to be tomorrow when addressing life's issues. It relates cause and effect.

The great money chase that modern man is engaged in is both a sickness, or syndrome, and an illusion, a historical illusion at that. The money chase has nothing to do with happiness. The chase itself inevitably destroys. It destroys all.

Decline is the precursor to final destruction. As with any disease, death is not immediate. It takes time, lots of time, perhaps centuries.

Now, to the book.

A far better understanding of the money dynamic for Americans was my intention when I started to write. It is for you to decide whether that has been accomplished.

In any case, I trust you will enjoy reading this work as much as I have enjoyed writing it.

David Barrett

INTRODUCTION:

# What in the World Is Driving the Money Mania; or, From the Garden of Paradise, How Did We Ever Get Here?

## From the Beginning a False God

After Moses descended from Mt. Sinai and with his own eyes witnessed the "Chosen People" abandoning Yahweh in favor of a hand-molded calf made of gold, he immediately understood that retribution was inevitable and his people would suffer greatly for this treachery.

As a man of faith, as a man who had the distinct honor of conversing with the God of Abraham, Isaac, and Jacob, he knew that this trial would pass in time and his people would survive, for that was the promise that had been made.

As a man of hope, he likely assumed that after godly retribution, the Israelis and their descendants would never again turn their backs on the Creator to worship another false god.

He could never have imagined that the later descendants of Abraham and their Christian brothers would pursue material gain with a vengeance. Was the eternal lesson never to be learned?

Those of us in North America, whose forebearers gave their all to create a God-fearing, independent, generous, and free nation, have demonstrated a good deal more faith than most. However, both the immediate and long-term outlook, even for this nation, is shrouded by a sordid love affair with money.

For Americans, at least for the great majority, this love affair is of recent vintage. Well into the nineteenth century, most Americans lived on farms, and few had ever held a gold coin.

Today the cry in many parts of America is no longer "God bless America," but "Get the money, as much and as fast as you can." People seem to believe that this insatiable drive will somehow bring the "goodness" Jefferson envisioned.

When and where did this love affair with the brothel begin? It was certainly foreshadowed with the decline and corruption in the West of faith and the rise of men such as Henry VIII in the sixteenth century, who turned the biblical advisory on its head by informing his subjects that in this life one can have it all, or to be more precise, first money, then God. Money was to come first of course.

Henry led the way by stealing the Church property of England for his own use. The peasantry in earlier times had been dependent upon that land for their livelihood. The result of throwing them off the land starved many and punished the rest for their failure to labor. He thus created long before the industrial revolution a large and pitiful underclass below serfdom, which had never been seen before in Europe.

Europe since feudal days was a world divided between the nobility and the peasantry. The nobility of course ruled, but it was the peasantry that gave the nobility its legitimacy. Any baron or duke who lost the support of his peasants was in the deepest of trouble. God's law was transcendent. His law, the moral law, was enforced by the Church. Excommunication stripped any man—noble, priest, or peasant—of his legitimacy. So stripped, one became an outcast and was typically removed from office. The threat of excommunication alone sent a chill down the spine of many a king.

With money and its pursuit clearly ascendant well before Henry's reign, nations with borders and colonies sprang to life. Trade, bringing with it new products and wealth, seized the minds of ruler, merchant, and seafarer with an unmistakable need or desire for more.

Time and distance made it impossible to exchange goods for other goods, and thus an acceptable medium of exchange was essential. Trade was not new; men had been trading since antiquity, using gold, silver, and other metals as a medium.

Coin has been milled for centuries, perhaps millennia. In the early days of Rome, it was of little matter the type of metal that was used in a trade.

Iron bars worked as well as silver. Iron had many uses, including weaponry. Value was in the eye of the beholder or the merchant. As Rome grew and coinage became a matter of state, coins were assigned a specific value by the emperor, and that was not to be questioned. The foreigner and the traders of course viewed the matter quite differently. They recognized that precious metal value was something quite different than the plated coin with a picture of the emperor stamped on it. Gresham's law is that undervalued money will drive out the circulation of overvalued money and the law applied with or without the approval of the emperor.

The Romans, though the finest of warriors, were otherwise lazy. They looked down their noses at those engaged in commerce or in any form of physical labor. Slaves performed such tasks. The Romans were of course pagan and totally materialistic; they yearned for those products coming from the East, most notably silk. The silver mines of Rome were enough to satiate the lust for such goods, and Rome began to experience a massive balance of payments problem. As a result goods were coming into the Empire and coin was flowing out, which destroyed the financial infrastructure of the Empire and led to its demise.

As the West passed through the dark ages, becoming a feudal society, invasions and the threat of starvation, if not massacre, were ever present. Humans' focus turned decidedly spiritual, and the Church and moral order dominated their brief lives. Their labors had a transcendental purpose, their very salvation.

However, as the invaders, be they the Moors or the Vikings, brought new methods and products of labor and industry, humans expanded their interest in trade in key centers, such as the Italian states, Kiev, Constantinople, and Byzantium. Wealth could be achieved this way, requiring neither land nor labor.

Distances remained a problem. Values shifted depending on location. There was a continuing need for a currency that all would recognize, be they Christian, Jew, Arab, Mongol, or Norseman. Thus began the search for the ultimate value, something that could be readily measured and accepted in trade.

## Barbarism and Progress

As the West industrialized, as modernity with all its promises seized the imagination of virtually every citizen, nation-states increasingly moved away from the land and sought the machine. The machine with its efficiencies provided humans with a better life, a life of ease and self-fulfillment. Everything had to be done to speed the process.

Much stood in the way of progress. The world as a whole was still a great feudal state, with ignorant and backward people populating most of it. This had to be changed. Change of course brought opportunity and for many, in the West in particular, the prospect of wealth.

Nation-states took every opportunity to grasp wealth. They readily rationalized their misbehavior, initiating wars, colonizing or slaughtering peoples, spoiling the countryside, and employing slave labor.

All of this could be justified in the name of progress. Evolutionists were having a field day. Humans were meant to advance by some hidden force in the universe. Humans' interests might change, but their ravenous behavior would not.

Judeo-Christian theology had put a spike through the heart of barbarism. But barbarism, like Rasputin, had not been silenced. It rose again with great force.

Henry VIII gave it true legitimacy when he disowned the moral order, replacing it with a philosophy that humans could have their cake and eat it too. The subordination of morality to wealth became the standard and battle cry of Europe.

Evolution had so developed the human animals that their brain for all practical purposes was set on a course that could not be denied. Western humans were superior. Evolution made them so. Their manners, their intelligence, the size of their brain, and their accomplishments and inventiveness were sufficient proof that they were to lead. Nothing could stop their progress, and since they were born with this mission, all obstacles had to be set aside that might constitute an impediment.

Unfortunately, Europe was not united. It was not singular. It was made up of cultures, peoples, and nations whose size, power, and sphere of influence was to be decided by a few men, such as Metternich in Vienna, Napoleon, or Bismarck.

## Gold—Madness Infects the West

Though the world has not been on the so-called gold standard for decades, if one were to question the populace at large today and ask them to describe real money, a substantial number would refer to gold.

If they were asked, "Why gold?" the response would be along the lines of, "That is the way it has always been." In other words, God created man, woman, the animals, fauna, cars, computers, and so on, and what brings this all together somehow is gold.

Gold is the driving force, the mainstay, without which everything would stop. That was the prevailing opinion in the late nineteenth century, perhaps less so today with a generation that has grown up worshipping the almighty dollar.

Even today there is widespread belief that beneath that piece of paper that we call money, but in reality is currency, lies this vague but nevertheless truth that if all else fails, if we are hit by a comet, life will go on and people will resort to the use of this precious metal to transact commerce.

There is faith that gold will always be with us as it always has been to guide us as we pursue our destiny. This may be comforting to some, but it is sheer nonsense.

## In the Beginning There Was…

To start with, gold has not always been with us as the measure of value. In the beginning humans exchanged goods with one another as the need arose. The mass of humanity was tied to the land. Serfdom, a step above slavery, was typical of humans' condition through the Middle Ages. One's life span, depending on the period, was thirty-odd years.

Men and women, for the most part illiterate, lived in hovels, plowed the fields, and performed various services for the landowning barons. They rarely left their community. They owned nothing of consequence.

During the Middle Ages the royals and the Church owned the land and everything on it. If you were a peasant, service was your calling in life.

To the extent that trade existed, it was carried from the earliest of times along the trade routes. This trade was intermittent at best. People trekked East, purchased goods that they knew were in demand in the West, and exchanged them at fairs and other meeting places.

Trade in spices and such things as silk to any degree was totally dependent on developments in the great land mass extending from what is today Eastern Europe across the great Russian steppe into Manchuria and China. Anyone traversing this enormous area had to have permission from the reigning tyrant and pay the necessary "tax" to continue on the journey.

The critical trade route from the east was the Silk Road, a four-thousand-mile journey, which only the strongest could survive.

## Black Pepper and Other Spices

Trade, however, was not viewed as a hit-or-miss business. For more than four thousand years, spices were the most important part of international commerce. Most of the world's spices were produced in southern India, the Moluccas Islands, or the Spice Islands of Indonesia.

In Rome black pepper was the measure of wealth. Spices were used for a variety of purposes, including medicinal purposes. "Alaric the Visigoth demanded three thousand pounds of black pepper when he held Rome for ransom in A.D. 408. In the Middle Ages a serf could buy freedom for one pound of black pepper. When people talked about wealth, they spoke about how much pepper a person had."[i]

The spice trade was originally controlled by the Arabs. "Merchants from Venice who bought spices from the Arab traders had a monopoly on the selling of spices in Europe through most of the Middle Ages. With Europe using an average of 6.6 million pounds of black pepper a year, Venice became wealthy."[ii]

Spices drove trade with the East for centuries, but with the arrival of the Romans, silk took center stage.

Silk had been discovered in China. It became a mark of distinction and of position to wear silk in ancient Rome. As a consequence there developed a natural nexus between Rome and China. Over the centuries this became

*Life, Liberty, and the Pursuit of Money*

known as the Silk Road to China. The Road rose and fell in importance as dynasties came and went. The decline of the Tang dynasty in the tenth century interrupted trade until the thirteenth century, when the victorious Mongols reopened the highway to the East.

This route began to decline in importance by the late fifteenth century, when extended sea voyages, which were far safer, supplanted the land route.

Thus there were many trade routes, some far more important than others. All served the same purposes: the exchange of goods and information and a rise in wealth.

It is believed that in antiquity the first usage of gold in exchange probably occurred along one of these routes.

One issue discussed over the centuries is the intriguing relationship between gold and trade. To put that another way, what was it about gold that people were willing to surrender other commodities, spices, primitive and advanced tools, jewelry, and almost any product produced by the hand of humans in exchange?

There seems to be a consensus that gold first came into wide usage in Sardis as a proxy for a given commodity in the sixth century BC. For ages gold had been sought after for purposes of jewelry and ornamentation and was regarded by all peoples as precious. Its scarcity added to its luster, and thus its value went unchallenged.

Perhaps it was in Sardis along a trade route that gold was shaped into coin and thus given its portability. It was a more desirable burden to carry than goods, which required oxen and could be easily lost or stolen or just rot. Gold coins greatly facilitated trade.

Coins ultimately replaced barter. Barter retained one important advantage. In exchange it was far easier to discern equivalence. With a bushel of corn for a bushel of wheat, equivalency is self-evident. However, if I choose to exchange wheat for gold, equivalence is far less certain.

Both parties are convinced that gold and wheat both have value. The wheat can be eaten or stored; the gold can be shaped into a piece of jewelry or exchanged later for a tool or fixture. Both parties thus recognize the concept of inherent value.

Inherent value is not dependent on opinion.

## Why Gold? Why Not Rocks, Dirt, or Air? Or Better Still, Paper?

To stay with the example of wheat farmers who are marketing their crop, exchange may be an imperative and not simply a matter of choice. They may not have barns of sufficient size to store the crop. Without proper storage it will rot. In other words, they are compelled to sell their crop. They have bills to pay and mortgages on their property. The choice is not theirs. They must act. They understand that they have a commodity with real value, but the value, as the crop ages, will decline.

The farmer next door may have nothing of value to exchange for the wheat, but may say, "These large rocks on my property could be used to build a wall." Thus he proposes his rocks for the wheat. Is this a fair exchange?

The answer is probably no. Why? Rocks litter the landscape. Similar to the air we breathe, rocks are there for the taking. As a wall that must be constructed, they may have some future value, but in their present state, they have no value in terms of exchange.

That which is free, like the air we breathe, is there for the taking. That which is free has no value in exchange.

If the next-door neighbor were to suggest that he would build the wall and has the knowledge and tools to accomplish the task, and thus the capacity, then an exchange could be arranged between the parties.

When we define the word *value* or *money*, we mean product and capacity. Capacity may be a skill, aptitude, or know-how, or a thing such as a machine, plant, or patented idea.

That which entails capacity is "money." Money encompasses capacity. Product plus capacity defines money. Demand determines the amount produced.

## Gold Is a Product; Refined, It Is Money

Clearly gold has beauty and is malleable. It can be shaped to make jewelry, tools, and assorted instruments and thus has potential. The rocks described above have potential, but in their free state would never constitute money.

Thus, gold "unto itself alone" is not money. Shaped into a piece of jewelry by the jeweler's skill and workmanship, capacity is subsumed into this metal, giving it value and thus making it capable of being used in exchange as money.

Perhaps because of its scarcity, the historical reality is that from the earliest of times, humans have used gold in exchange. Gold in its natural state is not money. However, it has been readily used in exchange as currency.

Thus, it is important we distinguish money from currency.

Virtually anything can be used as currency in exchange. Today the world relies on paper. The dollar is simply paper.

Since virtually anything can be used as currency, why the preference for gold or silver? The reason is that they are precious.

To be precious, a substance must be scarce and widely dispersed.

Water in the desert among thirsty men is precious. Under the circumstances, it has exchange value or currency, and having utility is money.

Gold is precious in that it is scarce and is widely dispersed. The absence of concentration enhances its acceptability.

The exchange value of gold, that is, the price, will change depending on time, place, and circumstances, but value remains beyond the control of humans.

It is this independence that has allowed it to be the objective standard to measure value in exchanges among all humans through the ages.

## Thus Gold Became a Standard from the Earliest of Times

The sea routes were as critical to trade three thousand years ago as they are today. Of course merchants and traders did not go as far or as quickly, but the sea was critical if they were to get there. Travel was very slow and very dangerous.

These merchants who traveled from afar brought with them goods that were of great interest to the locals. As the earlier description of trade suggests, spices and silk were always in great demand for millennia, as were pottery and cooking utensils and assorted primitive tools.

Within a community, barter was the only realistic way to exchange goods and services.

But once trade moved beyond the community, it became far more complex. The merchant could only carry limited amounts of goods on wagons or oxen. Anything perishable had to be sold quickly. There was the constant threat of marauders, highwaymen, and bandits. There were no highways to travel. Every day offered new challenges, not the least of which was the weather.

The nature of the business of the traveling merchants required that they receive in payment for their goods something they could easily carry and protect and that would be accepted in exchange no matter where their travels might take them.

In other words, the payment had to have universal appeal. Though gold's exact value remained undefined and differed from place to place, it contained elements that made it highly desirable. Due to global scarcity and universal appeal, it was in demand. Small amounts were widely dispersed across the globe. It was a prime metal. Every grain had significant value.

Gold did not stand alone. Silver and copper were also desirable. If a medium of exchange was used, it took the form of a given weight of metal. "Metals were handed about in ingots, and weighed at each transaction… The trade that was going on in the ancient world before the sixth or seventh century B.C. was almost entirely barter trade. There was little or no credit or coined money."[iii]

"These dates should be noted. The first recorded coins were minted about 600 B.C. in Lydia, while the great period of Egyptian civilization had been reached at least a thousand years before that date."[iv]

To facilitate trade merchants had to travel along routes that were safe and brought them into contact with those who had the resources to purchase goods. In the first instance, the merchant had to have the wherewithal to purchase, say, spices.

Merchants and traders stayed close to the waterways. Rivers and streams facilitated travel and trade. In antiquity buyers of merchant goods, whose occupation was most likely farming, had to live near the water, which was essential for irrigation.

As they worked their farms, they would come across grains of shiny metal, which they quickly learned they could exchange for tools, oxen, and farm implements.

From the standpoint of the farmers, they were simply making an exchange. In point of fact without giving it any consideration, they were developing the concept of currency.

They recognized that metal had acceptable value not only to one merchant but to all merchants, even as they disagreed among themselves as to its precise value.

As gold was not sufficiently plentiful and would never be, trade was thus restricted. This necessitated a broadening of that which could be exchanged for goods and services. That journey as of this writing has never run its course. Humans are still experimenting and devising new ways to exchange.

## Gold Is Not and Has Never Been the Only Standard of Value

For millennia gold has been used in exchange or, as we so blithely say, as money. However, it is the most serious of mistakes to confuse gold and money.

As was noted earlier, gold became a readily acceptable token for use in exchange because it was viewed as being precious.

There have only been approximately 160,000 tons of gold mined in recorded time, and 50 percent of that just in the last fifty years.

As a prime metal, it could not be extinguished. It could be easily carried; it could be shaped and made into attractive utensils; it served as the base for the finest jewelry. And it could be hidden away from crooks, robbers, and thieves.

As a base metal, there was no way that an alchemist by mixing chemicals could produce more than was taken from the ground.

Gold was always scarce. In fact, as we moved toward modernity during the latter part of the nineteenth century, it was precisely the scarcity that allowed gold to be made the world standard, which in turn gave rise to numerous economic depressions.

## The Standard

In a world of different cultures and peoples, value is perceived differently. Thus we look for a standard that embraces all, is acceptable to all. Gold and other metals met the test. It stands to reason that any object considered precious by all can be made a standard for measuring value. Gold is not unique in that regard.

Gold is still trumpeted today in many places in the world as the only *true money*. The so-called gold bugs confuse many concepts, the most important being that they do not distinguish the standard from the product. Money is the product; the standard is an objective measure of value.

The standard stands above the fray. All exchanges are tested against the standard. The medium of exchange and the standard need not be the same. Oil is frequently used as a medium of exchange, but the amount of oil is determined by the standard.

## Must the Standard Be Precious?

It is obvious that the *medium of exchange* and *currency* are synonymous. Value does not come into play. If this was not the case, we could never use paper. Currency does not have value. There is nothing valuable about a green piece of paper with Washington's picture on the front, though many believe to the contrary.

However, that is not the question. The question is, "Must the ultimate standard be precious?" Or can the world have a standard that is not precious?

To this day that question has not been satisfactorily answered. Can it be answered?

Humans decide what is and what is not precious, irrespective of the views of government or any other body. Their views about preciousness have changed and will change depending on the circumstances.

Today's world views oil as precious as it sits buried miles under the sea or ground. That was not the case fifty years ago.

The American Indian viewed wampum beads as precious. In fact, they sold Manhattan Island for them.

Experience tells us that preciousness, to a large extent, is dependent on supply versus demand.

As long as the test of universal acceptance is met, virtually anything and everything can qualify as a standard. It need not be metal or a refined chemical or some fine art. It can certainly be paper, though the purists find the notion repugnant.

The market will ultimately determine the price of everything, but the agreed standard is the ultimate measure of value.

## The Standard May Never Be Set by Fiat or by One Party to a Transaction

By definition, the word *standard* means "beyond the control of." If I have it within my power to control the standard, at that moment it is no longer the standard. The standard must stand alone, impervious to outside influence. A work of art by Michelangelo is the standard for the masters. The masters do not make the determination that this work shall be the standard. The standard stands alone and invites universal acceptance, which is readily given because one and all can see the majesty in the work. It is precious unto itself. A true standard can never be violated.

Does the fact that there is a standard exclude the possibility of other standards? Is there anything in the nature of a standard that requires singularity? Surprisingly, the answer is yes. The ultimate standard must be singular. There may be different standards for different societies; that is, the standard need not be universal. But there is only room for one standard in every society at any point in time.

This is a profundity that history has not been able to grasp.

Once society moves beyond barter, that is, the exchange of "like goods," such as a horse for a cow, we quickly move into the world of a standard. We test the equivalence of the exchange by an independent standard, over which neither party has any control. This standard allows for the measurement of equivalence.

This brings us to a universal principle that order requires balance. The universe, though constantly changing, is balanced, or as the philosophers would say, is ordered. The opposite of order is disorder or chaos, and chaos is irrational and destructive.

To maintain order, to make everything we do rational, comprehensible, and ultimately knowable, we must pursue equivalence and balance. The world of commerce seeks equivalence in all exchange. It is essential for progress.

Before leaving this subject, it is important to point out that though there can be but one standard for any society at any time, this does not mean that secondary standards tied to the primary standard cannot coexist.

Thus gold, which today is regarded as a standard, though not the universal standard, still stands as an acceptable measure of value.

## Gresham's Law: The Public Will Never Be Fooled for Long

Simply put, Gresham's law states that if I introduce a currency whose value is suspect, for instance, a plated coin stamped with a picture of the emperor, gold and silver will disappear from the market. People will hoard a currency with value.

CHAPTER 1

# The Sad and Sordid History of Money—Interlaced with Brief Moments of Enlightenment

ANTIQUITY AND THE ROMAN EXPERIENCE—HOW DID WE MANAGE TO GET ON A GOLD STANDARD IN THE FIRST PLACE?
As difficult as it is to believe, it was largely an accident, an accident of history. Nevertheless it is true that gold, silver, and copper were from the earliest of times universally accepted in exchange and in payment of debt. They became standards.

For such purposes gold was viewed as the most precious. Though it held this exalted status, it was not as widely used as copper or silver since it was not as readily available. It was indeed the most precious of the metals, due primarily to its scarcity, its intrinsic beauty, its universality, and its purity.

Desirability did not necessarily translate into broad-based usage. Due to its scarcity, an ounce of gold was worth many times more than an ounce of silver. As a rule of thumb, the value was twelve to fifteen times greater.

To the ancients, all metal was precious. Metal could always be put to use. It was easily identified, was portable, and unlike other commodities, was not perishable.

## THE ROMAN MONEY EXPERIENCE
The earliest human societies bartered in order to exchange goods and services. Every exchange, even the most basic, required a measuring device, a value yardstick. Coin, unlike bars of metal, was a perfect yardstick.

Something nonperishable would have been essential, and the best indications are that humans turned to a substance such as rock, and later metal engraved with oxen, to convey the notion of obligation.

The Hellenic world initially relied on barter, utensils, and cattle as mediums of exchange. Metals came into use, including iron, copper, gold, and silver, with value being determined by weight.

The Romans first used copper and later silver and gold in their trading and commercial activities. Rome treated copper as a precious metal.

Gold was later used in Roman coinage, but it was in short supply and the evidence is that its early use was for international trade purposes and for payments to the military.

Money usage in Rome was far from rudimentary. The merchants were quite sophisticated and were familiar with mortgages and bills of exchange.

The earliest use of metal for transaction purposes in Rome involved the taking of a piece of copper and placing it inside a leather pouch. This procedure must have proven to be cumbersome, and over time Rome moved to copper and silver coins.

In 269 BC Rome adopted silver as a medium. In the early years of the Empire, silver was abundant. The silver mines were rich in ore. The labor necessary to exploit the mines was performed by slaves, who were plentiful as Rome expanded the Empire.

The growth of this thriving and expanding empire brought about increasingly insistent demands for more from the Roman citizenry. As a people, the Romans looked down on labor. Hard labor was for the slaves and such types. The merchant class, to the extent there was one, were regarded as the untouchables of the time. Getting one's hands dirty was not a vocation for the average Roman.

This society, brutal and corrupt, focused all its time and effort consuming goods produced by others. From Caesar on down, it was a society dedicated to paganism and excessive, extravagant consumption.

Such a society was doomed from the start, but during its days of glory, it ruled the known world as a result of its magnificent military, better known as the Roman legion.

Before King Tullus Hostillius, who reigned in the seventh century BC, the currency used in trade in Rome consisted of crude copper bars.

Emperor Servius, in 3 BC, was the first to make an impression upon this metal. It weighed one Roman "libra" or pound and was named the "as."

The evidence is that the barbarian nations preferred gold and silver.

The first silver coin in Rome was the denarii and contained one sixth of an ounce of silver.

Emperors of Rome during the era of men like Julius Caesar and Augustus were supreme. They came to be treated as gods and, as we know from history, came to believe, as in the case of Caligula, that they were gods. Thus, any edict proceeding from the throne of the emperor was never to be questioned.

They and much of the citizenry fell prey to the illusion that it was within their almighty power to determine the value of "money."

As the demand for currency increased as the borders of Rome expanded and as imports surged, the emperor was ultimately faced with a dilemma. He could arbitrarily decide the nominal value of Rome's coinage as emperor, but he could not deliver the volume of coin demanded. As the mines were drained, the extraction of ore required more labor, but additional labor did not assure greater return.

The solution was simply reducing the amount of silver and copper in the coinage. This was necessary since all emperors, gods or not, depended on the support of the populace for their very survival. An emperor might be all powerful, but that did not assure his longevity.

The so-called Roman games, which involved unspeakable barbarity, stood as a continuing attempt to placate the populace. Keeping the folks happy, god or not, went with the job.

An emperor who dared to make the executive decision not to produce more coinage in the face of increasing demand was taking a risk, a life-threatening risk, for there was always another emperor waiting in the wings.

The key to Julius Caesar's power was his popularity with the have-nots. He saw to it that they were taken care of as a modern-day politician would.

Thus, the pursuit of a tight money policy was not in the Roman lexicon. Of course they had no understanding of money and assumed that once the emperor had spoken on the value of the coin, it was final. It was not to be challenged.

The problem was that Rome was not the world. As monetary conditions deteriorated, it became essential that the amount of pure metal in the coinage be reduced.

In 250 BC the amount of silver in the denarius, for example, was reduced from one sixth to one seventh of an ounce. The nominal or expressed value was not changed. In other words, there was to be less metal in the coin, but the coin was to have the same value.

Of course the great populace of Rome was not educated, and those tribes and inchoate states operating outside its borders, though not educated, were not stupid.

They recognized a scam when they saw one. They wouldn't challenge the emperor, but they would move to implement Gresham's law. The coin with the greater metal disappeared from the streets of Rome or fled the country. Coins were melted down to obtain the silver.

Exporters to Rome concluded that they were receiving less for their goods, and thus scarcity ensued. Though the meaning of the term would not have been understood, Rome had simply devalued its currency.

In 207 BC a gold piece was coined called a scrupulum. Additional coins over time were added, but reduction in the amount of metal in coin was to become de rigueur.

Silver was to play a pivotal role in Rome throughout its history since it was typically used to settle imbalances in international trade. In the early years of the Empire, metal was synonymous with currency. Merchants could haggle over metal value and undoubtedly did, but as a medium for exchange, it met the key standards.

The fact that copper played a role in exchange did not preclude the use of alternative mediums, such as silver and gold.

It was apparent to one and all that silver had greater intrinsic value, perhaps as a result of its relative scarcity, than copper. Silver was readily acceptable to foreign states in settlement of trade.

In addition to the intrinsic value, there was the matter of portability. Less metal was needed to complete a transaction with the use of silver. Safekeeping was less of a problem.

The mines of Rome before depletion were rich in ore. There was presumably magic surrounding the silver coin bearing an impression of the emperor. Coin had a designated value. At the same time, there was silver metal in raw form. This silver had a price that would fluctuate. If the mines were overly productive, the price of silver would fall.

The recipient of the coin was well aware of this and thus in exchange demanded more coin. This left the impression that the merchant was raising prices.

For the Romans this added up to a contradiction. The emperor had decided what the value of the coin was, and here were these merchants questioning value.

Resolution of this conflict would not come easy. One possibility was for the seller of the goods to withdraw them from the market if the buyer refused to pay the seller's price. This translated into a business slowdown or recession.

Another possibility was to arrange for exchange in a more stable currency, such as gold. Copper was cumbersome, and the value of silver was open to question. Gold was another story. There was no chance of it becoming too plentiful, for the very word *gold* implied scarcity. Scarcity brought price stability. However, scarcity also limited or restricted commercial development. With such limitation, dismal economic conditions would prevail.

As the ultimate standard, gold failed the test. It was not sufficiently elastic. As global commerce expanded, for the ultimate standard to remain a true measure, the price and its availability would have to move in tandem. Experience clearly demonstrated that it did not.

A related problem is that should a nation manage to gain a disproportionately large holding of the world's gold, it is in a position to manipulate the price.

A true standard or measure, one can conclude, is not in some instrument or product. It stands apart. It is independent. It is conceptual. A ruler isn't the measure. The ruler allows us to measure.

## The Ultimate Standard and Human Endeavor

Money is created through human endeavor. Currency was instituted by humans to simplify the process of exchange. There is absolutely nothing in these two concepts that suggests that people must suffer deprivation or shortage. Nature provides us infinite potential. That is all that we need. We must choose to use these gifts wisely. There is never a shortage of money. but people fail to utilize and allocate resources properly.

All value, real and potential, is stored in the globe's resources. It is not subject to assignment. Utility, value, and wealth are synonymous. They are independent; they lie beyond. They are not subject to capture to be placed in an object such as gold. Any attempt to do so misconstrues the meaning of money and restricts human potential.

This reality has not dissuaded people from attempting to locate the ultimate standard, the golden calf of life. It must be here somewhere, they reason. But where is it?

To put it simply, it is a violation of perfection ingrained in creation to attempt to identify or create a fixed or permanent store of wealth.

During the extended monetary conferences of the 1870s in Paris, the attendees attempted to do just that. They agreed that they had found the standard they had been looking for over the ages, and yes, it was indeed gold.

Henceforth, only gold would do. The prospect of utopia at last!

There was, however, a slight problem. Well, it was more than slight, but it was to be largely ignored in the face of utopia.

That problem, posed by a few of the delegates, simply put was if gold and not redemption was a human's salvation, what was gold's price? They pointed out that if it had a price, then it was not gold that was the ultimate standard, but the price.

One of the great lessons of history is that if people are bent on self-destruction, nothing should be allowed to get in the way, least of all common sense or critical reasoning.

Such thinking threatened to bog down the conference and thus had to be dismissed out of hand, which is what the conferees proceeded to do.

One American played a very helpful role in this regard. His name was John Sherman, senator of Ohio, nicknamed the "Ohio icicle," who would later be appointed the thirty-second secretary of the Treasury.

If the price of gold was a mystery to most, it was not a mystery to Sherman. He supposedly advised that gold had no price; it was "God's money."

The world adopted the gold standard and paid a whale of a price. Over the next three decades, the world suffered through something on the order of a dozen depressions.

As far as anyone knows, God was never consulted about any of this, and neither were the people, who were to suffer the consequences.

As economic circumstances worsened, nations resorted to the use of domestic currencies, which in the United States included silver.

A political contest in the United States ensued between the "eastern bankers" for their advocacy of a gold standard, which meant tight money for lack of availability, and the western silver interests, or the easy money advocates.

The battle between easy and tight money raged for decades, continuing to this very day. By the late 1800s, a man came to the forefront and set the stage for the modern Democratic party. His name was William Jennings Bryan. He became the Democratic candidate for president in 1896, 1900, and 1908. He failed, though, in his quest to bring some sense of reason to the endless debate about wealth, gold, silver, and currency.

CHAPTER 2

# The Collapse of Empire

## THE FALL OF ROME

Two millennia earlier the Roman Empire expanded eastward. At the height of its power, Rome by every measure of the time was a colossus. It controlled three and a half million square miles, with a population of fifty million. Its barbarian ways were swept aside under Theodosius the Great (378–395) as the Romans formally adopted Catholicity.

Rome had to constantly address invasion, civil war, the plague, and economic uncertainty resulting from a continuing shortage of labor and thus insufficient exports, which contributed to their balance of payments problem.

With the incessant demand for more currency from every quarter, including the military, the mines of Rome became overworked. In time this led to devaluation as less ore was introduced into the coinage and finally full debasement with the issuance of plated coins.

Gresham's law was triggered. Domestically the reckless increase in the supply of currency produced an inflationary surge, thus creating an artificial price structure for domestic goods.

Rome began to go down the road to insolvency. Coin with intrinsic value fled the Empire. The balance of payments became distorted, with Rome in no position to export, while import demand continued strong.

The average Roman citizen was confused by developments beyond his understanding. He did not see the fallacy inherent in his belief that wealth could be increased by simply increasing the measure.

From sheer ignorance and a misguided understanding of power, Rome sought by emperor diktat to fix the value of Roman currency. The value of currency cannot be decided by fiat. That decision ultimately rests with the market and those engaged in commerce, for they determine the price in exchange.

In 476, Emperor Romulus Augustus presided over the ultimate decline of Western Rome.

While it would take centuries before the final collapse, the seed of that collapse began with the consumption habits of the Romans, combined with the degradation of the monetary system.

Thus was ushered in the period known in history as the Dark Ages. Barbarism, starvation, and confusion. typified by migrating peoples. were the order of the day in the West.

In the East, Byzantium, with Constantinople at its center, thrived in comparison. Easterners viewed their poor cousins in the West with disdain. In later centuries the political and economic circumstances changed. The East was threatened and ultimately overwhelmed by the Ottomans. Border encroachment by assorted peoples and tribes began to eat away at the economic viability of the Byzantine Empire. But this was a long time in coming.

Internal economic weakness in time invited disintegration and assault from outside and ultimately collapse.

From a monetary standpoint, the Roman experience taught many lessons.

With all its failings, Rome was not doomed from the outset. Though the people were lazy, their military was a marvel. The Romans consumed but did not produce. In time, its economy fell victim to a collapsed currency. With gold and silver expatriated or hoarded and plated currency worthless, commerce simply ground to a halt.

The critical step that Rome should have taken was the issuance of a new currency, one that would retain value apart from any involvement of the state.

Seventeen centuries later, England, faced with similar difficulties, passed the Bank Charter Act, and Germany in 1946 did the same.

The United States in 2011, with massive debt, public and private, and with commitments it cannot possibly address, found itself in Rome's predicament. The world was in need of a new standard. Dollar liabilities, now virtually infinite, would prevent the dollar from remaining the reserve currency of the world for much longer.

This would require global restructuring, an event for which there is no precedent in world history, since the dollar has served as the critical standard for the better part of the century.

An important lesson to be taken from the Roman experience is that the state does not have the power to decide value. The state does have the power to designate a medium as legal tender, but it cannot determine value.

Value is a measure of equilibrium. Imbalance reduces interaction between parties. Absent equilibrium, commerce must suffer, and with it human progress.

Rome in the early years was a nation on a mission. Replacing the Greeks as the center of global power, this mission was expressed by pushing outward. As long as there was unity of mission, the continuing advancement of the state, the preeminence of Rome, would go unchallenged.

Personal desire, undoubtedly beginning at the highest levels of government with the emperor and slowly working its corrupting way through the body politic, would over time result in the loss of mission, and with it decline.

The grandeur of Rome was replaced by a rush for power and riches. This did not go unrecognized. Tiberius, by the second decade AD, complained that Rome's wealth was being transferred to other nations, including enemy nations. Today we refer to this phenomenon as globalization.

In the first century AD it is estimated that as much as 550 million sesterces were exported annually to India alone to pay for imports.

It would seem impossible that a nation with leaders as strong and determined as Julius Caesar, Trajan, or Hadrian could abandon the mission so completely. Clearly this happened, but why?

## The Road to Mediocrity and Decline

Systemic failure becomes inevitable when the focus of average citizens is directed inward. They no longer see a responsibility to be a contributor to society, but seeks satisfaction for themselves.

*Life, Liberty, and the Pursuit of Money*

Successful farmers consume more. They have parties and banquets. They begin to take holidays. They employ others to do the work they previously did themselves. With new employees, tools, and invention, production will indeed rise, but consumption is likely to increase more rapidly.

Progress invites consumption. Abundance fosters population growth, as the marvelous economist Malthus concluded. Humans are destined to never get in front of the consumption curve.

The most recent experience in America is that average Americans are consuming a good deal more than they are producing. They accomplish this by borrowing from the production of others, particularly foreign nationals.

We can be certain of this by simply looking at their rate of saving and the trade balance. Saving is a proxy for incremental production. A favorable trade balance suggests that they are working harder, being more productive, and consuming less than their peers in other countries.

In order for America to progress, it must increase domestic production at a rate faster than its rate of consumption to satisfy global demand.

It is fair to say that the average American today is not only behind the curve but is being buried by the curve. More about this problem later.

Returning to Rome, what held the Romans back was their attitude toward labor. They held manual labor in contempt. This contempt carried over to the merchants and others engaged in trade. The extent of the deterioration that resulted was not readily apparent, as it took place over generations.

The social structure of Rome was very rigid, a caste system totally dependent on slave labor, and morally corrupt. Collapse would eventually come, and the fearsome majesty and awe that this great power had projected throughout the known world would be no more.

Western civilization, or as I prefer, civilization itself, arose from the ashes of Rome. The death of paganism and the rise of Christianity allowed for the spirit of humans to break out of the darkness. It was from Roman rubble that the long trek to modernity began.

Without question, the decisive element, characteristic, or attribute that is essential to the advance of the cause of humans and the society in which they live, is wisdom.

It becomes clear that those peoples that see beyond greed, money, consumption, power, military might, and self-worship will prosper from generation to generation.

Many such peoples suffer from invasion, sickness, and starvation, but in the end survive. They become a beacon calling humans upward and forward. Oh, how wonderful it would be to be able to grasp that wisdom, define it, and share it in a convincing way with everyone. Such a task is for philosophers and theologians.

There was one American who, after great study and the gift of genius, when called upon by his people, sat and wrote words in a declaration that are certain to ring in the hearts of humans for all history. His name was Thomas Jefferson, and in four words he explains the full meaning of life as he spoke of "nature and nature's God."

Jefferson and his contemporaries understood the true quest of life. Unfortunately, there are too few who understand it today.

CHAPTER 3

# From the Dark to the Middle Ages

## War, Barbarism, Invasion, and Survival

The Dark Ages, a period lasting for centuries, were marked by migration, invasion, barbarism, and starvation. The West became the poor cousin of Byzantium and its crown jewel, Constantinople. Byzantium did its best to ignore the poor West. This can be seen by their turning away from the use of Latin as the official language.

The West accepted the authority of the Byzantine emperors but grew distant with the wealth disparity.

In the late fourth century, the Roman Empire began to show signs of rebirth, but the resources and imperial authority were directed to the East. A slave-state mentality persisted in the West, accompanied by barbarian invasion and Gothic plundering, with Christianity less firmly established than in the East, which now beheld a new capital, Constantinople, taking on a certain splendor and dignity.

Both East and West continued to be ravaged by invasion and the threat of repression. "The impression that emerges is one of consensus around the ideal of a God-appointed Christian empire, prosperity reflected in lavish building throughout Asia Minor and the dynamic capital of Constantinople, and political stability enshrined in the rise of a new breed of trained, dedicated bureaucrats."[v] The leaders were cautious and pursued policies including the reduction of taxes and control of expenses, "providing financial stability,"[vi] which set the stage for Justinian (482–565), a man of religious orthodoxy bent on the restoration of the universal empire, which he saw as the "terrestrial image of God's heavenly kingdom."[vii]

Justinian, a builder, spender, military leader, and autocrat, appeared by the time of his death, with considerable help from his powerful wife, to have succeeded in beating back the barbarians, under a magnificent general Belisarius, and in "restoring the glories of Rome."[viii]

"His ideals of autocracy and Romano-Christian universalism became a program to which all later Byzantine emperors subscribed."[ix]

Land translates into wealth—gold and silver are secondary—to be used in exchange. Land and the desire for more land remains the focal point and driving force behind the efforts of the warrior and petty tyrant. He pursues land holdings and titles to land by invasion, murder, theft, and destruction. Land becomes the raison d'être of his existence.

There is, however, a force that successfully challenges this animalistic urge and serves to the present as the irreplaceable compass to assure the survival of the European people, their cultures, their values, and their beliefs.

This is the Judeo-Christian moral code. It was challenged and sorely tested both within Christianity and without, but it survived intact. It is administered from the smallest of Italian states, known through history as the seat of Peter, the Bishop of Rome, the Papacy.

The long line of occupants of the seat of the Bishop of Rome failed with disappointing frequency, just as the first occupant, Peter, failed prior to Pentecost in living the ideal embodied in the code. Many succumbed to temptations of the flesh and failed at crucial moments to administer the code impartially and unhesitatingly, disappointing their Christian followers.

However, the Papacy never lost the moral authority embodied metaphysically in the seat itself. Papal authority remained constant, though its influence ebbed and flowed as human events unfolded.

That influence changed the fortunes of nations and peoples and went virtually unchallenged until the rise of Protestantism in the sixteenth century.

Though the Papacy would never field a great army, it carried the ultimate weapon for king and peasant alike—humans' fear of the eternal inferno once a sentence of excommunication was handed down.

Humans through the Middle Ages continued to rampage, invade, pillage, murder, and steal, but the threat of excommunication changed the habits of many a king, barbarian as well as the civilized, allowing Europe to progress.

In the eighth century, the Muslims occupied Spain and crossed the Strait of Gibraltar. Islam served to enhance global trade, bringing gold, slaves, China silk, porcelain, spices, Egyptian grain, precious stones, dates from India, and textile goods.

Suffering defeat at Tours, France, the Muslims' expansionist goals came to an end. Thus began the arduous climb toward European statehood with the arrival of Charles Martel, also known as "Charles the Hammer," as head of the Frankish Empire. He defeated Abd-er-Rahman of Spain at Tours in 732. In the future Christian civilization, not Islam, would be dominant across the European continent.

Constant warfare had bedeviled this continent; it was literally a continuing battle for survival. People whose hands were not on the plow were fighting or preparing for battle. War was sport. Byzantium and Islam held their culture and tradition together while the West was mired in disarray.

With the establishment of Constantinople, the West went into centuries-long decline, hastened by the barbarians from Scandinavia and the Muslim invaders in the early eighth century, bringing with it the collapse of the Visigoth Kingdom on the Iberian Peninsula.

Roman institutions disappeared or were replaced by the growing Christian influence, with the great emphasis on churches. The cities of Byzantium retained their grace as cities such as Rome decayed. The result was a sharp decline in population in the West.

From the rubble new towns in Italy emerged whose focus was trade. Salt became an important trading commodity. Byzantine Venice gained access to trading with the East, and new products for export and import brought a growing realization that wealth was inextricably tied to foreign investment involving trade.

From the standpoint of the struggling Continent, it was repeatedly assaulted from the inside and the outside. Invaders such as the Lombards, a Germanic tribe in Italy, denied Byzantium control of Italy.

"By the death of the prophet Muhammad in 632 the Arabian Peninsula was united behind the new faith which he had preached, and within ten years Persia and the Byzantine provinces of the east had succumbed to Islam."[x]

"A vast free-trade zone was established and local populations preserved their culture and their prosperity under a regime which resembled a benign protectorate rather than an empire…Its conquests would carry Arab forces to the borders of India and China."[xi]

This expansion brought Byzantium down and reduced it to an impoverished and militarized empire reminiscent of the West after the fall of Rome. "Byzantium was forced to turn in on itself, and any hopes it had of reasserting its authority in the west were dashed."[xii]

By the year 750, Islam began to fracture, bringing about a resurgence of local customs and practices. However, during its dynamic phase, Islam had greatly expanded the global trading world, making it possible for goods and peoples to flow over a far greater expanse, introducing new goods, and sparking advances in mediums of exchange.

Charlemagne, or Charles the Great, arrived in the early eighth century and proceeded to expand the Frankish Kingdom into a Western and Central European Empire and be crowned Emperor of the Romans (800–814). He served as both a conqueror and reformer, advancing the Carolingian Renaissance, a revival of culture, art, and literature. A stalwart defender and protector of the Catholic Church, he brooked no heresy and enforced Church doctrine across the length and breadth of his empire.

"Charlemagne was provided with an ever growing number of literate clerics who could be used in his administration and, in the newly reformed Latin and the new more legible script, had a precise and international written language that could be used throughout his multilingual empire."[xiii] The significance here is that he represented the first northern emperor,[xiv] and there was a shift in power from south to north, together with an economic resurgence. The West now had a ruler who could bring unity and purpose to the West and would prove together with his successors to be competitive, particularly when it came to the title of Roman Emperor.

"Suddenly, in the reign of Charlemagne, pirates crossed the North Sea to raid monasteries...."Indeed the word Viking may have originally meant traders, men who go to wics (trading places).... "Scandinavian merchants went to Russia and brought vast quantities of silver from the Abbasid Empire in the east to Charlemagne's kingdom. This silver did much to finance Carolingian church-building, and to stimulate both the Carolingian and the Scandinavian economies. The drying up of supplies of silver in the 820's and 830's caused by political troubles in the Abbasid Empire precipitated a crisis in the Carolingian Empire, and forced Scandinavians whose position had depended on the silver trade to turn to piracy."[xv]

These pirates were barbarians in every respect. Having no respect for life or property, they proceeded to destroy both people and culture, choosing to focus on centers of learning and wealth, which of course were the monasteries.

One can see during this extended period the importance of Christianity. At the very core of the Christian moral code was a genuine respect for the rights of people, even though the code was frequently violated by Christians as well as pagans.

The Christian violators, some quite renowned, pillaged for self-gain but implicitly recognized that such acts, as much as they sought to justify their own behavior, were morally indefensible.

For the barbarian, there was no code except for those rules that each tribe or warrior group might devise to hold its culture together. Thus, the Vikings did not draw a distinction between their acts as traders and their pillaging as pirates. Both were simply a means to an end.

Civilization formalizes this notion in the oft-repeated saying that the end never justifies the means. For the barbarian the end always justifies the means. Thus there was no way to reason with the Vikings; the answer lay in opposing force with force. An important breakthrough for the civilized world was the introduction of mounted infantry or cavalry. Knights on horseback greeted the invading Vikings, who, though expert in seafaring, were no match for what must have seemed to them an important advance in warfare.

The era of free-reign pillage was now drawing to a close. Increasingly the Vikings came as invaders but stayed and married into the local population.

Thus, Viking expansionism eventually ran its course. They were granted in 911 an area around Rouen, which became the duchy of Normandy.

"As far as the ninth century is concerned, the primary legacy of the Vikings was that of destruction."[xvi] However, "The raids brought Scandinavia into much closer contact with other parts of Europe which paved the way for conversion to Christianity..."[xvii]

"But it is difficult to imagine how England could have emerged by the late tenth century as a wealthy, powerful, and united kingdom had not the Vikings destroyed all native dynasties except that of the West Saxons. The English nation was in a sense created by the Vikings, with the help of the West Saxon propagandists."[xviii]

By the year 900, Christianity had extended its reach to the northwest and had even begun to spread into Scandinavia and Eastern Europe.[xix]

During this extended period, canon law became more refined for both East and West, and the world witnessed the establishment and spread of monasteries. In the West with the inspiration of St. Benedict and to counter worldliness in the Church, a blueprint developed where a community of men came together for prayer, work, and study, while in the East, monasticism grew, with substantial popular support for holy men.

With the rapid growth in monasteries as both religious retreat and centers of learning, whose members were the leading intellectuals of the time, it was inevitable that the wealth of the Church, most notably in landholdings, would expand at an exponential rate. The Church in every respect, both temporal and spiritual, was becoming increasingly powerful; thus appointments such as the abbot to head an important monastery became leading figures in the kingdom.

In the West the Church was viewed as the divine instrument that would lead men to salvation. In the East, though the people were very religious, mysticism ruled. On all matters, including religion, the people looked to the emperor for guidance.

A debate ensued on the power of kings and other nobles to appoint bishops and other senior church officials within their realm. The Church's position was simply that the matter should not be the concern of the temporal world. It was a Church matter, pure and simple. The issue referred to as lay investiture came to a head during the papacy of Gregory VII (1073–1085). It led to conflict between kings and popes. History reflected this in the continuing debate of church versus state.

Economic progress became visible in both East and West. It was Italy that would prove to be the economic standout, making efficient and moneymaking use of land capital.

While the early Middle Ages was a period of extended decline, disintegration, and Scandinavian and Muslim invasion, we were left with an inheritance of Roman law and administration, science and medicine from the Muslim world, and the urban life of Italy.

It should be noted that the Arab Muslims were an intelligent and relatively advanced people, and as they spread their influence, new wealth arose because they introduced products previously unknown in Europe. Not until 1492 did the Christians succeed in driving out completely the Muslims from Spain.

Middle East involvement in European affairs and the European Crusades served as a springboard for the mixture of peoples and customs, products, ideas, and beliefs. In this regard the translation of Aristotle from Greek to Latin revolutionized thinking in the world of philosophy and science.

The eleventh century witnessed Christian Europe on the march. Jerusalem was retaken in 1099. For the Middle Eastern Arab, these incursions were a threat to their homeland. They showed no lack of determination, and it is widely viewed that their defeat resulted from a lack of financial resources.

These conflicts brought great death and destruction but proved to be a boon to international trade. The Italian city-states were the principle beneficiaries. Trade begets trade, and the Italians expanded their contacts, reaching into the Byzantium Empire and other distant places.

Expanding trade brought profit and wealth, but distance greatly complicated the transactions. Risk of piracy or disaster on the high seas necessitated some form of insurance. All trade had to be financed. The Italians proved ready and willing to undertake the opportunity for a share of the profit. Thus, we saw the beginnings of instruments so commonplace in modern banking, such as bankers acceptances and bills of lading.

## Byzantium and the Italians During These Ages

The growth of the cities and towns in Italy led to the rise of communal government, where the most powerful families elected their own leaders. The rise in wealth and influence of the Italians, combined with a perceptible decline in the power and influence of the Byzantine Empire, resulted in the Fourth Crusade, with the fall of Constantinople on April 12, 1204. The fall of this great city to the Latins signaled an eclipse in Byzantine power.

The many crusades eventually ran their course, and after a brief interlude, the Latins exited Constantinople. By the second half of the century, Muslim forces were again on the offensive, expelling Christians from their Middle East enclave.

East and West faced a new threat. In the 1240s the Mongols crossed from Asia into Eastern Europe, displacing kingdoms and peoples on a scale never before seen. They continued to expand their empire in Asia and in Eastern Europe well into the fourteenth century.

## Progress of Sorts

"Alongside banking there were large scale manufacture and long distance trade. Ere there were three principal exports: slaves, taken by the Germans on their eastern border or by the Vikings, and particularly in demand by the Muslim caliphate of Cordoba before its collapse in the early eleventh century, Flemish cloths and woolens, increasingly manufactured from English wool, and silver, of which major deposits were discovered in Saxony during the eleventh century. Through Italy and the inland waterways of Russia these goods were traded for luxuries from the east, particularly silks and spices, which were at one valuable and relatively easy to transport."[xx]

"Kings and great lords were essentially military leaders; they were held in esteem, or not, according to their ability to fight, whether in defense of their rights and lands or in conquest…there was a general pressure for service to be rewarded by grants of land. Possession of land freed a man from accidents of life such as a quarrel with his lord or years of sickness and old age and it was essential for those who sought wives."[xxi]

"As primogeniture became the norm…there was a dual pressure on lords to find fresh lands both for members of their own families and for those of their vassals…Many went to fight the heathen in the Holy Land or Spain, as much to redeem their souls as to secure fresh lands."[xxii]

Economic progress was being made certainly by the eleventh century, and the source of this advance in wealth was agriculture.

"The control of local justice and of obligations to forced labor, the offer of 'protection,' and levying of taxation were the essential means by which free peasants were reduced to servitude, hereditarily bound to their tenements and liable to arbitrary levies and labor services."[xxiii]

"From the eleventh century lands began to be cultivated which had previously lain fallow…The process was partly a response to a growth in population but was also and perhaps more significantly, lords aimed to increase their revenues."[xxiv]

"With the growth in population came the growth of towns. They were supported largely by manufactures for the local market, such as utensils or cloths but income also came from offerings at their shrines and the expenditure of their lords, who for their part looked to raise revenue from market tolls, or from the profits of their mints."[xxv]

"During the twelfth century towns assumed further functions. Some, such as Paris, drew income from the students attracted to their schools. Others drew income from banking and mortgaging land, which could raise considerable sums when nobles were running into financial difficulties or churches were caught midway in expensive building programs. Jews unencumbered by the Christian prohibition of usury, played a prominent part in these activities and paid a heavy cost for it. They were liable to pogroms, such as those which swept the Rhineland cities in 1096, and to arbitrary levies by their lords. When the king of France arrested the Jews in the crown lands in 1180, he was able to ransom them for the considerable sum of 15,000 marks."[xxvi]

By the light of modern commercial standards, the Christian prohibition against usury appears to many to be irrelevant. However, the issue is still fiercely debated. Every state legislature has in the hopper or in law, restrictions on the level of interest that can be charged consumers. Usury is still very much a problem and is so recognized.

For some 1,500 years, the principal concern of society and the Church was not profit but salvation. The charging of interest was perverse, ranking with murder in terms of its moral consequences.

The difficulty was "It alters things…without toil. Man was intended to toil. To gain wealth without toil went against the very nature of man. The twelfth century Church Council denied Christian burial to usurers, which was later confirmed by The Church Council in the thirteenth century."[xxvii]

As Christian moral theology had no direct application to non-Christians, the business of lending was theirs for the taking. As they were arbitrarily excluded from many fields of human endeavor, moneylending became an important occupation for the Jewish community. Bound together by religion and tradition and shunned by society, they became an important source of capital, which was readily provided to the Gentiles.

Suffice it to say that anti-Semitism was both a Roman and multinational European problem centuries before the rise of fascism, as the above clearly indicates. Underlying the syndrome of persecution was the desire to extinguish debt.

Though a variety of reasons were often given for persecution of moneylenders, the desire to rid oneself of debt, most particularly during times of economic reversal, fed the syndrome and the inhuman practices that went with it. The creditor has few defenders. Invariably there are upward of, say, one hundred debtors for every creditor.

In terms of equity, debtor and creditor should be treated equally. Throughout history this very rarely has occurred. The creditor, when times are difficult, becomes the designated loser. Debt is perceived to be a destroyer of equilibrium and thus order, and therefore the creditor must go.

Debt must be extinguished if the debtor is to retain his or her standard of living without increased toil. Debtor nations resort to devaluation of currency. By this means, the creditor, presumably another nation, is not paid what he or she is owed.

## Kings and Lords—The Temporal and the Spiritual

The role of kings changed over the centuries. Monarchs recognized their dual responsibility: support of both the secular and the spiritual.

"Kings identified their duties to their subjects with their obligations to God, and defined them as the punishment of oppressors, protection of the helpless (particularly widows, orphans, and churches), and extension of the word of God to pagan neighbors. That kings might sometimes neglect or contravene these principles made them more rather than less significant, for without them there could be no justification for a permanent secular authority."[xxviii]

By the eleventh century papal intervention directly and through emissaries became increasingly apparent. During this period there was a considerable growth in papal authority to cleanse the Church of "worldly values."[xxix]

The two practices that caught the attention of the papacy were: first, marriage within the clergy, which translated into the use of Church property and goods to care for one's family; and second, simony or the obtaining of ecclesiastical appointment through the payment of money.

These practices raised questions about the role of kings when it came to the matter of clerical appointments. Putting his man in place as bishop extended the political influence of the king and perhaps as importantly allowed him at least indirectly to gain access to Church land. Bear in mind, land was the critical measure of wealth; it was for all practical purposes the principal source of income, and thus money.

In a series of pronouncements by Popes Urban II (1088–1099) and Paschal II (1099–1118), "The principle that kings could dispense ecclesiastical office was thus effectively rejected."[xxx]

Political intrigue aside, civilization was able to progress from the tenth to the twelfth centuries because of the great work accomplished by the monasteries. They continued their role as intellectual centers while preserving the literature and the works of earlier periods. By the twelfth century scholars from around the world visited these monasteries and began teaching for fees. These fees were paid by their pupils; "such were the origins of the University of Paris."[xxxi]

"An equivalent development can be seen in the art and architecture of the period."[xxxii]

"The twelfth century saw the emergence of a more secular, utilitarian concept of rule which evaluated the deeds of a ruler in terms of the benefits they brought to his people, and classified as tyrannical when harm resulted instead."[xxxiii]

However, great changes in Europe awaited the coming of the thirteenth century.

## The Thirteenth to the Fifteenth Century

As the world moved from the thirteenth to the fourteenth century, having experienced unimaginable challenges by today's standards, one might have thought that civilization was imperiled. This did not prove to be the case. The Mongol invasion, with all the death and destruction that it brought, reopened trade links with China and the rest of Asia. Similar to what occurred in the eighth century with the Muslim invasion, trade opportunities greatly expanded.

The dynamic is oxymoronic. On the one hand, we see widespread destruction, and on the other, unmistakable progress. In today's world we might use the descriptive aphorism or appellation "globalization" to describe these events.

In a strange way the world was coming together.

Though relatively small in terms of geography and population, the new wealth of the Italian states and their political and cultural influence grew exponentially, stretching from the Mediterranean to Constantinople and beyond.

As new centers of commerce came to life, we saw a marked increase in the inhabitants of towns and burgeoning cities. Trade, now extended over great distances, brought to these centers not only goods but human cargo, who were bought and sold as slave labor into the heart of Europe.

Accompanying this cargo were strange diseases that infected the local population, who had no immunity and thus fell prey to this wide-ranging assault. The greatest of these diseases, the bubonic plague, carried the name "Black Death." This plague, which it is generally agreed had its origins in the Far East, swept through Byzantium beginning in approximately 1347 and then through the Mediterranean and wiped out one third of the population of Europe. Some estimates go as high as 50 percent. Europe did not regain the population lost during this period until the eighteenth century. Like the great flood, it spared few families. Tales of this human carnage are truly gruesome. Unlike the flood, the plague, this harbinger of death, did not strike and then disappear.

The catastrophic drop in population made an equally severe drop in trade and thus in the generation of new wealth.

To make matters worse, the Muslim Ottomans now threatened the Byzantine Empire. Constantinople held out until the fifteenth century. It fell to the Turks in 1453.

The plague and the decline in population had a severe impact on Italy. Upheaval wracked Europe, impacting virtually everyone from the peasant to the Church.

This holocaust had a profound effect on the world of commerce. With commercial disintegration the leading position of Italy as financier and commercial underwriter evaporated.

## Spain—The Renaissance and Schism

The Kingdoms of Aragon and Castile now united. Working closely with France, they exacerbated the hostility existing between the Italian states and engaged in warfare, culminating with the conquest of Granada. Consistent with the resentment that accompanied foreign wars and the xenophobic reaction of the populace, the Jews were expelled in 1492—by happenstance, the year Columbus discovered America. Spain saw no inherent conflict in its lust for riches while proselytizing. A decade later the Muslims were given the choice of Christian conversion, as were the Jews, or expulsion.

Spain's explorations and colonizing opened new opportunities for trade, which became the driving force behind the actions of many nations in later centuries.

In Italy, stirrings of rebirth in law, medicine, science, art, architecture, and education began a new era, which in time would carry the appellation "The Renaissance."

Of equal importance were the steady gains in authority the secular world achieved, led by kings and their courts. There was at least at the outset no discernible decrease in religious fervor. Kings still recognized that their monarchial authority sprang from the fact that they were the designees of divine appointment, who were responsible for protecting and defending both the Church and, as well, the defenseless within their domain.

However, as the kings continued to involve themselves in religious affairs, particularly in matters of Church appointments, and as their military capability grew, their inclination to listen to and take instruction from the Church diminished.

No longer as the world turned to worldliness did kings proclaim service but increasingly felt it was their right, if not their duty, to distinguish their views on important matters from those of the Church. In a sense they began to co-opt religion. The clearest indication of this was their donning of clothes that resembled religious garb for important functions, including the wearing of crowns and the carrying of scepters.

Kingships formed for the purpose of service, particularly to the poor, which encompassed the concept of responsibility to a higher authority, and thus a divine appointment, over the centuries morphed into divine anointment. Duty in the minds of these princes translated into rights. They became self-empowering.

As popes, bishops, and clerics were anointed, these secular princes were anointed too, thus sharing the rights, power, and authority of those designated by ecclesiastical authority. They viewed themselves not only as princes but princes of the church as well, though perhaps once removed.

Though this self-empowering process took place over centuries, the right to challenge the Church on matters religious led Henry VIII of England to denounce the papacy when it refused to grant him a divorce from his lawfully wedded wife. This led to his declaring himself head of the Church of England while ostensibly remaining Catholic.

CHAPTER 4

# Henry VIII, King of England and Ireland, 1509–1547

## The Importance of Henry

Beginning with Henry VIII, England, while not abandoning its Catholicity, abandoned the Papacy and, in abandoning the Papacy, the strictures of the moral code. No longer did the sitting pope hold the keys to the kingdom, at least in the mind of Henry and his successors and followers.

The pope no longer stood in England as the vicar of Christ. Presumably, Christianity needed more than one. Henry, by making himself the head of the Church of England, was the "vicar" throughout his empire. By fiat, he and the pope henceforth were equals. Both were princes, and each should be treated with appropriate respect as such. The pope's views might or might not hold sway in other parts of Europe, but in England it was Henry's view that mattered. Anyone not inclined to hold with this was henceforth considered a traitor.

In England, Catholic theology was not to be abandoned, but the interpretation of that theology would be up to Henry. He decided what was right and wrong. The moral code could be altered or changed, dependent entirely on his perspective.

Thus, he could dissolve his marriage to Catherine of Aragon, shut down the monasteries, retire the clergy, steal all Church valuables, and take their land, which constituted some 20 percent of England's land, and the profits flowing from it and make all of it his.

With this land he built for himself great edifices as the pagan Roman emperors had done. The peasants who lived and toiled on the land in large numbers were considered trespassers. As such they were expelled, leaving them homeless and penniless, with no source of income. Starvation wracked the countryside.

This problem would not be remedied for decades. Only after Elizabeth I ascended to the throne was the problem recognized. Until her time, the unemployed were considered shirkers and were subject to the most barbarous treatment, including branding and beatings and, if circumstances suggested, death.

Parliament under Elizabeth ultimately passed legislation to address this horror. However, there were so many and their conditions so inhuman that even Elizabeth was shocked as she toured the countryside.

This pauper legislation had no title since help for the poor and indigent had no place and was largely unknown in English society.

English attitudes changed over the centuries, but labor was always treated with disdain. "Are there no workhouses?" would remain the standard, endorsed by governments conservative and liberal, until socialist pressures and depression conditions following the Great War finally give primacy to labor with the election of a Labor government.

There is no question that Henry VIII viewed himself as a prince. In the cold light of history, we can say he was a Christian prince of a different sort.

As one might expect, he was excommunicated from the Catholic Church, but this did not change Henry's ways. To gain wives and lands and great riches, he was willing to take his chances in the hereafter. Perhaps his calculation was that for a prince, within the hierarchy of heaven special allowances would be made.

If the moral code was to be cast aside or made subject to the views of princes, nobles, and merchants, but not peasants, since they were subject to the authority of their superiors, then the princes, nobles, and merchants should be able to pursue their interests without due reflection on the moral consequences. It was about this time that the light on hell began to dim in Europe.

For 1,500 years the code had been the foundation that allowed for the rise of civilization. If it no longer was the searchlight to guide humankind, what would take its place? What interest or interests would humans pursue during their comparatively short stay on this planet?

Humans' interests varied. Increasing knowledge allowed for continuing exploration and investigation. Society now focused on the finite. This provided people with the opportunity to raise their living standards and extend their lives.

This could only be accomplished through the acquisition of wealth.

This way of thinking was not new. Humans had from time immemorial sought wealth, but humans' priorities would now begin to fundamentally change. Led by Henry and noted philosophers, the pursuit of money and power henceforth took priority over the spiritual. The sixteenth century was the critical moment in history in that respect.

For this to be accomplished, a new philosophy was introduced. This period marked the beginning of relativism. Henceforth, right and wrong no longer stood as an objective standard against which humans could measure behavior.

Justification was to be found solely in the mind of the one acting. Thus Henry could marry many times and steal many times. He justified this by noting his stature as a prince, as was said quite clearly centuries later by Frank Hague, the mayor of a city in New Jersey, when it was pointed out to him that his actions contravened the law and he simply responded, "In this city I am the law."

Relativism allowed for the justification of all conduct, no matter how barbarous, as the world would bear witness to in the twentieth century.

No question the sixteenth century was the turning point in this regard. It stands as the beginning of fundamental change in the aspirations of society, bringing forth the best and the worst in humans, a trend that continues to the present.

The overriding question that this book cannot possibly answer but that lies at the heart of the debate over critical global issues today is the following: "Is this path chosen freely by humans to prioritize and pursue money and power above all other considerations sustainable?"

Henry's basic problem was one of extraordinary greed, which he combined with emancipation, a "right of kings" as God's designated prince to rule not only the people but the kings themselves.

In fact, a mural painted of Henry during his reign shows him sitting at the hand of God. He was engaged in self-delusion.

Implicitly he replaced the moral code with a regime, prioritizing self-interest and self-aggrandizement. Such a code brought a clash of interest between individuals and ultimately states. The greatest of these would have to await the twentieth century.

The espousal of personal freedom as defined by Henry remained closely guarded in England, being limited to the nobility. On the Continent the response was in general very similar. America made important distinctions.

## The Act of Dissolution

The pivotal moment for England, the Church, and Western civilization occurred in 1536. There is simply no way to fully estimate the repercussions that proceeded from the convocation of the clergy guided by Henry, which laid down the articles of doctrine for the Church of England and prefaced the Dissolution of the Monasteries, resulting in the closure of 563 monasteries within four years.

"In 1536, under the guidance of the King, Convocation (the official assembly of the English clergy) laid down the Ten Articles of doctrine for the Church of England, treading a middle road between the teachings of the Catholic Church and the more radical beliefs of the reformers. The Dissolution of the Monasteries began, and within four years every religious house in England—563 in all—would be closed and the inmates pensioned off, changing the landscape of England for ever."[xxxiv]

Henry, though he continued to profess his Catholicity and Christianity, in effect was moving to destroy all vestiges of traditional Christianity. The Judeo-Christian moral code had raised humanity from the darkness and barbarism that had enveloped the European Continent for thousands of years. The dignity of humankind had become an accepted principle, though frequently ignored and widely abused during humans' long climb from the depths of despair. The dignity of humankind would be accomplished under the watchful eye and guiding hand of the seat of Peter, that is, the Papacy, which would challenge any effort to adulterate the moral code.

In one fell swoop, Henry sought to destroy all of this. Turning humans away from their spiritual obligations of conscience while substituting a new philosophy involving not the pursuit of truth but materialism and hedonism, along with the advent of modernity, led to wholesale greed.

Until Henry, Western man, guided by the Church, first sought salvation and then the material goods of the world.

After Henry large numbers of Westerners used the Church symbolically to denote their Western identity but with no responsibility. This new "Church" allowed people to carry on their affairs strictly as they saw fit. Following Henry they would speak directly to the Creator, ignoring Him when it suited their purposes and calling on Him in an emergency.

The pursuit of self-interest set nation against nation, people against people. Nationalism became the guiding principle in international relations. People were enslaved, deprived, and slaughtered for money.

Money became the root of evil. That condition would not change, even after untold numbers of wars and unimaginable devastation inclusive of World War I and World War II.

This largely pagan philosophy would over time produce great disparity in income, leading to revolution and dissolution, and serve to give rise to alien and inhuman philosophies such as communism and fascism.

The very heart and soul of society were threatened as the money craze rapidly expanded. It led to social syndromes such as divorce and disease and offspring confused totally as to what was right or wrong.

## Henry Goes for the Gold, Church Land, and Valuables

Henry was driven by the need for money. This spendthrift never had enough for himself and his court.

Perhaps these circumstances pushed him over the edge. His self-appointment as head of the Church of England allowed him to deal with the Church land in the kingdom as he saw fit.

Henry had a fixation when it came to land and castles. Construction and renovation were his passion. He would build castles on immense acreage, insisting on certain designs and making minute changes to suit his tastes. Many were truly magnificent, and yet he would spend little or no time visiting them. Frequently he traded them for other properties, invariably getting the better of the bargain.

Land of course, as it had been over the centuries, was true money. Henry worshipped money and the things money could buy. The Church of England became the tool he used in order to advance this worship. Henry may never have loved his wives, but he certainly loved money. No one in history made an effort to accumulate it as he did. Money and the presumed power that went with it, false god or not, was all, except perhaps women, that Henry ever wanted.

Church land was the greatest source of wealth in England. It constituted 20 percent of the land. The income that could be derived from such vast holdings would satisfy any future need he might have, while impoverishing thousands who were thrown off the land and later prosecuted harshly for their idleness. (We are witnessing something similar today as thousands are fired to enhance the wealth of executives.)

"The vast revenues of the abbeys were diverted into the treasury, doubling the royal income and commensurately increasing the King's power... Henry also appropriated wagon-loads of jewels, removed from crucifixes, relics, shrines and altar ornaments, and a wealth of plate...The Crown also took possession of monastic lands worth £120,000 (36 million) a year, one fifth of the kingdom's landed wealth. The King redistributed a third of this land in order to secure the support and loyalty of influential men, and in 1536 a new Court of Augmentation, under Cromwell's control, was established to implement this policy...Most beneficiaries had to pay for the privilege...Most men of affairs were prepared to compromise their principles for the sake of gain, and readily identified themselves, through their new vested interests with the royal supremacy; opposition to the King's religious reforms, particularly in the south, was therefore minimal."[xxxv]

Christian unity, the moral code, and the guiding hand of the Papacy were all sacrificed for money. One is immediately drawn to the earlier example of Judas Iscariot. Henry's treachery, like the earlier one, would have titanic implications for the direction of society.

This is the pivotal moment in Western world history. In earlier centuries the Christian world had been beset by schism and frequently corrupt leadership. But the "Chair of Peter," with its power of excommunication, was not challenged even by the most determined of kings or emperors.

Religious schisms, some quite popular, would in time fade away. Henry's Church of England was schismatic, but unlike other schisms, it represented an alternative religion. One could pursue money, material goods, or a hedonistic lifestyle, while still claiming to be a member in good standing of the Church.

Being a member of this church had advantages. It allowed nobles, merchants, and peasants to do whatever they liked and not be subject to moral approbation. In addition, there was little prospect of excommunication, with all its implications.

Without question the corrupting influence of lust for power, money, and authority, combined with a misplaced sense by kings and princes of their own importance, had its final expression in the sixteenth-century religious schisms.

These schisms, combined with Church corruption and ignorance, led to the formation of a Christian philosophy that we have come to know as Protestantism.

CHAPTER 5

# Money and Banking

---

## THE RISE OF CREDIT AND THE CURRENCY FAMINE

The geometric increase in trade, both in terms of goods and services and slaves by way of the Mediterranean, placed Italian bankers in a most advantageous position. This position was furthered with the invention of "double entry book keeping, the letter of credit, bills of exchange and the deposit account."[xxxvi]

More sophisticated methods of financing were being experimented with, but Europe was slowly slipping into a currency famine. Silver had for centuries been the most acceptable currency in the world of trade and commerce. As stated earlier, silver met the key qualifications. It was precious. As a metal it would not spoil or degrade, and it was universally acceptable for purposes of payment.

Silver was more available than gold, and thus gold held a special place as a standard to measure value. Due to its scarcity, gold was not typically used to consummate a transaction.

A distant tribe or state might demand gold to settle disputes. Gold was frequently used to pay ransom, particularly if a major political figure, local lord, or perhaps king was involved.

An exchange for gold carried with it a special significance and lent importance to the transaction. However, for the typical commercial transaction, silver was the widely accepted medium for payment.

The difficulty in relying on gold and silver was that they required mining. The ore in the mines was finite. Thus, as world trade increased, there was a constant need for new discovery. Both metals were in great demand for the purpose of jewelry and for plate, as well as currency. They became important status symbols. Ore was critical to the money supply, but there was stiff competition for it. There was competition among goldsmiths to meet their customers' desires for ornaments, dishware, goblets, pins, frames, and a variety of trinkets.

Thus the price of gold and silver, responding to demand, was subject to constant fluctuation. There is evidence of major shortages of both metals during certain periods of the Middle Ages.

## Currency—The Great Enigma

The late Middle Ages ushered in a period of profound societal change.

The nobles typically treated the peasantry wretchedly by any standard of today, but there was a peculiar harmony. Men and women lived and worked mostly the land, while barons, kings, and earls sought to expand their wealth and power by fighting and seizing land. In the midst of this mayhem, chivalry, though too often glamorized, was both real and an important standard of behavior.

In large part as a result of ignorance and their station in life, the great bulk of the European population had neither the time nor the motivation to pursue money. The nobility held secular power, with the Church preeminent, until Henry, with respect to anything touching on morality.

Metal had its place, particularly in trade, but distant trade had no bearing on the lives of the many. Trade had grown, at first very slowly, after the fall of Rome. But with continuing invasions and mixing of peoples, a wider world with differing resources stretching from Mongolia and China in the East to the Arabian desert in the Middle East stimulated trade and the growing need for a universal currency, which unquestionably was gold and silver.

England, an island nation protected by the sea and a formidable navy, was harbored from the destructive invaders on the Continent. At the same time, England was an important producer of woolen products, hides, a variety of fine products, and coal, which was much in demand throughout the known world. England, with natural resources sufficient to feed and maintain its own population, could turn to exports.

England was an exporter, which meant that wealth, as measured in terms of gold and silver, was destined for London. London was not only becoming an important center of commerce but of finance as well.

One might readily conclude that over the centuries, this would have resulted in England becoming the wealthiest of nations. However, the English experience was far from linear. The English, just as the peoples on the Continent, were beset by the desire for foreign goods.

A ticklish problem was the constantly changing price of precious metals, both in absolute terms and against one another. No way could be found to fix the price of money. The value of money was in constant flux. A further complication was the fact that the value was not uniform from one region to another. Where there was an abundance of gold or silver, the price of both and the ratio between them, that is the number of ounces of silver to buy one ounce of gold, were subject to significant variance.

As the value of metal rises, it requires an increased amount of labor to accumulate the needed amount to repay debt. In other words, the creditor is the beneficiary whenever there is metal shortage or the price rises as a result of increased demand, as would naturally happen in a vibrant economy. The value of labor was a constant variable, and so was the value of money.

Thus, it logically follows that as the value of currency rises, a greater amount of labor is required in order to accumulate the same amount of purchasing power in terms of currency.

A simple example of this would be the debtor, who by the terms of a contract, having borrowed gold, at maturity must repay gold. At maturity if the purchasing power of the gold has doubled, then the borrower must expend twice the labor to repay the same amount of gold. Rising currency values have a profoundly negative impact on both labor and the debtor.

The creditor stands to benefit; although he will receive the same nominal amount when the debt is repaid, that is, the same number of ounces of gold, the purchasing power of the currency has appreciated. Gold now has twice the value, and thus he stands to realize gain both in terms of interest paid and the appreciation of the currency. Note, most of the gain in the illustration comes from the appreciation of the currency.

Appreciating currencies reduce the value of and increase the cost of labor, and enrich creditors, most notably foreign creditors. Appreciating currencies, as they represent the prospect of enhanced return on the one hand, stimulate investment; but on the other hand, they encourage outsourcing and the reduction of staff in order to minimize cost. As this condition persists, greater attention is paid to laborsaving devices. Invention takes center stage, as advances in productivity become increasingly important to profitability.

The implications of this are both meaningful and troubling.

## Measuring the Impact of Appreciating/Depreciating Currency Value in a Paper Currency World

I must detour briefly from a rendition of history to address certain concepts.

How does paper currency impact commerce?

Let us suppose Country A is on the gold exchange standard and its gross product increases. This gives rise to an increase in the value of the local currency. As a holder of that currency, I can exchange it for gold and with the appreciable increment buy more goods.

However, metal has built-in equilibrium. There is only so much metal available for purposes of exchange.

On the other hand, with a fiat or paper money standard, buying power is uncertain. It is entirely dependent on the emission of the central bank or government, which may or may not choose to increase the money supply. Currency is always available, but the price is uncertain.

In such a case, though my contribution in terms of labor has increased and thus I have more dollars, the paper in which the contribution is measured may or may not have greater value. That is up to the central bank and, to a lesser extent, the market. My wealth is ultimately determined by the action of the central bank and not by my contribution.

Earlier, we noted that through the ages a major problem with the use of metal as currency was shortage. A shortage of gold or silver on many an occasion throughout history brought economic expansion to a halt. This was recognized as a serious problem. In the early twentieth century, such a condition in New York prompted a bank to issue wooden nickels. This raised an outcry and calls for the creation of an institution to provide liquidity under such circumstances. With considerable opposition both in and outside of Congress, that led to the formation of the Federal Reserve.

It might be said that the driving force and purpose behind this creation was the continuing need for currency availability or liquidity. It was expected that in every other respect, this body would seldom be seen and rarely heard from. We now know better. The implications of this were enormous and not understood at the time; they are still not understood today.

If a central bank intervenes and this results in an upward movement in currency value, labor output must rise in tandem; otherwise the global gross product will fall. When the gross product falls, by definition, a condition of recession has ensued. It follows that under such circumstances, the value of the currency should then fall.

This is not happening today; though the US economy is in recession, the value of the dollar has been on balance stable or rising against other currencies.

This is bizarre; the reason for this phenomenon is clear. Central banks make this possible through intervention. They in turn are being driven by the continuing increase in global debt. Debt is the ultimate culprit.

Debt has the effect of driving the value of paper currency higher, not lower.

A shortage of currency gives rise to recessionary conditions, but so does appreciation in currency value not matched by greater output.

If we were today on a metal standard and there was no gold or silver available or the price rose substantially, commerce as in centuries past would have slowed precipitously.

In a paper system, there is never shortage; there is no liquidity risk, a condition that invites debt. Why not increase leverage when there is no possibility of shortage? Currency demand drives the currency price higher.

What is the end result? A currency bubble of course, best described as a profound condition of disequilibrium. It cannot last.

Nations strive mightily to have what they refer to as a strong currency. They seem to be under the illusion that a strong currency translates into wealth. Currency, as we have noted, is never wealth. It is true that a currency rising in value versus the currency of another nation will allow the former to buy more goods from the latter with the same amount of currency. However, the offset is an imbalance in payments, a trade distortion.

To avoid this distortion, the appreciating currency country must increase productivity, that is, must increase the units of output for the same amount of labor to offset the appreciation.

The world of business is in a constant search for ways to increase productivity. Invention and innovation are powerful tools in this regard. More often, this is accomplished by reductions in staff. Fewer laborers are producing the goods.

The few may be wealthier, but a greater number are sacrificed. The currency indeed may rise in value, but those who have been sacrificed will not benefit. The result must be a widening in the wealth gap, those who have versus those who do not, which is the global condition today.

Thus, one certain effect of an imbalanced appreciation in currency is to further stratify society, to widen the gap between rich and poor. The poor, in order to maintain their relative standard of living, enter into debt as the value of currency rises. These circumstances give rise to a massive accumulation of debt, both public and private. The bulk of this debt is for consumption and thus does not generate any return.

With the unemployed unable to repay the debt by virtue of the fact that they no longer have the opportunity to labor, the debt default rate rises exponentially, extinguishing capital and savings, and the world spirals into depression.

The long-term effect of global appreciation of currency is to throw the world into depression.

The central banks of the world attempt to maintain parity among currencies. Their policies are driven by this perceived need. Thus as the dollar, the world's reserve currency, appreciates, others will take steps to see that their currency remains in line.

As a result all currencies, at least the major ones, find their currency values appreciating though the economic fundamentals in their country do not justify it. Commerce becomes stunted.

This issue can be viewed from many different angles. Another way of describing conditions surrounding a world of appreciating currencies is that the cost of labor rises. As the absolute value measured in terms of goods and services paid to labor increases, employers seek to offset those costs by reducing the numbers of workers.

Paper currency value should truly reflect economic reality, in the same way that silver and gold did a century ago but it most assuredly does not today due to the capacity of central banks to manipulate exchange rates.

The experience of Germany post World War II bears this out. While the physical infrastructure of Germany was being destroyed, the money supply of Germany expanded at an ever more rapid rate. The result was that the currency was no longer acceptable in commerce. The other frightful possibility is that the amount of debt becomes so great that no one believes it will ever be repaid. Both conditions will bring commerce to a halt.

With infinite paper and debt, there is no mechanism in place to correct imbalance. At some point, the market will cease to function.

We are in the fix we are in today as the result of confusion over two concepts, money and currency. Money is the product of labor, and for equilibrium to be maintained, for progress to be made, labor must be the engine, for only labor is the perfect and true standard. Currency thus must be a measure of labor. Failure of currency to measure labor will in the end bring total disarray, if not dissolution.

## A History of Gold versus Silver, Price versus Availability

Though a universal commodity, gold has always been a scarce commodity. So has silver. But far more silver has been processed.

Though the price of gold versus silver has varied significantly, the ratio of 12–15 to 1, that is, one ounce of gold is worth twelve to fifteen ounces of silver, was typical. From the standpoint of mining, discovery was key.

In the modern world, we take it for granted that money will always be available at a price. This was not the case prior to nor during the Middle Ages.

In the late Middle Ages, most notably in the thirteenth century, the availability of silver improved. The effect of this was to drop the price of silver versus gold. Periodically gold became more available, and the price of gold would decline.

By the early fifteenth century, silver was in short supply, and the price of silver versus gold rose. During most of the fourteenth and fifteenth centuries, gold was to play a leading role in commercial affairs. Gold became the world's leading currency. Silver was simply unattainable.

The growing use of silver for plate and the continuing imbalance of payments in Western Europe would periodically result in the virtual disappearance of silver. The effect was to drastically reduce commerce, or in the less-traveled regions, bring it to a complete halt.

As nations, peoples, and tribes came increasingly into contact with one another as transportation improved and as the demand for different products from different regions increased, the need for metal increased.

Since either gold or silver was acceptable in payment, frequently a borrower would borrow in gold and repay in silver or vice versa. Meanwhile, holders of silver would secrete the metal as the price rose and then dump it as the price began to fall. All of this was very unsatisfactory. In all cases, lenders were certain to lose. They would receive in payment in the lesser of the two as measured by price.

## Where Have All the Goldsmiths Gone?
Many centuries before the world had ever heard of Herbert Hoover, FDR, or the New Deal, there came paper to the Western world via China. Paper would change everything, including currency.

Paper was invented in China in the second century BC. Felted paper was brought to Europe by the Arabs in the sixth century. There was no European paper until the twelfth century, and paper was still reserved for the elite until the fifteenth century.

We can credit the wide usage of paper money in the West to the most unlikely of trades, the goldsmiths. Goldsmiths were artisans; today we would call them jewelers. They practiced their profession through the network of guilds from antiquity through the Middle Ages.

Earlier efforts in antiquity and later to introduce coinage were always met with mixed results. Coin did produce a new industry, the infamous money changers, but coin always wrestled with the problem of value, which led to the creation of the agio.

The agio allowed bills to be in bank money or the standard of the mint. Bank money was money "on account" and thus received universal acceptance.

Most of the work of the goldsmiths involved precious metal, which was shaped and engraved to the specifications of its owners. There was an obvious need for the safekeeping of items and materials that were precious. To the owners of these materials, it made a great deal of sense to leave these items with the goldsmith rather than leave them at home or travel with them and risk having them lifted by highwaymen. Today we use safe deposit boxes for the same purpose.

Wealthy landowners would take their metal to the goldsmith to have it shaped and engraved and receive from the goldsmith a receipt with the goldsmith's name and address, a description of the item, and undoubtedly an estimation of value.

In their districts the goldsmiths were well-known—after all, they were very important people—and their official receipt was something that could be easily carried on the person.

Thus, if one ran into a highwayman, he would not lose his jewelry, and the highwayman would not steal the receipt because to be caught with it meant severe punishment, such as having one's hands chopped off.

Receipts obviously multiplied and were traded. In time they became goldsmith notes. Voilà! Paper currency was born. Goldsmith notes became the first bank notes, and bank notes, sans a picture of G. Washington or the King of England, were accepted as currency.

Goldsmiths were the true bankers. It didn't take them long to realize that it was possible for them to issue more notes than they had metal on deposit. They reasoned that since the owners of the metal would seldom come by to take the metal, they could loan the metal via the issuance of notes and be repaid before the true owner of the metal returned.

This was not banking fraud. They were not lending the owner's precious metal; rather, they were issuing their notes, which of course were supposed to be secured by the precious metal. Thus, it was imperative that whoever the borrower was, he had the capacity to repay the loan. If the goldsmith was not repaid, he would have to bear the loss.

If one did not have gold or silver at hand in order to buy or trade, the next best thing was a goldsmith's note. This note could be redeemed simply by taking it to the goldsmith.

This was a very profitable business just as long as everyone repaid their loans on time. Credit received a very big push from this practice.

Another important banking practice was that of guarantees, which were widely used, particularly where trade was involved. Since goods were shipped great distances, the Italian bankers who made trade their business would offer payment and other guarantees for a share of the goods or profits from their sale.

As was widely noted even at the time, the Italians became wealthy, though they owned little land. This fact fostered great jealousy among the Italian states and fierce competition with other centers of trade, most notably Constantinople.

This rise in wealth of the Italian bankers ultimately broke the monopoly that Jewish bankers had exercised over finance as a result of the centuries-old view on interest and usury.

The definition of interest began to change, and the charging of interest became more acceptable. The prohibition evolved into opposition to usurious practices. The crusaders' need for transportation and supply at the entrance to the Mediterranean gave the Italians a sweeping advantage and led to their domination not only of trade but of finance as well.

## The Crusades—Was This about Redemption?

Spiritual redemption and commercial redemption are two different things indeed. Modern banking is built on the concept of redemption, the commercial type. The instrument, the IOU, the bill, the note is symbolic and must ultimately be redeemed. The instrument doesn't determine value or wealth.

This has become impossible in modern banking. With "fiat" currency we have merged or at least have attempted to merge currency and value.

We fail to make the critical distinction that currency is only symbolic. The paper must be redeemed either in precious metal, scarce commodities, or goods or services. No methodology has yet been devised that would assure redemption, at least not since 1971.

Until the 1970s the Federal Reserve issued silver certificates. Silver certificates looked in every respect like ordinary dollars, with George Washington's picture on the front but also, and more importantly, "Silver Certificate" engraved on them. With enough certificates one would go to the office of the Federal Reserve in lower Manhattan, and the Fed would hand you a bar of silver in exchange for the certificates.

China, having invented paper, was well ahead of the West in terms of introducing it as currency. It is thought that paper money was introduced by Kubla Khan in China in the thirteenth century.

The Mongols made a considerable effort to reform currency practices when it became obvious that excessive emission of paper was impairing value. The poorest peasant developed an intuitive sense that the paper he was taking for his hard work was really worthless. It was at this point that the paper currency world collapsed.

## The Persecution of Creditors

Throughout history, moneylending was viewed as a less-than-respectable business. The widely held view that the lender did not contribute value to a transaction and thus was reaping a benefit that was not rightly his was the basis for periodic wholesale assault on lenders.

During the Middle Ages, kings relied heavily on bankers to finance their various activities, particularly their wars. Taxation had its limits. Therefore one had to turn to the so-called bankers for the needed revenue. The Jewish community played a major role in this activity. As debt mounted, a crossover point was reached where it became a great deal easier to renege on the debt than to satisfy the demands of creditors for repayment.

Sympathy for the debtor and the power of kings invariably put the creditor at risk when the creditors were a separate, frequently isolated community, as the Jewish community was in Europe. The simplest way to extinguish debt was to get rid of the creditor.

This course of action was often repeated, and it frequently took the form of expulsion of the lender. Edward I (1239–1307) expelled the Jews from England.

## Hitlerian Tactics before Hitler

Edward's war against creditors required the support of the populace. He made accusations of usury to engender their support. This of course was a popular position among the many debtors in the country.

This campaign was facilitated by Edward's accusation that it was all the fault of the Jews. In 1275 Edward issued the Statute of Jewry, which among other restrictions required that Jews wear on their outer garment a yellow star with a length and breadth of six inches by three inches. Each Jew, man and woman alike, twelve years and older, had to pay the bondsman three pence annually at Easter. Furthermore, Jews could not take the property of another in foreclosure or any other proceeding without the express permission of the king.

The Jews ran into continuing persecution and expulsion, in part because of race and in part due to the widespread belief that as lenders they were unfairly benefiting financially from the hard work of others. Many were arrested, and in 1279, three hundred were executed in the Tower of London.

This irrational bias reached a crescendo during the Hitler era in Germany. German propaganda successfully painted the Jews as being the beneficiaries of global banking techniques that gave the Jews control over industry and commerce. Thus they were held responsible for the outbreak and the loss of the First World War which justified the widespread murder and looting of their property, which we have come to call the Holocaust.

## The Edict of Expulsion, 1290: The Beleaguered Jewish Community

With the Norman conquest, the Jewish community arrived in England and were very successful in their commercial pursuits. They traveled extensively throughout Europe gaining wealth, returning to England, and living lavishly. Edward I concluded that such wealth must be due to usurious conduct, and this led to the Edict of Expulsion.

Edward I appears to have been driven to this decision solely by his need for money. In the end, greater taxation was the price paid by the populace for the Jewish expulsion. With expulsion all debts owed to the Jews were transferred to the king. As a result of this decision, Edward's popularity soared. Confusion abounded.

The guild system of Europe made it very difficult for the Jews to pursue other commercial ventures. Expulsion was seen by Edward as a practical solution to his and the nation's debt, which was the source of his political problems.

Anti-Semitism was of course not restricted to England. In Spain, two hundred years subsequent, an Edict of Expulsion was ordered. All Jews were required to leave the country and were allowed to take their property as long as they did not export gold or silver or coin money or other things prohibited.

## Modern Banking Comes to Life

The ever-widening circle of trade with participants of many different backgrounds necessitates a regularized system acceptable to all.

Among the events that signaled a new era in trade and commerce were the conquering of Constantinople by the Latins in 1204, giving the "westerners" control of the Black Sea and the Crimea, a major gold center. The gold florin was struck in 1252, which, as a widely accepted medium of exchange, was of great assistance in furthering trade.

In 1283 the Statute of Merchants recognized the rights of merchants. In the fifteenth century, the discounting of bills for foreign commerce became widespread.

In the sixteenth century, organized banking gained a foothold as the City of Antwerp became the center of international trade and the capital of the money market. Bills drawn on Antwerp became the international currency of the age.

Earlier the ever-reliable goldsmiths, scriveners, brokers, and merchants played various roles in providing financing for trade and commerce.

The sixteenth century was the turning point for another major change in the world of money and banking. The payment of interest became an acceptable practice.

## Interest—The Devil's Workshop

Long before the rise of Christianity, in both Greece and Rome, the notion of interest was identified with usury. Thus it was deserving of universal condemnation.

In antiquity those who borrowed were desperate men who occupied small plots of land and by borrowing found themselves in a state of virtual slavery. Though there may be more differences than similarities, today's consumer addiction to the credit card in the twenty-first century has placed many a family in serf-like condition.

Money, unlike agriculture or guild work, was not productive, and thus, to charge interest was nothing less than a violation of the natural law.

The Church viewed the "charging of interest as a vile crime comparable only to murder."[xxxvii] This view prevailed up to the time of Calvin. This strict prohibition and the consequences that flowed from ignoring this directive necessitated the money trade find refuge outside the Christian community.

As a result, the Jewish community by default inherited this trade. However, Jewish participation and ultimate domination of the money trade did not begin with the rise of Christianity. No less a figure than Cicero spoke of the Jewish bankers, and much was written in his era on the subject of money and interest.

Though the charging of interest was indeed viewed as virtually criminal up to the sixteenth century, there was no objection to making a profit. No one thought it scandalous to charge rent.

A further complication was that the greatest financial institution of the Middle Ages, namely, the Church, was indeed essential to the expansion of world trade. By the sixteenth century, the charging of interest morphed into a question of usury.

At one point Church officials concluded that the charging of interest was no longer criminal provided the rate did not exceed 10 percent. However, the rate would not be determinative of usury. Rather, interest became usurious if the rate was fixed and unconditional so that the amount had to be paid irrespective of the success or failure of the venture. In effect, the Church was investing, not lending.

In world affairs there would never have been an issue if it had not been for the geometric expansion of world trade that was a by-product of tribal ventures and conquering kings and, most importantly, the era of the crusades.

To finance a venture on a scale as large as the crusades, transnational in scope, required huge sums of currency. Taxation was never the solution since it is in the nature of people to take whatever steps are required to avoid handing over to monarchs and other authorities their hard-earned capital and receive nothing in return. Even the prospect of the return of the Holy Land was insufficient incentive for Christian men to part with their wealth.

Thus a question arose as to what it would take for men to come together to finance a venture. The answer lay in three critical words: "rate of return."

Rate of return could be distinguished from usury. Usury carried with it the notion of taking something from another, a form of stealing. Return, on the other hand, meant the taking of risk, an investment, a truly worthy and moral pursuit. Investment in the expansion of trade allowed for the landless to gain wealth.

The great transnational efforts that are so familiar to us in the modern world require staggering amounts of capital. The capital or money to carry on the venture requires both sufficiency and dependability. As it proceeds from numerous sources, it becomes concentrated for a certain purpose.

Thus a new term found its way into the commercial lexicon, namely, the concentration of capital.

In order to achieve this, there had to be an intermediary, and we call that banking.

Bankers and banking, both as entities and in syndicate, served the purpose of bringing together the sources of capital and the borrower, allowing for the building of structures or the massing of armies at agreed terms, satisfactory to both.

The rise of banking was the critical step on humans' seemingly inexorable march toward modernity.

This march was further stimulated as humans quickly learned that money begets money. Thus societies began to save capital rather than consume it, allowing for the process of concentration to take place.

Indeed, the rich got richer, and society prospered.

This process appeared to be unending, and perhaps it is. This climb to the mountaintop is certain if people can only avoid the fault lines. In their exuberance, in their desire to get to the top over the centuries, people have turned a blind eye to the dangers inherent in the climb. Instead of recognizing the fault lines for what they are, people see them as shortcuts to gaining immense wealth and power.

Unfortunately, as the world has learned, there are no shortcuts, but rather stumbling blocks, which herald disaster.

## The Fault Lines

The most destructive fault line is consumption. Consumption represents the final destruction of wealth.

On the other hand, production resulting from the efficient use of labor increases wealth. As long as production balances consumption, the global standard of living, assuming little or no change in population, remains intact.

Wealth expands to the extent that production exceeds consumption. The uncertain variable is population. We have learned over the ages that wealth increases at an arithmetic rate, while population increases at a geometric rate. This is problematic.

Those with future visions of prosperity fail to see that population growth is a hurdle. This is nature's way of maintaining balance among the species. Nature will seek to prevent any species from dominating the polity. Nature's role is to assure balance, not human domination.

Since the latter part of the twentieth century, and in earlier times, humans seem driven by the prospect of consumption. Most investment in public and private sectors appears to be consumption oriented.

Production is of secondary importance. We produce to meet our immediate need, and we work tirelessly in order to consume more. Self-satisfaction has become the purpose for living. Money/capital and consumption have synthesized. We find ourselves in a blind alley from which there appears no escape except more of the same.

Life becomes truly meaningless, a far cry from the moral code that dictated the behavior of humans for most of the first two millennia AD.

## The Production-Consumption Tie

We labor to survive. We produce in order to gain our share of the necessities of life. Those who do not labor must perish. Such is the lesson of life itself.

However, to produce amounts only sufficient to maintain the status quo means that humans' standard of living can never improve. All people regardless of nationality regard such a condition today as completely unsatisfactory. That was not always the case. Throughout history at least up to the seventeenth century, it was widely accepted that people were born with a role to fill, and to seek more than this in some respect violated nature itself.

That view still prevails in major regions of the undeveloped world, as the caste system of India readily attests to. In the United States, we base our constitutional government on the concept that the individual is supreme. The individual has "inalienable rights." Each of us has the right to progress. Progress is achieved through education and the application of knowledge.

With experience and dedication, we become wise. We no longer work to consume but to advance. We push ourselves in the direction of infinite wisdom, the Creator.

In order to accomplish this, we must lay the groundwork. As a nation we must invest. We must build. To build, however, we must have the resources, and those resources can only be obtained from the product of our work that is not consumed. This of course translates into savings.

Investment takes many forms; it gives rise to invention, which simply modifies labor practices or provides new instruments to accomplish labor's goals in a more efficient way.

Thus progress is a continuing process built on the freedom of individuals to pursue their goals within society, contributing to the total product of the nation through the utilization of their unique skills.

Production and human progress are synonymous. Production and wealth are synonymous. Wealth and progress are thus synonymous. Consumption impedes progress. Economic advancement is totally dependent on this symphony of interaction. For the melody to come through, each artist must perform. Their performance determines the majesty of the human spirit.

Clearly the performers must eat and sleep. Yet there can be no symphony while they do.

Thus production is not linear. Mixed in, if you will, will always be consumption. The greater the percentage of consumption to production, the less progress is being made, and the less wealth is being accumulated.

Wealth is destroyed by failing to produce or by consuming a greater percentage of the total product. Increasing production is the key that opens the door to progress.

## Capital versus Currency

As we can see clearly from the above, production and consumption are working against each other. No nation or society can move forward by increasing its consumption. Such a society is on the road to pauperism.

To move forward, we must find the most efficient means to increase production. The prerequisite of production is capital, that is, accumulated savings.

Thus the second great fault line is insufficiency of capital and/or its dependent, currency.

While the attributes of consumption are self-evident, the problems associated with the availability of money/capital/savings are far more subtle.

Allowing consumption to rule means a society will become bereft of money/capital. Such a society will not invest, for it no longer has the savings to invest. Such a society retains its currency, but it is worthless.

Thus currency and capital are not the same. Capital, accumulated savings, always has value, but currency may or may not. Currency is never value and at best is but a representation of value.

Governments of the twenty-first century have come to believe that if they flood their society with currency (liquidity), the effect will be the same as investing capital. Currency invariably fosters consumption. Capital fosters investment. Never the twain shall meet.

Of course, to flood a country with currency was a physical impossibility until the advent of paper. In point of fact, the problem throughout most of history has not been excessive increases in currency (the money supply), at least not up to the twentieth century. To put it simply, paper made all the difference.

Prior to the advent of paper money, there was total reliance on metal. All paper issued had backing. That is not the case today. Nothing backs the dollar today except the good faith of the US government. A frequently used expression in describing this is that the government controls the printing presses.

Thus the government will never default on the nation's debt since it simply has to turn on the press. Turning on the press results in more currency, but the value of the currency is diminished in tandem with the incremental amount printed.

Since equilibrium rules, the price of goods must rise to maintain balance. We call this inflation. Thus the currency is worth less after the flood. Creditors who made loans before the flood are now paid with dollars that are worth less. The expression that is used is that the creditor is repaid with a devalued currency.

On the other hand, the debtor, who is repaying his or her debt with cheaper currency, benefits to the extent of the devaluation.

As there are always far more debtors than creditors, political leaders always choose devaluation when the public and/or private debt of the nation threatens solvency. To put this in stark terms, nations never go broke. They simply turn on the printing presses.

This is an important fact that the Chinese and other foreign holders of the vast amount of debt that America has accumulated in recent decades appear not to fully understand.

It may surprise the reader to learn that America has neither the capacity nor the intent to repay its international debt obligations at current foreign exchange levels.

As this debt continues to mount, at some point holders will sell dollars to avoid devaluation. Alternatively, if the global economy goes into a tailspin, the government will officially alter the exchange rate, thus diluting the impact of debt. In either case, the holders of the debt will see their wealth diminished to the extent of the devaluation.

In a very real sense, the debtor, not the creditor, is in the driver's seat. Unfortunately, devaluation is enormously destabilizing. A nation such as China is not likely to sit idly by and see its wealth diminished through devaluation. Yet if history is the guide, they may not have a choice.

Such a convulsion, at the very least, would be destructive. Destabilization resulting from a massive buildup in debt and the destruction of capital resulting from World War I produced the collapse of the 1930s.

From the ashes came Hitler and Pearl Harbor. The response of the United States to modernize and construct a war machine that at war's end could be converted for peaceful purposes has given us the prosperity of the last seventy-five years. It required a massive buildup in debt that was repaid. Will our current debt, money largely spent on consumption and war, be repaid? Time will tell. Rest assured, we can never run out of currency, but we can certainly run out of money. We can go broke.

As was previously discussed in these chapters, the universality of two metals for both their preciousness and their scarcity made them an acceptable payment mechanism in any kind of exchange. Paper, on the other hand, is neither precious nor scarce.

Yet scarcity has its downside. Without access to the metal, commerce essentially ceases. The bankers, as we have mentioned, had a solution for this, as did other moneylenders, and made fortunes at various techniques that by definition were essentially bridge loans. The bridge was there until the goods were delivered to some far-off place or until one received payment from a debtor. This system worked fine provided everything was paid. On many an occasion it wasn't, which gave rise to a run on banks as people became concerned that they would not get their deposits back. The banks were forced to shut down. With no banks there is no lending, and when there is no lending, commerce slows perceptibly.

## Where Has All the Money Gone?

This critical question essentially went unanswered for centuries. Metal was king. Without metal, for all practical purposes nothing could be bought or sold. It was not surprising that people began to associate in their mind metal with money. Thus began the popular misperception that metal and money were the same thing. In other words, they were synonymous. This illusion of shortage gave rise to alchemy. Alchemists were in very great demand and were paid extremely well, at least until they failed to deliver on their promise to their employer, who was typically a king. The king, with his dreams of divinity, would then take what was viewed as appropriate action, which among other tortures was to burn alchemists in oil. I suppose the lesson here was to never promise more than you can deliver, particularly to old-fashioned kings.

Disappointment took its toll, but it did not do away with alchemy, though they are no longer referred to as alchemists. The modern-day investment fund, Ponzi schemes, and assorted money manipulators are still promising more than they can deliver.

Of course the earth can only give up so much metal, which is obviously the case when we speak of gold. If more gold were readily available, we would mine it. That is not to say that there aren't tons of gold in the bowels of the earth, but the money needed to mine it, the cost of labor in gold versus the price it could be sold for on the open market, is out of balance or, as economists would say, mining gold is a misuse of labor and capital and thus inefficient. The same capital and labor can be used for more productive purposes.

Suffice it to say there is always shortage, and thus there is a built-in or inherent problem in the paper and gold currency system.

Gold and silver as currency universals were transferable and could be carried great distances. In Roman times, metal mined in Roman mines made its way to the Far East as the wealthy of Rome sought out silk and spices and other commodities, which they proudly displayed in their vainglorious effort to impress neighbors, senators, emperors, and plebeians. Of course in that regard, little has changed.

Military conquest and a slave-driven society made it possible for an extended time for the Romans to maintain this lifestyle. Their economic system was very simple: the slaves produced, and the Romans consumed.

While America of the twenty-first century stands light-years away from the Roman experience in a million different ways, the fact is that today we increasingly allow others to produce, most notably the Chinese, and we consume.

Obviously the Chinese are not slaves and expect to be paid. We ostensibly pay them for their labor, but of course, not with metal, which we would have run out of a long time ago if we were still on a metal standard. That can be said with confidence, as America has approximately $40 billion in gold in reserve but owes China and Japan over $1 trillion each.

Instead of gold, both Oriental nations and many others receive IOUs, security, or bonds, in other words, a debt instrument that has a maturity date and that must be repaid with interest.

*Life, Liberty, and the Pursuit of Money*

China and others are doing the producing. We are consuming, and they haven't been paid. Clearly the Chinese are doing this voluntarily, but why? Well, at some point they expect to be repaid. They could demand repayment today but are unlikely to do this since the debt we owe stands as a political club over any action America might take on the international scene. China is much like the banker who has made a large loan to a company. When the banker calls, the company answers the phone.

This peculiar, distorted, and very uncertain method of engaging in commerce is part and parcel of the paper exchange standard. A related and most important question is "What constitutes repayment?"

The Chinese approach to international markets would lead one to conclude that repayment at some point would result in America crediting the bank account of China with the redemption value of the securities plus accrued interest. In order to do that, America would have to run very substantial surpluses in the federal budget. To accomplish this would mean that the government is taking in substantially more revenue than it is spending.

It will be either that or a substantial cutback in government programs to have the capital to repay our international debt. Neither strikes me as feasible. Talk of massive reductions in government spending carry the veneer of responsible government but are not realistic. No one in Washington or anywhere else truly believes that the United States government will ever reduce spending to such an extent, though they may tinker on the edges from time to time with small reductions in targeted programs.

Any public official who truly believes that reductions are possible is not being realistic or truthful. The only realistic way to generate additional revenue is to grow the economy. That means that America must dramatically increase domestic production.

The focus on globalization today precludes that possibility. One can project a time when rationality and common sense return to American policy, and we again become the great producer of the world.

Even under those circumstances, it is difficult to see how the federal government, given the demands of the populace and the proclivity of politicians of all stripes to spend, will ever get to the point where we balance the budget. Virtually all government spending is for consumption purposes. Foreigners produce, government spends, and we consume, an unworkable economic dynamic.

## Paper Negates Payment

Instead of payment in kind, producers receive a piece of paper, a debt instrument, which takes many forms, the most popular of which is that piece of plastic we call a credit card.

It will be quickly noted that banking and drafts have been with us now for centuries thanks to the goldsmiths of the world. That system, though imperfect, served its purpose.

Prevailing doctrine holds that credit cards and similar instruments are simply modern-day versions of the payment system.

At first glance, that sounds reasonable enough, but it is in point of fact hogwash. When the goldsmiths of old and their modern-day descendants issued drafts or checks on gold in the bank, it represented transfer of an asset. It might have been in payment of a debt; it might have been a gift; but it always represented a transfer of an asset. When the gold or silver coin or plate was deposited in the bank, the owner still owned the asset. The bank, on the other hand, was liable to the owner to return the asset on the demand of the owner.

This of course is the reason the word *deposit* was used. The bank, on the other hand, being liable to the owner, had a liability, which is the case today, for all deposits in a bank are liabilities of the bank.

Under the paper exchange system, the picture is entirely different. The party or owner of the credit card does not have an asset. He or she buys goods with a card that constitutes a promise to pay sometime in the future. Thus debt is created.

The assets are the goods, but they are not his or her goods paid for with his or her accumulated labor, though he or she now legally owns them. Though the credit card serves as the supposed method of payment, in point of fact payment has not been made.

An obligation or debt has been created. No payment has been made. The buyer gives the seller a promise to labor sometime in the future to pay the obligation.

Whether or not the buyer is trustworthy is not relevant. This transaction does not involve an exchange of assets. In such an exchange, I give you my accumulated labor or savings for your goods. With the credit card, an asset is exchanged for a debt obligation.

Fundamental imbalance has been created. In time the asset will be consumed. The debt remains.

As the seller is not receiving anything of value for the goods, the seller's solvency is totally dependent upon receipt of an asset at some point in the future. If the seller does not receive such an asset, he or she has nothing, for he or she has surrendered his or her asset. The seller's position is very similar to the farmer who has given away all his or her crops for a promise in return. He or she may be a great farmer, but in reality he or she has nothing. As a result of this interchange, the world is not wealthier but is dependent totally on the future ability of the buyer to labor. The buyer thus has expended both present labor and future labor. His or her capacity to labor has been exhausted.

The massive amount of debt that the world has accumulated limits capacity. As long as the world's debt is accumulating faster than its savings, we will continue down the road to pauperism. The system is dysfunctional and thus is unsustainable.

To reverse this threatening slide, we, the global community, must by the deployment of resources increase production dramatically.

China and others must insist that for world trade to expand, payment in kind be made. China must insist, and soon, if the global system is to remain intact, that in return for the sale of goods internationally, they receive goods in return and not debt securities.

China must spend the $1 trillion due them by purchasing goods, preferably American goods, since we owe this debt. Then and then only will they have been paid and debt extinguished.

This will stimulate American investment, labor, and production and begin the process of rebalance, which is absolutely critical if the system is to survive.

In answer to the question where has all the money gone, a good portion of the answer is that we have consumed it. The remainder is in the vast array of goods that people can least afford for the best of reasons: they do not have the savings.

Yes, the goods are money, but if I do not have the capital to conclude an exchange, the goods (including housing) will rest in place until they depreciate sufficiently in value as to be worthless.

Some would argue that balance can be achieved through taxation. Such an approach is simply not politically credible. History has demonstrated that people will not work unless they are paid (except perhaps at gunpoint). Compensation or pay means that they have the freedom of choice on how to spend their income. Suggesting that humans work and be denied the right to invest or spend runs counter to human nature.

As it was in the time of Rome, the world is increasingly broken down into two groups: those who produce and those who consume. America, from the time of its founding up to the latter part of the twentieth century, was the world's most important producer, innovator, and inventor.

Beginning in the late 1960s, we shifted our focus to consuming from producing. This resulted in the massive buildup of debt.

Don't misunderstand, this nation is still the leading nation in the world, with unmatched assets, but we cannot long remain in that position if we continue to consume at the current rate. Debt will simply overwhelm us if it hasn't already.

## Metal, Wherefore Art Thou?

It has been many decades since the leading nations of the world concerned themselves with the availability of metal. With modern technology, the mining industry of today can readily identify the sources of ore and deliver it to the marketplace in a timely fashion. It simply comes down to a matter of price.

Metal prices today are a function of supply and demand. Take the price of gold, for instance. As the price rises, the supply increases. There is plenty of metal in the ground, and if the price is high enough, the huge mining combines know where to get it. The same is true with other commodities, such as oil.

Earlier in world history, gold and silver were the safe havens, giving rise to the tendency to hoard. Hoarding produced scarcity. Economic activity thus dried up as there was little or no capital to finance commerce. That was at the heart of Franklin Roosevelt's decision to take America completely off the gold standard, call in all gold in the hands of the people, and raise the price to thirty-five dollars an ounce while expanding the (paper) money supply.

The effect of this decision was to put the nation and much of the world on a dollar standard. There was no issue at the time of there being too many dollars since the United States was a creditor nation. At that time with "one third of the nation ill housed, ill clothed and ill fed,"[xxxviii] to speak of too many dollars or the risk of inflation would have been laughed at. Nevertheless, a critical misstep was made. The mistake was increasing the price of an ounce of gold to thirty-five dollars.

The price should have been increased to seventy dollars or floated with an announced target in a range of sixty-five to seventy dollars, which would have allowed for a rapid increase in the money supply as the new gold price and currency in circulation were brought back into balance. At the new price, sellers of gold would have flooded the market. It would have been readily available. Such a step, combined with the decision of Congress to create the Federal Deposit Insurance Corporation, would likely have ended the money and banking crisis. The US Treasury could then have sold gold, pushing the price lower, providing the banks with plenty of capital as circumstances demanded.

The United States could have accomplished this because we were a creditor nation. Everyone owed us, the reverse of today.

The overriding need of the time was capital for investment, which would have meant immediate employment. However, the cognoscenti could not shake the belief that gold was true money and not just a measure or standard. In retrospect, FDR's steps were not radical. One could argue that they were too timid, but at least he tried and for that he is deserving of credit. His hope and determination and willingness to experiment, combined with his empathy for the common man and political astuteness and cunning, were sufficient to hold the nation together until the tragedy of Pearl Harbor.

It was war, with massive intervention of government in terms of borrowing, spending, and investment, that led the world over the course of seventy-five years to a level of prosperity unheard-of, unseen, and even unimagined throughout world history.

The Second World War and the Cold War resulted in the creation of massive amounts of money/capital, which in turn were used to rebuild the West and a goodly portion of the third world. It was accomplished with the best of intentions, to spread freedom, to alleviate poverty, and to sow the seeds of future prosperity.

CHAPTER 6

# Empires in Crisis

## Debasement of Currency

Over the course of English history, England suffered from the periodic shortages of coin, producing an economic malaise as the full force of the shortage took hold.

Such shortages brought both hunger and the threat of political instability.

England relied on a tried-and-true measure to relieve the pressure. The king would announce the minting of new coin. To accomplish this required substantial amounts of bullion.

Much like Rome, England had a balance of payments problem. This was not understood. For the English the reason for the shortage remained a mystery.

Coin, which of course was bullion, had universal appeal, and though it was minted in England, it could easily find its way to other nations. Coin shortage was commonplace.

The underlying causes for shortage were many, including warfare, famine, coin clipping and related forgeries, and melting down of coin for plate, jewelry, or anything else fashionable.

New coins with less bullion content, and thus less intrinsic value than the old, encouraged the holders of the old to avoid exchange in favor of meltdown. This debasement of the official currency, though, made it possible for many to pay for imports. The Lincoln advisory about fooling all of the people all of the time was in play.

The English, like the Romans, debased their currency by reducing the bullion content. Americans are doing so today by printing dollars. All three nations seem to be convinced that no one will notice.

## The English Moneyers, the Coin Makers

Prior to the twelfth century, people were plying their wares, but currency in bullion form carried with it many problems. The value of a piece of metal standing alone was almost indeterminable.

The metal had to be measured out so the parties to a contract knew what they were getting and giving. Necessity was indeed the mother of invention. Metal was ultimately reduced to set pieces, which were both portable and dependable in ascertaining value. These pieces became known as coins. Different coins obviously had different values.

The people who produced these coins in England were known as "moneyers." This title fits nicely. Moneyers were dealers in coins. Undoubtedly most were goldsmiths, but since this activity was a far cry from refining jewelry, this became a profession unto itself.

Their principle challenge was to guarantee that each coin minted retained the expected level of purity and fineness so that the essential value did not change from coin to coin.

One might expect that from the beginning, given the relative importance of this activity, the king might have played a major role. That was not the case. These men were in the early times locals who developed a reputation and would mark the coin with their identification. Their ID carried a certain weight of its own. It represented an informal guarantee of weight and purity. I might be willing to accept a coin with your mark since I know of your reputation for skill and honesty. This was a good business, and like any good and profitable business, it expanded quickly; and as one might expect when it comes to all things related to currency, it attracted the dregs of society.

Fees for service were one way to make coin, but a far easier way was forgery.

The king's interest was keen in this most profitable of businesses. Most importantly, taxes were paid by coin, and thus forgery was an effective way to beat the tax man. Unfortunately for many of the forgers, the tax man was the king.

Forgery continued to be a major problem, and perhaps with an eye to consolidating this activity under his auspices, Henry I took the matter on—head and limbs on, that is.

"Eventually Henry decided to act more drastically and at Christmas 1124 all moneyers were summoned to Winchester. According to the Anglo Saxon Chronicle, all were mutilated within twelve nights."[xxxix]

The local moneyers' days were numbered.

"1180 does mark the end of the feudal moneyer, with the introduction of a more modern contractual relationship between the Crown and those who administered and manufactured coinage…a separation of function between moneyers and money changers."[xl]

By the thirteenth century, die keepers were introduced to the money game "to police the use of the dies and the quality of the blanks."[xli]

Separation of function was viewed as another way to hold down the tendency to swindle, be it the crown or some poor merchant.

## Recoinage and Trade

Forgery might be dealt with by mass execution, but this would not solve the problem of shortage of bullion. Thus the technique of reminting was introduced.

Over time coins become worn, bent, and in innumerable ways defaced. Their intrinsic value may have changed as a result of wear and fraudulent acts of people.

Thus the work of reminting was introduced to the world and seen as a necessity, which of course it was, carrying with it ancillary benefits that the minting society recognized immediately. The moneyers were paid a fee to mint coin. Opportunities to remint were very good for business. Minters ultimately gained their authority through royal appointment.

The collection of taxes was the driving force that ultimately gave rise to the practice of recoinage.

Old coins, becoming worn, bent, and disfigured, increasingly were suspect. One undoubtedly has seen the picture of the merchant taking a coin, placing it between his teeth, and then biting down to test the metal content. Money traders at fairs and like events set up benches and then bounced the coin and listened to the sound, which supposedly allowed them to determine intrinsic value.

England had at least six major recoinages between the twelfth and fifteenth centuries. Such an event rid the world of some forgery. In addition, it served a far more critical function, namely the stabilization of the monetary system of the country.

There was now more coin available, allowing business to progress as the king, through his minions, collected the royal taxes. They would know for certain what they were getting.

Most importantly, it allowed for the great royal flimflam, which in today's world translates into running the printing presses.

Yes, there was more coin available, in some cases a great deal more coin. It was new and shiny. Everyone, it seems, wanted it. Only the most perceptive seemed to have noticed that the new coin had less bullion content than the old.

Recoinage was the method used for devaluation. Of course at first glance, one might conclude that was unfair to the holders of the old coin, but of course it wasn't. Their coins were supposedly no longer in use, but the intrinsic value, the bullion content of those coins, exceeded the content of the new coins.

If the domestic use of old coins was restricted, the holder had another option. The holder could import goods and pay with the old coin. Foreigners, unlike the domestic types, recognized the superior value of the old coin and naturally were more willing to trade for the old rather than the new. As the old coin became scarce, English imports fell. As the foreigner could now pay for imports with the new coin, the foreigner's cost of goods purchased declined, but he or she received less for exports.

In a sense it appeared that there were more winners than losers. Appearances unfortunately can be very deceptive. Recoinage left the English with less capital, the essential ingredient for investment and thus progress.

Capital is the seed of progress. Less seed means less production, less labor, and less progress and wealth. An increase in wealth is never a

Disney World event. Wealth never arises spontaneously. Capital formation is the key.

Capital formation in the United States as this book is being written is approximately 15 percent of our gross national product. In China it is 45 percent. In Japan, France, and England, it exceeds 20 percent. We continue to tilt the consumption-production ratio in the direction of consumption, a sure sign of a nation in decline.

## The Underlying English Problem

The balance of payments problem became acute in England in the fourteenth and fifteenth centuries, requiring a further reduction in the bullion content.

"The last three re-coinages each saw the pound weight of the bullion struck into more and more lighter coins, in response to increasing scarcity of bullion in Europe, in the latter fourteenth and fifteenth centuries."[xlii]

Bullion is scarce. The mines from which Europe obtained most of the ore were exhausted. Coins in Europe were disappearing.

The melting down of coin for the purpose of converting it into plate and jewelry would account for a certain amount of loss, but that would have been occurring in earlier centuries as well.

Perhaps foreigners were willing to pay more for silver than the market in London. If that were the case, the price in London over time would have adjusted to the global price.

The most logical explanation is that the nation was experiencing a serious balance of payments problem. In a sentence, over an extended period of time, they were spending more than they were earning. This was true of England and the rest of Europe.

Foreign invasion, civil war and strife, the plague, crusades, and changing weather patterns had for all practical purposes bankrupted England and Europe.

In the case of England, these events impaired the wool trade and other exports and thus seriously reduced the flow of silver into the country.

England had become less productive.

The shortage of bullion creates stress. In the early fourteenth century, Parliament petitioned for the use of gold.[xliii]

In a nation short on silver, by all means turn to gold. In this way the money supply might not fall. Bringing gold into play will alleviate the stress of shortage but give rise to a new problem or rather a complication: simply stated, how to officially equate the value of silver to that of gold.

By the nineteenth century, gold and silver price fluctuations were seen as an impediment to global commerce and led to decisions that arguably were catastrophic.

The impact of these decisions we will trace later in this book. Clearly they had a profound impact on Europe. In the United States, the gold/silver cleavage and debate would have a profound impact in the domestic American political arena that persists to today.

## English History and the Need for Coin

Roman suzerainty over England ended in 410 AD. However, it was over six hundred years before the famous and famed William the Conqueror, William I, landed on the shores of England and, with his victory in the Battle of Hastings, "took charge."

To demonstrate that he was in charge, he proceeded on a nationwide "castle building" effort that early in his reign included the Tower of London and Windsor.

William, whose title became King of England and Duke of Normandy, appears to have had a knack for planning. He always saw to it that his bankers accompanied him on his conquests. His bankers were from the Jewish community as a result of the Christian prohibition on the payment of interest. They were to play a key role in seeing that his financial needs were met.

They had little choice, as William was not known as an understanding sort of fellow. The methods used by his minions to collect taxes and "borrow" bear testimony to that fact.

He replaced the ruling class and brought to England essentially a new language.

William reigned for a little over two decades and was succeeded by Henry II, who expanded through marriage English power to the Continent, adding to his titles the Duke of Aquitaine. English power continued on the Continent until the fall of Calais in 1558.

Before the arrival of William, England survived six centuries of division, war, Anglo-Saxon carnage, and worst of all, the Vikings. William brought unity to the island nation.

## HENRY II CONSOLIDATED THE MONEY BUSINESS

Henry II of England (1133–1189) was the great-grandson of William the Conqueror, from the House of Plantagenet, a despot who seized the crown by force.

As was the case with monarchs before and certainly after, Henry's position was constantly threatened. Though he was fully capable of wreaking havoc in the countryside, he understood that in order to secure his position, it was important to get organized, and organization required coin.

Constantly in need of coin for his various ventures, Henry recognized that it was imperative that he gain control of the production and exchange of coin.[xliv]

To do so required sufficient justification. He could not simply move on the moneyers and take their business. The great expansion in the business of the moneyers gave rise to problems, the most important of which was continuing fraud.

One can surmise that customer fraud, particularly in those times, would have been overlooked by the nobility, but it was a horse of a different color to defraud the crown.

The king's lifestyle and perhaps survival depended on tax collections. Kings were not attuned or sanguine when they found out that the coin they received was not of the value it was professed to be or had been tampered with. Taking the king to be a fool had a certain career downside to it.

After all, who was in charge, the moneyer or the king?

Henry, who was most interested in centralizing and controlling the money process, saw this condition of money uncertainty as both a threat and an opportunity.

"The profusion of the moneyer presented unique opportunities for fraudulent gain whether at the expense of the crown or the mint customers. At times of general re-coinage however the execution of a moneyer cast doubt on the value of the old coinage and confirmed the king's good faith.

"The blackening of the reputation of the old coinage was a regular feature of the introduction of a new type and the gallows helped to establish the poorer quality of the old type in the minds of the public."[xlv]

"1180 does mark the end of the feudal moneyer and the introduction of a more modern contractual relationship between the crown and those who administered and manufactured its coinage. Subsequently a separation of function between moneyers and money changers 'royal salaried' was introduced."[xlvi]

Recoinage meant devaluation, clearly harmful to the body politic. Yet the king promised and delivered a brand-new shiny coin with his coat of arms or other insignia in place of the old, which was worn, clipped, bent, and otherwise destroyed.

Such a nice king to be so considerate, it was thought. The new was in. Peddlers, merchants, and ordinary folk flocked or chose new in place of the old and other suspect foreign coins.

The fact that the new coin had less silver bullion than the old largely passed unnoticed. Of course the entire business was a sham. The king would pay his debt down with the new coin.

As trade increased, as wars and assorted expeditions continued, and as the king's court needs inexorably drove the demand for coin, or in today's euphemistic language, demands for increases in the money supply, ore had to be found or new coin minted.

The value of all things is an objective concept. It is intrinsic. There is no such thing as the government assigning value to money (product). History is replete with examples of governments that have tried and failed to do precisely that, including of course the United States.

Fraud, including the widespread practice of clipping, was invariably sold as a key justification for recoinage, though the real intention of government was to surreptitiously and artificially increase the money supply. Increasing the money supply allowed for the continuing import of goods from faraway places, such as China.

China refused to respond in kind, buying little or nothing from the exporting European countries. Thus the outflow continued unabated, and the importing nation was left with few options.

Given the choices, weak kings and governments, fearing the wrath of the people, took what they believed to be the safer political but economically disastrous course, to debase the currency.

## Balance of Payments and Repercussions

Suffice it to say that over time, all nations have at one time or another experienced a balance of payments problem. Not all nations in history have chosen to reduce the bullion in their coinage. Some nations introduced tariffs so that the foreign goods were made more expensive and less attractive to the citizenry.

Others had special tariff arrangements with certain nations but imposed tariffs on others. Those that were given special consideration were said to have "favored nation" status.

The root cause of a balance of payments problem differs with the nation.

For Rome, England, Germany, France, and now the United States, the critical underlying cause is war and the cost of maintaining the military.

Rome greatly expanded its empire by military means. Romans, notoriously unproductive, used the military in far-flung ventures to secure property, plunder, slaves, and treasure. The cost of maintaining an enormous military by a country that existed to pursue materialism inevitably led to bankruptcy.

Nations such as England and France made good use of their empires, insisting that their colonial peoples produce materials and buy the finished products from their rulers or their appointed merchants. This brought gain to the mother countries, but it came at a great cost, namely, the maintenance of navies and armies that were needed to hold the colonies in a state of servitude. In time when these chains were broken, the respective empires simply collapsed.

Germany, an aggressor from its earliest beginnings, was in perpetual need of raw materials and other materials from outside its borders to sustain the military. Living totally beyond their means and unable to sustain aggression, Germany collapsed financially and militarily in 1918 and again for good measure in 1945.

The United States, with bountiful natural resources and a productive people, separated by a great ocean from the continuing friction of Europe, being largely left alone for most of its history, gained in stature and wealth by pursuing balance in its affairs until the coming of the Great War, which it entered in 1917.

As America increasingly became embroiled on the world stage, ostensibly in pursuit of world peace with justice, the financial cost bled the nation, resulting in an unimaginable imbalance of payments by the early 2000s.

## Money Troubles—Good King John and Other Kings

From the twelfth through the fifteenth centuries, money troubles wracked English monarchs. This was the era when English kings periodically engaged in wars on the Continent to secure their power in England and the Continent, which they managed to do until the fall of Calais in 1558.

This was all very costly and ultimately brought about a shift in power with Parliament, with King John being forced to sign the Magna Carta in 1215. This was a formal admission that the king was not above the law, combined with other concessions to the barons in return for their support in raising revenue.

It was for naught. Loss of their possessions on the Continent heralded and brought to power Henry VII after Edward II and a series of coups. The year 1485 marked the beginning of the Tudor dynasty.

Henry VII was a frugal man, unlike his famous son, rebuilding the treasury, which his progeny in due time would certainly squander.

Henry VIII came to power in1509 and, in the most extraordinary act of greed ever recorded, seized the English monasteries in 1538. His second daughter, Elizabeth, a bright and talented person, combined banditry, exploration, colonization, and victory in war to gain stature for England in the world.

Once again, world venture proved costly, and Elizabeth died with debt as her legacy. After her death dynastic uncertainty and religious bigotry plagued England internally.

Following the disastrous rule of James II, the last Catholic king of England in 1685, William of Orange, the husband of James's daughter Mary and ruler of the Netherlands, reigned in England.

At Mary's insistence, Parliament agreed to the rule of William but limited the power of the monarchy by introducing the English Bill of Rights. England passed into a constitutional monarchy referred to in history as the Glorious Revolution in 1688. Monarchial power would henceforth be limited. Taxes that monarchs could impose on their citizens would be restricted. English monarchs henceforth had to turn to Parliament in order to conscript an army.

Anne, Mary's sister, succeeded her brother-in-law William II on his death in 1702 as England's queen.

Of far greater importance, a man came into public view who would have as profound an impact on currency and the status of currency as he would on the course of science, Sir Isaac Newton (1642–1727).

## THE GREAT NEWTON—AND OH! THE MISTAKES MEN MAKE

The genius of the man is not open to question. As a teacher, he would set forth in *Philosophie Naturalis Principia Mathematica* the laws of motion and universal gravitation.

In mathematics he shares with Gottfried Leibniz the development of differential and integral calculus. His work with light, which he understood to be streams of minute particles and the passage of light through a prism, gave the world a theory of color.

He and Albert Einstein stand as the two most influential men in scientific history.

Far less well-known is the fact that Newton gave up teaching and became England's "master of the mint" in 1699.

The principal job of the master was to keep his eye on the minters to be sure that counterfeiting did not spin out of control. He was the king's man on the job.

The post was a sinecure. However, a more dedicated bureaucrat one would never find. Newton approached the job with the same determination that had made him the outstanding teacher and student that he was. As an intellectual, he was a man of fame in his own time.

The penalty for counterfeiting had not changed over the centuries, namely hanging, drawing, and quartering. In later years, few were forced to pay the supreme penalty for their crime, but the penalty remained in force. With the arrival of Newton, zealotry in the search for these crooks, robbers, and thieves once again come to the fore.

One of Newton's favorite guises was to go to the local taverns in London to catch the counterfeiters in action. He caught quite a few. During his tenure, some two hundred were tried and convicted and made subject to the death penalty, though few were executed.

It is hard to imagine Einstein being made head of the United States Mint and then spending his evenings going to discos and local bars on the chance that he just might catch someone slipping the bartender a counterfeit fifty-dollar bill. I suppose it is fair to say that life and fame are never what they appear to be. Newton was given the job, and by heavens, he was going to do it, even if it meant posing as a drunk. It can be fairly said that they don't make big league bureaucrats like they used to.

His drive for perfection came through in his titanic scientific work. He was to now put it to work in the service of England to tackle something far more plebian, currency.

As so frequently happens when people are appointed to a position that is foreign to their field or that they have little experience in, they rush to solve problems they lack full understanding of.

It would be accurate to say that Newton had but little understanding about the nature of currency. He shared with millions a lack of a full appreciation of the law of supply and demand. The consequences for England and the world proved disastrous.

*Life, Liberty, and the Pursuit of Money*

As noted, over the centuries, England and the Continent had been plagued by shortage of coin and bullion. It was a commercial plague that had to be eradicated. Newton believed that this was the work of counterfeiters or of merchants and others who were the equivalent of counterfeiters.

Gold and silver were coined at certain rates fixed by the indenture of the king and the master of the mint. "…between the two metals could not be made to correspond with the actual market ratio…the metal overvalued at the mint will tend to drive the other from circulation." Thus it stood to reason that imports of coin would be negligible.

Melting down of coin and similar acts were so un-English. Worse still, this was an insult to the king and would in its workings deny him important revenue.

By any measure, this was a form of treason. To be found guilty of treason in England could seriously impact one's longevity.

At any rate, "The Great Recoinage" that was underway as Newton came to the mint was in danger of failing. A significant amount of the coin that was turned in for recoinage purposes was counterfeit, foreign, clipped, or worn, and thus this important project was failing.

Charles Montagu, Chancellor of the Exchequer, was instrumental in getting Newton the appointment. As we will see later, a descendant of Montagu played a pivotal role in the Great Depression in the twentieth century.

It has been speculated that Montagu obtained the appointment for Newton out of fear that without a man of his talent, recoinage would certainly fail.

Newton seized the opportunity to direct recoinage and initiated a thorough study of the relationship of silver to gold throughout the world. Being the man he was of science and precision, he presented his findings in great detail.

He found that silver coming from the West Indies would arrive in Spain and travel through the Continent and then to Asia. Since it was moving away from its source, higher prices were forever being paid as it moved across borders and continents.

"And it appears by experience as well as reason that silver flows from those places where its value is lowest in proportion to gold as from Spain to all Europe to the East Indies, China and Japan and that gold is most plentiful in those places in which its value is highest in proportion to silver as in Spain and England."[xlvii]

If the gold/silver ratio is producing an outflow of silver, the value of silver must be greater elsewhere. The cheaper silver becomes, its ratio to gold will widen until it becomes more attractive to transact business in silver. At that point market forces will increase the demand for silver, pushing the price higher.

From the law of supply and demand, we know that "plentiful gold" or anything else will not serve to keep the price high, but to the contrary, will work to bring it down. Newton's analysis and conclusion only served to distort the gold/silver ratio. In short, all other factors remaining equal, since gold and silver were interchangeable, the equilibrium price in the end was the final determinant, not some artificial price set by a bureaucrat.

Newton was a bullionist at heart, believing that the wealth of the nation was determined by the amount of silver and gold it had, rather than by its productive capacity. His goal was to attract silver into the country by underpricing gold. People would sell silver to get gold.

In his mind, and in the minds of many then and now, the higher the price of the metal, the wealthier the nation became.

This misunderstanding remains with us. Today people argue for a strong currency. A strong currency is not indicative of wealth; to the contrary, it limits our ability to produce and sell goods.

England was a debtor nation. All debtor nations suffer an outflow of capital as payments exceed revenue. To cure the problem, a nation must improve its balance of trade. The English problem had nothing to do with the ratio of silver to gold.

As so frequently happens, Newton was a public official interested in pleasing the hierarchy, namely, the queen and her advisors. He was the master of the mint; having sufficient coin available was his job. The recoinage effort had to succeed; his position depended on it.

Newton was not about to lecture the queen on trade policy, even if he had a full grasp of the problem, which is questionable.

Silver over the ages had been dominant in England, as it had in most of the world. The English penny (silver) was the base standard in England.

A deficiency in the availability of silver would have major consequences on business trade and income. To take plate from the public and turn it into coin would not solve the problem. It would simply invite greater outflow. Thus his aim was to find a way to keep silver in England.

"And if gold was lowered [*in exchange*] only so as to have the same proportion to the silver money in England which it has to silver in the rest of Europe, there would be no temptation to export silver rather than gold to any other part of Europe."[xlviii]

"For as often as men are necessitated to send away money for answering debts abroad, there will be a temptation to send away silver rather than gold because of the profit which is 4 percent. And for the same reason foreigners will choose to send hither their gold rather than silver."[xlix]

The Newton solution was not to fix the problem but the effects of the problem. By artificially pricing gold, he expected to stem the outflow of silver.

"The re-coinage of 1696, a re-coinage which, being undertaken on a wrong basis, had its influence in making England, in fact or practice, a gold monometallic country for the greater part of the eighteenth century, and that long before the advent of any theory of gold monometallism."[l]

By altering the ratio of gold to silver in favor of silver, Newton inadvertently made gold more attractive. Given the importance of England to world trade, for gold to take on new importance had worldwide implications. England was not on a gold standard, but that was the direction, though unintended, that they were headed.

Suffice it to say that the decision was monumental. Speaking as master of the mint, Newton spoke for England. In a world of silver and gold, his ratio meant gold was to be favored. To this point the world's money supply rested on full interchangeability of silver and gold. Neither was to be favored. Since value was intrinsic, market forces would determine the ratio one to the other.

The ratio might differ from one locale to another. As Newton had speculated, plentiful silver arriving in Seville would produce downward pressure on the silver price there but not elsewhere. State intervention meant henceforth currency value would be distorted.

If silver was to fall into disuse in commerce, the downside would be a major reduction in the money supply at the very time when the population of Europe and global commerce were rapidly expanding.

In the late eighteenth century, when the world followed England's lead and officially adopted the gold standard, the adverse impact on the money supply resulted in a half century of global financial and economic crises.

## The Implosion of the Old Order

Over the centuries, from Rome through the Middle Ages, the nobility ruled Europe even during periods of barbarian invasion and supremacy.

The Papacy had successfully kept the royals in line more or less with the threat of excommunication, until the arrival of Henry VIII.

Beginning in the sixteenth century, the money dogs, witnessing the accrual of wealth and growing power of the Italian states, were determined to share in the largesse. The world became fascinated by profit through trade with the Far East.

The Portuguese, superior seafarers, gained the upper hand in what turned out to be a race for global dominance in trade. By taking the sea route to the East around the Cape, they were in a position to bring spices to Western Europe cheaply, eliminating the need for the Venetian middlemen.

During the early part of the sixteenth century, Portugal had a virtual monopoly on global trade. They made Goa the capital of India. They built forts and military outposts to assure that no one would challenge their dominance.

England entered the fray first by trying to establish routes north of Moscow, creating the Muscovy Company in 1555.

The Dutch in 1602 created the Dutch East India Company with its own army and navy and succeeded in ousting the English East India Company, whereupon England turned its sights on India.

Spain focused its attention on the Americas and in 1545 made a huge discovery of silver ore in present-day Bolivia and later in Mexico, which was transported back to Seville and then began its journey across Europe toward the East.

It is presumably this silver that later caused so much of the problem for Isaac Newton as it passed through England and resulted in his decision regarding the ratio of silver to gold. It was a decision, to borrow a famous phrase of Franklin Roosevelt, "that will live in infamy."

The abundance of Spanish silver and gold allowed for the financing of greatly expanded world trade, including the Americas, which was increasingly in need of goods.

This blossoming of trade required both the ships and the infrastructure to make it sufficiently profitable. This was aided and abetted by the mass movement of people from Africa on the order of some twelve million to labor in these new centers of commerce.

For the great states, and the select, namely the nobility, the outlook should have been bright, but conflicts abounded and wars were fought on land and sea over possessions and colonies.

The European view was that colonies were there to serve the motherland and the peasantry was there to serve the nobility. Injustice marked this extended period, ultimately giving rise to men of the Enlightenment, including Rousseau, Locke, and Voltaire.

England had a Parliament and France, the Estates-General, with its three estates—the clergy, the nobility, and the commoner—but men of privilege still held sway. The divine right of kings remained the prevailing philosophy.

While war, disease, and the unpredictability of nature complicated life, the eighteenth century turned out to be one of economic expansion.

Increasing population and the demands, particularly from the expanding cities, had by the late eighteenth century begun to impact the price structure.

In France the harvests were particularly bad in 1787–1788. As a result there was a slowdown in manufacturing, and poverty began to plague the country.

The Enlightenment philosophy and the successful American Revolution began to stir the French people. The French nobility, isolated as they were, seemed oblivious to this. On that famous day in July 1789 when the people of Paris stormed the Bastille, a government minister hurried to Versailles to alert King Louis.

On hearing the news, Louis is said to have asked, "Is this some sort of uprising?" The minister, it is said, answered, "No, sire, it is a revolution."

Indeed it was. It spelled the beginning of the end for the nobility of Europe. The chasm that existed between the nobles and the common man, the wealthy and the poor, now began to close, extinguishing the nobility in the process.

Bear in mind, it was the nobility, particularly in the person of Henry VIII, that had succeeded in undercutting the moral influence of the Papacy. European nobles had become a thoroughly corrupt lot.

A lazy, privileged class that lived off the labor of others without the slightest concern about their plight best summarizes the great nobility.

Deteriorating economic conditions and a new philosophy espousing the conviction "that all men are created equal" sounded their death knell.

With Christianity deeply divided and the money dogs loose, no prospect existed for the return of a moral code to guide the affairs of men.

As the old order perished or simply faded away, it was replaced not by another class of men but by a force, with dagger edges, that would in time result in a great continuing clash, one nation versus another. The world now witnessed the rise of nationalism.

## Nationalism—The Arrival of Napoleon

From its earliest days, humankind has had to wrestle with the conflict of peoples, tribes, and cultures.

Whether it takes the form of envy, zealotry, or more subtle forms of human failing, there lies an identifiable cause. Though it has many shadings, at the heart of virtually all conflict are religious differences and financial difficulty.

Given the stakes, the conflicts that arise over differences in religion can be readily understood, even as the horrors perpetrated in the name of religion cannot. Zealotry and the blindness that accompanies it will run its course unfortunately, leaving in its wake death and destruction. Financial difficulty, on the other hand, is, to use a popular expression, a horse of a different color.

Entire nations and peoples are involved. Survival is at stake. A fierce determination to right the wrong takes hold. War is thought to be the answer, and an irrational striking out at the perceived evildoers ensues.

This horrid state of affairs befell France on a fateful day in July 1789 when a great people, perceiving that they were on the point of starvation, rose up en masse to overthrow the ruling elite, namely, the nobility.

King Louis XVI, together with his courtiers and advisors, never saw it coming. They should have. With only the most superficial understanding of European history, they should have recognized that while a great people will willingly put up with adversity, no people will silently starve or allow their children to starve to keep in power the government of their time. Louis did not understand or grasp this unpleasant reality. He paid for his ignorance with his head and the heads of thousands.

In another time, some 144 years later, another man would come to power, fortunately for the nation and the world, who did understand this, and his name was Franklin Delano Roosevelt.

## The Financial Debacle—England Victorious

A cursory review of history might lead one to conclude that in the period leading up to the American Revolution, England must have been in decline, which might have accounted for its defeat at the hands of Washington. This was not the case. England was supreme. Mighty England had prevailed in the Seven Years' War or, as we like to describe it on this side of the Atlantic, the French and Indian War.

There was one slight problem that the English, of all peoples, should have been cognizant of, given the proclivities of Henry VIII. Wars are expensive. England, though victorious, had to find the way to pay for victory.

That meant new taxes. Taxation, particularly as administered by the British Parliament directed at the colonies, did not sit well with the Americans and was the straw that broke the proverbial camel's back and produced a full-fledged revolution.

"England's assertion of authority over its American colonies in the form of new taxes came at a time of British ascendancy and as-yet-unparalleled global influence that flowed from her spectacular victory in the Seven Years' War...To be sure, England had not won alone, but her allies colonial and Continental, had lost as much as her enemies. Virtually all of Western Europe lay ruined and impoverished. Vast armies of peasant soldiery had been marshaled all over Europe to decide which ruler should tax the most men. A hundred towns and villages had been burned to the ground. In many villages, only women and children were left to till the fields. One in nine Prussians, half a million, had been killed in seven years. The war had opened the doors of Europe to sudden and permanent changes. Sweden, once a European power, receded from importance. Russia lost a staggering 120,000 men but, marching into the west for the first time, opened a new era in European history. For France the losses were catastrophic: France lost her American empire.

"But the Seven Years' War and Britain's place as the preeminent world power were won not on the fields of Europe, but on the Atlantic and in the forests of North America. Colonial trade equaled imperial power. A century's expansion of overseas trade had financed the expansion of both the British and French fleets until, by 1758, England boasted one hundred fifty six ships-of-the-line, while France only had seventy-seven....France overseas trade had plummeted from thirty million livres in 1755 to four million in 1760."[li]

That same summer, 1760, after the fall of Quebec and Montreal, all French possessions from the Arctic Circle to the Falkland Islands fell under British rule.

France was bankrupt. Her colonies were lost.

"To gain its great victories, England squeezed its purses empty. Landowners had paid up to twenty-five percent of the assessed value of their acres each year in war taxes; poor men paid high new taxes on their beer and tobacco, and the middle class paid twenty-five percent of value on houses, deeds, offices, brandy and spirits. If a man owned a house, he paid a tax not only on it but on every window in it. No wonder they were resisting postwar proposals for further taxes to pay the bill for their great victory. The funded British national debt by January 1763, according to Exchequer accounts, had reached £122,603,336—a staggering sum that increased by £7 million in interest the next year and by that much again in the next six months. Instead of bringing a harvest of mercantile profits, the end of the costly imperial war brought a severe depression in British trade."[lii]

France was indeed bankrupt, though at the time the dire strait of affairs that the nation faced was not understood by the French peasant, the small merchant class, or the nobility. These people soon chose barbaric domestic violence and militarism in an effort to reclaim their dignity as a leading European nation.

England was bankrupt as well, but with its great colonial holdings, the English believed that the ship of state would be righted. All it would take, they thought, was the imposition of new taxes, this time on the colonies. They were dreadfully wrong and soon paid an enormous price with the loss of their American possessions.

This was the state of affairs when a puny Corsican military strategist with the ability to inspire led a takeover of France and in time all of Europe.

The overriding lesson, never digested, has plagued the world to the very present. National bankruptcy and the divisions that follow lead to militarism, which unchecked runs rampant, producing ever greater destruction and financial hardship in the absence of an overarching moral code to direct the affairs of men. That is the lesson of history.

## Pre Revolutionary France

Largely illiterate, the French people, led by tyrants and with virtually no say over their living conditions and subservient to the nobility, remained passive. It was accepted as their lot in life. The peasantry constituted 75 to 80 percent of the population.

The bourgeoisie or the middle class constituted approximately 8 percent of the population or approximately 2.3 million. This was too small a percentage at a time of complete social breakdown to moderate the extremes. They owned 20 to 25 percent of the land.

The clergy, which numbered approximately 130, 000, held 10 percent of the land; and the nobility, numbering some 250,000, held 25 percent of the land.

France was an agricultural nation, and thus land was its wealth.

The Enlightenment ideals expressed so forcefully and effectively and promulgated by Locke, Diderot, Turgot, Rousseau, and Voltaire began to move the French people. The inequities and injustices in life were being made visible in their writings and in their words, and were guaranteed to excite the passions of men.

The successful American Revolution against their archenemy, Great Britain, was a true harbinger expressing the possible.

Lastly, there was the slight matter of taxes. The clergy and the nobility did not pay taxes. The tax burden fell on those who could afford it least.

A nation in bankruptcy was a concept that would never have been understood in that era. On the surface all seemed to be normal. Louis and his consort, Marie, and the thousands of royals were still living well beyond their means, while the rest of France went about its business until starvation set in.

Somehow and in some way, everything would work itself out. Wasn't France a leading nation, to be emulated and admired? The French had demonstrated their importance in literature, art, and religion. France was identified with the greatness of Western Europe. It was expected that in the future the world would look to France to provide global leadership.

Unfortunately for France, reality was operating on another timetable.

The immediate cause of the revolution, it is widely agreed, was the financial crisis. The revenue picture was bleak. Louis, following European tradition, simply calls on the Estates General, the French Parliament, to raise taxes. The third estate moved to have the tax-exempt status of the first two estates removed. This motion was defeated, as the first two estates effectively vetoed the plan, each estate having one vote, so the final count was two to one. Louis then made what would prove for him personally to be a fateful decision; he sided with the system then in place.

Though France shared great power status with Great Britain, internally France lacked the dynamic of change that would shortly become a hallmark of Great Britain as it began to industrialize with the invention and development of the steam engine.

France was feudal. It saw the world in feudal terms. It identified wealth with land. Britain, on the other hand, appeared to grasp the reality that wealth was a function of production.

France had at best an antiquated governmental structure, highly centralized and thoroughly corrupt. The philosophy of the divine right of kings still held sway.

The French economy had not failed. To the contrary, it had been expanding for fifty years. The weather was for an extended period of time ideal for agriculture. The typical French peasant plodded his weary way on a small plot of land for livelihood.

French international forays culminating in the Seven Years' War were largely financed through borrowing. It has been estimated that the principal on France's national debt before the American Revolution was seven times its annual revenue. Of course this condition only worsened with its financial support of the colonists.

France acted on the principle that the United States is closely following as it carries on its affairs in the twenty-first century: that debt will never be repaid, or if it is to be repaid, it will be paid by a future generation.

For France matters reached their climax in 1788. With the treasury empty, unable to devise a fair and equitable tax scheme or attract additional monies through loans, France simply reached the point of no return.

I suppose the message is that all things must come to an end, even the financial tomfoolery of debauched nations.

Perhaps the monarchy and the system in place might have survived this deplorable state of affairs if it had not been for, of all things, the weather.

France experienced the worst of harvests in 1787–1788 and thus a slowdown in manufacturing and other business. For an agricultural nation like France, this meant famine.

Despite all the troubles, Louis XVI, the court at Versailles, and especially Marie Antoinette went on with a lifestyle that would have pleased Nero. Of course in the end, they paid for this, with their heads. That was the proper and right thing to do, or fair is fair; at least the French people thought so.

In point of fact, the French Revolution was a saga that lasted decades and had many complexities, including foreign invasion, but at the very heart of this horrifying spectacle was a financial crisis.

In 1783, with the peace treaty signed ending the American Revolution, America's foreign debt totaled $11.7 million. Of that amount, the French were owed $4.4 million.

With the support and political influence of men such as Lafayette, France provided critical support for the American Revolution in money, guns, and manpower.

Washington and the French finally prevailed in the war at Yorktown, Virginia, with the surrender of British General Cornwallis.

Though this has been appropriately hailed as Washington's greatest triumph, the French played a key role. A little-known fact is that France provided the navy under Admiral de Grasse, who successfully kept the British at bay during the battle. At a minimum, three fourths of the men who surrounded Cornwallis at Yorktown were French.

Indeed, the victory was as much a French victory as an American one, as Jefferson noted. "Jefferson seemed acutely aware that scarcely one-fourth of the allied force at Yorktown was American; that it was really a French victory…"[liii]

As Americans, we are deeply grateful to the French, but the cost to the French of their investment broke them financially and led to the horrors perpetrated during the French Revolution, wiping out the vestiges of nobility in France.

Though truly inspired by the courage and bravery of the American people in defying Britain, France under Louis XVI had other motives in mind as it extended financial support to America.

Under the British mercantile system, the colonists were prohibited from trading with other European countries. They were effectively denied the right to issue their own currency, were dissuaded from setting up their own domestic manufacturing, and of course were taxed without representation in Parliament.

In the view of the British, all colonists were to be subservient to the Crown. They would have little or no say in their own affairs.

The French saw in the American Revolution an opportunity to participate in a critical market through the expansion of trade, becoming a key partner in the revitalization of the French economy.

While France did virtually everything in its power to see to it that the Americans prevailed, it appears that they never seriously considered the implications of American independence. The French government, through Minister Compte de Vergennes, had reached what he considered to be a firm understanding with Ambassador Benjamin Franklin that should the British ever agree to American terms, particularly with respect to the matter of independence, Franklin would first advise Vergennes before initialing the agreement.

It was widely believed that Vergennes would have used his considerable influence both in London and with Congress to assure that France's interests, which included negotiations with Great Britain on a peace treaty and its territorial claims including its interests in Canada, would be satisfactorily addressed in a comprehensive treaty. France had no intention of simply being a bystander to a treaty between America and Great Britain.

France wanted America to succeed, but in a setting that advanced France's interests. Franklin had agreed unqualifiedly to these terms.

"The next morning, November 30, 1782, the American negotiators, along with their secretary, Temple Franklin, met with the British in Oswald's suite at the Grand Hotel Muscovite to sign the provisional treaty that, in effect, ended the Revolutionary War. In a nod to the obligations owed France, the pact would not become formally binding 'until terms of a peace shall be agreed upon between Great Britain and France.' That would take another nine months. But the treaty had an immediate and irrevocable import that was contained in its opening line, which declared the United States 'to be free, sovereign and independent.'"[liv]

"To Franklin fell the difficult duty of explaining to Vergennes"[lv] he "had breached his obligation to France…After sending Vergennes a copy of the signed accord, which he stressed was provisional, Franklin called on him at Versailles the following week. The French minister remarked, coolly but politely, that 'proceeding in this abrupt signature of the articles' was not 'agreeable to the [French] King' and that the Americans 'had not been particularly civil.' Nevertheless, Vergennes did allow that the Americans had done well by themselves, and he noted that 'our conversation was amicable.'"[lvi]

In addition, Congress had specifically instructed Franklin not to agree to a treaty without consultation with Congress.

"Only when Franklin followed up with a brash request for yet another French loan, along with the information that he was transmitting the peace accord to the Congress, did Vergennes take the opportunity to protest officially."[lvii]

The revolution in France less than a decade later swept aside treaties, agreements, diplomatic niceties, commerce, trade, debt, and other obligations together with the nobility of France as the people went on a slaughtering rampage symbolized by the infamous guillotine that would serve to change France, as well as Europe, forever.

This national rampage eventually exhausted itself, creating a political vacuum ready-made for a tyrant with the military might to enforce order, while appealing to the base nationalist interests of the people.

## Napoleon, a Name That Will Live in Infamy, Except to the French

Coming forth from Corsica stepped a military genius, manipulator, and narcissistic madman who led the French people on a journey, promising the restoration of French greatness through conquest, the "godfather" of the age, Napoleon.

No one can question his success; then again, no one can question Hitler's early success a century and a quarter later. In many ways they were like two peas in the same pod.

Napoleon's tenure on the world scene lasted from 1799 to 1815. He first succeeded in overthrowing the Government of the Directory and establishing a new government, the Consulate, which embarked on a codification of law and an expansion of the bureaucracy, the latter allowing him to exercise greater control over the conquered or otherwise dependent states. His legitimacy was greatly aided by the fact that as he came to power, France was at war with Britain, Russia, and Austria. He succeeded in bringing about a temporary peace in 1802, only to renew his warlike ways in 1803. Between 1805 and 1807, he defeated the Austrian, Prussian, and Russian armies, and his "Grand Empire" was a fait accompli.

The Grand Empire stretched from France to the Rhine and the western half of Italy. These states were ruled, so typical of modern-day godfathers, by his relatives. He moved to consolidate the German states, opening the way to their eventual union.

His real enemy, however, and a nation he truly despised, was Great Britain. Britain's power sprang from its advanced manufacturing base and extensive colonial empire, which paid "retail" on all goods being exported from England. From these same colonies, England imported the raw materials that, when refined, became the foundation for their exports. British commerce was protected by the formidable British navy.

For Napoleon to achieve continental dominance, it was imperative that he have the money and credit to sustain his ever-expanding army. To achieve this he imposed on the dependent or conquered states taxes that were euphemistically referred to as contributions. Since the successful invasion of Great Britain was critical to his vision of being emperor of all, he simply requisitioned whatever was needed for the cause, including demands on the Dutch that they build small boats, which he planned to use in the invasion.

"Since money was one of the most important factors constraining the development and use of military power in the first decades of the nineteenth century, Napoleon's ability to extort vast sums from reluctant allies allowed him to face a theoretically much larger and richer coalition.

"Napoleon effectively subordinated the economy of a considerable part of western Europe to the cause of French military power, thereby allowing him to maintain a higher degree of military power at a much lower cost to France than he would otherwise been able to do, a factor crucial to understanding his success in the first year of renewed continental warfare."[lviii]

Napoleon's primary goal was to fight Britain "to the death." One wonders how a country of some twelve million people could hope to defeat this continental colossus that could simply take or steal whatever was needed if it could not be produced.

Geography, of course, favored the Brits. To cross the English Channel, then land and supply an army of sufficient size to conquer this majestic island was a formidable task. As events unfolded, the task was beyond the reach of Napoleon and, in the twentieth century, the capacity of Hitler.

France had lost the commercial battle to Britain in the eighteenth century, but could Britain hope to prevail against this formidable adversary with its call on virtually all the goods and services on the Continent in the nineteenth? At first glance the picture looked rather bleak for the British.

Yet Britain held some formidable assets. Its navy was unmatched and inflicted a crushing defeat on the combined French-Spanish fleet at the Battle of Trafalgar. Britain had its colonies, with their extensive wealth in labor and raw materials, and an outlet for the goods produced in England, a society advancing steadily in industrialization.

However, the crux of the matter still laid with the matter of money. Both adversaries had to successfully finance this conflict.

For France, having lived through the bankruptcy of Louis XVI, and then having been torn asunder by the murderous revolution, money and banking had returned to something of a natural state.

The bankers of the time were more than reluctant to throw in their lot with Napoleon. Godfathers typically do not make the best banking clients. As the Continent increasingly became a war economy, traditional commerce suffered and the citizenry was deprived. However, his government imposed strict import controls from outside Napoleon's sphere of influence that protected and encouraged the development of French manufacturing.

Meanwhile, the government took control of major industries such as armaments, tobacco, forests, and mines among others.

They were incorporated in the "Continental system" designed to maintain the military at whatever the cost and obtain the capital to continue Napoleon's crusade through extortion and taxation.

This system, a throwback to the days of barbarism, allowed France to reassert itself by isolating Britain, thus preventing a massive importation of British goods, making it possible for France to take the critical early steps without the threat of competition from industrialization.

The years 1800 to 1810 were effectively a kind of takeoff of the industrial "Revolution in France, fundamentally made possible by population growth and greater rural consumption, but also by a host of factors directly related to the imperial government: extensive governmental patronage and, above all, stiff protectionist policies that completely insulated fledgling French industry against 'impossible' English competition."[lix]

"By 1810, French industrial production was 50 percent over what it had been in the 1780s, and if it was still nothing like the level of British production (nor growing at its rate), it was yet an accomplishment that should not go unnoted..."[lx]

The revenue gained from these various ventures, of course, fell well short of Napoleon's needs, forcing on France the need to sell the vast Louisiana territory to the United States at a negotiated price.

The need for goods on the Continent opened the door of opportunity for the smuggling of British goods, even if that was to be accomplished through gunrunning. Napoleon did not take kindly to such activity.

Napoleon sought to isolate the Continent, and through his embargo and related military activity, starve and defeat Britain. However, to enforce the embargo required that all the states in the Continental system adhere to the British embargo.

As fate would have it, Russia refused to go along, which invited an invasion by Napoleon with an army of one half million men, who reached

Moscow but failed to obtain the surrender of Czar Alexander I. This meant retreat and the death of most of Napoleon's army in the cold Russian winter, bringing to an end this great scourge of Europe.

Napoleon, though ultimately defeated, changed the face of Europe permanently. New philosophies for governance sprang from the chaos and dislocation of the Napoleonic era. Of particular significance was the coming on the world scene of socialism and the rise of nationalism.

European statehood had been coalescing over many centuries but was given a major push forward during the Napoleonic Wars. Napoleon's victories enhanced greatly his reputation in France but aggravated greatly the populace of the nations he conquered, giving rise to a determination to chase the foreign invader from their soil. Nationalism took hold in Europe, with devastating consequences in future decades.

## Deficit Financing Comes of Age

For certain, Britain had again prevailed against its archenemy, but what financial techniques did it use that allowed this rather small island state to prevail in this contest with a behemoth?

Britain devised something of a new technique with respect to currency, which as it spread in time would be given the appellation deficit financing. To achieve their aims and to deal with the shortage of metal, thus a shortage of currency that made recoinage—a tried-and-true technique from the past—virtually impossible, Britain turned to paper.

Taking after Rome, they discovered that by fiat they could issue paper and restrict convertibility during a period of crisis. This is referred to in history as the "Bank Restriction Act" and was in effect from 1792 to 1821.

England returned to convertibility with much hesitation only when it was faced with a massive loss of specie (coin) once again at the close of the nineteenth century when its desire for Chinese and Indian imports gave rise to another massive balance of payments problem.

England pleaded with China to buy English goods, but the Chinese had no need for them.

The English got even, however, by selling through India enormous amounts of opium in the latter part of the century, taking home silver and gold by the ton, leaving China ravaged with an indescribable drug problem, from which it didn't recover until the arrival of the Communist Party General Secretary Mao in mid-twentieth century. Many an Englishman and leading American prospered from this trade.

With industrialization, the demand for capital increased exponentially. Metal when truly scarce impeded investment.

Imperial expansion and war, most notably the Seven Years' War and the American Revolution, necessitated a reliance on imports from the Orient, which drained silver from Europe and North America.

Paper may not have been an ideal solution for the English, but it was the only solution open to them. It was certainly worth a try.

Paper money came to the West via China in the ninth century. Various governments in China found that paper was a convenient substitute for metal when metal became scarce. They did not grasp the inflation problem. The more paper printed, the less was the purchasing power. Though it may have taken centuries, even the Chinese peasant came to understand that this paper was essentially worthless. It ceased to be used as a medium of exchange in China.

In Western Europe, Sweden can claim priority for introducing paper money. In 1656 Johan Palmstruch established Stockholm Banco, issued credit notes that could be exchanged for silver coins, issued more notes than silver, and ended up in jail. [lxi]

## Paper Money Finds Official Favor—The Bank Restriction Act

As discussed, debt had resulted in bankruptcy for France, and a shortage of metal was stifling the commerce of Britain. Both nations found themselves in extremis in financial terms. France responded with revolution, and England with the passage of the Bank Restriction Act.

In extremis, any port in a storm as it were, will do just fine. Great Britain—having lived well beyond its means fighting wars that it could not afford, including the American Revolution; having imported from Asia silks and spices and everything nice, paying with silver and gold and thus so draining the treasury that it was forced to resort to the minting of smaller coins; and now faced with a threat to its very existence by Napoleon and an empty treasury—temporarily solved its monetary problem by continuing the issuance of Bank of England bills, having suspended convertibility in 1797.

Paper money was to replace gold, with an understanding that when the crisis ended, convertibility would resume. This was a very practical solution provided, of course, that the world was willing to accept these bills. Everyone understood that the bills themselves did not constitute payment.

Paper bills never constitute payment. Payment occurs when the bills are brought to the bank and exchanged for gold. Gold is payment, not the paper bills.

The bills were simply IOUs, much as a bond is, with some important differences.

In the fiat currency world of today, the holder of a bond paying interest exchanges it for paper that does not but carries the imprimatur "legal tender." Translated, this means that a creditor must accept this currency in payment of debt.

This concept of currency and debt has worked for decades but remains fatally flawed.

The flaw is that though a creditor such as a bank must accept the tender, a shopkeeper or others engaged in commerce do not have to. The shopkeeper will accept the paper, the dollar bill, only as long as he is certain that others will accept it from him.

Thus the paper isn't truly payment but remains an IOU. This in time becomes a gigantic daisy chain. The world of debt we live in today is precisely that.

The chain will hold as long as the links hold. With a major break, the entire system collapses.

Since we are all in this together, theoretically that break will never occur. The difficulty with this argument is that we are not all in this together.

*Life, Liberty, and the Pursuit of Money*

Excessive debt, funded by printing currency, brings ever closer the moment that though the currency remains legal tender, it is no longer accepted for fear that it will suffer a profound loss in purchasing value.

Internationally this has to be a major concern. Domestically the day of reckoning occurs when one goes to the store to buy a gallon of milk and hands the cashier a five-dollar bill, but the cashier reacts by saying, "This isn't five dollars but just a piece of paper." The consensus today is this will never happen; we shall see.

Thus the British decision to suspend convertibility was a risky business. The world just might not accept British paper.

Officialdom in London stated unequivocally that convertibility had temporarily been suspended and, further, the Treasury would retain enough bullion to cover the amount of bills outstanding. This should allay any fears that creditors might have.

Though this was comforting, in fact, Britain issued far more bills than they had bullion. This was not an immediate problem as convertibility had been suspended for the moment. Whether they had the bullion in their vaults, no one knew for certain. In the future, however, this became a major problem.

Britain of course continued to collect taxes, and as the leading industrial and colonial power in the world, had considerable credibility. The France of Napoleon had none. France was a questionable financial risk. Britain, on the other hand, was solid, or so it was argued.

However, there were real risks. The most obvious was the Brits might lose the war with Napoleon. It had been the intention of Napoleon to invade the British Isles and to occupy, if not to destroy, Britain, in which case Bank of England bills would prove worthless.

Then there was this matter of bills outstanding versus bullion in the treasury. War demands greatly increased the issuance of bills. The demand for British goods and trade at a time of severe shortages on the Continent and elsewhere necessitated substantial increases in the "money supply." Thus there was considerable uncertainty as to the amount of bank bills outstanding.

Britain issued far more bills that they had a call on in bullion. The risk thus lay with the billholders to the extent of the difference. However, Britain prevailed in the war.

With the end of the national crisis, the so-called restriction period had to come to an end. It lasted from 1797 to 1821.

## The Day of Reckoning—The Resumption of Convertibility

As the British Parliament approached the time for the renewal of convertibility, they were faced with a most unpleasant reality.

The ratio of bills outstanding to gold was estimated to be 28.4 million bills versus 2.2 million in gold reserves. This meant that billholders would get about 8 percent gold for each bill.

In other words, the stated value of the pound was less than was generally thought—a lot less.

In today's world when a business goes into bankruptcy, creditors come forward with their claims and are paid proportionately less than the amount of debt, except for those with statutory priority. The creditor is simply paid less than he or she is owed, and legally the debt is extinguished.

Do nations have the right to do this? Would Britain resort to this tactic?

Recently Argentina came to an agreement with bondholders of the sovereign debt to pay something over thirty cents on the dollar. The European Union is working with Greece currently, and it appears the bondholders will receive approximately fifty cents on the dollar. Agreement must be reached as there is no way to put a country into bankruptcy, or as has been frequently stated, countries don't go broke. The country and people survive and will continue to be part of the family of nations. The creditors must invariably bear the burden of loss or at the very least a major part of it. Better luck next time. As maddening as it may seem, this is the way the world financial system operates.

However, if one stops to think about it, there is no other alternative, except not to invest at all.

*Life, Liberty, and the Pursuit of Money*

This problem arises, however, only where there is no right of convertibility. If the bondholders had a right to the gold in the treasury or other assets, the problem would not arise.

Coming back to Great Britain, the English Parliament in 1819 passed an Act calling for the resumption of cash payments. In other words the bill holders were going to be finally paid gold upon the surrender of the Bank of England bills.

Again it was universally accepted that gold constituted payment. The bills, though they had been used as currency, were representations or IOUs.

The critical difference between Britain of 1819 and the United States in 2011 is that we and the rest of the world accept our "dollar bills" as payment.

On the surface this distinction might not appear to carry great significance, but to the contrary, it is critical. An independent measure or standard to equate value is essential if the world expects to avoid the distortions that are inevitable if one nation has the unlimited power to print currency while determining its value.

Value is never subjective; neither nation nor individual can determine value by fiat. If it were possible to do so, a government would theoretically have the power to declare any asset worth more or less than its objective or true value.

This is precisely what the modern world has done. We print excessive amounts of currency and declare the currency legal tender, which in turn distorts the price structure of all assets, altering the price but not the value of the assets. This in turn engenders widespread speculation as demand increases faster than supply. A "get rich quick" psychosis grips the country and the world.

The nation and its people in turn come to believe that the pot of gold is not through their efforts in production, but rather through asset acquisition and consumption, which as prices rise becomes affordable by taking on immense amounts of debt. A nation once prosperous becomes hostage to the debt and the holders of the debt.

With the domestic price structure distorted, the need to reduce cost to remain competitive becomes paramount. The transfer of productive facilities to other domiciles begins. Unemployment in the home country rises, debtors default in large numbers, businesses merge and then fail, and the global economy at first flattens out and then staggers, ultimately imploding as the debt pressure, which can no longer be financed, overwhelms nations.

Central banks, now acutely aware of the dangers, seek to ameliorate the catastrophic effects of this condition by extending more credit, printing more currency, and depreciating the currency, making it increasingly difficult to either produce or acquire as the gap between the value of currency and the objective value of assets widens.

The global economy enters a downward spiral that cannot be relieved, absent a fundamental restructuring.

This global ship, this modern-day *Titanic*, put together by many nations—the global economy better known simply as globalization—enters the phase of final collapse.

Indeed it will sink, submerged under an iceberg of debt and driven by the thoughtless, greed-driven misuse of currency.

## Addressing Reality

Fortunately, the end of greatness was not nigh for Britain and the civilized world in the early nineteenth century with the final defeat of Napoleon.

It was time to move on. With the return of peace, promises earlier made were now going to have to be met. The many creditors who had supported Great Britain during the long years of conflict were now looking to be paid.

A reasonable question that would be asked today is "Why?" Why would a triumphant Great Britain seek to complicate international and domestic commerce and further pressure business and government by living up to a promise made many years earlier in a very different world?

Clearly in a world dominated by metal currency, many in England and in their Parliament felt they had no choice. The world had accepted English paper. They had relied on this promise when credit was extended, and they expected the English, being an honorable Christian nation, to live up to that promise. Without convertibility the promise to pay would remain but a promise.

Clearly, if England had not lived up to its promise, obtaining credit in the future would have become problematical in a changing world that was increasingly mesmerized by mechanical invention and industrialization.

Under the fiat, or paper currency regimen, the ties that bind and assure equilibrium in society are broken. People no longer recognize that to consume they must produce. Instead of producing and living within their means, people see an opportunity to take and not give. As a substitute for giving of one's time, talent, and energy, that is, one's labor, people choose to walk down a road far more easily traveled, the world of speculation and debt.

Likewise government, which controls the printing press, encourages the citizenry to live beyond their means, encourages profligate spending, fights unpaid wars, makes no effort to balance revenue and spending, and meets growing debt demands by selling ever more Treasury securities.

The gap between the rising tide of consumption and stunted domestic growth in production is met by shifting the production imperative offshore to other countries.

Why work and produce when others are willing to do it for us—the Chinese, for example? All we have to do is give them artificially priced currency, and they will give us trinkets in return.

Of course this dynamic means that fewer Americans are needed in the workforce. Unemployment rises as speculation (such as in housing) surges, distorting the price structure. Who cares? Everyone is getting what they want, and the printing presses just keep rolling.

The first indication of major calamity is the bursting of the price bubble. Prices, having risen to a point that is unsustainable, now fall sharply.

People shed assets to mitigate loss, business slows and then enters a prolonged period of decline, unemployment rises, and the economy spirals downward. Sound familiar?

Who is responsible for this catastrophe?

Debt is obviously the proximate cause.

Clearly the individual is at fault for living beyond his or her means, and so is industry for its contribution to this obvious illusory economic condition. Government, state and federal, are the worst offenders. The federal debt in 2011 of the United States approximated $15 trillion and was growing at $3.9 billion a day. That is not million. That is billion. The printing presses are just rolling along.

Fortunately, for England and the world, England understood the problem. They had come through bankruptcy prior to Napoleon. Debt had to repaid. The future, if not the survival of the country's commerce, depended on it. England, the most powerful of nations as measured by the size of its empire and military and industrial capacity, could not change that.

## England Addresses Reality—The Year is 1819

Though long delayed, Parliament in 1819 after arduous and contentious debate finally passed "The Act for the Resumption of Cash Payments." England was about to engage in the process of getting itself out of debt.

In 1797 the suspension of cash payments was viewed as a necessity given the financial condition England found itself in. War gave the Brits no choice at all. Under the terms of suspension, it was understood that once the crisis had passed, convertibility would resume. Ah, the best-laid plans of mice and men…

The end of war, however, brought with it a new set of economic and financial problems. This encouraged Parliament to defer consideration of the matter, awaiting passage of the so-called Peels Bill. The year 1820 became the target date for conversion of large-sum amounts into gold bars, and 1823 for gold coins.

For years prior to the passage of the legislation, a debate had raged over the most important of details, namely, the price at which bills would be exchanged for gold.

At the time of suspension, gold bullion was "convertible in coin at the bullion office of the Bank of England at 775.6d or at the mint at 775.10 1/2d."[lxii]

The need for war materiel and the demands of trade and other commerce necessitated a substantial increase in currency, or the appellation for the time, the printing of "paper" pounds.

*Life, Liberty, and the Pursuit of Money*

But after suspension of cash payments, the price of gold reckoned in paper pounds fluctuated wildly.

A volatile gold price disturbed the ratio of bills to gold. As noted, there was considerably more in paper bills at the stated value outstanding than there was gold in the treasury. Thus a "haircut" was in order. The bills were going to be devalued.

This haircut would amount to some 30 percent. The billholders, domestic and foreign, would receive in exchange 30 percent less in principal than the amount stated on the bills.

Faced with this prospect, a furious debate erupted in Parliament. Creditors were outraged, and of course debtors, who would stand as beneficiaries, were greatly pleased.

Among the purists, particularly those in Parliament who represented the creditors, this seemed to be unfair and unjust. In a nation that had long held to the principle that failure to pay a debt was a serious crime, such a giveback was unthinkable to many.

What did this say about the creditworthiness of the nation? Could England be trusted in the future? What impact would it have on commerce? This was anarchical at best, barbarian at worst. What effect would it have on labor, who might well read in these happenings a new lesson and message carrying a quasi-socialist tinge that a commitment to work for one's livelihood was less than essential?

Suspicions that a scam was afoot here, including the possibility of corruption in government, raised the ire of many. However, what really set passions ablaze was the suggestion that new taxes had to be passed to account for this and future shortfalls in revenue.

To the landed gentry, the wealthy of the time, this meant that the tax burden would fall on them. They and their representatives would have none of it. This was a powerful constituency.

Legislators were at loggerheads, but finally legislation was passed, and 1823 was set as an end date for the resumption of convertibility.

This proved unsatisfactory to the board of directors of the Bank of England, who constituted the purest of the pure. They voted to resume cash payments by May 1821, at the pre-suspension mint price, which would have a significant impact on the money supply and thus the price structure.

This event carried such importance that one has to stand aside and view it from the standpoint of the historical developments that followed. The nations of the world, particularly in the West, began to adopt guidelines and principles, frequently puritanical and strict and very much at odds with reality.

In the case of Great Britain, the purists argued that the debt must be paid, irrespective of the impact on the people.

Of course the purpose of government is to serve the people, not to admonish them. The imposition of a strict moral code has absolutely nothing to do with government or the banking industry. It is not their role, or part of their portfolio, to determine that which is pure and principled and that which is not.

The English had no choice but to issue paper bills.

Debt and deficit financing, which this constituted as the Brits did not have the means to make payment against this paper, was unfortunate.

However, this did not throw the world into disequilibrium. It simply meant, to the extent that there was now more currency outstanding than gold reserves, devaluation of the currency. Britain was simply a poorer nation than it was prior to the war.

In balance sheet terms, the value of the nation's liabilities had increased far faster than the value of the nation's assets. Pretending that this was not the case greatly contributed to the economic stagnation that ensued after the Napoleonic Wars.

An adjustment in the value of pound sterling should have been made to account for this change in circumstances. The value of pound sterling was now worth less since, to put it in the simplest terms, Great Britain was now worth less.

It is impossible to overstate the importance of doing this. When one completes a financial statement, one lists assets and liabilities; the resulting balance is net worth. Ignoring one's liabilities will not increase one's net worth. To do so is fraudulent.

Failure of the government and subsequent governments of Great Britain to adjust the currency value was a fraud, both on the people of Great Britain and the rest of the world. Pound sterling was not worth what they said it was worth.

As a result foreigners had to pay more for goods produced in Great Britain than their true value or what they would have cost elsewhere.

This served to crush British exports. With an exaggerated currency value, internally people can only buy less, and thus the economy slows and unemployment rises. The overcapacity that had been set in place during the conflict to produce war-related materials further accelerated the downturn.

The decision to pay sterling bills with the reinstitution of convertibility at the prewar nominal value was a distortion of reality. It was a way of pretending that these events had either never occurred or the government and people of Great Britain and the banking industry were somehow not responsible. It resulted in a sharp increase in unemployment and sharp decline in prices.

Had the government moved on devaluation prior to the return to convertibility, major advantages would have accrued to England.

Across the world, people would have been buying British, and the long economic decline might never have ensued.

It was not to be. The sacredness of contract and the duty of the debtor were to take precedence. Rigidity, or as I prefer, blindness to the current reality was to mark the order of the day and century. There was no place for innovative thinking.

Great Britain was insistent on ignoring the critical changes that were taking place in industry and commerce. They refused to take stock of the change in their position and Europe's as a result of continental warfare.

This self-imposed isolation, blindness, and plain stupidity would result in policies that were self-defeating, creating a social and political vacuum that would be eagerly filled by a rising Germanic power to the east and ultimately lead to two world wars.

It would take a century and a half before England was ready, with the arrival of Margaret Thatcher in 1980, to take critical action. Of course by this time, it had long surrendered its world leadership in every sphere and now stood as a pygmy dependent on the United States, a mere shadow of its former greatness.

There is no question that there were other events in play. With the passage of time, Britain would have had to surrender its colonies as they pressed for independence. But British weakness, as measured by the decline in its financial condition, greatly accelerated this process.

It is a very sad yet true story, and from the vantage point of history, it may have been unnecessary.

## What Steps Might Great Britain Have Taken to Halt Its Inexorable Decline?

So much that transpired was by chance—the discovery of silver and gold in the New World; the egomania of Henry VIII and his break with Rome; his fascination with property, which set the money dogs of Europe and England loose; the appointment of Isaac Newton to head the British Mint and the miscalculations he made in pricing gold to silver; the unexpected American Revolution, the destructive French Revolution. Who could have known?

Britain before the onset of conflict had been a nation at peace for decades and as a result had prospered on the world stage.

Historians point to the mercantile system and the hostile manner in which England treated the peoples in their colonies; the caste system of France, which separated those of privilege from the common folk; and the American Revolution as the critical elements in the upheaval that followed.

All of this may well be true, but in the end, what assured England's decline and that of France was hostility to change, a denial of reality. The leadership of Britain and France refused to accept the dynamic of change and its inevitability.

The world might be changing, but they were determined to remain steadfast in their devotion to the past, or to be more precise, to their past glory. Both nations were broke and broken, but they felt it was imperative to carry on their pretensions.

For most of Europe, the nineteenth century was a horror. Even with the astounding technical advances and inventions, poverty spread like a great cancer, resulting in divisions, as nations attempted to separate themselves from their neighbors in order to ensure internal stability.

Beggar–thy-neighbor policies and territorial disputes grew as Europe fractured. It became an imperative for every nation to hold on to what it had and grab what they could; otherwise they ran the risk of being swept away or overrun by an aggressive neighbor.

The Congress of Vienna, with its overriding commitment to the past, had made a valiant effort to hold the line, to reestablish former spheres of influence, with their monarchal structures, in the vain hope that this would limit nationalistic tendencies that were sprouting, together with strange, new, radical philosophies across the landscape.

By holding with the past, Europe, in a word, was disintegrating.

This Continental "coming apart" meant a further decline in authority and international cooperation. There was no moral authority to point nations in the direction of peace and understanding.

If a nation was to survive, it had to look out for its interests. It had to protect itself, and that meant greater reliance on the military option.

Nations with a military bent, such as Prussia, now commanded far more respect in world affairs and wielded this newfound influence to unite the Germanic peoples in a German Union, with William I, a true German warlord, at the head.

Advances in technology meant advances in military hardware that was far more potent, and thus the threat was that much the greater.

France would forever be fearful of this new threat from the east and, with a smaller population, anxious, perpetually anxious, and paranoid about it. This bred hostility that inevitably led to conflict, a conflict that carried into the twentieth century.

## The Collapse of Europe—"Haven't I Seen This Show Before?"

The collapse of Europe did not result from a lost battle or death of a monarch, and took the better part of two centuries to complete, culminating in the battle for Berlin in 1945.

The collapse of Rome took centuries as well, but the ending was not quite as spectacular. The Western Empire died "with a whimper." Western Europe died in a cataclysmic show of men and arms, surrounded by newsreel cameras to forever testify to the ferocity of the event.

There was nothing left afterward to demonstrate the greatness of empire of either Rome or Europe, except perhaps a few monuments.

I make the argument that the death of both was inevitable. The proximate cause in both cases was financial collapse. Financial collapse for a culture, nation, people, or individual is calamitous. Moral collapse is the precursor of financial collapse.

We can forever speculate about what might have happened that could have radically changed the direction of history, and though convincing, the fact remains that with moral collapse, financial collapse was inevitable. It simply would have ended with a different set of characters.

Under the circumstances prevailing at the time, there was a crying need to reverse the direction of England, the world's industrial leader. Certainly others would have followed.

A consensus should have developed for new policies and new leadership to break with the past, to energize the more productive elements in society.

Incredibly the reverse took place. With prices falling, at the very least, one might have thought that it would have been widely accepted that increasing the so-called money supply was imperative.

In Gresham's phraseology, "The value of money is in the inverse ratio of its quantity, the supply of commodities remaining the same. Increase the quantity of money, prices rise. Decrease the quantity of money prices fall."[lxiii]

The issue for England and implicitly for the world after the Napoleonic crisis was a return to sound policies, which translates in monetary terms to the return to convertibility at an equilibrium price.

Fiat or paper money was an expedient. Keep in mind that neither the holders of the paper nor the government, neither the people nor the Bank of England, ever considered Bank of England notes as final payment. Of course this is in sharp contrast to the situation today, where the world accepts bank notes or currency as payment. Is it truly payment?

Though it continues to be a matter of debate, the 1819 Act for the Resumption of Cash Payments is widely regarded as the primary cause for the sharp decline in prices that ensued, in particular in agricultural prices. This would not have occurred if England had devalued the pound sterling prior to the return of convertibility.

The wealth, in financial terms, of Great Britain had declined by a measurable percent, but the English were determined to ignore this reality. Dynamic change was happening in front of their eyes, but England responded by closing its eyes. There were now more people and increased capacity to produce, but as notes were exchanged for gold, less currency. Gresham's rule went into effect: less currency, fewer jobs, declining prices, and less profitability.

At the very time the world, in worsening economic straits, should have been pushing to increase the availability of capital as an aid to business and production, they chose to go the other way. Yes, the attraction of gold and silver is that they are scarce, but scarcity does not make for wealth. For the sake of gold, the world would remain poor.

## For the Love of Gold

The Bank of England crossed the Rubicon in 1844 with the passage of the Bank Charter, when Bank of England notes fully backed by gold put England formally on the gold standard.

The rest of the world, including the United States, was on a mixed standard, that is, gold and silver.

Though the price of gold relative to silver in the future would be volatile, both were acceptable internationally in payment. Obviously the debtor would pay with the less expensive of the two at the time of payment.

The creditor thus felt cheated. This uncertainty bothered bankers as much as it did creditors. It led to hoarding of one metal or the other as the price fluctuated. All of this was so untidy and unpredictable.

Though the world was desperate for economic relief, for capital, the bankers blamed, not the lack of capital, but the dual metal payment system for undercutting commerce and creating the economic straitjacket they found themselves in.

The pristine reputation of the Bank of England, the gold-silver confusion, and the strengthening position of London in financial affairs exerted pressure on other nations to join England on the gold standard.

Though a few nations had gone to the standard earlier, the critical moment was reached in 1871 following the formation of the German Union. Before union, Germanic territory, until Napoleon, was a large conglomeration of small states.

The collapse of the Austro-Hungarian Empire provided Prussia with the opportunity to bring them together under Prussian leadership. Bringing them together and keeping them together were quite different matters.

The more western states of the Germanic states looked to Austria and France for commercial trade. The eastern states, those on the borders with Prussia, were dominated by Prussia and the Prussian militarist tendencies.

The Germanic states had different currencies, all convertible into silver. The Prussians believed that through the creation of a central bank with a single currency backed by gold, true union would be assured in the future.

Yes, England was on the gold standard, but England wasn't on the Continent. The states that made up the "Latin Monetary Union," led by France, remained an attraction for trade.

These matters would be simplified if the world went on the gold standard.

A series of conferences was held in Paris, with the financial leaders of the important nations in attendance. Their intention was to make gold the sole international payment standard.

In a world struggling with continuing depression, to cancel the bulk of the money supply was an idea that was both bizarre and irrational. To the Americans from the west, who looked for leadership in a future presidential contender, William Jennings Bryan, silver was not the enemy but the solution to the United States' currency money needs.

Their voice was not to be heard in Paris.

One was not necessarily wealthier by accumulating gold, for when the gold price went down, one was obviously less wealthy. Put simply, wealth was relative. For wealth to be measurable in terms of gold, it had to have a universal price of sorts.

The American representative reportedly brought this conundrum to the attention of the powerful American Senator Sherman of Ohio, who later served as secretary of the Treasury. The senator swept the problem away with the observation that gold had no price. It was "God's money."

The gold standard was here to stay. Following on the heels of Germany, Belgium, Italy, Switzerland, and France adopted gold in 1873, as did the United States when it adopted a de facto gold standard at a price of $20.67 per troy ounce. Others were Scandinavia in 1875, Spain 1876, Finland 1878, Austria 1879, Russia 1893, Japan 1897, and the United States officially de jure in 1900.

We were all to worship before the golden calf, and the world was about to pay an unbelievable price for this folly.

CHAPTER 7

# The Other Side of the Atlantic

### THE UNITED STATES OF AMERICA—A LAND OF THE F...

The eighteenth century witnessed the birth of America. While depression, monetary confusion, outright intrigue, and aggression dominated western and eastern Europe in the post-Napoleonic era, Americans as a people were building a nation.

A large majority of the three million-plus who settled the New World showed only passing interest in metal. They understood, however, the importance of having available a medium that would allow them to engage in business.

They recognized, at least from a governmental standpoint, the need for a medium of exchange but eschewed adoration of metal or currency. Prior to the period leading up to revolution, they accepted European coin as a standard without much fanfare. The difficulty lay not in the nature of the medium but in its availability.

The mercantilist philosophy and the law of Great Britain was that all commercial transactions except for local trade be with the mother country. Trade with other nations was unlawful. In the business setting that prevails today, the colonists were viewed as the retail buyers or consumers. They were to pay retail prices for the goods manufactured in England. They were to have no say in the matter. Domestic manufacturing was discouraged.

The colonist's role was to simply provide raw materials. As a consequence of this, metal flowed out of the country, leaving the colonists literally moneyless. They endeavored to address this problem starting in the seventeenth century by devising alternatives.

In the south the first currency was tobacco and rice. The Atlantic states focused on corn, cattle, and furs. New York and environs early on focused on wampum. We of course associate wampum with Indian trade.

It was serious money (currency) nevertheless. Wampum was a string of 360 black and white beads made from shells and was used principally in exchange for beaver skins; it served as a medium as far south as Virginia.[lxiv]

As commerce developed and with metal scarce, the rebellious Americans searched for alternatives, most notably in the north. On the surface it might have seemed very reasonable to the British, who did not object. After all, greater commerce meant that the colonists would be able to buy from London. At first that unquestionably was the case.

In discussing the subject of currency, it is most important that one never lose sight of the fact that mercantilism, together with bullionism, were both universally accepted at the time as the only way to engage in commerce.

The prevailing philosophy was that currency—rather than the goods or the capacity to produce goods through labor—was wealth. Thus for a nation to grow in wealth, it was imperative that commerce bring bullion into the country and take whatever steps were necessary to prevent it from leaving. The balance of payments in effect was to be a one-way street. China adheres to this philosophy today, though they pay lip service to balance in trade.

The logic of this philosophy meant that in the end, one country, perhaps the mother country, would have all the bullion and the colony would have none.

The bereft colony would then not have the capacity to buy anything further, leaving the mother country without a trading partner. Mother country and colony would thus suffer, leaving both poorer. Apparently the analysis of the Mother country and colony never got that far.

Spain, which directed all its attention and effort to bringing gold and silver from the New World into Spain, took steps to see to it that in international trade bullion never left the country. This is the classic example of this self-delusion.

If trade slowed as a result of these policies, so be it. In time, Spain would become the poorest nation in Europe. One might say that they never saw the big picture.

Spain was not alone in this. Though it was more bullionist than England, meaning that it had a greater desire to attract metal and to keep it than the island nation, both believed that currency was wealth and acted accordingly.

Thus their laws and attitude toward others were not founded on balance and equality but were driven by the imperative "get the money." Such was the ignorance of the time, and it continued until today.

Revolutionary America and Americans, except of course for the natives, were immigrants all. For the better part of a century after their break with England, this eager, determined, and courageous assortment, coming as they did from all parts of the European Continent, showed but little interest in what today might be described as an all-consuming fascination with money.

In that regard they were very different from their European cousins. Post-revolution Europe continued to decline, but America was becoming prosperous.

The new arrivals had an insatiable desire for land, having been denied such an opportunity in Europe, but never for currency, be it gold, silver, or paper, but rather for freedom and the opportunity to produce.

## The American Revolution, a Colonial Secession—Currency and the Banking Business in Revolutionary America

As noted, currency meant little to the colonists. The populace focused their effort and attention on their families and their farms. However if they were to prosper, a medium of exchange was necessary. The continuing absence of such a medium, many believed, was due to the efforts of the British, who expected their colonials to remain both poor and docile. Thus, if there was a shortage, the British must be responsible.

At any rate, short of a medium, the colony of Massachusetts instituted a private bank as early as 1681.[lxv]

Paper money issued in one colony in all likelihood was accepted by all, if for no other reason than "What was the alternative?" Since this paper could not be redeemed, it depreciated. This depreciation manifested itself in the prices charged for goods. This translated into inflation, which in turn, as bills continued to be issued, translated into more inflation, ultimately reducing the paper to a negligible percent of its nominal value.[lxvi]

"Dr. Douglas estimates in his Historical Summarization of New England that in 1748 more than 2.5 million in pound sterling was in circulation in Massachusetts. Prices were high, debtors demanded more currency, and the normal vicious circle of high prices, more money, and higher prices was in full swing."[lxvii]

"But the British Government became uneasy at the rapid depreciation of the currency and its instability and in 1720 a law was passed prohibiting the issuance of bills of credit for any but absolutely essential government expenses. For a while this law caused a painful deflation, and serious resentment against Mother Country. So much so that the measure was largely ineffective and in 1751, the British Parliament passed a new restrictive bill, this time prohibiting the further issue of legal-tender bills of credit by the New England states; in 1764, the restriction was extended to all the Colonies."[lxviii]

This act on the part of the British Parliament was universally considered a quite unjustifiable interference in local matters and was deeply resented. Nor was the act entirely effective in doing away with paper money. In 1774, between $10 million and $15 million worth of it was in circulation. It is not surprising that when the crisis came in the following year, the colonists fell back upon paper currency as the chief method for financing the war.

Hard money or specie became associated with Toryism, Monarchism, and oppression; and paper money with democracy, freedom, and the rights of the people. Mr. William Jennings Bryan in 1896, in accusing his opponents of Anglomania and referencing corruption by the "Money Lords of Great Britain," was running true to type.[lxix]

## The Beginning of War, Revolution, and Taxation

The American Revolution was such a momentous event in world history that it is easy to lose sight of the underlying causes. However described, the fact remains that the absence of a stable currency played a critical role. To be more specific, the issue of currency and taxation became intermingled. The current debate about taxes is almost child's play in comparison to the fury that raged during the course of the late eighteenth century.

When the French and Indian War came to a close in 1763, both nations were in extremis financially. The French were inclined, given the sublime attitude of the "Courts of Louis," to finesse the issue.

The British, the victors, decided to address the issue head-on. They embarked on a taxation program adopting the first principle of tyranny, namely, tax the "other guy."

Thus the decision to tax the colonists came easy. After all, the war in North America had been fought for their benefit. It is safe to say that was an argument that did not sit well with the colonists, more so because they had no say in the matter.

In their condescending way, the British ignored the American protests and proceeded to pass two Acts that harshly stirred the revolutionary pot, namely, the Stamp Act in 1765, followed by the Townsend Duties in 1767.

For the Americans "taxation without representation" became the battle cry, and battle it would be, and what a battle at that.

"Almost the first step that Congress took after hostilities began was to sanction the issue of paper money. A week after Bunker Hill the emission of £2,000,000 worth of bills was authorized. The lesson of the depreciation of the colonial paper currency had evidently been well learned. But what was the Continental Congress to do? It was more or less a make shift body, without power or desire to impose taxation on a people in revolt, partly against taxation without obvious borrowing facilities, and it naturally seized upon the first thing at hand, the printing press. Between 1775 and 1779 Congress issued about $240,000,000 in bills of credit. Of course, value depreciation of the paper ensued..."[lxx]

"After 1780, the depreciation of the currency was more rapid than ever and in 1781, it ceased to act as currency at all. At the end of the war there was a distinct reaction against any further issue of bills of credit. The indescribable chaos had changed the attitude of a large section of the public, and the 'cheap money' champions had little to say in drafting the Constitution. That document denied any state the right to coin money, issue bills of credit, or make anything but gold and silver legal tender. Soon the worthless continental and state fiat currency disappeared."[lxxi]

The rather casual use of the euphemism "disappearance" understates the facts. One must bear in mind that these were indeed perilous times. The war was going badly and Congress had little revenue. Paper currency or fiat money wasn't the solution. The following passage makes this abundantly clear.

"Financial matters, however, most occupied Congress, most concerned the public, and most required [James] Madison's attention in Philadelphia. [At the time Madison was a member of Congress.] In March Congress devalued Continental currency by a ratio of 40 to 1, but the move, a desperate effort to prevent further inflation, failed completely. By the end of the year the actual depreciation had reached 100 to 1; in the spring of 1781 the states began to repeal their laws, designed to support the Continental paper, and in May the bottom fell out. One dollar in specie would purchase $1,000 of currency and soon thereafter the phrase 'not worth a Continental' literally meant 'worth nothing.' Thus shorn of the vital source of its financial independence, the power to emit negotiable paper currency, Congress had to beg for funds."[lxxii]

France came to the aid of the United Sates with money and supplies, including the critical difference at the battle of Yorktown, namely, the French fleet and of course the magnificent Marquis de Lafayette.

It was not the French alone who bailed out the American government. American merchants led by Robert Morris, who was one of the wealthiest men in America at the time, provided critical aid to the new nation.

As Mr. Ketcham points out in his biography of James Madison, "In fact, without the private merchants who 'lent' their credit and connections to the public, both government and the war would have collapsed."[lxxiii] The crucial question was not whether formal "conflict of interest" opportunities existed (they usually did), but whether he (Robert Morris) used information obtained in confidence as a public official for his personal gain, or whether his operations in balance gave the public a "fair" return for their money.

## The End of the Beginning—Alexander Hamilton

The war was won, independence was achieved, and now the difficult part of governing began. Of course that meant that the new nation, deeply in debt, had to focus on the most taxing of all problems, money. The experience during the war made it clear to the founders that government fiat or paper money would never do, irrespective of intentions.

Bank money, on the other hand, which meant specie, that is gold or silver, would work well. The nineteenth-century fascination with gold had yet to begin. Silver was still dominant. In fact, until the arrival of Queen Elizabeth I, silver was the universal standard for measurement. Payment of gold was determined by the current value of silver.

Of course other metals were popular in the Far East, such as bronze and copper, but that may have been due to the fact that they did not have ready access to so-called precious metals.

"The fundamental distinction between these two [government money versus bank money] was stated clearly by Hamilton in 1790. Speaking of the issue of paper money, he says:

"'…the wisdom of Government will be shown, in never trusting itself with the use of so seducing and dangerous an expedient…The stamping of paper is an operation so much easier than the laying of taxes, that a government in the practice of paper emissions, would rarely fail, in any such emergency, to indulge itself too far in the employment of that resource, to avoid as much as possible one less auspicious to present popularity…in the first case (viz., a paper currency issued by the mere authority of the government) there is no standard to which an appeal can be made, as to the quantity which will only satisfy, or which will surcharge to circulation; in the last (viz., one issued by a bank payable in coin) that standard results from the demand. If more should be issued than is necessary, it will return upon the bank.'"[lxxiv]

For Hamilton, as Treasury secretary, and thus for America, fiat money was out of the question.

The problems associated with fiat or government money were also apparent to Robert Morris, the American financier who played a critical role in seeing to it that the American cause did not collapse. In 1781 as Superintendent of Finance, he had introduced legislation to Congress that resulted in the creation of the Bank of North America, which issued notes that "circulated at par" and "inspired public confidence."[lxxv]

The First Bank of the United States, the Hamilton plan with specie as currency, is viewed as an unqualified success. The nation's debt was paid down, the price of money stabilized, and credit was again available to merchants. There was, however, at least one fly in this ointment. The bank was private, which was inconsistent with a fundamental principle of Jefferson and Madison, who believed such an institution would favor the wealthy. The stock was subscribed to by people with money, and that included foreigners, many of whom reportedly made a fortune from their holdings.

Congress passed the Bank Act with no votes to spare, and it was never endorsed by the "Jeffersonians," centered as they were in Virginia and the South, whose antipathy to the idea was based on fundamental principle. The argument that the "times" required the taking of unusual steps was not persuasive.

The charter of the bank was for twenty years, and the Jeffersonians could barely wait for the time when the bank would be an unfortunate episode in American history and pass out of existence.

The Americans were going to maintain tight control over the money supply, while their European cousins were more like the Romans, described so accurately by H. G. Wells. "'Money floated the Romans off the firm ground,' as Wells puts it. Everyone was getting hold of money, the majority by the simple expedient of running into debt; the eastward expansion of the [Roman] empire was very largely a hunt for treasure in strong rooms and temples to keep pace with the hunger for the new need. The Equestrian order, in particular, became the money power. Every one was developing property. Farmers were giving up corn and cattle, borrowing money, buying slaves, and starting the more intensive cultivation of oil and wine."[lxxvi]

Europe seemed determined to follow in the steps of Rome. Both would ultimately collapse, much like exhausted stars, whose heat and energy dissipates but at a pace sufficiently slow so that the casual observer is unaware.

In one important respect, the collapse of Europe differed greatly from the collapse of Rome. The Roman Empire was pagan, completely pagan. On the other hand, Western Europe was Christian, at least on the surface, though it increasingly worshipped the golden calf.

Rome in time was reduced to dust, but Western civilization not only survived, but reached levels of prosperity and a standard of living for the average person unheard-of in the annals of humankind. This was made possible by the rise of a new power across a great ocean, beginning with the arrival of a few poor but deeply religious settlers on the eastern shore of North America in the seventeenth century.

They brought with them the Judeo-Christian principles embodied in Western civilization, namely, fear of God and obedience to His will; love of neighbor; and an unshakable belief in life, liberty, and the pursuit of happiness, which when translated meant the pursuit of good, rather than money.

*Happiness* derived from the Greek word that means the ultimate good.

This philosophy allowed the North Americans, with unswerving determination, to become the greatest of all nations, and when called upon, willingly to give of themselves and their wealth in sacrifice for the preservation of those principles.

America nevertheless had to engage the world. To do this at first meant the adoption of a standard that commerce would have ready access to, namely, a metal coin. The Spanish milled dollar of 1785, a silver coin minted in the Western Hemisphere, was the immediate answer.

In 1792 Congress passed legislation creating a mint to be located at the seat of government, adopting the decimal system, and authorizing the minting of certain coins in the 1792 Mint and Coinage Act.

We can thank Thomas Jefferson for the currency system we are familiar with.

"In *Notes on Coinage* he proposed a decimal system; the world's first, based on the dollar. 'Everyone knows the facility of decimal arithmetic,' he wrote. 'The bulk of mankind is schoolboys through life…In all cases where we are free to choose between easy and difficult modes of operation, it is most rational to choose the easy.' His simple system was a currency based on tens: one-hundredth of a dollar; the dime; the dollar; ten dollars; etc. Congress agreed with his clear mathematician's logic and adopted his system in 1785. Jefferson's brilliantly uncomplicated system of coinage was one of his great legislative achievements."[lxxvii]

## Currency and the Banking Business—Thomas Jefferson, James Madison, and Alexander Hamilton

Historians speak of and reference Jefferson and Madison when discussing early America with such frequency and something close to adoration that they have almost become mythical figures. Less so Hamilton, though his involvement and contribution in the design of the governmental structure is compelling.

Jefferson and Madison were blood brothers philosophically. They were close friends, were both from Virginia, served together in the design of government, and with Washington shared a vision for America that completely broke with the past.

It was never their intention that America would simply become a separated nation among many others. It was to be a unique state among nations, committed to individual liberty and freedom, that would advance in a fundamental way the cause of humanity.

They believed that if the mix of immigrants on this side of the Atlantic, uncorrupted by heritage, power, or money, could fully come to grips with true freedom, the limitless potential of all men could be achieved.

The colonists' grievances against Great Britain were multitudinous. The breach between them could never be healed, not because the Americans were unreasonable, but because the Americans had yet to be corrupted.

Implicit in their thinking was that the corruption of Britain and Europe had gone so far that there was no possibility of reformation.

European man had failed because he had been corrupted, presumably by power and money. This would not be tolerated in America; hence the need for revolution.

The thinking of both men was heavily influenced by the English philosopher John Locke, who argued that for man to find himself, he must return to his true nature.

Both men were truly God-fearing and believed deeply in the continuing role of the Creator in the lives of men, using nature as the vehicle for the sharing of His blessings. Both Aristotle and Thomas Aquinas would have been proud to have known them.

Man could advance if he relied on "nature and nature's God" in pursuit of his destiny, as Jefferson so eloquently put it in the Declaration of Independence.

What was man's destiny? Happiness, the perfect good, not materialism or hedonism or the corruption spread by kings such as George III, who was responsible for bringing slavery to the shores of America, or other foreign nobles and churches, such as the Anglican Church with its bigotry and practice of self-interest.

## Philosophy in Practice, the Presidents

Jefferson and Madison went on to become presidents, chief executives of the new nation; others, philosophically their soul mates, followed over the course of the next two centuries.

However, it was their governing philosophy, and those standing in opposition, that would lie at the very heart of virtually all future national elections or confrontations.

It was never their intention to divide the nation politically. Yet at the same time, governmental action could never be allowed to impede the march of men in their search for happiness.

When threats to the "inherent rights" arose, they had to be opposed, violently opposed, if necessary. Government had no inherent rights. It had no right to rule. Thus the people had to be wary of all government action, though well intended.

Jefferson and Madison believed that governmental action must always be suspect, for "the road to hell is paved with good intentions."

Jefferson formalized this philosophy in the Declaration of Independence when he wrote that all men come into the world with "inalienable rights." These rights are natural to man, spring from the benevolence of the Creator, and can never be taken away.

Man enters into society voluntarily. He accomplishes this by way of contract with his fellow man and creates a government with specific and very limited powers to facilitate the pursuit of his goals and to defend his freedom.

In order that this never would be misunderstood, governmental powers were to be enumerated in documental form and experimentation with a state-dominated confederation was to be formalized in a Constitution.

We speak today of Republican and Democrat or Conservative and Liberal as if such designations had been with us from the beginning. At the outset there were no political parties. Washington for one was concerned that the unity required could be shattered if political parties representing competing interests were to come into being.

However decisions had to be made, and thus interests were to be contested.

This book is not intended to be a political treatise, but to fully understand the development, challenges, and crises the country faced over the course of the next 235 years, it is imperative to have a firm grasp where the critical leaders, past and present, stood in relation to the philosophy of Jefferson and Madison.

The founding fathers were indeed a brotherhood. Yet the only political experience they knew well was that of Great Britain. They lived and worked under British law, a British bureaucracy, the Anglican religion, and British customs and traditions.

The founding of a new nation could not change that or habits developed over a lifetime and that of their forebears—or at the very least, not change them quickly. Many would see the future in terms of independence, but independence, particularly in matters commercial, closely aligned with the interest of Britain.

Those who were of a British mentality were to become known in this era as Federalists. Hamilton, though a revolutionary of the first order, was a dyed-in-the-wool Federalist.

Washington, though wary of Britain in every way when it came to custom, was a Federalist.

Jefferson, on the other hand, despised the British and everything about them and, after his long service as ambassador to France, developed a deep respect and regard for France. Jefferson understood that without France, the revolution would never have succeeded. France was our true friend, even as they pursued their interests when supporting the Americans, and should be favored over the British, who were still the enemy even after the signing of the Treaty of Paris. In his mind the British would remain the enemy as long as they continued to occupy American soil and threaten American interests.

Jefferson and Hamilton both served in Washington's cabinet, Jefferson as secretary of state and Hamilton as secretary of the Treasury. They had many disputes, but push would come to shove and ultimately political division over the matter of the creation of a central bank.

Jefferson presented his strong views to Washington on this matter, arguing that for the government to create such an entity was clearly unconstitutional. No such power was designated in the United States Constitution, which was adopted in 1789, replacing the Articles of Confederation. Without this designation such power remained with the states.

Hamilton argued that if the nation was to establish a reputation for becoming a reliable credit, it must deal with the debt it had accumulated during the revolution, and to do this and to advance commercially, it must align itself with the wealthy interests and merchants, which of course included the Brits. Thus there was a need for a national bank, he argued.

He contended that the power to create a national bank, though not specifically designated, was implied, being necessary to accomplish the end as specified under the powers of the legislature in Article I Section 8 to pay debts and borrow money.

Jefferson argued that implied powers had to be necessary, not simply a convenience, to accomplish an end. In this case it was not necessary, for there were many other ways to accomplish this end without intruding on the inherent powers of the states, rather than through the creation of a new and potentially powerful institution. *Necessary* as used in the text did not mean the end to be accomplished, but the means used, and clearly there were other means available to accomplish the goal.

Washington was hesitant but, seeing no other option, signed the legislation creating the First Bank of the United States on the last day available for signing.

## A Breach Forevermore

The decision to move forward with the bank made it clear to Jefferson that the Federalists were intent on the recreation of a little Britain. So disturbing were the implications that he moved to form a new party, the Republican Party.

If the end could justify any government action, be it included or not included in the designated powers as set forth in the Constitution, then the Constitution was more form than substance.

Jefferson could never accept such a proposition, and thus felt the need for a party to stand in opposition. Madison agreed, and began to refer to Federalists as the British Party.

Thus began the political system that we know today, the two-party system. Though over the course of the next two centuries, many a political party sprang up, they only faded away after the issue and consternation that brought people together in the first place had run its course.

However, the two-party system remained. The names, designations, and issues may change, but on the national level, two parties invariably dominate.

Interestingly, the Republican Party of Jefferson morphed into the Democratic party of a future president, Andrew Jackson.

The special interest-oriented Federalists in time faded from the political scene after being trounced at the hands of Jackson. There was continuing suspicion regarding their pro-British stance, which many, particularly outside of the Northeast, including Jackson, regarded as treasonous.

The Whigs, their successors, who looked to Congress for leadership and favored internal development, met with a modicum of success, only to be swept aside as the debate over slavery in the western states divided its members.

Lincoln, running in 1860 on the Republican Party ticket, swept to victory, and the two-party system that we know today was here to stay.

Over the centuries, not only have party names changed, but regional and ethnic preferences have drastically changed and continue to do so. African Americans from the time of Lincoln until the election of John Kennedy voted Republican. Today they represent the most important voting bloc within the Democratic Party.

What has not changed and rages today as it did at the time of Jefferson is dispute over the so-called powers of government, specifically those not clearly set forth in the Constitution.

The last word on this would be determined by the Supreme Court, or so it was decided by John Marshall, a renowned Federalist and Chief Justice of the Supreme Court. Since his tenure, the Court has on numerous occasions engaged in the most convoluted reasoning to find Acts of Congress and states constitutional.

The Federalists on the Court, currently referred to as liberals, seem willing to stretch the Constitution as far as necessary to justify governmental action. This has given rise to the accusation that they no longer interpret the law but make the law.

The Jeffersonians on the Court are called strict constructionists. There is considerable accuracy in that description, for Jefferson would have invariably come down on their side in many an important decision.

Thus the debate goes on. A brief sidebar look at certain presidents is informative.

Madison of course was a Jeffersonian, a tried-and-true Jeffersonian, as was Jackson, at least philosophically. Madison might have been slightly left of Jefferson, willing to make an occasional exception, as he did when he signed the legislation creating the Second Bank of the United States.

Jackson was more centrist. He trusted completely the concept of a government of the people, but if circumstances demanded, he was willing to take the action he deemed necessary.

Like Jackson, Lincoln was a centrist. He believed in the people and the right of people to decide their future. Nevertheless, he fought the Civil War and emancipated the slaves.

In the twentieth century, Woodrow Wilson, who fought the First World War, was an internationalist and a Federalist, as was Theodore Roosevelt, though neither were anglophiles and both were thought of as populists.

Franklin Delano Roosevelt was a Jeffersonian internationalist, motivated by strong empathy for the common man.

Harry Truman was Jeffersonian and a centrist very much in the tradition of Jackson whom Truman emulated.

Ronald Reagan was Jeffersonian and a centrist in the Jackson and Truman tradition, though a staunch Republican.

George H. W. Bush was a Federalist and an internationalist, with a striking interest, much like Hamilton, in the moneyed class.

His son, George W. Bush, was an internationalist, with Jeffersonian tendencies in the sphere of presidential appointments. A Federalist for certain when it came to moneyed interests, he embraced OPEC and China.

William Jefferson (a misnomer) Clinton was a Federalist posing as a populist when it came to policy. Though a Democrat, he would not be included among the Jeffersonian presidents. He appointed to the Supreme Court members whose writings and statements suggested that the Constitution was in dire need of updating, a most revolting thought to his namesake. In an idyllic rush to globalize society, Mr. Clinton, as president, was willing to sacrifice the immediate interests of the Americans for a new world order, including most notably China.

## Jeffersonian Policies, Britain and France, and the Matter of Tax, Trade, and Money

Prior to the revolution, the British view of the colonists was rather simplistic. They were British subjects who by chance occupied America. America was now unmistakably British, as France had been defeated in the French and Indian War, thus surrendering their land claims from the Arctic to the Falkland Islands.

The colonists living here were expected to behave, that is, to restrict their commercial activity to Britain alone. They were to sell to Britain raw materials, including produce, tobacco, and wood for the British ships.

In turn they were to buy from the Brits all goods, including luxuries.

In short, the colonists were expected to sell wholesale and buy retail. Such an arrangement meant that the Americans would remain the poor cousins, struggling to survive, without a currency of their own, flirting with bankruptcy, in order to make the mother country prosperous.

As one might imagine, the colonists saw this as a form of vassalage, serfs to be treated by their betters with appropriate scorn.

The Seven Year War with France had been expensive and had to be paid for. Taxes in Britain by today's standards were exorbitant. Property owners paid an annual tax of 25 percent on the value of their property. Virtually everything was taxed. The colonists, being British citizens, though not treated as such, should pay their fair share.

Revolutionary fever gripped the colonists with the passage by Parliament of the Stamp Act, the first internal tax.

Till the passage of this Act, internal taxes had been set by the colonial governments. As famed Federalist, Chief Justice John Marshall would later say, the power to tax is the power to destroy. The colonists feared the worst. At the very least, the Brits were taking over.

Adding to the colonists' misery, Parliament passed the Currency Act of 1767.

The colonists, out of sheer necessity, had issued paper money. There were no silver mines in operation. Gold coin was scarce, and thus hard money or specie was nowhere to be found. This condition didn't seem to bother the Brits, but paper money obviously did.

British merchants were quick to pick up on the fact that paper money depreciated and thus the value was always in question. Simple solution? Do away with it.

From now on it would be cash on the barrelhead, British sterling or gold coin or credit that had been arranged with British merchants.

To be certain that they got every penny, they placed customs collectors on American shores, another act of imperial aggression.

The colonists were penniless. Prices fell, deflation set in, and few had money to buy anything.

All peoples in history, faced with the prospect of economic disaster, have moved against the ruling class. The Americans, of all people, would not prove to be the exception. They would never accept the argument that they should starve for that class. Faced with the prospect of hunger and tyranny, they revolted.

Though the Stamp Act would be repealed, other duties were substituted, and domestic clashes ensued, making conditions further ripe for revolution.

Successful revolutions require leadership. That leadership was available in abundance as the founding fathers sprang from virtual obscurity in America to lead the cause. Among them was a man whose enormous intellect has few comparisons in world history. He came forward from Virginia to provide the philosophical basis in the cause of humanity, personal freedom.

It would be a revolution like no other. This was not a battle over land or goods or money, but a contest for the very soul of man. The struggle, which continues, would rage over the years domestically as well as internationally.

To fully understand the American struggle now, as in the past, one must understand Jefferson's philosophy.

His philosophy and the principles that flowed from it are the distinguishing features of America.

## "THE PURSUIT OF HAPPINESS"

*Freedom*, a word brimming with hope, is understood by everyone, feared by tyrants, dismissed or minimized by snobs and arrogant intellectuals, and misused by many to justify their own predilections and questionable behavior. It is the foundation, the unbreakable stone, upon which the great American Republic was to be built.

According to Jefferson, man does not earn freedom or receive it as a gift that may or may not be dispensed by family, community, or government.

All men are born free. Nature bestows freedom. Nature does this, but nature acts at the direction of a benevolent being, omnipotent and omniscient, which wills that man, through the use of reason, endowed with a free will, shall pursue goodness, and in that pursuit will experience happiness.

Jefferson believed that the purpose of life for every being was to attain the "good." However, life on this planet was always the pursuit, and not the realization, of "perfect goodness." That was not achievable, for that was beyond the scope or capacity of finite man.

Thus reason led him to affirm the existence of a being who is "good" since perfection was not achievable in the here and now; the pursuit itself is the happiness of which Jefferson speaks.

In the mind of this magnificent man from Virginia, reason alone led him to accept the existence of the perfect good, but he refused to take the matter further, as there was no empirical evidence for him to work with or to reason to. Theologically, he was a deist. Intellectually, Jefferson was constrained by the limits of reason. Faith was largely absent from his intellectual portfolio. Though he was very familiar with the Bible, the evidence contained therein was insufficient for him to cement faith. He placed reason over faith.

As a personal matter, he saw in organized religion a threat to the "pursuit." He reserved most of his condemnation for the Anglican Church, which he believed was both bigoted and corrupt. The Anglican Church was simply a religious extension of British tyranny, led by the worst offender to the rights of men, namely King George III. A happy life was one of striving, a reaching for, a giving, working together with one's fellow man to produce progress. In a very real sense man is on a team, a team in search of greatness requiring total commitment. Success is assured when each and every member gives his all.

Team members never take; they give. Freedom is the natural right to be on that team, pursuing greatness, becoming good, giving one's all. Goodness does not allow for taking. Thus we are not free to take whatever we want. That is not freedom as Jefferson would define it. It is a form of anarchy. It is destructive.

Selfish interests run counter to the pursuit. Obesity, greed, and inordinate desires run counter to the goal and will destroy the team and ultimately each of its members. Goodness and the pursuit of happiness are synonymous.

## Freedom in Action

Personal freedom, the right to reason, is consistent with our nature, with our humanity.

Though self-evident to the early fathers, this was taken by the British as a direct threat to their authority.

To their way of thinking, colonists were free only to serve the king and his interests. Thus Parliament by law could impose taxes, duties, and restrictions as suited them.

While it was true that the colonists were British nationals, they had no representation in Parliament. As a people, they were something less than full Brits. This notion embittered leading Americans, Jefferson and Madison of course, but also colony leaders the likes of Samuel and John Adams, Washington, later Franklin, the elite of Virginia and Massachusetts, and men from the other colonies.

The public man from the thirteen colonies resented British interference and particularly the mercantile practices that kept them in a state of semibondage to British merchants. Trade was restricted. Thus they were highly dependent on London for credit at terms disadvantageous to the colonists.

British taxes were arbitrary. The redcoats had rights that violated the colonists' sense of dignity, such as the right to post soldiers in the homes of colonists and Lord North's infamous decision to close the Port of Boston after the Tea Party.

The colonists were in bondage. They remained poor financially, and there was no doubt in their mind that their condition resulted from British domination. To groups like the Sons of Liberty in Boston, the solution was to take matters into their own hands, meaning violence.

To many in America, particularly among the landholders and other elite, such as members of the House of Burgesses, the state legislature in Virginia, revolution might come, but it must be a last resort.

Men such as Jefferson, Washington, and Madison believed that entreaties to the king, olive branches, were a waste of time. The British had made it clear over the decades of occupation that rights were reserved for the king and might be dispensed as he saw fit.

The implacable position of Jefferson and his followers was that the British king had no rights in America, none whatsoever, never had, and never would, and neither should Parliament.

Only the people had rights. No government had any right unless it was specifically ceded by the people to the government, and then it could be removed if said government misused or abused this right.

The purpose of government was to serve the people. It was the people who ruled, and this right to rule sprang naturally from their birth. No one had a right to interfere with it.

Americans weren't British except to the extent that they chose to follow certain British customs. They were free individuals who had the right to form a society in compact with others, coming together as a team, while appointing representatives to serve their interest.

If the representatives did not so serve, then they must be replaced. If they ignored the wishes of the people and clung to or abused their authority, then the individual had the God-given right to remove himself from this society. The individual had the right to disband the Constitution, revolt, and return to his natural state.

A slice of British opinion in and outside Parliament was empathetic. They believed that Americans were British citizens and their rights should be respected. London was thousands of miles from American shores, and it was far wiser and less costly to give these colonists latitude.

*Life, Liberty, and the Pursuit of Money*

Those in Britain who held to this view were mindful that America was not just another backwater. It accounted for one third of British trade, and trade was essential to British world dominance, and ultimately its prosperity.

Though entirely speculative, it is unlikely that Britain would have ever mounted the very expensive campaign to quash the revolution if trade had not been in issue. Simply put, given the financial straits of Britain after the French and Indian war, it was trade and their need for revenue that set policy.

General Howe, the British commanding general in North America at the time of the revolution, and his brother, the senior admiral, had sympathy for the American position. However, even among the peaceniks, revolution could never be countenanced, and any American effort in that regard should be put down, by force if necessary.

To Jefferson, none of this bore any logic at all. To begin with, America was inhabited by peoples of many lands, and thus with the same misplaced logic, we should be following the laws and ordinances of Britain, France, Germany, and Spain.

In history, kingship meant the right to serve the people, particularly widows and orphans, not the reverse. The king of England, like all kings, was meant to be a servant of the people.

By gaining the throne through inheritance, he took arbitrarily from the people the right to choose their representatives, and thus he was by definition a tyrant.

As the American Revolution was about to enter the violent phase, Jefferson sat down and wrote on behalf of a Congressional committee of five what is now considered a document of universal importance. It served as the cornerstone of the American Constitution.

In the fullness of its meaning, it would free man from any form of bondage, opening to him for the first time the prospect of continuing progress and prosperity.

Praised endlessly and read by all peoples from one generation to the next, the Declaration of Independence at the core is an indictment of tyranny, specifically the tyranny of King George III.

The abuse the colonists had borne was his fault, not the fault of the British people or the Parliament. Among their grievances was that it was he who brought slavery to the shores of America.

On his strong conviction on the subject of slavery, Jefferson later wrote to a French diplomat, "And can the liberties of a nation be thought secure when we have removed their only firm basis, a conviction in the minds of the people that these liberties are the gift of God? That they are not to be violated but with his wrath? Indeed I tremble for my country when I reflect that God is just…"[lxxviii]

Americans had to go their own way, severing all ties with the mother country in order to pursue happiness.

Jefferson's philosophy guided the revolution.

## Paying the Price

This revolution meant war, and war was expensive. The Continental Congress and the colonies adopted paper money to pay the bill. As noted earlier, they had no other option. Specie, which had always been in short supply, combined with the contraction of London credit, meant insufficient arms and supplies for the fighting men throughout the war and declining trade.

The wealthy merchants of America, led by the famed Robert Morris, footed the bill until France was finally persuaded to open the king's purse to finance the war. The legendary Lafayette played an important role in this regard, as did Benjamin Franklin, whose diplomatic skills were truly extraordinary.

It was hard for the French minister to say no to Franklin, as he was the most popular man in France besides the philosopher and author Voltaire.

France had enormous internal problems and, as we noted earlier, was bankrupt. Jefferson, after returning to the United States having served in France as ambassador, noted that nineteen million of the twenty million French were "more wretched" than the "most…wretched" in the United States.[lxxix]

The king of France was persuaded to provide the critical financial aid to the Americans, but he had no intention of backing a loser. In the end it took American success on the battlefield to finally convince him. France invested in America.

In the end, France paid an enormous price for this decision. The French Revolution took the head of the king himself, as well as the head of his despised Austrian wife and their noble friends.

Prior to the Constitutional Convention, Congressional options were limited. Congress could plead with the states, but had no power to tax. It was up to the states to decide how funds were to be raised. The states were highly reluctant. There were three major problems. First, there were many loyalists who wanted no part of revolution. Second, the new nation's farmers for the most part lived a hand-to-mouth existence. Taxes? No thanks!

In addition, there was the problem of Washington coming out on the short side of virtually every battle he fought.

The power to tax thus became the centerpiece of the reform movement. To have a nation, as Hamilton argued, there must be a central government to bind the states, both large and small, which would share power. The equitable sharing of power was critical to the formation of a new government, but so was the need for revenue to pay the bills, as the war so clearly demonstrated.

In this argument, Hamilton took the lead, and in the end prevailed. However, his solution, which included a national bank and which both Jefferson and Madison saw as an unconstitutional grab for power, ruptured the cabinet and led, as mentioned, to the formation of political parties.

However, long before any of this came to pass, the only option that seemed to be available at the time was paper money.

Make no mistake about it; paper money had its advantages. For one, you could print all you needed. This stimulated commerce. The creditor had little choice but to accept paper money, which was being issued by both the states and the Continental Congress.

This also served political purposes as a ruse on unsuspecting British merchants, some of whom were still trading or exporting during the revolution. The downside was that there was no way to assure currency stability.

Was this currency intended to be payment that would be redeemed by specie as soon as the conflict came to a close and normalcy was restored? In other words, was this a promise to pay or payment? With war front and center, the issue was never addressed.

We do know that Jefferson, who was forever in need of money, sold land and accepted in payment this paper that over time lost most, if not all, of its purchasing power. When his life ended, he was deeply in debt. Paper money had not proved to be a boon to him at all, nor for that matter anyone else except perhaps for a few debtors.

Bear in mind that there was little or no choice in the matter. You either accepted the paper or nothing at all, a point the Continental Army frequently made. Men such as Jefferson, who were themselves in debt, took the only avenue open to them.

Unexpectedly, the Hamilton Plan provided the answer, which was simply a plan for convertibility. The matter got resolved in favor of hard money or specie.

How did Jefferson deal with all of this? He recognized that currency depreciation necessitated another solution. When it came to money, as to most things, Jefferson sought simplicity. Nevertheless it was the British coin sterling that ruled commerce both before and after the revolution.

Jefferson appreciated better than most men the need for national solvency. America had to rid itself of debt. Revenue had to play a major part. To secure that revenue, British duties and taxes, internal and external, were to be set aside.

In the future America would trade with everyone. Jefferson was willing to trade with anyone including the British, but *the trade must be balanced*.

Trade with Britain had never been balanced. The imbalance in trade meant there was never surplus specie in the country. Mercantilism strangled commerce.

Today America implicitly accepts the mercantilist philosophy, as it is a boon to the large international institutions and corporations. Imbalance in trade is strangling America, though we herald free trade.

Open trade is essential, but so is balance in trade. Jefferson was particularly insistent when it came to Britain that perfect balance be maintained. If he was here with us today to witness policies adopted by Reagan, H. W. Bush, Clinton—particularly Clinton—and George W. Bush that favor world trade even if not balanced, he would be arguing that such a policy is suicidal.

America was rendered destitute through mercantilism, the heart and soul of which was imbalance of trade. Imbalance of trade ultimately translates into bankruptcy. Welcome, Mr. Jefferson, to the financial condition of the United States in the twenty-first century.

A reasonable tariff that would on the one hand encourage trade and on the other provide the revenue the nation needed to carry on its affairs was of primary importance, he believed. The dispute that arose with the South during the Jackson era concerned the level of tariff. Northerners, who controlled Congress, insisted on raising the tariff to protect northern manufacturing, which in turn hurt the South, which was more dependent on exports and imports. The trading counterparties of course retaliated.

Jefferson agreed that the debt of the United States and of the individual states should be paid. The nation should not dishonor its debt simply because it had been accumulated during conflict.

The credit of a nation was a critical feature of nationhood. Other nations would never take America seriously in world affairs if it was willing to default on its debt.

On this score Jefferson and Hamilton were in total agreement. They were in agreement on most points regarding finance, but where they disagreed, the disagreement was profound.

## The Jefferson-Hamilton Divide

Both leaders were critical to the success of the revolution and to final state passage of the American Constitution. They knew each other well and had worked closely together before and during the war. Both served in Washington's cabinet. They were friends, if not close friends. Jefferson's help was critical to Hamilton, who led the charge with regard to the structure of the US government and its adoption by the states.

However on the most fundamental questions, they parted company. Their relationship was analogous to two compatriots who worked closely together, respected each other, and were successful. However, they belonged to different churches. They didn't discuss religion very often, but when they did, their philosophies clashed. Neither was about to compromise because on matters as important as religion, there was no room for compromise.

For Jefferson, America wasn't just a new nation but a new creation, fundamentally different from everything human society had experienced before. Man, as nature and nature's God had intended, was free of corruption, which had been visited upon him by governments and other self-seeking forces.

Ordained with the capacity to reason and a free will, man was free to break the chains that bound him. This opportunity and responsibility were his birthright.

The individual might not live up to his potential or might fail completely, but the failure and responsibility would be his and his alone. The purpose of life was the pursuit, the pursuit of perfection.

Hamilton had a far more worldly view of America or, as Jefferson would have argued, a corrupted view.

To Hamilton America was to be a "little Britain." The colonists had not fought the revolution to free themselves from the customs and traditions of England, but to break with the power of the king, the nobility, and Parliament—in short, the power of London to tax and direct affairs.

Hamilton was suspicious of government, all government to be sure, which was why he insisted on the separation of powers, but otherwise the individual was free to do whatever he chose, associating with those he chose to advance his wealth and power, including the British, as long as it did not threaten the revolution.

He fully intended to be part of a domestic aristocracy. The aristocrats were those who would advance the commercial interests of the new nation in order that it might grow in wealth and power. Their wealth would separate them from the common man, and they were to be their representatives. They were to be the leaders. As he saw it, in the end all would benefit.

You might say Hamilton was a trickle-down theorist.

## THE NATIONAL DEBT

One of the issues that had to be resolved was the question of the national debt, which had accumulated during the revolution and was owed to creditors domestic and foreign.

The matter had to be satisfactorily addressed.

"In January 1790, before Jefferson was sworn in [to Congress], Hamilton, in charge of creating a financial system for the new government, had presented his first report on the public credit to Congress, which divided sharply over his proposals to fund a national debt and have the federal government assume the unpaid debts incurred by the states during the Revolution. Southern delegates, including Madison, opposed allowing speculators from New York and New Jersey who had bought up depreciated securities to make huge windfall profits by being paid off at par value with accrued interest. Madison's proposal to distinguish between original bondholders and speculators was voted down, but Hamilton's proposal to assume the northern states' debts had been defeated by the southern states, which had paid their war debts already. With Congress deadlocked, Jefferson feared that, if there was no compromise, the funding bill would die and the national credit would 'burst and vanish and the states separate to take care everyone of itself.'

"One day Jefferson ran into Hamilton outside Washington's door, looking 'somber, haggard and dejected beyond description.' Hamilton urged him to use his good offices with Southerners in Congress. It was part of Jefferson's job to handle domestic as well as foreign diplomacy, but he refused to appear directly involved in Hamilton's affairs. He did agree to invite Hamilton, Madison and delegates from Maryland and Pennsylvania to his house for dinner the next day to discuss the impasse. That night and the next day before the dinner meeting, he worked out a compromise that led to Congressional passage of Hamilton's debt-assumption act and location of the new national capital on the Potomac after a ten-year stopover in Philadelphia.

"In July 1790, when the debt funding, debt-assumption, and capital-location bills came before Congress, all three sailed through to passage. In exchange for the siting of the capital in the south, two Maryland and two Virginia members changed their votes on funding and assumption of debts to support Hamilton and the northern financial interests in Congress."[lxxx]

Hamilton has always been treated as the financial wizard whose policies advocating responsibility, trustworthiness, and dependability would stand as the permanent foundation of future commercial dealings of the new republic. History makes clear that Jefferson played perhaps the critical role in bringing this financial structure into being, truly a man for all seasons.

Though both men found agreement, there remained a marked difference in philosophy.

## For Jefferson, Aristocracy? Hell, No!

"Hamilton's isolationism could not have been more antithetical to Jefferson who, with Madison, was working to create a republican system based on an entirely different set of assumptions. While Hamilton preached adjusting to 'the general policy of nations,' Jefferson sought to revolutionize it. Since before the Revolution, he had believed that Anglo-American commercial ties were inherently unequal and exploitative. He contended that England actually depended on American commerce, which gave the United States a weapon vital in reforming foreign-trade policy. As Madison put it succinctly, England supplied Americans 'chiefly with superfluities.' [This is the case today with China.] Trade with America employed a large part of the British workforce. England depended on the Americans, among other imports, for the grain to make her bread, the whale oil to light her lamps, the wood to build her navy. If the United States played its card of nonimportation, Jefferson believed, the great mass of English workers would be thrown out of work, West Indies planters and their slaves would go hungry. But it was only necessary to threaten these two pressure points, Jefferson argued, in peacetime to persuade the British to open all their domestic and colonial ports to American goods and shipping, and, in wartime, this would force the British to respect American neutral trading rights. Jefferson was relying on his memory of the effects of revolutionary nonimportation in 1773–1775 to gauge the impact of his theory. At that time, fully one-third of British trade had been with her American colonies. By 1792, trade with the United States was only about one-sixth of total British imports and exports, while fully one-half the value of all American trade was with England and her possessions. This worsening imbalance worried Hamilton and the Federalists, who pointed to it whenever the hint of commercial war came up. Hamilton argued that Americans would feel the effects of a commercial war long before England. Jefferson countered that, in a contest of self-denial, Americans would, as they had in the 1770s surely make the sacrifices necessary to prevail. The threat of peaceable coercion conceived by Jefferson and pursued by Madison became the centerpiece of their Republican foreign policy."[lxxxi]

Any form of aristocracy or privilege was an anathema to Jefferson. "All men were created equal." Talent was distributed as the Creator saw fit, but each and every man was given the cognitive power to pursue happiness. The proper use of talent facilitated the pursuit.

Wealth was a disincentive, a peculiar form of debauchery. It only served to corrupt the individual. He became vain and indolent, developing a distorted view of his importance. He would begin to believe that he was better than other men. Never satisfied, he would increasingly take what was rightfully due others because he was better than other men. Justice and fairness escaped him.

Inherited wealth passes along this deformity to succeeding generations. In time a social divide develops, which cannot be breached, and social breakdown commences, producing violence and revolution. Money was the root of evil not because it was tied to wealth, but because it corrupted, distorted man's perception of himself and the purpose for his being.

This new republic could not survive if personal gain was substituted for happiness. Personal gain separated and reduced men. Happiness raised them.

Under no circumstances could institutions be established that would foster corruption. Institutions created for the benefit of an established aristocracy constituted a denial of freedom.

Under the Constitution, no government had such power. Government powers were specific and very limited. They were spelled out with great clarity. There was no room for error or misunderstanding.

Hamilton and Jefferson went their separate ways, and the great political divide began that continues to this very day.

Jefferson was in agreement with Hamilton that it was essential to pay off the national and state debt, but a national bank owned by the rich and serving their interest—never.

Jefferson lost the argument.

CHAPTER 8

# The Debt Is Paid—A New Nation Begins Its Journey

## The Nation Has a Soul—It Is Called Thomas Jefferson

Though a number of states initially objected when it became time to pay off the debt of other states, since they had through their own resources paid theirs, the motion carried, and with continuing revenue from tariff, duties, and excise taxes now flowing into the coffers of the Treasury, the debt was paid.

The second argument advanced against paying state debt was that speculators had purchased much of it in the market at a substantial discount and should not now be rewarded for their speculation. This was simply overlooked.

With the passage of time, we have come to understand that the contribution of Jefferson to a full understanding of freedom is unparalleled. The soul of every American is stirred by the Jeffersonian ideal.

People from all parts of the globe, now as in the past, flock to our shores in search of Jeffersonian freedom. We speak proudly of this heritage, but we practice and have practiced since his day a quasi form of the Federalist doctrine.

We mix concepts and seem to be unaware that these societal contradictions exist. We rationalize this behavior. In a sense we live a schizophrenic existence.

We preach equality but practice discrimination. The profit motive carried to the extreme divides the community but, under the guise of freedom, is used to justify the most corrupt behavior. "If it is legal, it must be right" is the slogan of the modern day.

Thus senior corporate executives take millions from the treasury of companies they did not create, while firing thousands whose contributions have made these companies successful, denying so many of them income and equity.

Taxation is constitutional if in the application of the law it is universal and equitable. In practice, laws are regularly passed intending to benefit one group over others.

We relish having the biggest house or car to demonstrate our superiority over our neighbors. We yearn to become aristocrats, to be better than others. We appear mesmerized by those who have made large sums of money on Wall Street, Hollywood, or corporate America. Not only do we not challenge the notion of an aristocracy; so many of us appear to worship it.

The important question is, can this divide that exists in America today continue? Can we preach universal freedom as Jefferson believed in and then violate it consistently?

Does the soul of Jefferson still tremble when he matches our actions against the backdrop of a just God?

After his election to the presidency, Jefferson speaking to Congress said, "Today we are all Republicans, all Federalists."[lxxxii] If he was with us today, would he have to say we are all hypocrites?

## James Madison and the Soul of Jefferson

Though Jefferson had lost his battle over the national bank, he had only begun to fight.

Under the terms of the Treaty of Paris, which gave America independence, British merchant rights to payment were officially recognized. In addition, the loyalists' right to regain property lost in the war was formally recognized. In the meantime the British continued to occupy large portions of the North American Continent.

Defeated by Adams by three electoral votes in his challenge for the presidency, Jefferson led the opposition against the infamous Jay Treaty, which favored British claims, allowing them to refuse to accept payment in colonial paper. Further, the treaty allowed them to sue in American courts for hard money payment.

Jefferson saw the Jay Treaty as undermining American interests.

If any nation deserved favor, it was the French, certainly not Britain, but what could be expected from this pro-British party the Federalists? In the hearts and minds of these rascals, the British monarchy reigned.

Jefferson and his Republicans got their revenge. He was elected the third president of the United States, serving from 1801 to 1809 and pursuing policies oriented to full recognition of the rights of men instead of government.

He cut internal taxes, expanded trade, shortened the time required of immigrants to gain citizenship, adopted a defensive posture with respect to the military, slashed public spending, and lastly purchased the Louisiana Territory, which included land as far north as present-day Minnesota.

Was this purchase constitutional? Congress, prior to this purchase, had never authorized such an acquisition. Napoleon, planning to restart his war with England, was in desperate need of money, so Jefferson made the $15 million deal, constitutional or not.

This was subsequently legitimized with the argument that this was a onetime event, a matter so extraordinary that the opportunity, so beneficial to Americans, had to be handled in secret. There the matter ended. Congress later ratified the purchase.

Internationally, the Jefferson presidency was challenged. Britain's victories at sea and Napoleon's control of the Continent put the United States, though neutral, in the middle. Neither Britain nor France was willing to accept America trading with the other.

The Brits seized American ships and impressed our sailors. The French pirated American vessels, seized the goods, and ignored American pleas. Neutrality did not impress either country.

Perhaps a boycott of both would end their hidden war and intransigence. Boycotts, as Jefferson was to learn, are easy to promote but hard to enforce. With money at stake, many merchants, particularly Federalist merchants, ignored the edict.

The war in Europe came to an end. Thus the need for American products at the war's conclusion dropped sharply.

This ultimately produced a domestic depression, but Jefferson and the Republicans did not suffer at the polls in this time of international turmoil, and he was reelected in a landslide.

The Republicans went on to later victories, but economic stagnation and international uncertainty, highlighted by a worsening relationship with Britain, continued. Then there was the problem of debt. America was back in debt as the economy soured.

Madison succeeded Jefferson as president. The man, like his mentor, was a profound thinker. The foundation of his political philosophy, like that of his predecessor, was John Locke. Nature had determined that man was born free and no power on earth had the right to change that. Madison was destined to become the architect of the Constitution, and on virtually every important matter, he sought out and accepted Jefferson's view.

When it came to Constitutional matters, Jefferson was, by any standard, a strict constructionist—Madison slightly less so.

On a fundamental question such as a national or central bank, their views were identical. The federal government had not been given the power to create corporations. Thus a national bank was unconstitutional ab initio. The argument of implied power as a necessary means to an end thus could not be raised.

Madison noted speaking before Congress "a proposal to grant the federal government power to charter corporations like the national bank had been rejected at the Federal Convention…Efforts to enlarge the specified powers of Congress by loose construction endangered the very notion of limited government…Under this [loose] interpretation, generally accepted by the Federalists in 1787, the necessary and proper clause merely permitted Congress to pass laws explicitly and necessarily related to its enumerated powers…

"Mark the reasoning on which the validity of the [national bank] depends! To borrow money is made the end, and the accumulations of capitals [money is implied] as the means. The accumulation of capitals is then the end, and a Bank implied as the means. The Bank is then the end and charter of incorporation, a monopoly…implied as the means.

"The only safe role of interpretation was to take the word 'necessary' seriously."[lxxxiii]

The matter in Madison's mind was of critical importance because he feared a "privileged financial aristocracy."[lxxxiv]

Hamilton believed that to move the nation forward, it was critical to wed the wealthy and their money and influence to government.

Of course this orientation was very European.

## The Second Bank of the United States

A private bank, with stockholders, men with money, including foreigners, was an early step to setting the nation in the direction of monarchial government, which is what Jefferson and Madison believed. This was the reason they had opposed the bank in the first place. They thought the creation of a private bank would lead to division in society with haves and have nots.

Their opposition was pushed aside. Thus the first Bank of the United States was created. However, it was given only a twenty-year charter, a testing period of sorts.

The organizers went along with this, assuming that after the twenty years had run, Congress would clearly see the advantages of a central bank, and it would be enthusiastically renewed for some indefinite period.

On matters of trade, Jefferson and Hamilton were in agreement. Mercantilism as practiced prior to independence, the sending of raw materials to Britain and receiving back finished products at retail prices, clearly inhibited the growth of domestic industry.

Production and the benefits that flowed from it, namely jobs, an improving standard of living, the prospect of owning one's business, the exercise of talent in developing new products, and invention were denied to the colonists under mercantilism.

To the colonists, the British mandate, the denial of freedom, not only meant subservience but poverty. Independence meant the opening of trade to the world and the prospect of prosperity.

Thus Jefferson and Madison were both in favor of free trade, with an important caveat. Trade was never free if the shores of one country were open and the other closed. This is the problem with our current trade policy. We are open to imports, for example, with China, but China is closed to American products produced in America except under the most stringent conditions. As a result, the trade balance favors China by a ratio of at least five to one, and this has been allowed to continue for the better part of two decades.

Both founding fathers demanded that bilateral trade be open and thus fair. This policy proved viable and successful and was maintained, becoming a fundamental tenet of American foreign policy. Insisting on balance with all trading partners, including those designated as most favorite, was policy until the late twentieth century, when increasingly "internationalists" came to control foreign policy. The same proselytized globalization, which had the effect of destroying large segments of American industry.

Jefferson put this succinctly with an eye toward Great Britain and distrust of the same when he said, "Free commerce and navigation [should] not be given in exchange for restrictions and vexations, nor are they likely to produce a relaxation of them."[lxxxv]

At present, the principal argument advanced by those who oppose taking action to defend our interests, imposing tariffs if necessary on excessive imports of Chinese goods, is that this could stimulate a trade war.

Trade war? We are at war, with American jobs at stake. Their solution is to sit back and wait for the day that China changes its policies. Change? They have no intention of changing. The current arrangement benefits them greatly. Further, as we have recounted in this text, the history of trade between the West and China does not support such a conclusion.

As matters stand today, China is the beneficiary of trade, the mother country, and America is the vassal state. The very high unemployment in the United States is the direct result of this self-destructive policy.

Madison, though a strong advocate of trade, commented, "What can be more absurd than to talk of the advantage of securing the privileges of sending raw materials to a manufacturing nation, and buying merchandizes which are hawked over four quarters of the globe for customers."[lxxxvi]

In the simplest of terms, history instructs us that open trade that is not fair begets serfdom.

Tariff is the mechanism for equalizing trade.

A nation employing unfair tactics in pursuing trade policy, such as dumping goods below market value in order to eliminate competition, or through manipulation of currency by keeping their exchange rate at an artificial level, stifles global growth.

In a world dominated by unprecedented levels of debt, the outlook must be for increasing default as people and nations increasingly surrender their potential for profit.

Tariffs will not impede trade as long as equilibrium is maintained. The issue is not a tariff versus the absence of a tariff; the issue is balance.

Thus a nation without tariffs can safely do business with a counterpart with the same policy, but not with one that has restriction on imports. Balance, as we have emphasized before, is key. Balance assures growth; imbalance stifles trade and hence progress.

It should be noted that America in the Jefferson era derived a large portion of governmental revenue from duties and tariffs, internal and external. Income taxes had yet to see the light of day.

Madison advocated "mildly protective tariffs. He considered the general principle of free industry and fair trade 'unanswerably established'... The only industries that might be protected indefinitely Madison wrote to [Henry] Clay, were those producing military supplies, other 'indispensable' strategic materials and goods calculated to be so expensive in wartime as to justify the higher cost of tariff-protected domestic manufacture in peacetime....In every doubtful case Madison wrote the government should forbear to intermeddle...'particular caution should be observed, where one part of the community would be favored at the expense of another.' A 'moderate tariff' Madison asserted would 'answer the purpose of revenue and foster domestic manufactures'..."[lxxxvii]

The Madison presidency was a disappointment to his admirers given his capacity to reason and persuade. He seemed incapable of taking his genius and fully utilizing it during his tenure as chief executive. He proved indecisive and though the War of 1812 was finally won during his watch, on the most important of issues he equivocated.

He never developed a comprehensive plan to fund the war. Debt more than tripled during his watch. Caught in the debt bind, he rationalized his opposition to a national bank. Perhaps a central bank would find a satisfactory way to deal with this problem. He signed the legislation creating the Second Bank, though he had adamantly opposed the creation of the first central bank, arguing strenuously that it was unconstitutional.

His cabinet appointees were less than distinguished. Many believed that his secretary of war had traitorous inclinations. He finally relieved him of this portfolio, but enormous damage had been done as a result of incompetence, including the burning of Washington.

The one bright spot, a very bright spot indeed, was the arrival of Andrew Jackson, who was appointed major general and senior officer of the southern command, replacing Henry Harrison.

The Second Bank of the United States became the centerpiece of enormous controversy, dividing the nation and Washington, unlike the First Bank, which as it turned out was an unmitigated success. Revenues flowed into the Treasury principally through the collection of tariffs, sufficient to pay off not only the federal debt but also state debt, which was concentrated in the north, as previously noted. The southern states, with the exception of Virginia, had earlier paid off their debt.

In 1811 the bank's charter expired; opponents to the bill cheered as the death knell rang. Liberty had vanquished the profiteers and speculators.

However, new, unforeseen problems had arisen in the twenty years since the establishment of the First Bank, the most important being war, namely the War of 1812.

CHAPTER 9

# The War of 1812—The Republic Staggers: Will It Survive?

### Andrew Jackson—A legend for All Time

The efforts of Washington and his men provided us with a country. It was Andrew Jackson that gave us a nation. When we speak of the republic, these two men, together with Lincoln, who later sustained the nation, stand on a pedestal by themselves.

In a world fascinated with "things" together with the endless search for more, thus requiring an infinite supply of money, it is hard to relate to a man who despised money. Better than any man who ever served as the nation's chief executive, Andrew Jackson of South Carolina understood the corrupting influence of wealth.

The secondary classrooms across the nation, as they study American history, tend to gloss over the Jackson era. Unintentional as that may be, they are left with, at best, a skewed version of his importance to the cause of liberty and thus the nation.

To put it very simply, without Jackson there would be no America.

Everything about the man is a demonstration of his uniqueness. He is Yankee Doodle Dandy.

No question that Jefferson, Madison, and others provided the intellectual prowess and leadership that shaped the country. No doubt about their critical contribution to the concepts of liberty and freedom that we hold so dear today. Without Washington and Jackson, however, there would have been no union of men and women of common cause to unite. There would have been no independent nation. Their battles on the battlefield and off made the difference.

Though George M. Cohan wrote his patriotic ballad some one hundred years after Jackson's passing, Jackson's spirit embraces the song.

America has known a great number of patriots, but none finer than this man who was in the fight for freedom before he was a teenager. In the eternal fight for freedom, and with it the cause of humanity itself, it was Washington, Jackson, and Lincoln and in the twentieth century Franklin Delano Roosevelt who played the decisive roles.

In point of fact, it was Jackson, not Washington and the French at Yorktown, who fought the last decisive battle of the American Revolution. After the battle at New Orleans, neither foreign nation nor domestic political group would challenge the independence and unique character of the American Republic.

America would now be universally recognized as one nation and a formidable one at that, both at home and abroad.

The Treaty of Paris, which followed the battle of Yorktown and was negotiated patiently by Benjamin Franklin, assured American independence. However, as the British continued to hold a broad swath of territory, it was clearly their plan to remain on the North American Continent. They had no intention of leaving.

In the end a treaty is simply an agreement on paper. In a world comprising kings and empires, paper is perishable. Boots on the ground determine the course of events. Britain was in the driver's seat.

This former colony, which had embarrassed them on the battlefield, might well implode, aided and abetted with British pressure. The British were in no rush to reassert dominance.

As the fortunes of France with revolution had greatly diminished and with the British "rules of the road" determining the direction of trade, the prospects for a truly independent America were less than bright.

After the War of 1812 and the Treaty of Ghent, which followed, Britain accepted final closure on the issue of American independence.

Yet it was the Battle of New Orleans that was being fought as that treaty was signed that foreclosed any future possibility of the British—or for that matter anyone else—returning and laying claim to American territory.

Jackson's victory and with it the destruction of the British army outside New Orleans forever changed Britain's attitude toward America.

Washington and his confreres initiated the American Revolution, and Jackson ended it.

## Jackson the Man

There is no phrase or simple sentence that can adequately describe the man. He was first and foremost a warrior. He fought from the moment of birth until his death. At the same time, he was the shrewdest of politicians and the most popular chief executive in the nation's history.

His numerous battles were public and private. His time-tested solution to private insult and slur, particularly if directed at his wife or family, was to challenge and to duel. He feared no one and was always willing to accept the consequences for his actions.

In one case late in life, he was challenged by a man by the name of Charles Dickenson, a crack shot.

Though dueling was against the law, Jackson accepted the challenge, and when they met, Dickenson fired first, hitting his mark, a bullet that Jackson carried in his body for the rest of his life. Bullet wound and all, he then took aim, firing on Dickinson, killing him instantly. This wasn't a Hollywood thriller; it was Jackson. He never changed.

This warrior at the same time was a man with extraordinary love and devotion to his wife and family, to the cause of liberty and justice, to America. He was a nationalist of the first order and proud of it.

In every respect he was Jeffersonian, but his manner was very different from that of Jefferson or Madison.

He was not particularly liked by either man. With more than a tinge of snobbery, Jefferson made disparaging comments about him with a decidedly political motive in mind.

Though a Jeffersonian, he was not from Virginia but originally from South Carolina. He was from the backwoods. In the minds of the establishment politicians, that fact alone should have barred him from the presidency.

Jefferson demonstrated this snobbery by supporting John Quincy Adams in the 1824 campaign for president, an election decided in the House of Representatives after Jackson, the popular vote winner, failed to garner the necessary electoral votes.

By the time Jackson succeeded to the presidency in 1828, secession was on the horizon. This time the antagonist was neither Britain nor France, but domestic revenue, tariff revenue, which was the principal source of government income.

South Carolina, led by John C. Calhoun, threatened secession if the tariff terms were not substantially modified. Talk of dividing the union was treasonous in Jackson's mind. To make matters worse, Calhoun was Jackson's vice president. Jackson got word to Calhoun that talk of secession was unacceptable, though Jackson, being a Southerner, understood and perhaps sympathized with the southern point of view.

He was an advocate of states' rights but union first, union before all else. In case Calhoun didn't understand his message, Jackson promised to come to South Carolina and personally hang him.

No one doubted that he meant it, certainly not Calhoun. Threats of secession simply faded away, and the tariff was modestly modified.

With the coming of Lincoln, secession would again come to the fore, bringing with it civil war. Had Jackson lived until 1860, few doubt that his voice would have been dominant in the South, quieting those advocating separation.

Slavery in many ways was an impossibly divisive issue and had been since the birth of the nation. Yet given his genius for leadership, war might have been averted and the slaves freed with slave owners compensated, as had been envisioned by Jefferson.

Unfortunately, we shall never know.

Jackson as a boy served in the militia. His military career appeared to be on the verge of being snuffed out when at age thirteen he was captured with his brother in Waxhaw, South Carolina, in a sweep by British dragoons.

*Life, Liberty, and the Pursuit of Money*

At this point a British officer made a mistake of historic proportions. He ordered Andrew to clean his boots. Andrew of course refused. The officer took his saber and sliced into Jackson's head, leaving a deep gash and permanent scar on his face.

Of course Jackson saw the British as the enemy, but this act, and the subsequent death of his brother, and later his mother from exhaustion, served to make the British his enemy for life.

To be completely fair, Jackson disliked all foreigners, including of course the British. The European states, he believed, did not have any right whatsoever to be on the North American Continent.

Before her passing, Andrew's mother successfully negotiated the release of her two sons in exchange for two British prisoners. His brother soon died from neglect and exposure, but Andrew survived, only to see his mother die shortly thereafter.[lxxxviii]

At fourteen, Jackson was alone in the world, penniless, but with complete devotion to a new nation, then still very much under the boot of the British, other foreigners, and Indian tribes. As fate would have it, he received a small inheritance from his Scottish grandfather and went to live with his uncle on the frontier between North and South Carolina until maturity. On the frontier the demands and needs of settlers attracted him to the law. After study, he was admitted to the bar and began his practice.

He met and married the love of his life, Rachel, to whom he was totally devoted. Rachel had been married earlier to a man who abandoned her, telling her he was getting a divorce. Rachel and Andrew married not knowing that the divorce had not gone through, making it possible for his political opponents to accuse her of bigamy.

Intolerant of any personal attack, it was an invitation to war to slander Rachel. Jackson greeted such attacks by inviting the slanderer to duel.

Dueling, though outlawed, was still widely practiced in the state that became his permanent home and farm—the Hermitage in Nashville, Tennessee.

Known for his military prowess and increasingly influential in political circles, Jackson went to Congress and then the Senate, but found the pace and palaver unsuitable. He yearned to return to Rachel, which he did, and was made a judge and general in the militia.

Scarcity of currency had always been a serious problem for farmers and settlers in the South and the West.

The First Bank of the United States and its privileged customers had a virtual lock on specie. This institution, as Hamilton and the Federalists had envisioned, was intended to be the foundation and bridge allowing for the convenient marriage of money and wealth. Everyone else was left out in the cold. This was Federalist doctrine. It still is.

From the outset, most Americans outside New England viewed the Federalists as simply pawns of the British Empire. Centers for commerce, trade, and market speculation specie migrated east to Philadelphia, New York, and New England.

The political power of the Federalists was centered in New England, with men like John Adams at the head. However, its tentacles extended into Pennsylvania, New York, Maryland, and as far south as Virginia.

To be a Federalist meant you were pro-British, versus the Jeffersonian, who was accused of being too close to the interests of France. The British had been the enemy, supposedly the defeated enemy, but were still by far the largest trading partner of a new and yet untried "state" called the United States.

Would this new republican state, a union, survive or simply implode and return to its former status as a colony of Great Britain? The British absolutely thought they would regain political control, and the rest of Europe was not at all certain. Britain with its great navy controlled the seas and imposed its will on those wanting to traverse the Atlantic Ocean.

Under the heel of Napoleon, France controlled the Continent, insisting on his terms for trade. As the war in Europe raged, both Britain and France were viewed as enemies, or potential enemies, but the prospect of profit encouraged exporters and importers to look the other way.

Federalists and Jeffersonians felt that we should not be taking sides in this largely European conflict, but trade was king, particularly in this relatively small country of three million people, with little or no domestic or manufacturing base.

*Life, Liberty, and the Pursuit of Money*

The future prospects for this new republic begin to change when Napoleon, in need of money, decided to sell the Louisiana territory. The prospect of the United States becoming a continental power was made possible. The British stood in the way, as did the corrupt Spanish and the Indians, but the dye had been cast. What was now needed—besides the people to occupy this immense territory—was leadership.

The Virginians hardly gave that matter a second thought. It was understood that Madison would succeed Jefferson, and after that perhaps Monroe.

It was widely expected that Virginians would continue to dominate the political scene, and then out of nowhere came Andrew Jackson.

## From Out of Nowhere…

Jackson was a Jeffersonian through and through. With identical political philosophies, one might have assumed that the two men were close allies.

That was not the case. Jefferson was quite critical of Jackson in his public comments at the time of Jackson's first run for the presidency. One suspects that only a Virginian would have met the Jeffersonian standard, but he apparently said that he believed that Jackson had insufficient regard for law or the Constitution and was "a dangerous man."[lxxxix]

However, events beyond the control of Jefferson or Jackson led the new nation in a completely different direction.

As the charter of the First Bank expired, President Madison, a leading Jeffersonian who had opposed its creation, was faced with the hostility of the British and French. War, bringing with it a financial and commodity collapse and soaring government debt, in desperation signed the legislation creating the Second Bank of the United States, much to the dismay of his supporters, again with a twenty-year charter.

The Second Bank, unlike the first, was met with scandal and corruption. Searching for integrity, the directors chose, first as a director and then president, the infamous Francis Biddle. Biddle and Jackson were destined to lock horns. The issue that created a political firestorm between the two was over the meaning in a democratic republic of a central bank.

Before the Biddle-Jackson contest began, Jackson, victorious in the presidential election of 1828, set out to confront the nation's many problems head-on. This required stern leadership, and he was up to the task.

## The Tariff Takes Center Stage

America in the early years had adopted European methods in commercial affairs.

With Jackson as president, it took a new direction, no longer imitating big brother, but in search of a new destiny where the people ruled, as Jefferson had conceived it.

It would be a nation of laws, not of men. It would no longer be a nation with a constitution, but a constitutional republic, democratic for certain, but not a democratic republic of the kind that brought tyranny and self-destruction to France after their revolution.

The law would bind all, rich and poor alike, and justice would be the standard. In this union liberty would be assured. True freedom would triumph.

All men were created equal, but were not equal in talent, commitment, or opportunity. It would be up to the individual to make his way, to find his destiny, and Americans in the succeeding generations would do that with abandon.

Government was representative of the people, their spokesman, not their overlord. Government had a role to play for sure, but its power did not stand alone. To the extent it had power, it was limited to those specific powers set forth in the Constitution, together with the means to accomplish them.

The central government would have the right to create currency, a standard to facilitate trade. It was to be a bystander, not the driving force.

If wealth was acquired, it was to be the result of hard work, innovation, invention, and a purposeful life.

Money for the sake of money, non-Christian in its orientation (taking rather than giving), was like slavery, a corrupting influence, and like concupiscence, had to be shunted and diminished where possible. Jackson was determined to accomplish this.

Jackson despised money and money interests, as his mentor had, considering them both corrupting and divisive. He intended to be the white knight, to free the people, thus allowing them to achieve their destiny.

President or not, he was first and foremost a man of the people. Where power came into play, it had to be limited. Thus he argued for passage of a law to make the presidency a single six-year term.

The tariff, the principal source of revenue for the government, was revenue, but it was also a source of wealth. The crisis surrounding it became one of Jackson's earliest challenges and a serious threat to national unity.

## Freedom Springs from Undivided Unity—The Matter of Nullification

The Jeffersonian ideal required that all submit to established law and play by rules that recognized the equality of all men. Each man would enter the fray and then proceed to demonstrate his ability.

This fact alone distinguished America from every other nation. No one was to have advantage. Those who gained great profit did so as a result of invention, ingenuity, commitment, and plain old hard work. Their profit was well-deserved.

The Jeffersonians did not anticipate nor could ever have foreseen the development of an industrial society. In any case it would not have mattered to them, for favoritism had no place in America.

Thus banks, particularly a central bank, represented a real threat to their ideals.

Banks by their very nature were designed to favor the few over the many.

I am reminded of a meeting many years ago with the late Aristotle Onassis, who married Jacqueline Kennedy after the assassination of the president and who had developed a worldwide reputation as a shipping magnate. Virtually everyone believed that he had made his fortune shipping oil around the world.

He told me that this was not the case. Having married well and come to the United States during the war, he made his initial fortune in, of all things, the US government bond market.

During the Second World War, the Treasury was running up debt much as it is doing today, and needed to place that debt in large amounts. China was not available at the time.

In those days interest rates were "pegged," fixed by government edict.

Onassis as a result of his reputation could borrow huge sums from the New York banks at rates sufficiently low that he was guaranteed a profit.

This is happening today as the government funds the Wall Street banks. Onassis thought this arrangement was wonderful.

He said to me with a huge smile that he benefited and the government benefited. In fact, the government was so pleased with the arrangement that they gave him a medal.

I have often wondered what those who landed on Normandy or Guadalcanal would have thought of all of that had they known. At the time he was a Greek citizen to boot.

A central or national bank with the power to collect most of the revenue of the national government and to invest and lend it as it chose to those they knew or favored defeated the very concept of democracy. They would become the elite of society, the new nobility. They would profit though others might starve.

Such an institution was the darling of the Federalists, who did not see the inequity. They argued that commerce and America could only advance this way and thus be taken seriously by other nations.

Hamilton strongly believed this and managed to persuade Jefferson to go along, at least in the creation of the First Bank of the United States, which under Congressional mandate would expire in twenty years.

Jefferson and his followers were very wary, which is why the First Bank's charter was set to expire in twenty years.

When it expired, the country finances were again in turmoil, forcing Madison to sign legislation, much to the dismay of the Jeffersonians, creating the Second Bank of the United Sates, with a charter that would expire in twenty years. By this time presumably, the crisis would have passed.

As we neared the end of this second twenty-year run, Jackson was serving as president.

Jackson's position on the bank and banks was unmistakably clear. He told Francis Biddle, The Second Bank president, in no uncertain terms, that he, Jackson, was not just opposed to Biddle's bank but to all banks.

The bank issue was only simmering when Jackson was called upon to address the serious matter of secession.

When we speak of secession in contemporary history, we invariably think of Lincoln and the Civil War. The push in South Carolina for secession began long before Lincoln.

This threat, led by John C. Calhoun, was every bit as serious as the latter. It too involved both the threat of force and disunion.

The United States government depended on the tariff for revenue. Prior to the War of 1812, we were an agricultural nation. Staples such as tobacco, wood, and cotton were exported, and scarce European goods were imported. A tariff was imposed on imports.

Tariffs invited a retaliatory response from nations we were exporting to. Thus the level of tariff was a major concern. For the North, high tariffs protected domestic industry. For the South high tariffs limited their ability to export. Thus the issue was divisive, giving rise to sectional discord.

A tariff was in a sense essential, but high tariffs were self-defeating. There was widespread consensus about this, at least until the outbreak of the War of 1812. During the war, Britain insisted the United States, though neutral, not trade with Napoleon's Continent. Napoleon insisted we not trade with Britain or risk capture on the high seas by French naval vessels.

America was in a tight spot. The only avenue open was to look inward and begin to manufacture critical products, particularly armaments, domestically. These new industries were domiciled in the North. They hired workers and became a political force. These industries and their workers were here to stay. On a score of matters but most importantly on the matter of tariff, the southern view was a minority view. Thus a cleavage developed between North and South.

The North was pro tariff, and the South, at best, saw the tariff as a necessary evil. The reason for the divide is self-evident when one considers the fact that to the South, exports were their lifeblood. As they saw it, their rights were being trampled on.

In 1828, the year Jackson was elected, the tariff was raised to the highest level ever. The issue reached its crescendo as the British financial crisis collapsed the price of cotton. The South was in an economic bind, with no place to turn.

President Jackson, a Southerner, understood the plight of the Southerners but put the union first. He argued that the Constitution was not a compact between states but a contract between the citizens of the nation, that is, the people who through their representatives wrote the law, which respected the rights of all. Should tyranny return, the people had a right to secede.

John C. Calhoun, a politician, on the other hand, preached divorce. He argued that the states had the right to secede. He wanted to take the easy way out. The South must go its own way. He saw no other solution. The answer—the only answer in his mind, as he recognized that southern views would forever be in the minority—was secession.

Though such a step would have the most extraordinary ramifications, the right to secede, he argued, was implicitly given to the states in the compact known as the Constitution.

Confrontation appeared inevitable. The nation was spared by the election of Jackson. Compromise on the tariff was reached and secession was avoided, for the moment.

However, another challenge awaited Jackson. This time it did not deal with states' rights but the vesting of power in an institution.

CHAPTER 10

# The Matter of a Central Bank

## A Death Struggle

At first blush it would seem that matters involving a central bank might be of interest to economists, political scholars, and legislators, but would pass unnoticed by the general public. Banking, the most mundane of businesses, is for the most part simply dull. Who could possibly get excited over some opaque banking issue?

The European nations always had central banks. They were designed as clearinghouses for international commerce and the conversion of debt paper into specie. As the reach of nations expanded, they became a useful tool.

To the Americans such as Jefferson, Madison, and Jackson, they represented a threat to liberty.

The First and Second Banks of the United States had come into being during periods of extremis.

Hamilton had convinced Washington that to bring order to the nation's finances required such an institution. However, the notion of permanence was never in the cards, and the Jefferson Republicans couldn't wait for the twenty-year charters to expire.

They were confident the charter would never be renewed.

Jackson shared this view. He believed a nation consisting of those with money and those without posed a true threat to the liberties of the people.

The war came to an end, and the great American trek west began. The banking business exploded. Though fraud became the most visible characteristic of the business, it nevertheless was profitable.

*161*

A central bank with government deposits and specie in abundance is in a position to monopolize the entire business. It has a unique product, currency, and it is very much in demand.

Money divided people. It did not unite them, Jackson believed. The idea of a central bank acting in concert with the moneyed class was a prescription for disunion. "Union above all" was his motto. When the time came, he was willing to lead the charge against this bank, this monster, and its corrupt sponsors, many of whom were powerful, including Henry Clay and Daniel Webster.

Many a legislator, lawyer, or important businessman had become dependent on the bank for credit, and with self-interest in mind, they were not about to oppose the bank, its charter, and its determined president, Francis Biddle.

Biddle joined the bank as a board member in 1819. He assumed the presidency in 1822 at age thirty-six. He did not support the election of Jackson in 1824 and may have regarded him as the new boy who had not yet been taught the lessons of Washington and power.

During the twenty-year period of existence, the Second Bank handled the financial affairs of the United States. It was the government depository. State banks issued paper bills, which could be converted into specie upon demand. To obtain that specie, the state banks were dependent on the central bank.

The bank was viewed by the states as a prime source of revenue, and thus the states attempted to tax the bank. This raised an important constitutional question: Do the states have the right to tax agencies of the federal government? The Supreme Court decided they did not.

The Second Bank went out of existence. A third Central Bank was created by Congress in 1913, the Federal Reserve System, which would in turn favor the few, including national banks, Wall Street dealers, and foreign interests.

CHAPTER 11

# War: Biddle versus Jackson

## Privilege versus Equality

Americans by and large opposed the Second Bank, recognizing it for what it was, a privilege-oriented, corrupt hydra, sapping the innovation and American productive spirit for the benefit of the very few, who later in the century would be given the appellation robber barons.

Though Biddle did not actively oppose Jackson in the 1828 election, it was widely understood that he did not favor him. Renewal of the charter, at the time, was not immediately pressing since it was not due to expire for a number of years.

With the goal of renewal in mind, Biddle decided on a strategy that was essentially one built on persuasion.

He kept up a barrage of letters and writings pointing out the advantages, if not the necessity, of a central bank, including the argument that without one the United States would be the only leading nation in the world not to have one.

Of course when he spoke of the world, he meant Europe. One can't help but believe that Jackson, on hearing this argument, would have experienced a noticeable increase in his blood pressure. He was in effect being told that we should follow the European example.

What Biddle did not understand was that as fearless as Jackson was, he was fearful of banks. He was familiar with scams in history. He was suspicious of the banks and their motives, including Biddle's.

Though Biddle may not have realized it, Jackson was beyond persuasion. This iconic general, fearless in battle and just as determined, was not going to be moved by a Washington bureaucrat.

Biddle had an important ally in Congress, a man who yearned to be president, the influential senator from Kentucky, Henry Clay. Clay probably recognized that Jackson would never voluntarily change his view. He suggested that the matter of renewal be brought to a vote in Congress before the expiration of the charter and the 1832 presidential election.

If it was approved and then vetoed by Jackson, this would give Clay an issue to run on for president in 1832.

Biddle was hesitant, recognizing that this would certainly raise the ire of Jackson, making him more determined.

However, Clay and Congress, with support from the likes of Daniel Webster, who was on the bank's board, decided to push ahead. In 1832, the petition to recharter passed both houses of Congress.

Though any institution, including a central bank, that was widely opposed by the people should have cautioned men like Biddle, Clay, and Webster, there were, as Alexis de Tocqueville noted, many who believed "that the people were too ignorant to manage the affairs of the country, certainly on matters as technical as the operation of a national bank."[xc]

The question remained, what was the alternative to a national or central bank? The only viable alternative was state banks. With the receipt of government deposits, their growth potential was virtually unlimited. Such a prospect was inconceivable to Biddle, as many of the state banks were fly-by-night institutions.

Yet decentralization had advantages, as the local banks were closer to the people and in a much better position to evaluate credit requests. Regulatory oversight—not centralization—was the best antidote to irresponsible behavior. Management would be held responsible for their actions.

Clearly there were risks, but the alternative was an all-powerful institution out of touch with the people, an institution for the elite. This was not Jackson's America. Led by Thomas Benton of Missouri, the opposition to the charter renewal in Congress had one persuasive argument: there was no constitutional basis for such a bank.

The bank was not neutral in the sense that a clearinghouse is neutral. It was not simply an agency that facilitated commerce.

It had one truly enormous and deleterious effect on the nation, which was to draw capital from the rest of the country to its coffers in Philadelphia. This served to deprive the rest of the country of capital. Money flowed to the central bank since it was the safest institution from the depositors' standpoint and the best capitalized.

In turn this money was not loaned to farmers and small businessmen, but to the moneyed class, that is, the market speculators in New York, as well as to friends of Biddle.

Loans to large market speculators were attractive from the bank's standpoint. They were referred to as "call money" loans. They were short-term in nature, paid high rates, and provided liquid collateral that the bank could readily sell in case of default. There was very little risk in making such loans.

On the other hand, loans to small businessmen and farmers were unpredictable, dependent not only on economic conditions but on variables such as the weather.

Call money loans had maturities of a few days. Thus financial speculation dominated commerce, and the wealth in the country came from the ranks of the speculators, not the producers.

Such a condition was bound to create imbalances, which in time would repeatedly bring the economy to its knees as market bubbles burst and prices, particularly commodity prices, went into sharp decline.

Men like Biddle could not see this or chose not to. His bank was very profitable. The state banks he did business with were profitable, having ready access to the liquidity he provided them.

The less-favored banks were deprived of capital and were just out of luck.

Life was never fair. Of course money would trickle down to the farmers provided commodity prices stayed strong, as they could sell their produce profitably. However, if the market bubble burst, they would not only be hurt financially, but would face bankruptcy.

This is a brief summary of the unfortunate history of banking in the nineteenth century before Andrew Jackson arrived on the scene.

Given the facts, how is it possible that a central bank survived legislative scrutiny? Bear in mind that both the First and Second Banks were approved during times of crisis.

There was never a time when "the bank" had popular support. To the contrary, the bank was highly unpopular but received the necessary legislative support because economic conditions were chaotic at the time.

Further, the votes of legislators were secured by promises made or, in the worst of cases, outright bribes.

Those who favor a central bank, both then and now, inevitably speak of an orderly process and control. What right gives a select group the power to control the public? Where does this authority spring from? Is there a valid argument for constitutionality?

The argument that there was global precedent did not influence Jackson. For Jackson the measure was popular support, not precedent. Jackson believed that there was no constitutional basis for a federal bank outside the federal enclave, the District of Columbia.

This constitutional question has yet to be resolved. Simply stated, does Congress have the power to give a third party power over credit, money, and banking?

The Second Bank had twenty-five directors, five of whom were chosen by Congress. The rest were investors, and thus the money interests controlled the bank.

That issue may well come before the Supreme Court within the next decade given recent economic and political developments.

This critique of the central bank and implicitly banking in general is not an argument for doing away with banking. Bankers are not infallible and will make mistakes. It is by nature a risk business. Banking is crucial to business, since it is the only way yet devised to allow for the bringing together of borrower and lender. It is an efficient mechanism for the formation of capital.

Loan losses are the cost of doing business in banking, in much the same way that waste and depreciation are a cost to commerce.

## The Dye Is Cast

With his efforts to convince Jackson of a renewal of the charter failing, Biddle was drawn by Henry Clay into a decision that proved fatal for the survival of his bank. Clay would see to it that legislation was brought forward prior to the time of expiration of the charter to force Jackson's hand.

Neither Biddle nor Clay believed that Jackson would veto legislation authorizing a renewal of the charter. This was a major strategic mistake, because that is exactly what Jackson did.

Biddle was conscious of the risk though. Should the bill pass and Jackson veto it and be reelected in 1832, Biddle, his cronies, and the bank were finished. Biddle meant to fight, and fight he did, taking the extreme step of calling in the loans of favored legislators and others who could influence the process, including the banks that had depended on the Second Bank for liquidity.

He would break the nation, if need be, to preserve the bank.

Jackson would not be moved. He said to his vice president, Van Buren, that it was their plan to kill him, but he would kill it, meaning the bank, and kill it he did.

The avenue for slaughter went through the state banks.

During the early years of the republic, there was little or no regulation over the banking industry. Virtually anyone or group could start a bank. Bars, barbers, and blacksmiths were active in the banking business. Thus a state bank was not the pristine institution we think of today when we speak of the banking industry. Officially there were three state banks in 1790 and eighty-eight by 1811. As the central bank was the depository for government revenue, the state banks looked forward to the day when they would share the bounty.

The state institutions, if one can use the term, ran the gamut from fly-by-night to reputable. The key to successful banking was access to specie. Depositors and noteholders expected to be able to present the instrument to the bank and receive gold/specie in exchange. If the bank had a reputation for good banking practices, it could in turn take these notes to the central bank and obtain the specie needed for payment.

If it did not have such a relationship, the depositor or noteholder was taking his chances. He might never be paid, at least in gold or silver. New banks aplenty were coming on stream during the Jackson years, all of them issuing banknotes.

In order to avoid having to make payment on their notes, some would hide their bank headquarters in the woods. If you couldn't collect on your note, you simply used it to pay a creditor of yours. Thus notes and bills from the far reaches of the country were actively traded.

One could gain some idea of the notes' true value by way of a book that was published listing note values. Some were worthless. Some were worth 10 percent of their nominal value, and some 100 percent. It paid to have an updated edition of the book.

Thus these bills or notes were the currency of the time. There was no national currency apart from gold and silver.

The value of notes and bills was totally dependent on the integrity of the issuing institution. In practical terms this meant did they have the gold or silver to redeem them, or did they have access to liquidity, which meant Biddle's bank. Since the central bank was the recipient of all government revenue, Biddle was the kingpin.

If he decided he was not going to have any further dealings with your institution, you were in deep trouble. He was thus in a position to put you out of business or to make you successful.

Biddle by his actions appeared to believe he was as powerful as the president of the United States. He reported to no one. The president had to run for election every four years. Biddle might have been president for life.

Jackson ran for reelection in 1832, defeating Henry Clay, decisively carrying sixteen of the twenty-four states, including certain New England states, the Federalist bastion.

Both the secessionists in the South and Biddle were now going to find out just how powerful the president of the United States was.

The so-called "nullifiers," southern secessionists, faded away in time, mindful that Jackson was prepared to use force if necessary to collect the tariff in South Carolina and "hang" the culprits.

*Life, Liberty, and the Pursuit of Money*

Mr. Biddle, on the other hand, did not fade as quickly. The bank charter had yet to expire, and he remained determined to pursue a scorched earth policy to force Jackson's hand even after the election.

Mr. Jackson was equally, if not more, determined to destroy the bank, if not Mr. Biddle.

He accomplished this by simply moving all government deposits from the central bank to the state banks. This effectively put the central bank out of business.

On October 1, 1833, Jackson ordered that government deposits be transferred to the state banks.

The coercion of the central bank and its threat to liberty were thus effectively extinguished.

Unfortunately, the transfer did not mean that state banks would now act in a more responsible fashion. With money flooding in, they proceeded to flood the country with notes and bills. With Americans moving west in pursuit of manifest destiny, land loans exploded, bringing speculation and inflation.

Recognizing the danger, Jackson issued his now-famous "specie circular," requiring speculators who borrowed to purchase federal lands to pay their loan in gold or silver. This brought the land boom to an immediate halt, and with it, economic recession.

His successor, Van Buren, paid the ultimate price for this in terms of his popularity, but the battle for freedom had been won. Federalist power had been broken, and there would be no central bank, at least until the creation of the Federal Reserve in 1913.

The Jackson era, truly unique in world history, to this day serves as a dependable guide in the pursuit of freedom and democracy. H. W. Brands, in his book *Andrew Jackson, His Life and Times*, captures the true spirit of the man when he wrote: "Democracy made mistakes; Jackson didn't deny that. But its mistakes were the honest and correctible mistakes of human misjudgment, not the interested entrenched mistakes of selfish elites. Did the people know what was best for them? Not always. But they knew better than anyone else knew for them. God alone was perfect, and He ruled in heaven. Below the people ruled, if imperfectly."[xci]

CHAPTER 12

# Manifest Destiny

---

### THE AMERICAN PEOPLE TURN WEST—WILDCAT BANKING

With the conclusion of the War of 1812 and the Jackson victory over the British in New Orleans, every nation in the world not only recognized the United States but considered it folly to even contemplate engaging the Americans on the battlefield, certainly over territory. The Monroe Doctrine embraced this understanding.

The Americans now turned their attention west with a vengeance.

Land was available and cheap, and the Americans were going after it. No power and certainly no institution was going to stop them. For this momentous push westward, money and credit were needed in extraordinary amounts. The state banks were there.

The number of banks doubled and credit expanded tenfold. Sale of public land effectively eliminated government debt. Unfortunately the circular letter slammed on the brakes of this expansion, which had started in 1820.

The "specie circular" popped the inflation bubble and brought the economy down, but Jackson was not held responsible. He was succeeded by his vice president, Van Buren, and the public blamed Van Buren for the recession.

So admired was Jackson that typical Americans, when reminded of the fact that it was Jackson, not Van Buren, who had issued the circular that caused the slowdown, their response was typically that the slowdown would have happened anyway. Jackson and his policies were above criticism or reproach.

## Immigration

A confident, dynamic, and increasingly powerful nation was about to take center stage on the world scene. America lacked nothing. It had the natural resources, land, genius, inventiveness, and determination to seize a continent and shape it according to the principles laid down by the founders.

Everyone with guts and drive was welcome. Immigration exploded. The poor, tired, and detested sought refuge and sensed opportunity. However, this phenomenon did not take hold until the mid-nineteenth century.

The vast increase in numbers beginning in Jackson's time suggested that Jacksonian policies and his legacy as the defender of freedom were major contributors to this extraordinary migration. From 1836 to 1914, over thirty million Europeans migrated to the United States.

The prevailing attitude regarding immigration began to change in the twentieth century. The Immigration Act of 1924 limited the number of immigrants to the United States to 2 percent of the total number of people of each nationality in the United States as of the 1890 census. This served to discriminate against entry of southern and eastern Europeans and completely excluded immigrants from Asia.

## Financial Reality Post Jackson—The Panic of 1837

However when the subject turns to money, Jackson's legacy is hotly debated.

For the remainder of the century, Jackson had successfully removed the greatest threat to the personal freedom of the man on the street, namely, a central bank.

Jackson had defeated the special interests, and the people reigned supreme.

Jackson did not, however, succeed in solving a conundrum: how to maintain balance between the supply and demand for goods on the one hand and the supply of money (currency) on the other. To achieve balance requires restriction.

Without currency limits the demand for goods becomes infinite, while the supply of goods remains limited. Thus the money supply must be restricted in order to keep pace with the supply of goods. To achieve perfect balance, a way must be found to limit the growth in currency to the capacity to produce. Someone will be denied.

Accumulated money is savings or capital.

In 2009–2010 the United States did not, as is frequently stated, attempt to stimulate the economy by spending our savings, but relied on money borrowed from Asia. As these sums had to be repaid, the United States was furthering the imbalance. In the long run, this will make the problem worse, not better.

Stimulus will work only if the one providing the stimulus has capital and does not look to be repaid. Such a person is not a creditor, but an investor.

Prior to and during the Jackson era, notes were issued with the promise to redeem in specie or real money, which the issuing institution did not have. This currency that had nothing behind it was called money, when in effect it was simply a disguised form of credit. These credit bills, which neither the issuer nor the holder can expect to redeem, are a sham or fraud.

The bills or notes are worthless. However, the daisy chain or sham can continue as long as no one breaks the chain. The break invariably comes when the creditor, recognizing the "bubble" as we euphemistically refer to a spiraling price phenomenon, insists on payment.

The Jackson "specie circular" demanding payment in specie broke the chain and popped the bubble.

Speculation had given rise to false, nonexistent wealth, which in turn fed speculation. The end was predictable, but no one quite knew when or the event that would bring the debauchery to a close.

Post Jackson, the end came with the depression of 1837.

A synonym for depression is dislocation. The level of production and supply of goods must now revert to and approximate the amount of capital or savings left in the hands of the public. This inevitably translates into a high rate of unemployment and depression, which in this case lasted five years.

Virtually all analysts of this period are in agreement that speculation fed the property boom. Land, urban and rural, was available for sale.

However, the greatest speculation was reserved for the purchase of government land, which paralleled the railroads in the great migration westward. State and local banks of every size and dimension were there to make loans to the settlers, who in turn would buy property and then sell it for a profit, moving further westward. As long as property could be bought with mortgage paper, profit was more or less assured. The Jackson circular, insisting on gold or silver in payment, broke the back of the boom.

Why was this so? What is it about precious metals that thwarts speculative impulses? The most obvious and correct answer is scarcity of metal.

There is no limit to paper, but metal is hard to come by. Unlike paper it has intrinsic value. Scarcity is indeed part of it.

Further, investment and intense labor are required to mine this metal. The cost of mining is high. Production fluctuates. The intrinsic value remains the same.

Money is the capital and savings that result from laboring. Currency, on the other hand, simply facilitates exchange. Money and currency on occasion may serve both functions. This causes confusion. If I were to sell you a Picasso for a ruby, both are money, yet they are the currency in this transaction. If I buy a Picasso for gold, both are money and currency, as this is what the bargain calls for. If, on the other hand, I sell a Picasso for dollars, for paper, the bargain is not for the paper but rather those things that paper can buy. The bill or note is not payment but an implicit promise of payment.

I am willing to make this exchange since the government describes the currency as "legal tender." However, if I have doubts about my ability to use it in the future in trade, then I will not accept it, legal tender or not.

The paper has no intrinsic value. This is a system based totally on trust. Should this trust be broken, however it may occur, I am left with nothing but paper. In which case, if I go to a store and attempt to pay for a quart of milk by handing the clerk a five-dollar bill, the clerk will ask, "What is this?" My response would be "Five dollars," and the clerk's, "No, it isn't. It's just a piece of paper."

After a five-year duration, the imbalances that had arisen as a result of the speculative land boom had been sufficiently excised so that the economy was once more in balance and thus in a position to move forward.

The five-year economic collapse had left a legacy of bankruptcy, closed businesses, rampant unemployment, stagnation, and despair. The situation was untenable. What to do?

The money purists would focus on gold and silver, but specie was in short supply, as it invariably is.

Given the amount of specie in circulation in the United States, if specie was to constitute the money supply, growth would stagnate, and unemployment would remain high. There had to be another solution! But what, pray tell, was it?

Must we await discovery of new sources of metal? Perhaps we should experiment, or as Franklin Roosevelt supposedly told his advisors during the depth of the depression, "Try anything."

The "try anything" philosophy might sound like panic, but for elected officials, the price for doing nothing meant, at the very least, certain defeat at the polls.

In world history there is not a case where the citizens of a country sat back and virtually starved as their leaders did nothing to relieve the pain. The immutable fact of history is that starvation brings revolution. It may not be a full-blown revolution of the type experienced in Russia or France and in thousands of other countries down through history, but at the very least it means "the ins are out."

If you wish to remain in power, you'd better do something.

During periods of severe downturn, fear takes hold. People do not spend; rather, they hoard. Credit becomes impossible to obtain, and thus even less money is available.

The New York banks during the depression of 1837 stopped making payments in specie, and the banks failed.

As banks failed, the federal government, which had embraced state banking, sustained heavy losses. To cauterize the wound, Van Buren proposed an independent treasury to handle the money and banking affairs of the country.

"The new President, Van Buren, after providing for the emergency issue of treasury notes (between 1837 and 1843, $47,000,000 worth was issued, about one-third representing reissues), turned his attention to this problem. He recommended that the government should break off all connections with banks, should collect its revenue in specie only and should keep the same in an independent Treasury until the time came for disbursement. In 1840 a bill to provide for the establishment of an independent Treasury was approved by the President. Clay, now the spokesman of the soft-money interests called the policy 'a selfish solicitude for the government and an evidence of a cold and heartless insensibility to the sufferings of a bleeding people.'"[xcii]

Van Buren, it appeared, was going to isolate the government from the national problem. Though hardly his intent, it appeared that his goal was to make the problem the peoples' problem, not his. Such a message was politically fatal.

"The next year, the Whigs came into power and repealed the Act. Led by Webster and Clay they now insisted that the only solution for the present difficulties was a National Bank—it would provide a sound and uniform currency and would regulate the issues of the local banks. The bill for the establishment of a National Bank passed Congress but was vetoed by President Tyler on the ground that the Constitution gave Congress no right to create a bank."[xciii]

The Jackson legacy survived. Biddle and his Federalist ilk were not coming back into power, at least not yet.

"The Democrats came into power in 1846, and from that date until 1861, the government at Washington did its own banking, handling practically nothing but specie and keeping it in its own vault under lock and key. The dominant party (concerned chiefly for the safety of its own deposits) was still unwilling to admit that some control over the issue of notes was necessary, and continued to maintain, in the face of 1781 and 1837, that the public interest was best served by leaving to the banks themselves the regulation of note-issue."[xciv]

CHAPTER 13

# Nineteenth-Century State Banking

## A Lesson in Speculation and Chaos

History repeats itself, not exactly of course. The characters will be different, and the circumstances will change. However, if one pursues the same misguided strategy, the result must inevitably be the same.

The principal purpose of banking is to channel the savings generated through labor for which the owner does not have an immediate pressing need into productive loans and investments that will generate positive returns, including plant, equipment, and goods. In this way new wealth is created without destruction of the old. In a few words, this constitutes economic growth.

Without savings there can be no investment. That must be the starting point.

Entrepreneurs, with savings, then get together and form an institution to make investments and to extend credit. The savings they bring to the table, which is their money, is the capital required to bring the institution into being. As they make loans and investments, it is their capital that is at risk. In addition, to expand the business, they accept deposits from customers who see the bank as a safe place to keep money. It is not their intention to take risk. The bank promises to give them their money back when they need it, and thus their deposits are referred to as demand deposits. Banks compete for demand deposits in order to increase their business.

Thus the rules of banking are fairly clear and straightforward. The difficulty is that the rules are constantly being violated. This unfortunate fact is the base cause of the turbulence and failure humans have had to live with since the first lender met the first borrower.

The intent of banking was never to make it into a spirited form of gambling. It was to become a gambler's paradise in the nineteenth century, the twentieth century, and to no surprise, the twenty-first century. The latest editions are Merrill Lynch, AIG Insurance, and MF Capital, which not only lost a large amount making a market bet with a large percentage of the money borrowed from other banks, but can't find, at this writing, $1.3 billion in customer funds. Speculation has its downside.

In the nineteenth century, to open a bank meant that you and your partners had specie, which as we have noted was always in short supply. Thus the partners would get together and, instead of pooling their savings, would put down, say, 2 percent and give a promissory note for the rest. The note had value only as long as the banker could come up with the specie if called upon. In effect 98 percent of the capital, the money at risk, was borrowed money.

When the bank opened for business, the depositors would deposit specie and would be paid an attractive rate and given a bill or note that stated that the bank would redeem in specie at a time of the depositor's choosing. The bank then proceeded to invest or loan the specie for a fixed term, even though the deposit was a demand deposit. The bank would earn the interest differential between the cost of the deposit and the rate of interest on the loan.

Under the above circumstances, the so-called Murphy's law will invariably come into play. The law states simply that if something can go wrong, it will. For those banks that were highly leveraged, unfortunately everything went wrong.

On a date uncertain, the depositor showed up and wanted to withdraw his money, in specie of course. The bank didn't have the specie; it had loaned it to a misguided borrower who had invested it in land. If the bank had a backstop, that is, the capital of the founders or Biddle's bank, then the depositor got his deposit back. If not, well, he was just out of luck.

Thus the depositor was taking a gamble, which was never his intent. He thought his money was safe. What a surprise.

The bankers were certainly gamblers. In some cases, a more apt term would be "swindlers." As a group they were far better at swindling than they were at banking.

They had many a trick up their sleeves. One of their favorites was to issue bills for deposits that could only be redeemed at the headquarters of the bank, which could not be found. That sure sounds like a swindle to me.

In those states that had bank inspectors, the banks were required to maintain a reserve in specie in their vault. One ploy was that they would tip one another off when the inspector was coming and simply move the same specie from bank to bank. The inspectors had no idea that they were looking at the same reserve. Well, at least they could find the bank.

This madness, this chaos, led over time to the creation of clearinghouses to assure proper handling and settlement of interbank notes and bills. In addition, banks were also required to publish financial statements.

Not all bankers were swindlers. They ran the gamut from the good to the bad to the ugly. Effective regulation and inspection were in order, but that was to be long in coming, as recent events clearly illustrate.

Is there something in the American psyche when it comes to money that allows us to turn a blind eye to misdeeds? I suggest not. However, a pioneer country on the move was ready-made for speculative enterprise.

"As Professor Dewey points out, in passing judgment on the defects and shortcomings of banking at this time, we must take into account the fact that probably any system would have broken down under the 'reckless spirit of speculative enterprise' which sought an outlet through the channels of credit. Inflation is a contingent danger of any pioneer country; and if that country be, in addition, a democracy unfamiliar with the intricacies of Gresham's Law, and the circumstances of whose development have associated sound money with political tyranny and loose banking with 'the rights of the people,' there indeed is the danger very greatly enhanced."[xcv]

At moments of crisis there is a good deal of weeping and gnashing of teeth, and after a time, as memories fade, the swindlers are back at it. If the truth be known, the public ignores the swindler. The public expresses less outrage if a third party is swindled. However, each of us is justifiably appalled if we are the subject of the swindle.

It could be readily argued that the doing away of Biddle's bank facilitated the chaos. However, swindling was going on big-time during the era of the Second Bank. A central bank did not end swindling and, in fact, may have encouraged more of it as it sponsored select constituents.

CHAPTER 14

# Lincoln, the War, and Finance

## Thank Heavens for the Railroad

State banking, free from Second Bank restraints, now greatly expanded its reach, resulting, as noted, in gigantic currency fraud.

The federal government fortunately had no part in this. As fraud became widespread, the federal Treasury isolated itself from any contagion through total separation. Henceforth it accepted revenue payments in specie only, paying its bills and placing the reserve under lock and key.

Banking in the countryside, in sharp contrast, was a madcap and very profitable business.

Unlike the enormous excesses visited upon us recently in housing, the "core" and thus profitable business of the age was the railroad.

America was a nation fixated on railroads. Railroads and everything revolving around them were fair game for the bankers and speculators. Investment, notably from Great Britain and Europe, rushed to get a piece of the action.

Credit swirled around railroad enterprise.

During much of the nineteenth century, if you were drawn to the banking business, in effect you became a railroad connoisseur and land speculator.

Even with runaway speculation, there did not seem to be enough money for the railroad magnates, who among their many tricks would sell and then resell the same stock certificates. The crooks were out in full force.

*Life, Liberty, and the Pursuit of Money*

The end result was railroad overbuilding, creating a nation with lines that made no economic sense. Yet this great continent needed to be brought together, and by hook or by crook, we were going to get lines even if they went nowhere. America became a railroad heaven.

Of course in the end, many failed. In the meantime, there was a great speculative boom. Everyone was becoming rich, and there was plenty of employment for the masses. These workers included a large number of Orientals, mostly Chinese, whose labor exceeded that of their peers. They were never recognized for their contribution and were not eligible for citizenship.

The bankers just had a ball issuing worthless or almost worthless paper as they took depositors' money and mortgaged property on or near the lines.

This indulgence simply continued a pattern of fraud and continuing excess that inevitably arises whenever greed is rewarded and regulation is absent.

I believe it was Montesquieu who observed that if men were angels, there would be no need for government.

Given the opportunity for fortune, should we have expected that men without scruples would have behaved in any other way?

Abuse became widespread as currency issued by these banks ballooned. The effect of this was to awaken state legislators from their slumber, and they started to take action.

Even at this early date in the country's history, it was understood that regulation, transparency, and openness were powerful antidotes to fraud and abuse.

In this regard an important step taken was to institute clearinghouses, which provided a regional mechanism for the clearing of bank paper originated across the country. New England took the lead in this regard, followed later by New York, which by midcentury had in place a banking department and clearinghouse.

As the saying goes, all good things must come to an end someday. And indeed this "monopoly money" banking system crashed and resulted in a slowdown in investment due to a combination of high rates and a severe balance of payments problem due to an outflow in specie. Business failures followed, resulting in systemic failure. With this failure banks ceased making specie payments. After all, one cannot get blood from a stone.

In the world of 2008, Congress would step in. However, in the nineteenth century, such a move was out of the question. The Constitution prevented the national government from invading what was clearly seen as a state preserve.

On the national scene, the US Treasury witnessed a sharp decline in revenue. The cupboard was bare and revenues were falling just as Mr. Lincoln took office. He had a good deal more than war to think about as he entered the presidency.

## LINCOLN AND MONEY—WHATEVER WORKS!

Lincoln had a war to fight. As his predecessors and foreign kings, queens, and assorted tyrants would have certainly told him, wars cannot be fought without money.

I suspect he knew this, and the evidence is that this fine lawyer from the backwoods didn't have a clue as to what to do about it.

There is universal agreement that he was blessed with an outstanding cabinet. Men such as William H. Seward, secretary of state (1861–1869), and Edwin M. Stanton, secretary of war (1862–1868), were men of exceptional ability.

Another member of the cabinet, who had sought the Republican nomination in 1860, was the irrepressible Salmon P. Chase. Lincoln concluded that the best way to keep this fellow out of harm's way was to welcome him into the cabinet.

Chase was not of a kind that a president would offer a lesser job to. He thought of himself as a very important personage, deserving of wealth, respect, and important assignments.

Of course no one would argue that the Office of Treasury, particularly under the circumstances, was not an important position.

In fairness to Chase, when he was asked to take the assignment, he revealed to Lincoln the truth, namely, that he did not know a thing about money. To which Lincoln is said to have replied that neither did he, so that made two of them. Lincoln, being president, had other matters to attend to, presumably more important, such as civil war, and thus the job was Chase's.

Chase did not abandon his desire to be president nor his intention to run in 1864. Quite the contrary: he expected to get the nomination and to win election. This did not seem to bother Lincoln. At any rate Chase took the cabinet position, believing that this would give him visibility and stature for his planned run in four years.

## Taxation? Oh, No!—This Is America

Kings of old, embracing conflict and in need of revenue, simply increased taxes, borrowed, or stole. This would never do in America. Not only were the American people of different stock, but the revolution was largely fought over the issue of taxation.

Historians believe that had America been offered representation in Parliament, we might have acquiesced to Britain's imposition of taxes. There is scant evidence of this, however, Benjamin Franklin being a notable exception.

The patriots, such as the Sons of Liberty, wanted no part of Britain and certainly not their taxes.

Revenue was garnered through the payment of custom duties and other tariffs. It's fine to tax the other guy, but don't tax me. Not much has changed in the past three centuries in this country in that regard.

The most certain way to political defeat in America is to propose an increase in taxes. If one has any doubt about this, he might ask Walter Mondale, who proposed increasing the income tax in his 1984 campaign against Ronald Reagan and proceeded to lose forty-nine states.

Yet this war was a serious financial problem, and it had to be addressed. America was a nation of farmers. There was simply no concentration of capital that could be easily tapped. The money had to come from somewhere. Weapons had to be paid for. The patriotic soldiers, though largely uneducated, insisted on being paid. If the war was to be carried forward, sources of capital would have to be found. The only viable alternative to taxation was to borrow, but how to borrow vast sums was the question. In this regard the state banks were there and ripe for picking.

The state banks, a group maligned as nothing more than profiteering rascals, corrupted by undeserving gains reaped by taking advantage of poor farmers, widows, and orphans, were now going to have the privilege of lending to the United States government, like it or not.

Until now the government, fearful of some fatal infection, had divorced itself from the financial world and had managed its own affairs in a tightly controlled fashion.

For the state banks, this recognition was an unimaginable change in their social standing. To this point they had fought the establishment, specifically the First and Second Central banks, and had been treated with disdain by men like Biddle. They were now about to become the cornerstone of the establishment.

Of course the government would make the rules, the most important being that all loans to Washington had to be made in specie.

There was a slight problem with this rule however. The Lincoln Treasury was bare, and so were the vaults of the state banks. At the outset some specie was paid in, but when the point was reached where Washington could no longer obtain specie from the state banks, Washington suspended specie payments and so did the state banks.

Loans simply became book entries. Everyone was going into debt—together.

The ledgers across the length and breadth of the nation showed dramatic increases in liabilities. Debt would lead the way. Redemption in specie was out of the question. When would this debt be paid? A simple answer at the time was that after the crisis had passed, normalcy would return.

How was it to be paid? No one had a clue. The United States was adopting a strategy very similar to the one adopted by England during the Napoleonic Wars.

Though the state banks became willing partners, it was important to find investors to invest their savings in the United States government. Small-denomination bonds were issued in 1863. They became the unofficial

*Life, Liberty, and the Pursuit of Money*

currency of the day. Taxes could be paid with these notes, and they earned compound interest.

This required the skill of a true marketing executive, and Chase had just the man for the job. He was a wealthy Philadelphia banker by the name of Jay Cooke. As one might guess, Cooke received "a lucrative Treasury Department contract to sell government bonds."[xcvi]

Cooke did not want to let anyone down, particularly Chase, and it was widely rumored that he was to have been rewarded with gifts, which allowed him to live comfortably in the style to which he had become accustomed.[xcvii]

With war continuing, the demand for money never subsided. The tax structure was modestly revised to generate revenue. Though the Treasury had borrowed $150 million from the banks and Treasury notes sold, more was needed, a great deal more.[xcviii]

Mr. Chase, with perhaps nowhere else to turn, turned to the printing press. Implicit in all borrowings to this point was ultimate redemption of the paper at a time uncertain.

This was not only costly, but there were limits—psychological and real—to the issuance of paper. At some point the debt of the government becomes so large that the paper loses its credibility. People simply stop believing that it will be paid.

For the moment at any rate, the printing press was beckoning. Keep your head down and just print currency. Redemption, forget it. Welcome to fiat money. Oh boy, does this sound familiar.

## Fiat Money—The Unbreakable Daisy Chain

The world experience with paper money informs that it has the characteristics of a daisy chain. With no alternative readily available, it will serve the purpose intended and function well moving from hand to hand. However, the transfer chain must never be broken.

John Maynard Keynes, addressing the subject of liquidity, put this phenomenon very well when, in search for a definition of "liquidity," which in commercial terms roughly translated means facility, he found that definition incomplete. He said liquidity was closer to the card game *Old Maid* or

*Musical Chairs*. In other words the holder of the queen or the one without a chair at the end of the game is the one who loses.

If the standard paper was money, no one in theory would ever be stuck. Unfortunately the paper isn't money. It remains a mere promise. Currency, to be a true proxy for money. must have intrinsic credibility.

The price of gold will change, but gold has value unto itself. Paper bills or similar instruments have extrinsic credibility, which means that its true value is totally dependent on the credibility of the issuer.

Once that credibility is successfully challenged or more likely in this age becomes suspect, the possibility then exists for the chain to be broken. The breaking of the chain translates into systemic collapse. God forbid in the modern world such an event should occur.

The printing of paper money, since it proceeds without restriction, allows for the infinite expansion of debt. Many believe that debt can continue to expand without ramifications.

Collapse is the inevitable outcome when questions arise concerning the ability of the issuer to make payment. At that point the holders of the paper run for the doors.

Under the gold exchange standard or gold standard, conditions at times might have been very difficult, but the possibility of global collapse was never present. Today that possibility not only exists, but we had a taste of it in the United States housing collapse recently.

This currency, authorized by Chase and not redeemable in specie, was issued to the tune of $150 million in 1862. By 1863, $450 million had been issued.[xcix]

This currency was a loan, an IOU. It was not backed by anything. The problem is that the taker of the currency didn't know it was a loan. He thought it was money. He thought he was being paid. In fact, he was in receipt of nothing but a piece of paper.

He took the paper believing he could spend it, and perhaps he could under the greater fool theory. A gigantic daisy chain was created until people stopped accepting the paper.

Money is product. The taker of the paper believes that there is product behind it. Of course this is false. There is nothing behind it. The holder has an IOU, a liability, not an asset.

With demand falsely stimulated, people increase their borrowing to participate in what appears to be a windfall.

With prices rising and profits resulting from speculation increasing, ever more is borrowed. Everyone wants to get into the act. Buy more, buy larger, buy anything, Utopia at last.

Then the music stops. The entire system, based on promises that cannot be fulfilled, namely, borrowing without anything to borrow from, simply collapses.

Predictable? Of course, but great fun while it lasts.

At this point, the massive accumulation of debt, which both was real and remained a burden, could not be paid, and the economy fell into depression.

Depression is the inevitable result of a debt-oriented monetary system. Greenbacks, that is, fiat currency, had brought the United States through the Civil War, but they also made inevitable the depression that followed.

## Debt—An Aphrodisiac of the First Order

Debt of itself is not an evil, but it is insidious. It works like alcohol. A little is fine. In fact, a little might even be healthy. Once it becomes habit-forming, though, watch out!

When people borrow, they are borrowing the product of another. The one they are borrowing from, the one who has labored, has the money, has the savings. That person is transferring those savings to the borrower for a price. The price is called interest.

The one who has labored forgoes the use of the money, and the borrower takes the laborer's place. The transfer is one for one. The borrower may invest it provided he or she can return it.

If the money is consumed or lost, the laborer has lost, the borrower has lost, and the economy has lost, since the product of labor no longer exists. We are all poorer.

Consumption is the way to the poorhouse. If you have any doubts on that score, simply ask those who have rung up substantial amounts of debt on their credit cards.

A vacation on a credit card may be invigorating, but when it is over, you have nothing to show for it except the debt that remains. You may be more relaxed, but you are poorer. Debt plus consumption is the money equivalent of alcoholism. It can be fatal. It is always fatal, unless steps taken for rehabilitation are taken in time.

It would be fair to characterize the credit card as the greatest threat to the health and well-being of the average consumer ever devised, given the economic tragedy that is still unfolding. The fault does not lie with the card. The fault lies with its misuse and abuse.

In the nineteenth century, the fraudulent banking practices so prevalent among state banks were not indicative of a fundamental flaw in the nature of banking, but unregulated practices fed by ignorance and greed that produced economic disaster for the nation.

It is critical that the consumer learn after this recent experience how to manage his or her credit. He or she must know when credit should and should not be used.

For the future it is a positive development that consumers have access to credit. However, the consumer must understand the pitfalls inherent in all debt.

For the nation's benefit, government must have a regulatory role.

Consumer credit as practiced today is usurious. Not all consumers qualify for credit. The laissez-faire attitude of government toward this industry has served as an open invitation for abuse. All of this having been said, the fact of the matter is, debt is not evil.

Debt entered into to make it possible to produce may be wise. Case in point, a corporation buys land to build an auto plant. It hires workers and produces a product. The debt has given rise to enhanced value. The global economy has expanded to that extent.

The workers in turn save. This allows their children an education, which will contribute to further production in the future. They will buy and use the products, and to that extent they are consuming. But this consumption is essential for them to become productive.

A good example would be education as an engineer. The course of study allows for the development of new products and invention, which in turn result in greater employment, which in turn raises the level of wealth in the world.

Debt under these conditions is a positive force for development. It is the mechanism for increasing the standard of living for everyone. To get to that point, we must also consume, a cost of doing business. It is not consumption for the sake of consumption. It is consumption for the sake of production. This must be the standard for government, business, and the consumer.

The massive debt that has been accumulated by the United States government and the states for the most part is consumption-oriented. Thus we have little to show for it, and the nation is less wealthy than it was some decades ago.

Yes, we have made progress in many fields. Our standard of living, measured by conventional standards, has improved. Yet the debt remains, and the impact of this burden going forward on each one of us has yet to be tolled.

The United States debt combined with consumer debt is so massive that the economic future is at best clouded. "The sun will come out tomorrow" does not apply.

The fact that the government expenditures are well-intentioned is totally irrelevant. The nation is poorer. We as individuals are poorer, and we owe the debt still. The reality is that uncontrolled debt is the death knell for a great nation.

Nevertheless, collapse is never inevitable. Wrongheaded policies extending over decades will precipitate decline, but collapse is a process of fragmentation that will be addressed in more detail in a later segment of this book.

Debt is the precursor, the underlying cause of decline. Nations, unlike individuals or commercial endeavors, cannot experience bankruptcy. They remain in place or are absorbed by other nations.

Yet the organism as a unit no longer functions properly. Internally it fractures. Regional interests begin to dictate policy as the central government, debt-burdened, no longer has the capability of influencing local or regional decisions. This process of separation ultimately produces disintegration.

In a global context, massive debt produces separation, and with separation, antagonism—and antagonism leads to war.

## IOUs Produce Decline in Stages

The immediate impact of printing IOUs, as we noted, is a change in the price structure. Additional paper in the hands of consumers stimulates buying, which raises prices, fostering a "buy now before prices increase further" mind-set that in turn leads to shortages.

Though this exaggerated demand condition is unsustainable, business ramps up production and hires new workers to meet it, only to be left with excess inventory and the need to release staff as buying tails off.

The entire dynamic is artificial, but as I said earlier, it is fun while it lasts.

For many, the process is harmful. It was estimated that during the war years, from 1860 to 1865, real wages or purchasing power fell by one third as a result of higher prices due to printing IOUs, that is, currency not supported by savings or capital.[c]

Soldiers and those living on fixed income bore the burden, and in the end the nation had little or nothing to show for the debt incurred in terms of physical plant, with the important exception of the armor factories and the guns and cannon that were produced.

In effect the printing was a tax on those who could afford it the least. The cost of the war was borne by them, not by the profiteers or the eastern bankers.

Printing currency was the ruse used to finance the war. To the surprise of many, it appears to have worked. The likes of Chase and Lincoln defended these practices by insisting that it was the only option open.

The war was successful. The nation was spared secession. The slaves went free. But the cost was not evenly shared.

## Time for Seriousness

The financial condition of the nation leading up to the war, together with the massive proliferation of bank paper and the great greenback scheme, forced the politicians to get serious as the war was coming to an end.

It was estimated that "there were now 7,000 kinds of paper notes in circulation, not to mention 5,000 counterfeit issues."[ci]

In 1864 the final version of the National Bank Act was passed. Banking was to become a regulated business. Virtually all banking practices would fall under the purview of the regulators.

Banks across the nation were offered the opportunity to become national banks. Six hundred and thirty-four banks joined by 1864. Being a national bank gave the depositors confidence that their hard-earned money was being handled properly.

State banks were reluctant to join; after all, they had a good deal going for them.

However, a critical step was taken in 1865, when Congress imposed a 10 percent tax on the notes of all the state banks. This served to extinguish their issuance.

"The National Banks now had a monopoly of note issue…The foundations of the American monetary system had been soundly laid."[cii]

## National Unity Necessitates a New Money System

Post-Civil War America and the Western world began an extended period of consolidation.

America was reunited, in fact, if not in spirit. Before the Civil War, in casual conversation, one might have heard in any sector of the country, the United States *are*…After the war people said the United States *is*… Nationhood and union were to take precedence.

The belief grew that for true unity, one and only one money system must exist in the country. Proliferation of bills and other instruments were symbols of disunion.

Across the great pond, a similar event was occurring with the uniting of the German states under the forceful hand of the Prussians.

CHAPTER 15

# Europe—1860 and Beyond

## Eighteenth- to Nineteenth-Century Europe

When one contemplates the enormity of the destruction and killing that descended upon Europe after the French Revolution (1789–1799) and continued with little respite for a century and a half, there is a strong desire to find the culprit or culprits responsible for this madness.

Barbarism dominated the history of the European Continent well before and after Rome. The centers of barbarism merely changed over time.

Given the central role Germany has played in Western affairs, it is hard to believe that there was a time when there was no German state as such, but rather a conglomeration of small entities not much larger than little communities. However, they shared a culture and, from the tenth century until the early nineteenth century, referred to themselves as the Holy Roman Empire of the German Nation.

The critical event that changed the face of Europe, creating and later dispensing with countries, cultures, and peoples, was the French Revolution.

In 1789 during the revolution the French Assembly adopted the Declaration of the Rights of Man and of the Citizen. Many of the provisions in the American Constitution were incorporated.

Men had natural rights. All citizens were equal. Man was due popular sovereignty and was equal under the law, as opposed to the prevailing doctrine of the age, the divine right of kings.

The seeds of democracy were thus sown into the fabric of French society by the revolution. As Napoleon later took his army across Europe, these ideals went with them, even though Napoleon and his administrators and generals were Mafia tyrants.

The monarchs of Europe and the royalty and nobles never endorsed this concept and saw in this revolution of the spirit a real threat to their supremacy and position.

It was their intention, with the defeat of Napoleon, to restore Europe to a pre-French Revolution political condition.

To accomplish this required a redrawing of the map of Europe. The groundwork for this continental effort was set forth at the Congress of Vienna.

The Congress was given this unique opportunity as a result of two critical developments. The first was the final dissolution in 1806 of the Holy Roman Empire. The Empire had a Central European orientation, did not include Rome, and stretched from Italy to Poland.

The second was the defeat of Napoleon.

The final Act of the Congress, which redesigned Central Europe, was actually signed nine days after Napoleon's final defeat at Waterloo on June 18, 1815.

The Congress began its work in November 1814 and concluded in June 1815. It was attended by many nations. However, five principal powers directed its work. They were Austria, United Kingdom, Prussia, Russia, and France.

With the defeat of Napoleon, and thus the defeat of France, it was never intended that France would play a major role in future European affairs. However, the powers to be underestimated the cunning, persuasiveness, and diplomatic skill of the French representative Talleyrand, who managed to work his way into the inner circle and succeeded in exercising considerable influence on the final design of the map of Europe.

The Congress was chaired by another historic figure, a diplomat of the first order, the famous Austrian Clemens W. von Metternich.

The purpose of the Congress in theory was to secure future peace and harmony by responding to the demands and claims of the attendees.

An important result included the establishment of the German Confederation, made up now of some thirty-nine states, down from some three hundred previously, ostensibly under the suzerainty of the Austrian Emperor but sufficiently independent to allow Prussia and Austria to exercise influence in their respective theaters.

Prussian territory was expanded, and Russia annexed much of Poland and was allowed to hold on to Finland.

These territorial arrangements would, by the end of the nineteenth century, produce explosive friction, continuing well into the twentieth and serve as the raison d'être for the two great wars, culminating in the destruction of Europe and the final defeat of Germany.

With the earlier defeat of France, the ideals that had moved the French people, the concept of popular sovereignty, was dealt a sharp setback.

The Congress of Vienna thus endorsed the restoration of the old order, the conservative order, which translated into a restoration of aristocracies, deemphasizing liberty and civil rights, while embracing the restoration of tradition, obedience to political authority, and the states' interests above the interests of the individual.

## The German Confederation

A confederation is a workable political entity as long as all party participants see in the structure something beneficial. Its organic ties may be loose, as is the case with the British Commonwealth of today.

Any attempt to force confederation, which is what the Nazis and Bolsheviks endeavored to do by military force, will result in violence and, if history is to be one's guide, revolution. A confederation has to be voluntary, a natural event where all the parties recognize that by working together they will attain more than if they pursue their objectives separately.

The founding fathers viewed this nation that way and, in the earliest of documents, referred to the country as a confederation of states. The persistent argument over states' rights retains that notion of a great joint endeavor, with each member reserving the right to exercise judgment and perhaps proceeding down a different course if its interests so require.

It was on this principle that the breakaway states, beginning with South Carolina, fearful of northern domination, attempted the break.

*Life, Liberty, and the Pursuit of Money*

The Civil War settled the matter for the United States, and today we universally accept the principle that the United States is one nation, indissoluble.

Thus it was inevitable that the decisions of the Congress of Vienna, which involved many compromises by the "core" states attending, might look fine on a map but would be a serious cause of conflict on the ground, which was precisely what happened in Central Europe beginning with the formation of the German Confederation.

The Confederation brought together two very different peoples and cultures. Austria was suave, urbane, romantic, absolutist with an all-powerful monarch, Catholic, but in economic terms backward, and from a military standpoint nonthreatening.

Its partner was Prussia.

Prussia was the cultural antithesis of Austria and Western Europe. It was Teutonic. Prussia meant military, and all Prussians were to adhere to a severe, unforgiving, all-powerful, ruthless rule by an aristocracy that was military. There was at all times a very high proportion of military to the population. When speaking of the Prussians, one is reminded of the Spartans of ancient Greece.

In Prussia there was no middle class. Almost the entire state budget was earmarked for the military. A merchant's work was to make goods for the military. The army was staffed by the landowning gentry, the Junkers. The Junkers were prohibited from selling their land. There was no way to move up in society, and to make matters worse, the peasants were ruthlessly treated. Class structure was frozen. There was no independent wealth. The religious orientation was Protestant.

The supreme virtue was service to the state or the king, who retained absolute authority over the serfs. In periods of peace and war, the overlords of these desperate people wore uniforms. Prussian land was barren, and the people were dour and austere.

Prussian land had important natural resources. Thus it was economically viable. It was rich in coal and iron and focused, developing a railway network that would prove decisive in case of war.

## Metternich and the Confederation

Metternich, the great diplomat of the age, was an Austrian. He chaired the Congress of Vienna and was most conscious of Austrian interests. The Empire being created would have an Austrian emperor, and thus Austria's interests would be protected.

Did he not grasp the barbarian philosophy that motivated the Prussians? Did he not see the potential threat to Austria of such an alliance? If he did, it would have been the least of his concerns. Real power rested with the Czar of Russia and Talleyrand of France, along with Austria and of course England. Prussia was of secondary importance.

Return to monarchial rule would restore authority and absolute rule. Prussia was a showplace for absolute rule. It was another buffer or barrier to French influence, which was dangerous—so dangerous in fact that it took the combined forces of Europe to defeat that influence during the Napoleonic Wars. France must be contained, and the Confederation would serve that purpose well.

## The Best-Laid Plans

By 1851 with the formation of the Confederation, Austria was the dominant power, and most German states looked to Austria for leadership. Yet it was clear that Prussia was the dominant economic power.

For the German states to trade with one another without tariffs required a customs union. Prussia would soon dominate the customs union, and this in time would allow Prussia to begin a process that would end in political hegemony.

Growing pressure for unification lay with German nationalists, who harbored the dream of a unified state of German-speaking people. Bismarck, chancellor of the German Empire and a Junker, was in every respect a militarist. He presided with Von Moltke over the Prussian war machine. With two powers competing, the result must be a growing rivalry, which came to a head over a dispute over the state of Schleswig-Holstein. This led to the Austro-Prussian war of 1866, which brought to an end the Confederation conceived of at the Congress of Vienna.

Prussia mobilized and quickly defeated Austria, giving rise to the North German Confederation in 1867. This was the political fortress of Prussia until the onset of the Franco-Prussian War in 1870.

The North German Confederation was an alliance of twenty-two states that had sided with Prussia during the war. The southern states, such as Bavaria, though not part of this Confederation, were bound to it by the customs union. A new constitution was written, creating a bicameral legislature or council, and as one might suspect, Prussia was the dominating power. Executive power resided in the king of Prussia, who would appoint the chancellor. Bismarck was the designee.

States retained their own governments, but the military rested with the federal government.

## Expansionism

With increasing anxiety this new union with a militarist drive was viewed as threatening, particularly by France under a weak leader, Napoleon III.

Prussia and France had been enemies during the era of conquest by Napoleon I. The ultimate defeat of the Grand Armée served to stoke the fire of hostility among Frenchmen.

In addition, a new and expansionist empire was making a shambles of the balance of power in Europe.

This spark for potential conflict smoldered not only in the hearts of Frenchmen, but in the heart of the Prussian military as well, who effectively used a dispute between the two countries over who would succeed to the throne of Sweden to inflame animosity, leading to the outbreak of war, which France declared in July 1870.

The war ended with the complete and total defeat of France. The inefficient French were no match for the well-organized Prussian-led armies.

With the conquest of Paris in 1871 and its brutal embargo and isolation resulting in dislocation and near starvation for thousands, accomplished by the skillful use of the railroads and advances in the quality of artillery, France had no choice but to accept Prussian terms.

Bismarck reached a negotiated agreement to withdraw his troops from Paris as soon as France paid 5 billion francs.

This disgraceful and complete defeat created a huge backlash among the French people, who strongly objected to any surrender, but the reality on the ground left the government with few options.

As the Prussians withdrew their forces, they continued to occupy Alsace-Lorraine, a territory where the majority were French- and a small minority German-speaking. It does not appear that it was Bismarck's intention to occupy permanently French territory, but Moltke and the generals claimed the need for a buffer state and Bismarck consented.

This occupation continued up to World War I. It bred deep resentment and hatred among the French and was a major underlying cause for the outbreak of conflict in the West at the beginning of World War I.

## The German Empire

In the Palace of Versailles in January 1871, a union of all German states was proclaimed under the Prussian King, Wilhelm I. This Empire had Russia to the east, France to the west, and Austria-Hungary to the south.

The Vienna balance of power had been shattered. Prussia with its annexed states ruled central Europe and dominated Western Europe.

Europe clearly understood that Prussian dominance had been achieved by the force of arms. Thus Europe began to adopt a defensive posture, with increasing emphasis on weaponry and conscription. Nations began to pull apart, and alliances, in many cases unnatural alliances, began to take shape.

## The British Empire

Within the German Empire, there was much work to be done. Proclamation of empire and the tools for implementing empire are very different.

Across the English Channel lay Great Britain, which was, and would remain at least for a time, the world power.

If Germany was to be regarded as world-class in a league with the British, it must at the very least mimic what Britain had successfully accomplished over the centuries.

Britain had and had had a formidable military, largely undefeated, except for that unfortunate experience in North America. The French had been their principal adversary; however, with the French Revolution and the later defeat of Napoleon's army led by Britain, there were few willing to question British supremacy.

Britain was the leading nation in terms of the industrial revolution. The quality of its manufacturing was world-renowned. Though Britain had lost America, it had not lost its far-flung commonwealth and numerous colonies, including the pearl, India, to whom it sold its manufactured goods and from whom it purchased raw materials.

The East India Company and other trade organizations saw to it that these colonies adhered to London's dictated terms of trade. They were there to protect British interests, backed by a military and a navy that had no equal.

If Germany was to ever match the commercial dominance of Britain, it too must have colonies to which it could dictate terms, and this meant extending German power, including military power, well beyond its borders.

Thus the German Empire came into being with a ready-made adversary on its western border and the potential for another more powerful adversary over the issue of colonization.

## A New Germany—The Infrastructure

For eons the Germanic peoples had occupied Central Europe. These peoples lived in states, many of which were quite small. One of those states, Prussia, had a long tradition of militarism. Like the Greek state Sparta, the military was all that counted. Boys wore uniforms from the time they could walk. If one wanted to get ahead, the military was the only way to go. Nothing else mattered.

However, any military to be worth its salt must battle, and as Europe convulsed, Bismarck and his followers saw their chance. Empire was to be their goal. A nation as small as Prussia, though militarily supreme in that part of Europe, did not have the commercial viability or potential for empire. To accomplish this, a union of German states must be achieved.

This meant *anschulss*, the incorporation of German states into a new confederation, a new union, whose future would be determined by Prussia.

If such a union was to succeed, it had to be so bound that future separation would become virtually impossible. This was never intended to be a democratic state. The people were to have virtually no say in the political direction of this powerful, both militarily and commercially, new state.

However, Prussian power and influence had its limits. In time these states might easily chafe at being under the thumb of Prussia and begin to pull away. Treaty alone would never suffice. There had to be an instrument that so bound the people together that, irrespective of inclination, there was virtually no possibility of disunion.

Thus one of the first Acts after the declaration of union was the creation of a central bank, the Reich Bank. The Reich Bank would issue currency in whatever form it chose, and it would be based on gold.

For these formally independent German states, this was to be a dramatic and fundamental change, for up until now silver had been their currency. These states would be expected to divest themselves of silver and substitute gold in all of their dealings.

The new Germany was going on the gold standard, come heaven, hell, or high water. Yes, England had been on the gold standard, but most of the nations of Europe had not, and German commercial dealings were invariably with these nations and not England.

With logic born of necessity rather than reason, if Germany was going on the gold standard, for trade purposes others must as well. It seems clear that is what the Germans believed. That required persuasion. Thus began a campaign to put the world on the gold standard, a campaign, though illogical in most respects, that would eventually succeed.

## A Gold Standard for Europe and America

With the conclusion of the Franco-Prussian War, a victorious Germany, led by Chancellor Bismarck, was determined to make Germany a respected and powerful state. Using the Bank of England as a guide, Germany created its own central bank, the Reich Bank. This proved to be a fateful decision for it allowed this new union to have gold as the currency standard. In the minds of Bismarck and his advisors and bankers, this was critical to achieving a true German union.

The most bizarre aspect of this decision was that the German states, as well as other European states and most certainly the United States, trusted in the silver standard.

For the previously independent German states, their coins differed in denomination but were based on silver content.

Bismarck obviously concluded that to meld many states into one required the introduction of one supracurrency for all, and thus the reichsmark was born. It is probably more correct to say that the mark was imposed on these states.

While all went along, they had no choice. The Prussian mentality did not understand nor would it tolerate minority views. Though the legal procedures were carefully followed, the end result was never in doubt. If silver had been left as the base standard, people in each state might have been reluctant to surrender their currency. Under such circumstances, the unpredictability of future events might at some point have produced secessionist tendencies.

Thus what was needed were both a new currency and a new standard. The choice of that standard was never in doubt, at least not in Bismarck's mind. He would follow the example of Great Britain. Why Great Britain?

London was the financial center of the world, and if Germany was ever to rival Britain as a world leader, it must seek status and hopefully become a financial center.

It was widely understood that finance was critical to the expansion of trade and economic dominance. A secondary but very important consideration was the overriding need to create "a more perfect union."

There was always a danger of disunion, particularly under Prussian leadership, which was both militaristic and Protestant, versus Bavaria, which was Catholic. To limit the danger of thus pulling apart, it was essential to create a new currency. With all of this in mind, the gold-backed reichsmark came into being.

## The Reichsmark

Great Britain, at least implicitly from the time of Newton, recognized gold as their standard.

The British pound was the currency of trade and was held with such respect by nations, business, and wealthy merchants that the right to convert British notes to gold was viewed as a secondary consideration.

To the world British banknotes were the equivalent of holding gold. In the mind of many, the pound sterling was superior to gold. The price of gold could fluctuate, but the pound had the great British Empire behind it.

Sterling was supreme and would remain so indefinitely, unless somehow challenged by an outside force.

It is doubtful that Bismarck ever seriously planned to challenge Great Britain for world supremacy. However, there is no question that he intended to occupy the same stage.

To accomplish that, he must at the very least copy those attributes of power that distinguished Great Britain from everyone else. The military was not the issue at the time since neither nation was likely to engage the other, but commerce was another matter.

Would it ever be possible for Germany to contest commercial power on the world stage with the likes of London and that rising power across the Atlantic Ocean, the United States?

Germany had a viable industrial base, but that was not enough. Commerce demanded the trappings, and that meant among other critical measures a widely accepted global currency in which to contract and pay for trade commitments to other nations.

The reichsmark needed to gain wide acceptance, global acceptance, and to accomplish this meant convertibility, the right of the holder to exchange freely reichsmarks for the standard. Then what must the standard be?

If Great Britain was supreme, if the pound sterling in determining value was unchallenged, if gold, precious and pure, stood behind sterling, then gold must stand behind the reichsmark.

The pound sterling was the currency of international trade and exchange. In a real sense, the world revolved around London. Certainly Paris had an important diplomatic role to play and had its colonies, but it was no longer in competition, at least not since the defeat of Napoleon.

British power went unchallenged.

At the core of Bismarck's new union was military power. There were only two possible uses for military power in the nineteenth century. The first was to quell internal dissent, if any existed, to the reigning power structure. The second was to be prepared to fight wars for the purpose of expanding the wealth, power, and influence of the state.

Warfare was accepted as the natural state. It would be defined as diplomacy by other means, a form of chess where nations achieved political goals, enhancing their status and reputation among their peers.

In Europe human rights and concepts of democracy, where they existed at all, were neither understood nor accepted. Such ideals were viewed particularly after the French experience as truly threatening to the power structure and not to be tolerated or encouraged.

The rules of the warfare game were really quite simple. The victor received payments of varying size depending on the wealth of the defeated warring nation and of course land. War was about the accretion of land. To the victor went the spoils.

As late as the First World War, the extension of empire was the purpose of war.

This contrasted sharply with the views of a future American president, Woodrow Wilson, who held that the limits of statehood were ultimately to be determined by the citizenry of the state. No nation had the right to gobble up another, and certainly not a nation of a different culture, without the consent of the people.

This democratic ideal, applauded publicly by the various participants in the First World War, including Britain and France, was privately viewed as American naïveté by the most powerful in Europe.

To both Lloyd George, the British prime minister, and Clemenceau, the French premier, during the Great War the sole purpose of war was to exercise power. The single best way to exercise that power was in victory, where the victorious received land grants and payments. This was the way it had always been and, in their mind, would never change.

After the First World War, the victors received mandates. It was expected that the United States would have a mandate over Constantinople, perhaps Rumania, and certainly Albania, and if we wanted, parts of Russia and other diverse places around the globe. It was to be ours for the taking with the approval of Britain and France.

The nation of Iraq came into being as a result of a mandate given Great Britain at the Paris Peace Conference. The Brits had an interest in the Middle East because of oil and the need to control the strategic gateway to India.

War was all about land, as it had always been, stretching back to antiquity. Democracy, as set out in Wilson's fourteen points, with emphasis on self-determination, was exciting and new and applauded by peoples around the world, but dismissed as unrealistic in the power centers of London and Paris.

War was part and parcel of life. Men would die by the thousands, if not by the millions, and such death was honorable, particularly if war was fought on behalf of the victor.

## Ready or Not, a "New" Germany

With the creation of the German Union, Bismarck began the process of moving Germany into the status of a great nation.

Chancellor Bismarck was both a militarist and a statesman. "Deutschland Uber Alles" did not yet ring in German ears, but the imperative to show the world the greatness of the Germanic peoples in full union, led by a military man and a military history that had been very recently demonstrated on the battlefield with the defeat of the French, was the responsibility of a great leader. There was no question in the mind of Bismarck that he would be seen in history in precisely that way.

If Germany were to be truly great and so viewed by the rest of the world, it must have the trappings of power. Trappings included military, economic, and financial power.

Economic conditions prior to the 1870s were very unsatisfactory. The world yearned for both stability and prosperity and seemed to get neither. Periods of rapid expansion were followed with economic depression.

There were many informed industrialists and statesmen who blamed confusion over currency as a contributing factor. Thus internationally there was a willingness to streamline and unify the West's standard of money.

With both silver and gold being used to settle international trade contracts, it was in the debtor's interest to settle in the cheaper of the two. Creditors around the world felt as if they were always being cheated.

Thus as Germany announced that the standard for the reichsmark would be gold, the world quickly followed.

Nations drawn by the prospect of a single world currency ignored the obvious deficiencies of a single standard, the most obvious being the scarcity of gold.

At first there was enthusiastic support, except from the British colonials, many of whom favored silver, such as India, who had no intention of making a fundamental change in the way it carried on its affairs.

Through their British representatives of these colonies, they posed unsettling questions at the conference meetings. The attending nations embraced the idea nevertheless and moved within their own political sphere to make gold both their and the world's standard.

This initial enthusiastic support began to fade as global economic conditions worsened. With the limited supply of gold in central bank coffers and with no expectation of major new discovery, it became apparent that the gold standard, instead of facilitating world trade, would actually serve as a retardant. Those who had loudly hailed the prospect of a new era of prosperity with gold leading the way found themselves wrestling with economic stagnation and decline.

Economic decline did not lead to global renunciation of the standard, though in light of history it should have, but to halfway measures, including increased reliance on the domestic currencies and, in the case of the United States, a de facto acceptance of the continued use of silver to bolster the money supply.

Thus the West was left with an uncertain international monetary system that might be best defined as a quasi-gold standard.

Under these circumstances nations turned inward to protect domestic commerce. Nations felt a compelling need to protect themselves as an increasingly militaristic and competitive economic environment took hold.

The world lurched from one crisis to another, spurring nationalism and labor dissatisfaction, which would ultimately culminate in the First World War.

During the years that gold reigned, it never occurred to the nations' leaders that by removing silver as an acceptable standard, effectively reducing the world's money supply, the consequence would be a drastic negative contraction in economic activity.

These men of limited understanding believed as their forefathers had that gold bullion meant wealth. They blindly accepted the notion that the metal was money, whereas common sense should have informed them that money had to be the product of labor.

Spain had set out after Columbus to bring as much wealth in the form of precious metal back to the mother country as they possibly could. A century after Spain had set this course for itself, it found that it was not the wealthiest country but had lost its leadership status and was sinking deeper into poverty.

Spain failed to invest domestically and build a productive infrastructure. Ignoring the lessons of the past, this appears to be the policy China is currently pursuing. In time they will pay a severe price for this lack of foresight.

CHAPTER 16

# Gold and Wealth

## METAL AND WEALTH DO NOT EQUATE

From the days of antiquity, it was recognized that gold was precious. Preciousness, as we have recounted, embraces the notions of universality and scarcity. Thus it is widely accepted as a medium of exchange.

The medium or measure of exchange is, however, never wealth. Wealth springs from the goods produced and exchanged. Spain, by hoarding gold, was not becoming wealthier, but as a result of its failure to deploy these resources was in decline. Gold does not equate to wealth.

This idea that wealth is inextricably tied to metal accumulation was not the singular failure of Bourbon monarchs, but was widely accepted or went unchallenged from the earliest of times through the First World War. One could readily hear the anguish of Moses in despair.

Among the myriad of articles agreed to at the Paris Peace Conference in 1919 following World War I was a provision that provided that Germany may not market or sell goods beyond its borders.

This was intended to not only prevent competition, but to prevent the victorious Allies from suffering a loss of capital, in other words, gold.

Foreign goods could flow into a country, so the thinking went, but gold should never leave. The victors did not grasp the meaning of currency.

Currency hoarding impedes economic progress; does not simulate it. As a result, the long-term effect on Germany and the world was tragic. This truly self-defeating belief of nations based on the false assumption that currency meant wealth spelled their doom.

Such a mindless notion is still alive and well on the world stage in the present time. It is indeed a form of protectionism, but should not be confused with steps that every nation is obligated to take to protect domestic producers from unfair competition and trade policies. Failure to render such protection will stand as an inexplicable failure of the Clinton and Bushes administrations. American leaders embraced the globalization strategy, which translated into favoring the foreigner over the domestic producer, and ultimately resulted in a decline in the power, prestige, and wealth of this nation.

## Late Nineteenth-Century Turmoil

The world's population was increasing, but the standard of living for most was falling due in no small part to misguided monetary policies.

As a result national antagonism took center stage. The politicians of the day were to learn an obvious lesson: that people will put up with tyranny, disease, poverty, and other ills, but never with the threat of starvation. A political synonym for starvation is revolution, and revolution as the world moved toward the twentieth century was what we experienced on a grand scale.

Broad segments of society stretching from Central and Eastern Europe through Russia into China, including advanced nations such as Britain with its caste system offering the poor nothing but hard work and an early death, needed but a spark to turn people and nations into raging fanatics.

This spark came with an assassination in Sarajevo in 1914, and gave rise to a new politician by the name of Vladimir Lenin preaching a doctrine of world revolution.

## Late Nineteenth-Century Monetary Policy Assures Twentieth-Century Disaster

The corrupting influence of wealth and power should never be underestimated. This stands as a universal lesson of life. Greed knows no bounds or limits. It is never satiated.

As people advanced up the economic ladder, from the most humble of beginnings, as hunter or scrub farmer, they sought to acquire. The measure of success in this effort, the measure of wealth, was my holdings versus my neighbors'.

Never mind that each had enough to meet his and his family's needs. If my neighbor has more, be it land or goods, then I must have more. Thus, I must strive, fight, steal, or corrupt in order that the world recognizes me and ultimately the state I represent as supreme.

Prussia, the force behind the German Union, was now a military force to be reckoned with. It had raw materials but little visible wealth, but that could be changed by simply absorbing its neighbors.

Now the stage was set for imperial dominance. The reichsmark, paper gold, would become an attraction for one and all. Merchants and bankers would come from great distances to feast at this new center of power.

In Europe both Germany and England could not reign supreme. It would be one or the other. In this international contest, Germany was totally committed. They had no idea of the long-term consequences.

England was not overly concerned about this challenge. They were watchful, but they shared a common bond with the Germanic background of the royal family.

France was another matter entirely. Their concern and envy eventually led to warfare with their eastern neighbor.

However in the early years of the German union, it was neither warfare nor competition that was stressed; rather it was opportunity. With invention, industrialization, and the drive for new markets, modernity was on the march. Other concerns would wait.

Most privileged Europeans still viewed this American experiment as anarchist, another word for threatening. The great danger was they would lose their status in society, their position, and God forbid, their wealth.

As the world approached the last third of the nineteenth century, the caste system mentality remained in place.

The rabble must never come to power. The nobility must retain the wealth. The modern nobility were the creditors. The poor, the lowly merchants, and those in search of a better life were the debtors. The wealthy were few, the debtors many.

Many a debtor, seeing no chance to free himself, got on a boat and came to America, where the streets were lined with gold, presumably.

The creditors had the money in Europe, but they also had problems. The challenge was to increase returns with a secure investment. This required caution and care.

If the creditor was to be certain of getting back the money loaned and invested, he must have control over all the levers of power. He must control the market. There must be no room for miscalculation. Until the Paris Conference, he found control of the market difficult to achieve. For example, he would lend gold, and the debtor would repay silver. The debtors were taking advantage of the market. "Ruinous," cried the creditors. "We must put an end to this."

There was no logical reason at all for the United States to go to gold. The United States had been on a bimetallic standard since Alexander Hamilton had set the currency standard in 1786, with a ratio of equivalence of silver to gold of 15 to 1.

In addition, the mountains of California and the hills of Nevada were chock-full of silver, and many a miner and farmer depended on this precious metal for a livelihood and liquidity.

At any rate, the world bought into gold mania. Within a decade, the world was on the gold standard: Germany, 1871; France and Spain, 1872; Russia, 1873; the United States, 1873–1874; Austria, 1877; and India, 1898.

The bimetallic standard died, hastened along by the Germans, who on turning to gold, proceeded to dump silver on the market, greatly depressing the price. This had an enormous impact, particularly on the western economy in the United States. This dumping moved the silver to gold ratio from 15 to 1 to as much as 40 to 1 by 1900.

Since 1834 the United States had officially priced an ounce of gold at $20.67. However, it was formalized in 1873–1874, post Civil War, when in legislation, silver as a measure in coinage was omitted. This drift to gold was further aided by the discovery of gold in California in 1848.

To finance the Civil War, as previously noted, the United States, with no place else to turn, issued Civil War greenbacks, which were not convertible into gold, at least not during the years from 1862 to 1879. Convertibility resumed in 1879, facilitated by discovery of gold and a significant decline in the market price, which served to bring the stated price of the paper and gold into parity.

On the international level, life became a pursuit of gold. Industrialization, which required increasing amounts of capital and liquidity, found none to be had. Prices fell, and as they did, labor had to bear the burden. Wages were severely squeezed, and unemployment rose. Nations withdrew to protect their interests. Friction between nations increased. Nations warred over colonies as they sought out new markets and cheap raw materials and labor.

The world went into a downward spiral. The United States suffered deflation from 1875 to 1896. With the money supply reduced by 50 percent, the gulf between those who have and the struggling majority intensified.

Radical economic policies were increasingly embraced. Cries for socialism, for more equitable distribution of the world's resources, dominated economic debate. A cleavage, hatred between labor and management, became the practice of the day. Could war, perhaps a world war, be far behind?

## Gold Masters Humanity

The enthusiasts for the gold standard, who had visualized a new and more prosperous time, concluded that the downturn must be due to some unseen force. After all, wise men do not make mistakes.

The consensus as economic conditions worsened was that all downturns are inevitable. This group, which previously had focused on purity of currency, now directed their attention to the concept of "cleansing."

Economic expansion brought with it excess. The supply-demand ratio would, over time, be out of balance. This could be seen in shortages, which always developed. With shortages came increases in prices, the mark of an unhealthy economy.

With a rationale that seemed to parallel the gold-silver debate, all the excess had to be excised, in the same way that a doctor has to remove a cancerous tumor.

Businesses must close, unemployment must rise, and as spending diminished, prices would fall back to their "correct" level. During this period, which was inevitable, everyone just had to make do. The world must diet and be on a stringent diet at that.

In the United States, as in Europe, there were no social safety nets, which simply meant that a large number of people would find themselves close to starvation. The strong would survive; the weak presumably never should have been occupants of the planet in the first place.

It was during this period that rugged individualist, tighten-your-belt thinking, became fashionable. Those who had shown great courage by taking to the prairie had to brave the elements and the Indians, and the strong had made it. City dwellers had to do the same.

The industrial revolution had wrought great change and brought major advances. Unfortunately it had a dark side, namely, periods of economic downturn. It was indeed troubling, but it must be the way the Creator wanted it, and thus we had to learn to live with it. Certainly we would be a stronger people for undergoing this trial.

The so-called classical economists embraced this philosophy, as did government leaders, including men such as Winston Churchill and Teddy Roosevelt. Later, in the 1930s, as the Great Depression worsened, Hoover embraced the same logic.

Simply put, downturns were inevitable, and there was nothing, except perhaps prayer, that could be done about it.

It took an English economist, who in time would play a most important role in many an economic debate in the early twentieth century, the man from Cambridge, John Maynard Keynes, to lead the charge in opposition to such thinking.

Keynes was a man who relied on logic to discover the truth on many an issue.

On the question of whether a downturn was inevitable and with it the social ills that followed, Keynes agreed that a cyclical downturn would produce a decline in prices, but arrived at a different conclusion from other economists of his day.

Certainly if goods were again attractively priced, people would buy them, but the unemployed could not buy at any price, attractive or not, and thus the solution could never lie in higher unemployment.

Keynes did advocate government intervention, but not as the solution but rather as an actor on the stage during periods of distress. Since the Second World War, his thinking has guided policy in the United States.

Europe, on the other hand, adopted social welfare after the Second World War as a result of the socialist influence on that continent.

Keynes, though arguing for limited government intervention, could never shake the tag of being an advocate of government intrusion, though he steadfastly disagreed. He believed in the private sector but would never accept the argument that government was somehow the enemy. The enemy, he believed, was poverty and despair.

Relief, in whatever form, was a solution. A dollar was a dollar, irrespective of where it came from. If the private sector could not deal with conditions, then government had a role, though it might be a temporary one.

The mind-set that downturns are inevitable and we must accept them, of course, has changed and modified over the years to the point where today such thinking is in full retreat. However, it has taken the better part of one hundred years of analysis and creative thinking to overcome that view.

Coming back to the gold standard, clearly the shortage of currency, that is, gold, was the underlying cause of the economic distress that plagued the West during the latter part of the nineteenth century.

Given that length of time, one might have thought men might have changed their thinking and perhaps reversed gears, embracing silver again. No such luck. Darwinian thinking had settled in. The strong survive. Gold was currency, and nothing more should be said about it.

The classical gold standard lasted from 1886 to 1914. As conceived, a nation with resources and labor, attractively priced, was an inviting place to invest. As investment was made, men were employed, business picked up, spending increased, and prosperity settled over the land.

As prices inevitably rose, other venues became more attractive. Gold left the country, seeking greater returns elsewhere, a nice simple system. Unfortunately, men were involved. Unemployment was never popular, and governments were overturned as gold exited the country on its way to greener pastures. To prevent this, governments began to tinker with the system. One ploy was to sell bonds at attractive rates to keep gold in the country. Import restrictions bolstered in-country activity. The classical gold standard was never fully embraced by any country.

Whether embraced or not, it was the system, and no amount of tinkering or manipulation could overcome the fact that there was a worldwide shortage of gold. Gold and only gold constituted final payment.

In an industrializing world, ever in more need of capital, such a shortage could and did finally prove catastrophic.

## America and the "New Gold World"

America was less enamored than others with this desire for monetary purity but went along in part because of the misbehavior of the American state banks and the debt it now had to address.

Germany and the rest of Europe endorsed this measure for reasons of power. Power of the state would be uncontested and rule over the people assured if the state controlled the purse strings.

For Europe it was about power and greed. Not only would but a few rule, but they and they alone would have access to capital. These men were both vain and greed-filled. Greed by definition means to be an idolater.

If there ever was an example of the best-laid plans going awry, this was it. The world would not, in the end, accept the suicidal implications of a gold-only standard, which meant poverty if not starvation for a goodly portion of the Western world.

Nations, while publicly endorsing the standard, began to move away internally to a more diverse and flexible system. Gold would stand as the universal money standard for paying down international debt while presumably providing some liquidity for growth and employment. However, the world's gold supply was unmistakably insufficient to accomplish these goals. There simply was not that much gold in the world.

There never was a time in history when gold bullion alone would have been sufficient to meet the legitimate needs of humanity. The gold standard subordinated humans to metal. Gold was to rule, and people were to serve this master. The madness of this, one might think, should have been readily apparent. What was it about silver that made it less acceptable as a standard than gold? Why did the standard have to be metal in the first place?

Today, with the advantage of hindsight, the absurdity of all of this speaks for itself. Yet the world went on to live with this suicidal system until the Great Depression.

## THE UNITED STATES CONFRONTS THE GOLD STANDARD

America's greatest challenge immediately following the Civil War wasn't gold or the rumblings for changes in the standard, but how to pay down the debt burden that had accumulated during the Civil War.

It is estimated the government borrowed three dollars of every four dollars loaned during the war. The bulk of the money borrowed was in the form of fiat currency, better known in that age as greenbacks.

It had been widely expected that they would be withdrawn from circulation with the payment of specie by the Treasury once the emergency had passed.

Confusing money with currency and suspicious of governmental intentions, the agrarian interests let out a hue and a cry as business turned down following the war. There was no way to persuade them that recall of greenbacks somehow would help business. Thus paper money was going to be with us indefinitely.

Further, the nation's farmers and westerners understood quite well, based on their prior experience, that withdrawing the greenbacks and replacing them with gold bullion and coin would, over time, result in the movement of this money east. Again they would be deprived and suffer at the hands of the eastern bankers.

There was, however, a slight problem with paper currency. Greenbacks were trading at fifty cents to the dollar. In other words, the value of gold and greenbacks did not equate. The value of gold was twice the value of the paper.

If paper money was going to remain legal tender and the value of this paper in terms of gold was only fifty cents to the dollar, then clearly the value of gold, which was limited in supply, must appreciate in price.

This was the conclusion of the renowned speculators Jay Gould and James Fisk, who saw the opportunity to buy gold and in effect corner the gold market for their own benefit.

The government and the people could have their paper, but Gould and Fisk were going to control the real money, namely, gold. What they hadn't planned on was that the United States Treasury would take this opportunity and sell gold in 1869, thus collapsing the price, which had been driven artificially higher by one third due to their speculation. This produced a severe market reaction to be known as Black Friday on Wall Street.

The concerns and suspicions of the farmers regarding paper money were well-founded. Gold had twice the value or purchasing power of greenbacks. Market speculators could buy greenbacks and wait for the day of redemption, when they would receive the nominal value or 100 percent in gold. From the standpoint of currency availability, since one unit of gold could purchase two units of greenbacks, a recall of greenbacks, if attempted by the government, would have resulted in a major contraction of the money in circulation.

Fortunately for all, it was never seriously attempted, though such a move had considerable support in Washington, which recognized that greenbacks were only intended to be a stopgap measure.

There was an important and enduring lesson that should have been learned at this juncture. The American economy, which had expanded its commercial and manufacturing potential in order to meet the war emergency, was now dependent on those same measures for future growth. Clearly, fiat money had played a critical role. To withdraw the same would be the equivalent of cutting off one leg of a four-legged chair.

This matter was the subject of considerable discussion for years. However, support for action was never garnered. As the depression lingered, the price of gold and other commodities fell. Eventually gold and greenbacks achieved parity, and greenbacks were slowly withdrawn from circulation.

CHAPTER 17

# The Extended Depression

## Confusion

A world in confusion: the blind, following the blind, following the...It is frequently said that ignorance is bliss. But ignorance pursued with passion and determination must have unimaginable consequences.

The world now entered a period stretching from the late 1870s to the early 1900s that for the great majority in this country and Europe could be summarized in a single word: despair.

There were moments that must have seemed to many, particularly those children and their exhausted parents laboring twenty hours a day for a pittance, as if the devil was managing events behind the scenes.

Certainly many twentieth-century "isms," which were born at about this time, must have been the devil's work.

Though the gold-greenback divide would fade in time, the money debate—West versus East, in America—would go on. To the westerner, the eastern argument for sound money, gold, was nonsense. Gold may be fine for the big-city types, but to the farmer, such an imperative threatened his solvency.

## The Demonetization of Silver—The Crime of '73

The hard money advocates might have to live with greenbacks, but this did not change their fixation with gold.

In the Coinage Act of 1792, Alexander Hamilton, in accordance with Western European standards, had endorsed coinage of silver and gold at a ratio of approximately 15 to 1.

Thus our system by definition was a bimetallic system. There was no purpose served in changing it other than to award the greed of those eastern bankers who did not understand the needs of the farmers and other hardworking Americans.

Though widely recognized but less often discussed, there was a continuing problem with the Hamilton Plan: the 15 to 1 ratio could not be assured in the marketplace.

For example, after German unification, when gold replaced silver as the money of the German state, huge amounts of silver were dumped on the market, resulting in the collapse of the silver price.

Though this was in fact a problem, it was not one that was insoluble. What was needed in a world undergoing massive change was innovation and imagination. Greater flexibility was called for, with elasticity of the money supply so essential for orderly growth.

Instead, the world looked to the past for guidance.

In 1873, ignoring the obvious consequences of doing away with a major portion of the money supply, Congress votes to demonetize silver.

The sweep of gold madness was in full force. We were going to worship the golden calf with our European brethren come heaven, hell, or high water. The result was hell indeed.

For the farmers, for the manufacturers, for the silver mining interests, for the small businesses in America, the only capital available to them would be gold, and gold was controlled by a very few bankers and money interests in the East and in London.

Their position was hopeless and remained hopeless not for a few years, but for decades. The world entered a period of depression that appeared interminable.

Since gold was as scarce as hen's teeth and the demand kept rising, the price per ounce soared. By the mid 1890s, the unemployment rate in America neared 20 percent. With business on its back, prices kept falling.

Economic stress was briefly alleviated when crop failures in Europe sparked demand for American agriculture, bringing gold into the country, thus allowing for limited expansion.

It surprises to this day that the circumstances of the time did not stimulate calls for secession in the West. The atrocious living conditions in the cities in the East might have produced revolution. Yet the nation held together. One might have thought, under these conditions, that the tight money interests, the goldbugs, would have at the very least been swept from power at the first possible moment.

However, the money interests controlled the press. Memories of the destabilized conditions in banking and finance after the Civil War and the widespread belief that westerners at heart were ignorant anarchists, if not socialists, interested in getting something for nothing, were sufficient to elect William McKinley twice, defeating a brilliant American, William Jennings Bryan.

Bryan's populist views, which in many ways mirrored those of Andrew Jackson when it came to money and his political philosophy, served as a guide for a later popular and long-serving president, Franklin Delano Roosevelt.

Standing before the delegates at the Democratic Convention, Bryan gave what is generally regarded as the finest political speech in American history. His words captured the moment and have that distinctive ring of truth even today as he said:

"Upon which side will the Democratic Party fight, upon the side of the idle holders of capital or upon the side of the struggling masses?...Having behind us the producing masses of the Nation and the world, supported by the commercial interests, the laboring interests, and the toilers everywhere, we will answer their demand for a gold standard by saying to them you shall not press down upon the brow of labor this crown of thorns, you shall not crucify mankind on a cross of gold."[ciii]

In league with Jefferson, Madison, and Jackson, Bryan was a man of the people. The people were above the money interests, not subservient to them.

The western interests were not entirely defeated. They did manage to have passed in Congress the Bland-Allison Act in 1878, requiring the Treasury to purchase between $2 and $4 million of silver at a ratio to gold of 16 to 1, double the market price.

Further, as depressed conditions pressed down and money remained scarce, the Sherman Act of 1890 was passed, requiring the Treasury to purchase 4.5 million ounces of silver a month, with the Treasury issuing notes to pay for the purchases.

## Goldbugs in Power

As one might imagine in a world in full worship of gold but with limited supply, accelerating demand, and silver an outcast, the US Treasury was faced with a redemption problem.

By late in the century, Treasury notes were money good, meaning that they could be exchanged freely for gold. People insisted on taking down the actual bullion. Unfortunately there was only so much gold to go around.

President Cleveland continued the legislatively mandated purchases of silver paid for by the issuance of Treasury notes, while the holders of government securities retained the right to redeem those notes in gold.

By the late century, net redemptions served to reduce Treasury holdings of gold by two thirds. The unintended effect of redemption was to further contract the money supply, certainly as measured in terms of gold.

The monetary system was further distorted as the Treasury accumulated silver. It appeared it might soon be faced with the necessity of making government payments in silver.

We were on the verge of coming full circle. While in other fields the world may have been making progress, when it came to currency, confusion abounded in America.

Shortage of money and the economic disequilibrium that resulted finally produced economic collapse, which has become known as the Panic of 1893. At the height of the crisis, unemployment approached 20 percent, with people walking away from their homes as they do in the current crisis.

The proximate cause of the crisis was not housing, but the collapse of the railroad bubble. Massive overbuilding, which financed the great railroad expansion, was fed to a considerable extent by European investment.

Faced with domestic pressures and gold in short supply, they witnessed the spate of securities being issued in America for silver and decided it was time to sell their securities for gold and return that gold to Europe.

The crisis worsened, with no visible signs of relief, until the discovery of gold in Alaska, which produced sufficient gold in tonnage terms to alleviate some of the pressure.

Yet the liquidity crisis was never relieved. If the immediate cause of the Panic of 1893 was railroad speculation, the underlying cause was a shortage of gold, so as liquidity pressures built, there was no way to relieve them.

This problem of liquidity struck again in 1907. This was not a railroad problem, but a speculative problem that led to what is now called the bankers' Panic of 1907.

On this occasion, the failure of the Knickerbocker Trust Company in New York set off a financial contagion that was contained by the noted intervention of J. P. Morgan and other New York investment bankers.

These panics were avoidable. The blind adoration of gold, which was the underlying cause of much of the tragedy, cannot be rationally explained. By this time in history, greed had been so burned into the psyche of the ruling classes that no amount of logic, no amount of common sense, could dissuade them from the path to self-destruction.

However, a few things were learned, very few perhaps, but important ones nevertheless.

In 1908 the Aldrich Commission was created to look into the crisis. In the report that detailed events, it became clear that a mechanism was needed that would prevent the failure of one financial institution from infecting others, and thus threatening the financial system. If a bank failed, it did so because it did not have the capital or the liquidity to meet its obligations. This failure would invite other failures. Thus a stopgap measure of some sort was needed. The stopgap would provide the temporary liquidity needed until the crisis passed.

This did make sense, even to the traditional bankers, giving rise to the prospect of a new entity, the Jackson bête noir, a central bank.

Many were fearful. They had every reason to be. Unless it was carefully regulated and controlled, it had the potential of becoming the monster Jackson feared.

## Voila! The Federal Reserve—A Magic Wand at Last

The power and preeminent standing of gold in the affairs of men, now certified with the victories of McKinley, were formally celebrated on March 14, 1900, with the passage of the Gold Standard Act.

The dollar henceforth was to be measured in terms of gold, and all those wishing to redeem Treasury notes or bonds would receive gold in exchange.

The United States was officially in the gold club. Henceforth monetary purity would reign, though it would never be defined. The money interests, the Federalists of old, the eastern bankers, and the creditors were victorious, but what in real terms did their victory mean?

For the many, it meant hardship. The fact was, had been, and remained the same, namely, that there was a shortage of gold in the world. A shortage did not herald greater prosperity, but the very opposite.

A shortage of money, if gold was literally thought of as money, or currency meant that the many would be denied access.

That had to mean fewer business formations, less infrastructure development, higher unemployment in a world with a growing population, less education, a dearth of inventiveness, and in short, less progress. In a very real sense, the plan was for the world to just stand still.

The shortsightedness of this is self-evident. Progress requires change. Perfection embraces the notion of change. Nothing finite can ever remain the same. Failure to move forward must result in decline. We are either moving forward or backward. There is virtually no such thing as maintaining the status quo.

For the bankers, market speculators, and the well-to-do, who had been at the forefront of this drive for pure currency that is gold, life was not about to turn out as they had planned.

Within a relatively short period of time, they witnessed and were severely impacted by two financial panics. This was far from Utopia.

It appears they were determined to ignore the obvious, that the problem lay with gold as a single standard and in short supply. No, they argued, the problem lay with this movement of gold across national boundaries.

When investment opportunities appeared in Europe, all the gold fled across the pond. When Europe was in need of American products, particularly produce such as grain, the gold came here. The global economy was on a permanent seesaw.

Gold, "God's money," could never be the problem, they reasoned, only this flow to and fro. What was needed, it was felt, was a stopgap measure to bridge periods when the flow was exiting the country.

What was the answer? A central bank, of course.

One might have concluded that sufficient time had now passed since the Federalist battles had been waged between Jefferson and Hamilton or between Biddle and Jackson. Passions might have cooled, they thought, so reason might now prevail. No such luck.

Bankers across the nation did not want a new big brother looking over their shoulder. The West and South, struggling as they were, would not accept a central bank aligned with eastern money interests, making their miserable lives more miserable.

However, there was one new factor in play this time that may have been decisive.

Note or currency circulation was limited to bank holdings of Treasury securities. With scarcity of currency, the banks had not the means to buy Treasuries.

The reserves of the seven thousand odd banks invariably went east to the New York "call money" market, which paid handsomely, at least till 1907–1908.

Suffering from this profound shortage of reserves, the banks accepted the legislation, and President Woodrow Wilson signed into law the Federal Reserve Act on December 23, 1913.

On the surface the Act as implemented was to be very democratic. It was never intended to be a replay of Biddle or Hamilton.

This Act called for the creation of a Federal Reserve Board of seven members. The country was to be divided into a maximum of twelve districts.

Each district was to have a bankers' bank, which would accept reserves and make loans to member banks. All national banks were compelled to join, and state banks were given the option.

The primary purpose of this Act was to provide temporary credit to those member banks short of currency or reserves in exchange for commercial paper, that is, loans on their books.

It would provide the banking community with what was most needed, namely, liquidity or currency to tide them over the periods of currency tightness. A single new United States currency was created, the Federal Reserve Note.

To be certain that this would not lead to a condition where the banks, in order to take advantage of this new facility, would simply make loans that would then be rediscounted with the Fed, it was required that such loans be backed with a 40 percent gold reserve.

The commercial paper acceptable in exchange for such loans had to meet certain criteria and was to be of short-term duration. This is still the requirement today.

Conceptually the idea was very sound, and it worked well. However, implicitly it recognized gold as the ultimate monetary reserve, which would prove to be a serious problem in the decades to follow.

Through this Act, the continuing nineteenth-century problem of illiquidity had been addressed. Unintentionally, the Act would justify actions that would be taken to move the commercial world market away from bullion or an inelastic system, to a paper system, that in the hands of government, or to be more precise, in the wrong hands in government, would produce, to be kind, bizarre results.

The vast majority of the people from the very beginning opposed the creation of a central bank. It was widely felt that such an institution would serve only the wealthy interests and be a hindrance to the workingman.

This was still the case when this Act was passed. However, as was the case in the creation of the First and Second Banks, the crisis of the times dictated passage. In those two cases, a charter for twenty years was approved. The Federal Reserve was to become a permanent institution.

At the time of enactment, it was thought that with the creation of twelve districts, power of these bankers' banks, central bank power, would be widely dispersed.

This turned out to be a miscalculation of the first order. The power of the director of the New York District, with the backdrop of Wall Street and money center banks, was in a far stronger position to wield power than any of his contemporaries. In the wrong hands, the misuse of this power would prove catastrophic.

## Late Nineteenth-Century Panics

The economic and financial collapse that engulfed the United States in the latter part of the nineteenth century, in retrospect, was a mild precursor of things to come.

The world had little or no grasp of the workings of currency and money or the importance of the money supply. The role of government was limited to protecting the interests of the powerful. With the exception of the cry for socialism by a few writers, intellectuals, and sociologists, mostly of European origin, widely viewed as both revolutionary and anarchist, there was no concerted effort to involve government in the affairs of men.

This laissez-faire philosophy was deeply ingrained, a holdover of the cultural great divide, stemming from the Middle Ages, the separation of the nobility from the peasantry.

This divide would slowly be called into question in Europe over the course of the past two centuries.

In the United States, a nation of immigrants, there was no such tradition. Men came here to free themselves from this caste system and religious bigotry. Success was to be measured strictly on what one accomplished, and the measure would be wealth. Wealth translated into access to capital, and capital meant access to cheap labor, cheap land, and gold.

The industrial revolution, giving rise to mass production, greatly expanded the potential for wealth, and for this wealth to be recognized required new markets.

Cross border trading had been well-established, but the Western nations were determined to protect their domestic interests by whatever means was necessary.

The time-honored way for a nation to protect its interests meant the acquisition of military power. If all else failed, you simply bludgeoned your neighbor. Warfare was and had always been a winner takes all proposition. The loser paid, surrendering lands and all the costs associated with the conflict.

In the Franco-Prussian War, France lost its position as the power on the Continent, its honor and dignity, land (Alsace-Lorraine), and a $1 billion indemnity to Germany.

Prussia, having been consolidated into the German Union, became the real power in Europe, leading to unbridgeable hostility between Germany and France, making World War I inevitable.

As this tragedy unfolded, the nations of Europe became consumed with the desire for wealth, thus the need for new markets.

The contest for colonies engendered continuing confrontation, thus feeding the desire for advanced weaponry. Smaller nations aligned themselves with the larger.

Across the ocean, the United States, with a continent to conquer, had no interest in this pursuit, with the notable exception of Teddy Roosevelt, who, with his Rough Rider personality, was determined to conquer the West, that is, the Western Pacific, if not the whole of Asia. At the same time, the United States was determined to keep the rest of the world out of the Western Hemisphere, or, as the Roosevelt policy in this regard would become known, the Monroe Doctrine.

Global imperialism was the order of the day. However, success was far from assured. The undeveloped world was there for the taking, but domestic conditions had to be in place to generate new wealth. This meant that every nation had to have sufficient capital to push forward. This required a healthy domestic economy.

There was no shortage of land or labor, particularly in the United States, but gold was another matter. Without gold every economy would falter sooner or later. Gold was critical. As previously noted, at the very time when the world needed an expanding money supply, silver was excised, resulting in a far smaller monetary base. Global economic expansionism was somehow to be achieved with less money.

Gold went from the status of being precious to a metal that was super-precious and scarce and for which there was no substitute. Silver could be converted into gold, but the ratio was no longer 15 to 1; by the turn of the century, it approached 40 to 1.

Defying common sense, the world chose to ignore this condition.

Making matters a good deal worse, the banking industry was fragile, ill-informed, and corrupt.

Banking was part and parcel of the private sector, which meant that government had no role to play except in cases of outright fraud, which might result in some light legislation from state legislatures when and if political pressure became intense.

As the demand for capital continued to press down, the banking industry, sensing profitability, was more than willing to serve as the intermediary making loans, backed ostensibly with nonexistent gold in a global daisy chain that would disintegrate with the breaking of the weakest bank.

There were no assurances or deposit insurance, and at the first sign of trouble, the savvy would run to their bank and withdraw their deposits and savings. Thus when the bank had exhausted its reserves, depositors were left stranded.

Loans, particularly mortgage loans mostly to farmers, were seasonal; though most were not long-term, none could be immediately called by the banks. Thus the system would grind to a halt as depositors fled.

A related problem was commodity prices. As the economy slowed, commodity prices fell, and this meant that farm revenue was insufficient to repay the loans. Collapse of the banking system throughout rural America and most of Europe was just a season away.

Gold was not evenly distributed across the globe. As precious as it was, it hopscotched around the world seeking the highest returns and the safest investment. That was not rural America or rural Europe.

Invariably it found its way into the financial markets, where the money center banks operated. Their portfolios consisted for the most part of "call money" or broker loans that paid high rates of return, were of very short duration, and were supported by securities that were readily marketable, a truly safe investment.

Thus a concentration of capital in New York and London took place under the watchful eyes of a few bankers, with names such as J. P. Morgan, who could pick and choose among their friends, classmates, and cronies, and the ever-present industrialists such as John D. Rockefeller and Andrew Carnegie.

It was a club, with the club members deciding who was to gain entry.

Initially, commitments of capital went to the club members, who then pursued investment strategies. These strategies passed through the ever-functioning and liquid securities markets. As a result, the daisy chain widened exponentially. Each link of the chain was driven by the prospect of higher return, and thus was slightly less secure than the previous.

The chain was widening exponentially, but money, that is, capital in the form of gold, was not keeping pace. In fact, with the death of silver, the money supply had long been in decline.

Each link of the chain was dependent on the last. Over time, the chain, under constant strain from exogenous events, including natural disasters, snapped at its weakest point.

With a desire to limit loss and protect oneself, the participants attempted to disgorge their holdings. However, each link was dependent. The house of cards teetered and then fell. This resulted in the closing of businesses, bankruptcy, massive unemployment, and depression. The bottom fell out.

The reaction of the private sector, the only sector in the game as it were at this time, to this unpleasant phenomenon was quasi-religious. The so-called wise men simply concluded that these developments were cyclical.

Translated, this meant that they were in the natural order of things. With the same sort of absurd reasoning as Sherman's "God's money," they concluded that the Creator had intended this result or else it would never have happened.

Though most difficult for one and all, it was a cleansing exercise, and presumably we would all benefit over the long term for it. As one contemplates this, I suppose the watchwords of the times were "purity" for money, which meant gold, and "cleansing" for the economy, which meant unemployment, poverty, and starvation.

Such nonsense guided the critical decisions a century ago, and we see and hear, at least at the extreme, the same message today. Europe and America are presently cutting public spending in order to reduce debt. By a reduction in spending, won't this increase unemployment? Greater unemployment produces revenue shortfall, resulting in more debt. Are we making any progress?

People are hopeful that this experiment will work, but it is far from a sure thing. At any rate, as their argument goes, there is no other solution. Really? I somehow hear the echo of purity or cleansing again.

I am reminded of the martini drinker, whose daily quota has now reached double digits, being told that all will be well if he cuts his intake back to, say, seven a day. What else could he be expected to do? Of course there are an infinite number of possibilities that haven't been considered. It may be true that this reduction might prevent his immediate demise, but death will certainly come, though perhaps more slowly.

In other words, the cutbacks in spending as agreed within the European Union and proposed for America are not necessarily the answer, but the public is being assured that they are.

The nineteenth century's dependence on gold had some positive aspects, including advances in productivity. People worked longer hours for the same compensation. This in turn drove invention, the need to find efficient tools to do the job.

The love affair with gold reached its apex with the passage by the Congress of the United States of the Gold Standard Act in 1900, which provided for the redemption of paper money, that is, the dollar, into gold at $20.67 per fine ounce.

In this country, the matter had apparently been finally settled, or so it seemed, until a series of failures and the need of the United States government for gold resulted in Rough Rider Roosevelt having to go hat in hand to Wall Street for assistance in obtaining gold from the club by selling them government securities.

This proved too much for Roosevelt and Washington, neither of whom had any use for competing power centers and other monopolies, private or public.

As the crisis atmosphere continued into the Wilson Administration, the need for a solution gave rise to the passage of the Federal Reserve Act in 1913.

To be sure, the bill creating this new entity passed over strenuous opposition in Washington and throughout the country. No one at the time could have foreseen the next chapter in this epic saga, the reincarnation of Francis Biddle. Had they been able to obtain a preview, I am certain the Federal Reserve would never have come into being.

The man appointed to the critical job of managing this new entity, the new Biddle as it were, was the infamous Ben Strong.

CHAPTER 18

# The Twentieth Century

## World War, the Great Depression, and Oh, Those Germans

There is no question that the wars, misery, and economic upheaval that the world experienced during the course of the twentieth century began long before the start of the century. Arguably they became inevitable with the formation of the German Union. This world-shaping event, which paralleled the collapse of the Austro-Hungarian Empire, remade the geography of Europe.

Germany, the new power in Europe, was flexing its muscles.

Union had not been accomplished through the use of diplomatic niceties and mutual considerations. It had been imposed by Prussia. As has been frequently said, Prussia was a military looking for a nation.

Prussia would demonstrate to the world both its brutality and determination to conquer when it engaged France in the Franco-Prussian War, 1870–1871. Occupying France, including Paris, starving the population, stealing territory, and forcing France to pay a huge indemnity resulted in lasting French hatred and fear of invasion, which resurfaced in 1914.

Between the Franco-Prussian War and 1914, a rigid and certainly divisive atmosphere prevailed on the Continent. Nations joined alliances—just in case. Hostility was the watchword. Feeding this hostility was insufficient currency and the increasingly intense competition for colonial markets.

Between 1914, with the outbreak of war, and American entry in 1917 into the conflict, the military battle ebbed and flowed, both sides suffering catastrophic losses, aided of course by the advances in weaponry, resulting in human tragedy and destruction never before seen in the Western world.

The financial cost was astronomical, almost immeasurable, and the debt burden that accompanied this holocaust essentially bankrupted every participating nation except for the United States.

The world never comprehended the extent of the disaster.

In 1919 the victors gathered once again in Paris to discuss the terms of the "truce." What would become known as the Treaty of Versailles was about to be imposed on the Germans. If the word *treaty* implies an understanding with both parties working out their differences, this was no treaty. This was surrender.

The Allies decided on the terms, and the German delegation was given the choice of signing or else. The Allies determined that Germany was solely responsible for the conflict, and in the long-established tradition involving European conflict, the loser pays for everything.

In order to decide on the amount of reparations due for the losses sustained, the conferees appointed a commission that, in 1921 dollars, decided on a figure of 269 million gold marks or approximately 100,000 tons of pure gold. Was there this much gold in the world? Whether there was or was not, it was well beyond the capacity of a defeated Germany to pay, but it was nevertheless treated by the Allies as fair given the level of destruction visited on France, and Belgium in particular, and the losses and costs of war absorbed by Great Britain.

The United States, now the most powerful country in the world and the principal creditor who had funded the participants, declined reparation payments. However, the United States and its private banks were owed a great deal of money and expected reimbursement. On this score they were going to be sadly disappointed. In time this disappointment proved calamitous.

Popular German feelings and attitudes were completely ignored. By the terms of the treaty, the Allies were telling the Germans to go to hell. In point of fact, they did not have the power to send them there. The Germans were going to remain with us, feared and despised.

*Life, Liberty, and the Pursuit of Money*

Unlike the Allies, the Germans took the word *treaty* to mean truce, not defeat. This belief was fostered by the fact that the Allies never occupied Germany, though they did occupy the Rhineland. Hitler later embraced this notion of a truce upon coming to power. During the war Germany had been successfully blockaded. The blockade was not lifted until nine months after the war had ended. This only served to further complicate the domestic condition of Germany, fostering unemployment and destitution.

As consumer and luxury goods began to flow back to Germany in 1921, the demand was great, and prices quickly doubled. Germany was about to get its first taste of inflation.

### The Question for Germany Was "Who Has Gold?"

One fact is certain. The German people did not have the gold. It is ironic that Germany, who had led the parade in 1870 in adopting the gold standard, was bereft of gold.

In 1914, just before the war, the Reich Bank, the central bank of Germany, had approximately $1 billion in gold.[civ]

There were approximately $550 million of gold coins, $150 million of silver, $500 million of banknotes, and $48 million of Treasury notes in circulation.[cv]

In total, the Germans had a little over $2 billion in gold or gold-referenced certificates and silver circulating.

With war, the German government canceled convertibility and called in gold on a voluntary basis. The people, as good and obedient citizens, responded and were given "paper marks" in exchange. With war's end, the German people were holding paper, but by some estimates owed $147 billion in gold marks. Something on the order of $89 billion of these liabilities were funded with long-term loans, but over $50 billion was floating-rate short-term debt and was coming due.

The treaty, of course, was no help at all. Under its terms, Germany was dismembered. It lost its merchant marine. It had to surrender approximately 11 to 15 percent of its most productive territory, mostly to the French. It surrendered its colonial investments, depriving it of some $75 million in annual income. It was forced to transfer to the Allies rolling stock, chemicals, and coal, and to put the icing on the cake, it was prohibited from exporting goods, that is, selling to other countries, which would have generated foreign exchange.

Under these conditions Germany had three options. It could default on its debt; it could raise taxes; or it could print paper. It chose the latter, as the first two were politically impossible. Germany printed and printed and printed some more. As this turned into an inflation rout, the government, to protect the worker, indexed his wages, assuring hyperinflation.

This resulted in the collapse of the currency. However before final collapse, the currency over time suffered a shocking loss of value.

In July 1921, one dollar would exchange for 81 marks. In June 1922, one dollar would get you 600 marks. In November 1922, one dollar would exchange for 8,000 marks. In January 1923, the Reparations Commission, determined to find ways to make Germany pay, severed the Ruhr, and one dollar now equaled 10,200 marks. By July 1923, one dollar equaled 1 million marks, and the decline in the exchange rate was accelerating.

The currency collapse, euphemistically referred to as hyperinflation, had insidious ramifications. In dire need of currency with value, Germans were forced to sell their heirlooms and other treasure. Foreigners simply looted the country. Under the financial strain, institutions collapsed. The middle class, the bulwark of every society, became impoverished.

The resulting trauma played no small part in the Germans later striking out at everything foreign as well as their domestic enemies. Though they were certainly German citizens, the Bolshevik-led German communists and the most prominent minority and scapegoat throughout Western history, the Jews, became the prime targets of German rage.

## The Prelude to the Great Depression

Two facts became immediately clear with the onset of war: it would last a long time, and it would require expenditures far in excess of the world's accumulated savings and investments. This meant debt, money to be borrowed to meet the needs of the private sector, however restrained, and the military. As England's industrial capacity had been stretched to the limit, the only option open was to borrow from the one nation that could deliver the goods. That, of course, was the United States.

The financing for these purchases fell on the private sector since intergovernmental loans were virtually nonexistent. After America's entry into the war, Congress provided limited financing. The key credits came from the New York banks.

As the war went on, the capability of Europe to pay its short-term obligations was exhausted. Ben Strong, as president of the Federal Reserve Bank of New York, recognizing the financial difficulty, stepped in to encourage further lending by the New York banks.

Debt was simply being piled up on debt.

Though Britain owed American institutions large sums, they had expected reparations payments and were thus victimized, caught in the middle; not able to collect from Germany, they couldn't pay what they owed.

The bankers, who were certainly caught in the middle, joined forces with the war hawks, encouraging US entry into the war as the battle of the Atlantic heated up in 1916.

The armistice did little to change the facts on the ground and the financial picture.

Britain was broke. The physical ravages of war had severely impacted France and Belgium, and the British naval blockade was hurting all of Europe. By war's end, Central Europe faced starvation. The need for assistance was widespread. American production had made it possible for Europe to sustain the conflict, and now only America had the resources and the capital to repair the damage.

The American Relief Administration, under the direction of Herbert Hoover, played the most prominent role in coming to Europe's aid. Eventually America contributed significantly to this rehabilitation effort. This undertaking was financed through more loans, not grants, increasing further the debt burden emanating from the war.

These demands, combined with those of the American consumer, contributed to an inflationary boom through 1919 and 1920.

Given these demands and the mountain of accumulated debt, it became imperative for the Federal Reserve Board to keep rates low. Expanding the money supply was an invitation to price inflation and unacceptable, violating the argument for the creation of the Federal Reserve in the first place. Thus central banks began to take steps to increase rates to slow credit demand. Though their intentions were the best, this was precisely the wrong medicine.

The global economy slowed, but global debt remained. Inflation wasn't the problem. Debt was the problem. Debt as a percentage of disposable income was too great against the resources available to the war-weary citizens of the world. In Europe and the United States, a certain rationalization took hold.

Somehow the Treaty of Versailles and the payment of reparations by the Germans would solve the problem. As the statistics previously addressed clearly show, Germany could not possibly have paid off the debt during the lifetime of its citizens.

The world had to face up to the unpleasant reality that it had but two options. The first was simply to write off the debt. If that course of action had been taken, the private lenders around the world, including a large segment of America's banks, would have faced bankruptcy. The second option was devaluation. Devaluation is not a judgment about a people or nation. It is recognition of reality. The world was not about to face the facts. The massive accumulation of debt had changed everything.

The second critical factor was that monetary gold had not kept up with the marked increase in the demand for capital. Gold was the world's payment standard. The amount of gold in the world available for commerce was critical. As the United States had been supplying most of the world's goods, the movement of gold to the United States, prior to and after our entry into the conflict, was dramatic. The United States had not only become the largest holder of gold, but held twice as much as the next nation. Gold was indeed the standard, but its relative scarcity necessitated that nations depend on their domestic currency to carry on domestic and international trade.

In accepting payment in another nation's currency, the holder had the right to exchange that currency for gold. Gold was not keeping pace with debt accumulation. To borrow from Mr. Keynes, we were in a game of musical chairs. At some point when the music stopped, someone was going to be without a seat.

A further complication was the position of Great Britain. With gold scarce, more sterling bills were entering the world's money market.

This combined with the crisis in Germany forced Great Britain to abandon the gold standard in September 1931, and sterling suffered a 25 percent decline in value.

Years earlier Winston Churchill, Chancellor of the Exchequer, had aggravated conditions with an enormous blunder in 1925, reestablishing convertibility of sterling to gold at the prewar level. At prewar parities, gold was sufficient to cover about one half of England's trade imbalances.

War had changed the world and trading relationships. Empires were gone, and new and much smaller countries were now printing currency, whose value was questioned.

With the pent-up demand for goods, nations turned on the printing presses. With war, global commerce had increased enormously, and thus the amount of gold needed to support business at the ratio that existed prior to the war would have at the very least had to double. As a result the price of gold kept rising.

The world was in desperate need of rebalancing. The central banks of the world should have ushered in a measured process of devaluation of their respective currencies against gold or moved away from gold as the payment standard. The exception was the dollar, which had appreciated during the Great Conflict, with the United States now holding most of the world's monetary gold.

At the beginning of the war, there were three great countries; and at the end there was just one, the United States. This was not recognized, and with the central banks leading the way, a series of fundamental mistakes were made that within a period of nine years brought the world of commerce to its knees.

The decline in reserves of the European nations was self-evident. There was nothing opaque about what was happening.

These nations had suffered massive erosion of reserves as they increased debt and the money supply. Something bordering on common sense should have instructed the central bankers that the time had come to devalue their currency.

Since no one would accept in a commercial exchange something less than equivalent value, it meant that nations such as the United States no longer engaged in trade with, say, Great Britain at the current currency level. The conversion price of sterling had to be adjusted to reflect the change in circumstances.

When a host of nations finally went off the gold standard, it was implicit recognition that their currency was worth less. In the case of Britain, the official exchange rate for gold had been $4.86 per ounce, the prewar exchange rate.

By 1919 sterling was worth $3.81 per ounce of gold. This of course meant the savings of the average Brit on the world stage could buy 25 percent less than they had prior to the war. Wars are expensive indeed. In the end, if you borrow money and deplete your savings, you have to pay the piper, and that applies to individuals and to nations.

By 1920 it cost the average Brit twice the 1914 prices to pay for the identical amount of goods. As the world entered the 1920s, the shooting war had ended, but stability, or anything approaching it, was at best a distant dream. With empires broken and the great European nations wallowing in debt, social cohesion was called into question. Staring into the face of starvation and having no place to turn, the people turned to strange new economic philosophies. The leaders looked to their central banks for an answer.

The peacetime battle cry was "open the printing presses." Germany, which had suffered defeat and loss of territory and was faced with the prospect of paying reparations three times greater than their annual gross national product, led the printing charge.

The price level in Germany by 1922 was over one thousand times higher than the prewar level, and by 1923 was over a trillion times higher. Many of

*Life, Liberty, and the Pursuit of Money*

the smaller countries in Central Europe suffered a similar fate. This period from 1922 to 1924 was referred to as the period of hyperinflation.

The United States, though a major contributor to Europe's reconstruction, was able, as a result of the gains in savings and trade during the war, to minimize the price effects here. In order not to catch the European disease, the Fed adopted a strategy of keeping the amount of credit constant during this period of turmoil. In other words, to be certain that we would not suffer a bout of inflation, the Fed, or to be precise, Ben Strong, decided to restrain the growth in the money supply.

Prior to 1924 this policy, though cautious, was logical. By 1924, when it became clear that agricultural prices were in free fall with most Americans living on farms, this was troubling. Exacerbating the problem, governments without revenue, which necessitated sharp cutbacks in spending, could no longer be depended upon to drive the world's economic engine.

Strong, now sensing deflation, reversed policy by adopting an easy money strategy with the explicit intention of holding the price level.

This was a critical step for business, as declining prices meant a reduction in sales and higher unemployment.

In Europe hyperinflation brought with it exchange rate instability. The uncertainty surrounding the price of currency had a major adverse effect on investment. With no certainty as to the correct currency price, one could not evaluate risk. Thus investment was constrained. Without investment, without certainty of exchange, there could be no trade.

Certain countries had not suffered through hyperinflation, such as Italy, which simply accepted the new price structure as a given. Others, Germany and Austria among them, pegged or tied their currency to the value of gold and the dollar. They would no longer print money without restraint. They would print enough to keep the value of their currency stable against the dollar and gold. Contrary to popular belief, after the period of hyperinflation, economic conditions in Germany stabilized until the crash in 1929, which ended foreign investment and led to the rise of Hitler.

The remaining nations, including Britain, the Netherlands, and Scandinavia, allowed their currencies to float, meaning it would be left to the market to set the price.

CHAPTER 19

# The Price of Currency

## I Guess We Need a New Currency

That was for certain. However, before the Germans issued a new currency, the rentenmark, temporary money, in 1923, the Reparations Commission had managed to collect from Germany approximately 1,400 million gold marks in 1921 and 1922.

In 1924 Germany replaced this temporary money with a new reichsmark, which was assigned the value of the prewar gold mark. Supposedly nothing had changed. The absurdity of this speaks for itself. The creditors were going to get their pound of flesh.

By the mid twenties, with the newly introduced reichsmark in place, the economic picture began to brighten as foreign investment began to pour into Germany. It was as if the world finally came to the realization that global prosperity was in part dependent on German recovery.

After all, France, England, Belgium, and others expected to be paid. The American bankers wanted to be paid, and Germany offered enormous potential for business after their extended period of depression.

The central banks couldn't resist getting into the act, and they encouraged through their easy money policies more lending and investment to Germany.

The year 1924 was a year of currency realignment for the Allies as well. The gold standard morphed into the gold exchange standard. The persistent shortage of currency finally forced a critical rethinking of the matter. The British pound and the US dollar henceforth stood with gold as investment currencies interchangeable in trade. Led by Ben Strong, president of the Federal Reserve Bank of New York, easy money was now pursued with a vengeance.

With stability, a boom in the German economy stimulated by foreign loans and investment ensued. In 1926 and 1927, industrial production increased by over 30 percent. With money to be made, loans and investment from the United States, London, and France flooded Germany.

A bubble of the first order was being created. No one seems to have noticed, and certainly no one seems to have cared. This bubble rivaled the stock market bubble, which started shortly after, and much later the infamous housing bubble in the United States in the early years of the twenty-first century.

This massive amount of investment destabilized Germany. Liabilities exceeded assets by a ratio of 3 to 1. The Germans used money intended for long-term investment to cover short-term operating expenses. Germany was borrowing enormous sums but was making inadequate provision to repay.

All it took was a crisis elsewhere for the global economy to unravel.

## All Good Bubbles Come to an End

History records that the global crisis began in 1929 with the panic on Wall Street. Before it ran its course in 1932, it extinguished the capital reserves and savings of untold numbers of people across the globe and broke the American banking system in the process.

In point of fact, the crisis began with a far less celebrated event in 1928, the untimely death of Ben Strong of the Federal Reserve Bank of New York. Strong, a secretive man, had an unusually close and cordial relationship with Mr. Montagu Norman, governor of the Bank of England.

Strong had run the New York Fed from the time of his appointment as if it was his private bank. He had attended the organizing conference in Georgia that paved the way for the creation of the Federal Reserve that became law in 1913 when President Wilson signed the legislation.

It could be said that Strong was there from the very beginning and he and he alone would set policy.

As a confidant of J. P. Morgan, and with his influence, Strong was made head of the New York Fed in 1914 and basically developed its open market operations, which meant the buying and selling of government securities as he saw fit.

An Anglophile, he did everything in his power to ease the financial pressure on England, pursuing an extraordinarily easy money policy that was never subject to review.

With his demise, his successors sought to take corrective action, which literally meant closing the barn door after all the horses had fled. This gave rise to monetary tightening that had profound international implications.

## Mr. Winston Churchill, Chancellor of the Exchequer (1925–1929)
### "Winnie" Breaks the World, and the World Will Never Be the Same

Mr. Strong's easy money policy inflicted extensive damage. However, he had help. Mr. Strong, like so many other bureaucrats through the ages, proceeded with the best of intentions, but wreaked havoc instead of progress. At heart he was a true Federalist.

His intention was to restore England to greatness. His partners in this great scheme were Churchill and Montagu Norman, the governor of the Bank of England.

Great Britain, with its far-flung empire and its reputation as the world's leading financial center, was keen on returning to convertibility, a critical step in the return to world power status. Convertibility had, of course, been suspended during the war.

In the mind of the London government, the war years had been an aberrant period that should be put behind them.

Great Britain and the Allies had been victorious in the Great War, which translated meant the reestablishment of the power, influence, and world domination that had existed before the onset of hostilities in 1914. In the minds of men like Churchill, pound sterling had been supreme before the war, and by jove, it was going to be supreme after.

It was simply a matter of wealth. Yes, the war had been costly, but that somehow should be put aside, and whatever losses had been incurred should be borne by the Germans, who were obligated under the treaty. English wealth should not be disturbed. Thus convertibility must take place at the prewar exchange rate.

Mr. Churchill and company failed to look closely at the statistics. World trade, which had experienced a significant expansion after the war, beginning in 1925 and in subsequent years began to flatten out. Britain's trading partners were not interested in exporting goods to Britain and being paid in overvalued sterling.

Overvaluation had a profound impact on the financial state of Great Britain well into the future. Worse still, an artificial exchange rate was a rogue wave, destabilizing and making vulnerable the global ship of commerce. From this point on, the world was held hostage to unforeseen economic developments.

Clearly Churchill felt that Britain still ruled the world, at the very least the world of commerce and finance. Reality could be ignored, presumably for the greater glory of England.

England was no longer the center of the universe. That was for certain. International politics required that England go on pretending. To accomplish that required outside help. That help would come in spades from the one entity in the world that had the capacity to provide it, the Federal Reserve Bank, the central bank of the United States, and its Anglophile president, Mr. Ben Strong.

Churchill may have been living in the past, but the man in the street, the producers, weren't fooled for a second. They and the market participants across the world immediately recognized that this artificial conversion price for the pound meant that gold and other currencies were cheap in relation to the pound.

Monetary reserves fled Great Britain, the largest amounts coming to the United States.

Mr. Strong and the Fed understood that if this continued, Britain would be forced to devalue. That of course would have been the intelligent thing to do, but devaluation meant a reduction in wealth. Instead, Mr. Strong and the Fed decided that the mother country and its currency needed defending. The best defense would be an aggressive offense.

This gave rise to a two-pronged strategy. The Federal Reserve adopted an easy money strategy, keeping rates artificially low, and the money center, New York banks, were encouraged to lend and invest incremental reserves in England.

This policy was put into effect, though Strong and the bankers knew they were overextended to Great Britain. Debt was to be piled on debt.

Meanwhile capital was fleeing Great Britain. A flood of reserves, combined with easy money, found its way into the US stock market. We refer to this period as the Roaring Twenties. At this point nature's God may or may not have intervened, but certainly nature did. To the surprise of associates and friends, Mr. Strong died in 1928.

His successors surveyed the monetary wreckage—given Strong's penchant for secrecy, many for the first time. Genuinely dismayed, they proceeded to cut back on the rate of growth in money.

New York loans to Great Britain virtually ceased by 1928.

However, the money horses were running wild. The overextended American banks expected to be repaid; otherwise they would be in financial difficulty.

Great Britain, France, and Germany were up to their ears in debt. Europe was in a liquidity bind. Gold reserves were no match for the international capital demands resulting from the massive overhanging debt and easy money.

All it would take was a catalyst to bring the house down. That was provided by the largest Austrian bank, Creditanstalt, which failed in early 1931. The storm quickly moved to Germany in May 1931, and to Britain by the fall of that year.

The London money market was roiled by this chain of events. Withdrawals of capital escalated as depositors, fearing the loss of everything, began to run for financial cover.

Britain turned to Germany, but as Germany was in a bind, as previously described, Germany froze its debt payments to Great Britain on July 31, 1931.

Britain, faced with serious capital demands from all sides, finally faced the inevitable and allowed its currency to float, the exchange rate being set by the market, to relieve this pressure. This resulted in a devaluation of as much as 30 percent.

The Brits literally did this as a last resort. Earlier they had raised rates from 2.5 percent to 4.5 percent and then to 6 percent after the initial devaluation, attempting to forestall further capital outflow. These decisions were Britain's way of saying, "We are not in this together; every man or country for himself." They shortly abandoned the gold standard, a standard, it might be said, they had initiated in the first place, under Newton.

It could be said that 1931 was the year of universal pulling back. Europe ran for cover, and so did America. Though it wasn't widely recognized at the time, or for that matter understood today, the steps Britain took, including floating the currency, allowed it to escape the worst of the ravages of the Great Depression.

## France Stands, Waits, and Stagnates, Then True Leadership Provides the World with the Answer

French hatred and fear of Germany is renowned. It transcends the typical friction and competition that naturally occur between nation-states and peoples.

France's defeat in the Franco-Prussian War, the goods embargo and starvation of Paris, and the punitive terms exacted on France at war's conclusion certainly played a role.

From the formation of the German Union, Germany united, measured by population, was twice the size of France.

After the Great War, driven by lingering fear and revenge, France was determined to get the last drop of blood from the German people.

Efforts in the private and public sector to relieve famine conditions in Germany were resisted by France. Much of France was destroyed during the war, and the French believed that they alone deserved relief. Germany and the German people should be treated as outcasts. As far as the French were concerned, the Germans were to have but one role in the life of Europe: to pay reparations. Unfortunately, reparation payments were not forthcoming as France had expected.

France was thus forced into the "debt trap" and began to borrow heavily. Sovereign debt doubled between 1919 and 1923. This in turn forced a government deprived of reparations revenue to inflate the money supply. At the time there appeared to be no other alternative.

With economic conditions worsening, a new government under Monsieur Poincaré came to the fore on July 23, 1926. It "enacts heavy taxes and balances the budget for the first time since 1913."[cvi]

Poincaré, unlike Churchill and Montagu Norman in 1925, got it. He recognized that it was impossible to deflate the economy to the prewar level in order to bring into balance the productive capacity of France, minus government debt, with currency value.

To return France to prosperity, he recognized a two-step process was required. He increased taxes to pay debt and devalued to recharge the economy and reduce consumption. In June 1928 France devalued the franc by 80 percent.

Poincaré demonstrated extraordinary leadership. I think it is fair to say that what America needs today is this type of leadership. Without Poincaré France would have descended into the abyss. His foresight and courage prevented France from falling into a chasm, from which it might never have recovered.

"Keynes hailed the decision as visionary, with the implicit write-off of debts and the return of confidence, the French economy boomed. From the second semester of 1927 to the first semester of 1930, French industrial production increased by 30 percent. And the French economy proved resilient to the Depression until 1931."[cvii]

CHAPTER 20

# Depression Overwhelms the United States

## Central Bank Madness

At the outset of the twentieth century, the United States was the only major country without a central bank.

This was possible because the world was on the gold standard. As stated earlier, reserves or gold moved to the place of greatest opportunity. For much of the nineteenth century, that had been the United States. As opportunities arose these reserves would shift to a new locale, depriving the former of the seed needed for investment, resulting in a slowing of their economic growth.

The dynamic had one major advantage: it served to correct imbalances and rising costs, particularly labor costs, which inhibited further investment.

It was a semiautomatic system, not requiring a gatekeeper. It was far from perfect. In a world of limited international economic activity and that being mostly agricultural, this system worked.

Gold was the critical reserve. In 1913 the United States held approximately one third of the monetary gold reserves, while Europe held 60 percent. Financial power thus rested in Europe, with London at the center.

The First World War totally shifted the balance of financial power. By 1925 the United States held 43 percent of the world's reserves and Europe but 32 percent. In addition, since the United States provided the financial wherewithal for the combatants to prosecute the war, it would become the dominant creditor nation. Everyone owed America.

In 1919, though it still had to carry an impossible debt load from the war, much of Europe needed rebuilding. Having been starved during the conflict for consumer goods, demand quickly outstripped domestic supply.

In 1920, with an eye on inflation, the Fed increased rates. The money supply fell by 9 percent, and the United States economy contracted.

By mid-1921 the Fed decided to reverse course. Industrial production began to surge, and the money supply grew rapidly, most notably from 1921 to 1925. By 1924 the Fed policy focused on the British problem and began encouraging capital outflow to facilitate the return to convertibility by the British in 1925. Further, Mr. Ben Strong on his own was determined to return Great Britain to its prewar greatness. He sought to accomplish this through low interest rates and easy money to stifle London capital coming to the United States.

Behind the scenes a bizarre series of events was taking place, which to this day defy rational explanation. There can be no question of the nature of the close relationship that existed between Mr. Montagu Norman, head of the Bank of England (1920–1944) and Mr. Ben Strong, the singular power at the Federal Reserve Bank of New York.

In Norman's mind, a full recovery from the cataclysmic event known as the First World War meant that Britain must regain its rightful place as world leader and London as the leading financial center, which it had been for generations. Mr. Strong agreed with this view wholeheartedly.

Their subsequent decisions resulted in global disaster. A third person of influence who shared their view was Winston Churchill; though birthed by an American mother, he was a direct descendant of the first Duke of Marlborough. Soldier, writer, artist, historian, orator, and famed leader of Great Britain as prime minister during and after the Second World War, Churchill served during the interwar years in a number of capacities, including Chancellor of the Exchequer. In that role his influence was paramount.

Appointed by Parliament under the government of Stanley Baldwin in 1924 to serve in an office comparable to the secretary of the Treasury of the United States, Churchill was determined to see Britain returned to former greatness. How strongly he felt can be read into a statement he made many years later while serving as prime minister that he would never preside over the dissolution of the British Empire.

Under the British system of government, officeholders serve under the prime minister but are appointed by and report to Parliament. They can only be removed by Parliament. Thus they hold power in their own right. The decision thus to return to the gold standard in 1925, as Chancellor, was Churchill's to make.

For five years London had been pressing deflation on the British population in preparation for the day that it returned to the gold standard. By keeping rates high and slowing the growth in the money supply, it was expected the prewar price of sterling could be reestablished when the suspension of the gold standard expired in 1925.

To bring this about, great hardship was to be visited on the people, with prices falling, bringing with it unemployment, most notably in the coal industry. This set the stage for a social explosion.

Such an explosion in fact took place when coal miners briefly struck, bringing a suggestion from Churchill that machine guns be used to force them to return to work. The message? Anything to restore Britain to greatness.

Many economists advised against returning sterling to a fixed level to gold at the prewar level of $4.86, including the sage of the age, Lord John Maynard Keynes, who endeavored to explain the insanity of this and the hardship in loss of wages and decline in prices that were certain to follow.

Montagu, together with his associates at the Bank of England, prevailed on Churchill to go forward; after all, the greatness of Britain came before everything, including the people.

Churchill took this absurd advice, and Britain, together with the Netherlands, returned sterling to the exchange price that existed against the major exchange currencies, such as the dollar, prior to the war on April 28, 1925.

Completely ignoring the reality of enormous debt from the war, having lost its manufacturing and trading primacy to the United States, this action would effectively raise the real cost of British war debt. The cost of British exports would be higher and, in this still fragile global environment, less competitive.

Later Churchill, recognizing the enormity of the mistake, blamed it all on Montagu Norman. This decision, on top of the immense European debt, assured the coming of the Great Depression. In fact, it hastened it.

As difficult as the situation was, it might still have been possible to avert a global crash if the United States, and specifically the Federal Reserve, had been able to rise to the occasion.

## Mr. Ben Strong at the Helm

Once the decision was made by the British government to reestablish a fixed exchange regimen, with gold priced against sterling at the prewar level, then it was assumed by the British that their global friends would cooperate.

Montagu looked to Ben Strong to influence decisions in New York in order to shift to London much of the financial activity that had migrated to New York during the war.

Strong shared the British goal. And what was that goal? To demonstrate conclusively that Britain was still the preeminent world power. Never mind that Ben Strong was an American and the most powerful and influential person in finance in the United States. American interests had to be subordinated to those of Britain.

Britain was big brother, and apparently the Americans were to be treated as the poor second cousins. This bias of Strong alone, while harmful, might not have resulted in great damage if it had just remained a bias.

However, in a further marvelous demonstration of ignorance, both Strong and Norman accepted as a given the underlying principle that the price of gold was immutable, standing presumably alongside the Creator in that respect.

The war had been a brief aberrational event that had interrupted the good and presumably ordained order of things. They would jointly endeavor to put Humpty-Dumpty back together again. Ignorance bordering on insanity was at work.

In the light of history, it is easy today to point out the serious misunderstandings, miscalculation, and mistakes that were made during the interwar period. The irony is that men such as Strong saw themselves in a positive light, acting with the best of intentions to bring all of us and our children a more prosperous and peaceful world.

These were men of considerable renown hailed, at least initially, by their peers in the financial industry as well as academia and government. There were no signs of venality. Stupidity, yes, of course, but stupidity is not a form of absolution.

Certain questions demand answers. Why was there not an ongoing comprehensive review process in place in Congress? Congress has a duty of oversight under the Constitution. Certainly the speculative fever in the stock market and the associated debt should have alerted that body that not all was well. Congress eventually moved to rectify the problem and passed in 1935 an Act creating a Federal Reserve Board in Washington, where policy would henceforth be made and reviewed by a committee whose members would be appointed by the president. Unfortunately by 1935 the depression was well along.

The formation of a committee—was this enough? I would suggest the answer is a resounding no. The difficulties that will be addressed later, post the Bretton Woods Conference, clearly indicate fundamental weakness in the decision-making process. That remains the case today.

What is the fundamental problem?

The underlying problem is power. Great power can never be centralized, placed in the hands of one or, for that matter, a few men in a democratic society when their decisions are not subject to review and reversal and they are not subject to removal by the governed if necessary.

The reason that Andrew Jackson vetoed the Biddle legislation renewing the charter of the Second Bank of the United States was because he could clearly see, as none of his advisors did and as most of the rest of the world has yet to grasp, that all power is corrupting. Centralized power is a death knell.

Jackson referred to the Second Bank as the "hydra of corruption." He saw it as a private bank benefiting the wealthy at the expense of the working class and, as such, a threat to democracy.

At one point he put it succinctly that private, monopolistic, independent of government regulation should be denied access to the public's business. Lord Acton, the British philosopher and statesman, put it most succinctly: "Power tends to corrupt, and absolute power corrupts absolutely. Great men are almost always bad men."[cviii]

What is corrupted? The answer to that is reality. The powerful decision maker does not see the distortion. He sees nothing wrong in buying a $50,000 shower curtain or hosting a $6 million luncheon or a $12 million wedding or in subordinating the interests of the United States to those of another nation. In his stupor a new reality sets in, justifying any action as he surrounds himself with sycophants and those attracted by power.

The problem of the Strongs and Normans of the world is that their unrestrained power, with its consequent abuse, invariably produces disaster as they and their organizations self-destruct.

As an excuse for this behavior, they will later argue that they were acting under orders or with the best of intentions. Dante dealt with the matter of intentions very well when he simply concluded that hell was filled with people of good intentions.

## STERLING TO GOLD AT $4.86

To the rest of the world, the Churchill-Norman decision did not appear to be a great moment. Wasn't this a British matter? It would impact the Commonwealth for sure, but beyond those borders, did it have any significance?

The first indications that it did were immediately evident in the decisions made by the Bank of England and British business.

The world's commercial interests, together with speculators and traders, recognizing that the real value of sterling was nothing like $4.86 per ounce of gold, simply began selling sterling to get the gold.

Sterling was worth by most estimates 30 percent less than $4.86. The average price of sterling during the early twenties was $3.80. If the British were willing to pay more for sterling than it was worth, then by all means the rest of the world would sell it to them.

Notice the law of value and equilibrium at work here. Not only would the British sell it now, but they would keep selling it until the equilibrium level was reached. At the same time, British business was endeavoring to sell its domestic products overseas, priced in sterling, which was overpriced by 30 percent. This of course was impossible in a world of global competition. One simply cannot compete if one's goods are priced 30 percent higher than one's competitors; in most cases that meant the Americans.

Thus British exports went into steep decline. In response to this, the Bank of England should have immediately reduced the gold-sterling exchange rate by 30 percent. This would have been an admission that the net wealth of Great Britain was not what it was prior to World War I. Instead, the British set out to reduce prices and wages by 30 percent to remain competitive. This was madness carried to the extreme.

British businesses informed their workers that they were henceforth going to work the same hours for 30 percent less in pay. This produced a worker revolt and led to work stoppages, particularly in the coal industry, an industry that was feeling the pressure of global competition, which intensified postwar.

The great coal strike that occurred and the government's reaction with threats, including the threat of force to bring the workers back, was a scandal that Churchill and the Conservatives would never live down; it undoubtedly played a major role in their defeat at the conclusion of World War II.

From the viewpoint of the government and the Bank of England, a substantial cut in wages was essential to bring prices down to a level that again would make British products competitive. In the light of history, it is fair to say that they had the entire dynamic backward.

In reflecting on this today, it is inconceivable they were so blind to the reality, but one must keep in mind that this was a time when labor, particularly in Britain, had limited bargaining rights. The caste system was in place.

If starvation was needed to keep Britain great, then so be it. The profound change in attitude regarding the rights of labor had to await the fallout from the Great Depression, with legislation adopted by the United

States and Britain after the Second World War. Labor came to power in the person of Franklin D. Roosevelt in 1932, and socialism came to Great Britain in 1945.

## The Highway to Disaster

From a strictly monetary standpoint, the problem was equally severe. Britain was in great need of investment, and as sterling was being sold and gold transported to other parts of the world, particularly the United States, Britain experienced a net outflow of capital that threatened to derail and perhaps even sink the British economy. Without capital Britain would simply have become a third-world country. This was the antithesis of greatness.

Britain was suffering a financial hemorrhage. In order to slow the bleeding, the Bank of England began imposing restrictions on the movement of capital and proceeded to raise rates in order to make investment in Britain relatively attractive. The impact of this policy can be seen in the increase in the unemployment rate, which stood at just 2 percent in 1920.

For this self-defeating policy to have any chance of success required cooperation from other countries, particularly the United States.

Norman turned to his friend Ben Strong. Ben would not let him down. Britain's primacy had to be secured, apparently at all costs, and Ben, as I have noted, was willing to take whatever steps were necessary to see that this was accomplished. American interests would have to take a backseat for a time. Ben Strong was about to show his friend Montagu Norman that he indeed was an Anglophile through and through.

In this connection the first decision he made was to take the gold that was flowing into the United States from Britain and hold it off the market through open market operations and place it in reserve, a form of safekeeping to be held for a later date for the British, for it was in his mind really their gold.

As he withdrew gold from the market, he increased bank reserves, which created liquidity, a quasi form of debt, offsetting this withdrawal.

However, as these reserves were introduced into the system, they flowed into the coffers of the New York banks, which proceeded to lend in large amounts on margin to participants in the stock market. Had the gold been allowed to stay in the system, it would have trickled down to the farmer and other consumers, who would have purchased consumer goods from around the world and invested in the United States, fostering global recovery.

By providing liquidity, that is, bank reserves, the Federal Reserve expands the credit mechanism but doesn't decide who will be the beneficiary.

In the twenties the credit went to Wall Street, not to the nation's farmers and businesses. It was used for speculation in the market, which at the time was the safest investment offering the highest returns.

Credit was available, but it was going to the wrong people and for the wrong purpose. We have numerous examples of this today. Companies buy back their stock instead of investing it in plant and equipment, which would provide jobs. They are simply speculating on the market. Their assumption is that the market for their stock will trade higher in the future. However, if that is not the case, that capital is permanently lost.

By 1927 as Britain continued to struggle, Strong introduced a policy euphemistically called "credit inflation." Stock prices zoomed, but production languished. Agricultural prices continued to decline, and farm values declined with them.

The year 1927 became the year of the bubble, a year of fundamental disequilibrium. Some areas of the economy appeared to be doing well, particularly Wall Street. The wealthy were enhancing their wealth by buying stock on margin. As credit was readily available, there developed a housing boom and a consumer credit boom. Credit for consumption, not production, took hold. In 2007 the United States faced a very similar problem.

Increasing debt furthered dollar devaluation, which again was not recognized in trade since the dollar-gold exchange rate was fixed at $20.67 per ounce.

Thus we entered a period when the dollar and sterling were both overvalued. International trade was further constrained. Margin interest rates were low, which encouraged more borrowing. Behind the scenes Strong encouraged the banks to increase their loans to Britain.

On the surface all appeared to be sanguine as Americans in particular became enthralled with the stock market. No one apparently saw the dangers inherent in an economy that was totally imbalanced.

This would become apparent to all in October 1929 with the stock market crash.

The end of the superficial boom in the United States was due in part to the impact of assisting in the European recovery. Sterling at $4.86 was a fictitious rate, requiring an expansion of American credit to keep the discount rate low.

Strong never lost his British bias, and until his death in 1928 as a result of complications from tuberculosis, he remained an advocate for short-term loans to Europe for food and necessities and long-term loans for investment. He also sided with those who supported the cancellation and reduction of war debts to the United States.

CHAPTER 21

# Before the Depression, the Roaring Twenties—A Great Misnomer

## The Last Party

To describe the decade of the twenties as "roaring" or "flourishing" is a manifest oversimplification, mostly a falsehood. One would be a good deal closer to the dominant condition if one were to describe that period as one of contradiction.

History teaches that the decade of the twenties was dynamic in terms of change; it was a period of severe imbalance that would be the precursor of economic collapse.

Granted, there were impressive gains. The most obvious was the stock market, which flourished under Ben Strong as he maintained an exaggerated easy money policy in order to help Great Britain stem the outflow of capital. This money did not find its way into the hands of farmers and city dwellers, as we have noted, but flowed unceasingly into the coffers of the Wall Street bankers and brokers who peddled stocks, theirs and others, with the promise of riches.

As the market scaled new heights, riches for the asking appeared to be available to all. People, rich and poor, young and old, in all parts of the country and internationally, including the likes of Winston Churchill, joined in.

What was particularly enticing was that no one needed savings of consequence to participate. One could buy stock by borrowing the money at very low rates. This was termed borrowing on margin. Since there was no limit to the amount of money that could be borrowed, speculation reached fever pitch. The stock market of the twenties was akin to today's credit card mania or equity loan craze. Until recently, if one owned a house and was in need of cash, one simply drew down on the equity line or second mortgage without restriction for vacations, new cars, and so on.

How was this money to be repaid? In the twenties the money was to be repaid by appreciation in the stock market. The market would have to appreciate, it was reasoned, as virtually everyone was a participant, including the Wall Street barons of the likes of J. P. Morgan, who supposedly had unlimited wealth. They would see to it that the market would never decline. The average man in the street became an eager participant.

A far greater threat to the health and welfare of the nation was that virtually all the banks and related financial institutions were participants as well. The banks were speculating with depositors' money. Everyone was speculating, and few had any clue as to the ramifications implicit in any market downturn. A crash would not only ruin the participants but would bankrupt the banks and the savings of families would be wiped out, even for those who chose not to participate. A crash was simply unthinkable.

Blinded by greed and the prospect of wealth, those who bothered to consider the matter must have concluded that "nature and nature's God" would never allow for such a calamity. They were all wrong.

## CALAMITY

The depression era began. Congress moved to protect American industry and jobs with passage of the infamous Smoot-Hawley Tariff Act on June 13, 1930, raising tariffs on 20,000 imported goods.

France, on whose territory the Great War was largely fought, no longer held great power status. In financial terms neither did Britain. From now on trade was a matter of bilateral arrangements.

In the year 1930, the gross national product of the United States dropped 9.4 percent. Unemployment increased from 3.2 percent to

8.7 percent. Bank failures accelerated. This was but the beginning of a tragedy.

Virtually everyone in a position of power contributed to the disaster. The disaster was an orgy of excess.

The Federal Reserve, under the tutelage of Mr. Ben Strong, managed over the course of the decade to increase the money supply by 60 percent. This was to be more than enough "gin" for everyone, including the many that preferred drinking it straight, by leveraging debt.

By the way, leveraging remains alive and well today just as it was in that bygone era. Borrowed money pours into the market. In the twenties, why wasn't action taken? Who was to do it? There was no board to balance Strong's influence. Congress had the responsibility. What about the president? The president had the clout to put an end to this madness, this folly, but there is no indication that he was aware of the danger.

Even if he had misgivings, would he have interfered? The answer is likely no, since everyone was prospering. No one and certainly not a second-rate president and politician the likes of Calvin Coolidge (1923–1929) would have dared to attempt to take the punch bowl away from the party.

Upon Strong's death there was a dearth of leadership at the Fed. It could be said that he died at the worst possible time. He would not be there as the world went into crisis, and decisions henceforth would be made by committee.

By the early thirties it was widely agreed that the easy money policy of the Fed had contributed to the exuberance that led to the crash; and the Fed, at the worst possible moment, endeavored to reverse gears and began to raise rates in order to prevent what they feared was a bout of impending inflation.

Between 1928 and 1932, the Fed raised interest rates by 25 percent. This represented a belated attempt to offset the 60 percent growth in the money supply earlier. At the very moment the Fed moved to tighten money and thus slow the economy, the world was facing impending economic disaster. This later was seen as the worst possible series of decisions at the worst possible time. Disaster indeed would ensue.

## Quicksand, a Synonym for Debt
Debt spun out of control.

During the twenties, though laborsaving devices such as the assembly line, advances in machinery, and the introduction of the auto reshaped the nation, labor was not the beneficiary, as real income remained flat.

Farm income fell as other nations, now at peace again, began to rely on domestic production. During the twenties farm income declined from 15 percent of national income to 9 percent. Farmland value fell by 30 percent.

As business conditions were peaking, merger mania took hold. Two hundred major companies merged, one half American, placing added pressure on employment.

American corporations focused attention on profitability, at employee expense, in order to foster higher stock prices. Corporations engaged in stock buybacks instead of investment to push stocks higher.

The primary focus of industry in the early twenties had been auto and construction. Between 1926 and 1929, construction fell from $16 billion to $9 billion.

The widespread use of credit in the twenties, which had stimulated the demand for consumer products, became a burden as the borrowers defaulted. Auto sales declined by one third.

Organized labor was set back, membership declining from 5.1 million to 3.4 million. The wealthiest 15 percent held 40 percent of the nation's wealth.

As is invariably the case in times of disarray, the rich got richer. Those with incomes of $500,000 or more increased during the 1920s from 150 to 1,400. The top tax rate was 25 percent. Ninety-three percent of the population held 4 percent of disposable income.

The Fed, in an attempt to reverse the frenzied monetary policy, raised rates in 1929 and again in 1931.

Who was to pay for this tragedy, with its black-hole dimensions? Germany?

By 1933, the year of Hitler, Germany had paid one eighth of the amount agreed upon at Versailles. The Allies earlier agreed to a suspension of payments in 1932.

The fact that they had paid that amount was something of a miracle. The Germans were starving. The creditors were certain to lose, as they had throughout history, and this meant the banks in the United States and their depositors. A global calamity it was indeed, though some nations were spared the worst of it, such as Great Britain, which by floating sterling, never felt the full impact of the collapse as did the United States.

The debate goes on as to what was the ultimate cause of the Depression. The answer is clear. It was the war, and the proximate cause was debt. Debt has many dimensions. It will bring down governments; it will produce tyranny, starvation, unemployment, despair, and the financial ruin of millions who played no part and bore no responsibility for its creation.

Through it all Calvin Coolidge, a strong believer in the philosophy that government should keep its hands off the private sector, an advocate of a laissez-faire approach to economic development, idled his time in office away from the scene. He chose not to run again.

He was succeeded by a man of culture, decency, and broad commercial experience, whose name will always be associated with disaster, the ill-famed Herbert Hoover, who presided over the Great Depression.

CHAPTER 22

# The Horrible Thirties

## CHINA AND SILVER

One of the little-known facts of the depression era is the silver crisis in China. The Chinese monetary system was based on silver. Gold fever had never quite made it to China.

Given conditions as they were, the voices of the silver advocates were going to be finally listened to in the United States. In 1934 Congress passed the Silver Purchase Act.

The Act authorized the government to purchase silver until it equaled one third of the monetary value of gold or the market price increased to $1.29. In addition, the government nationalized silver stocks at fifty cents an ounce. The Treasury issued large quantities of silver certificate bills, thus adding to the monetary base. The unforeseen consequence of this was to drain silver from China to the United States.

This resulted in an appreciation of the exchange rate of the Chinese currency and a reduction in the Chinese stock of silver, which wreaked havoc with their ability to export.

This forced China to abandon the silver standard, and with that a progressive deterioration in the Chinese economy set in. This, combined with the dislocation caused by the Japanese invasion, destroyed completely the credibility of the Chinese government and was the primary cause of the communist takeover in 1948.

The United States had no appreciation of the impact the Silver Act would have in Asia. The purpose of the Act was to put more dollars in circulation by buying silver at an artificial price and thus increasing the seller's buying power.

However, by raising their exchange rate, the unintended consequence was to impede China's ability to compete by making their goods more expensive.

## Herbert Hoover, a Man of His Time

Debt plentiful, equity scarce, and the world's two principal currencies overvalued produced a recipe for global contraction and, at the very least, a major recession, if not a depression.

Rather than address the underlying problems of debt and currency, the world chose to tinker at the edges. As a result the decade was one of lost opportunity and hardship, which would establish the conditions necessary to produce another global conflagration.

The popular impression of the thirties is that the world suffered through an extended period of deprivation that came to a conclusion with the start of the Second World War. This is a misleading and simplistic picture of what transpired.

The underlying condition, when all is said and done, was widespread ignorance. At the very heart of this ignorance lay inexcusable rigidity. Men rarely questioned the logic or rationale for their positions. Those who challenged orthodoxy were considered outcasts. Change was threatening.

Implicitly they accepted the notion of a global caste system. If you were born poor, presumably this was what the Creator intended, and thus you should remain poor. This system of course benefited those who were wealthy or in power or were the scions of power.

The caste system mentality, with its profound resistance to change, is alive and well across the globe. The dynamic of life itself, when defined, means change. Life is a process of change.

As the world economic system began its long contraction, humanity cried out for leaders to awaken them from this nightmare.

In Germany they swallowed Hitler; in Russia, Lenin and Stalin. In Britain they ran through a series of prime ministers, all tinkering on the edges, none able to break with the prevailing economic philosophy.

The philosophy accepted recessions and depressions as the norm. These were cycles of life, which we should accept and muddle through, recognizing that they were inevitable. With falling prices and slowing demand, commerce would eventually right itself given sufficient time and patience.

This meant poverty, starvation, and great suffering, of course, but that was to be reserved for the working class; it was, after all, their lot in life. The upper classes were to be largely spared, which was fitting and presumably their lot in life.

However in Britain, a man would come on the scene, an economist of great renown, who would very effectively challenge the orthodoxy and be a major influence going forward right up to the present. That man was the venerable John Lord Maynard Keynes.

Keynes was not influenced by orthodoxy or the conclusions that flowed from it. In his mind logic or reality should dictate all decisions. Nothing can be right because we have always done it this way. It had to make sense, and it had to fit into reality. In his simple but profound analysis of money and interest rates, he took a syllogistic approach to the matter.

He challenged the conclusions of economists such as Ricardo as being simply illogical. He made the simple point that as prices fell and unemployment rose due to lack of demand, a bottom would never be reached since no one at the theoretical bottom would have the money to buy anything. More about Maynard Keynes later.

In the United States, as business conditions worsened and the recovery, which was "just around the corner," never arrived, a troubling anxiety and despair gripped the public.

At the time of the presidential election in 1928, the full extent of global disaster had yet to unfold. Though there was considerable anxiety, the public retained confidence in its leaders.

The Republicans nominated a man of considerable experience, the urbane, cultured, and very decent Herbert Hoover. Hoover had played a major role as the leader in the European recovery program. He had most recently served as secretary of commerce in the Coolidge administration.

His opponent was the well-known New York City Democratic leader and New York governor, Al Smith. Hoover won the election in a landslide, in part because of his appeal to the broad sweep of the American middle class, who identified with his philosophy and his Protestantism. Smith, in contrast, was a big-city figure and political boss who happened to be Catholic. While religious affiliation may have influenced the outcome, it is largely agreed it was not the decisive factor.

Hoover was a man who was stereotypical of his age, the period running from 1890 to 1932. This time frame is often referred to as the Progressive Era. Hoover was a progressive. He might well have identified with and certainly been influenced by the most popular political figure of that age, the famed Teddy Roosevelt.

Progressivism, greatly simplified, meant out with the old and in with the new.

Everything that was old was probably inefficient and wasteful. The world needed technocrats who would solve the aggravating problems of society. Hoover was a strong advocate of education, particularly technical education. Like Teddy Roosevelt he was a committed conservationist.

He believed in efficiency and believed that experts should identify problems and then solve them. He was a dry, favoring prohibition, opposing debauchery in all its forms.

He was a supporter of women's suffrage. He strongly believed in individualism. All men of this view should be able to stand on their own. Too much government, he would have argued, kills self-reliance and individuality. The best government is the one that interferes the least. However, unlike his predecessor, he was not laissez-faire.

He came to moderate his stance as conditions worsened and opposed his secretary of the Treasury, Andrew Mellon, succeeded by Ogden Mills, and their approach to solving national problems, which was "just leave everything alone."

His approach would be labeled "voluntarism." Public and private cooperation, particularly at the state and local level, was the best way to address all problems.

His great failing was that at heart he was a bureaucrat. He may have publicly heralded change, but feared the prospect. Men such as Hoover become conditioned and insistent on changing little and frequently become dogmatic in support of their methods. They believe they can do no wrong. They are profound egotists at heart.

As early as December 3, 1929, just three months after the crash, Hoover thought the worst of the crash was over. Hoover clearly saw himself as a reformer. Consistent with his belief in voluntarism and as a reformer, he expanded civil service, proposed a Department of Education., fostered a good neighbor policy toward South America, and signed the Norris-La Guardia Act, which limited judicial intervention in labor disputes. As a conservationist he set aside three million acres of land as part of the national parks program. As a builder he initiated the Boulder Dam project. He negotiated the St. Lawrence Seaway Treaty.

Consistent with his philosophy, he opposed direct relief from the federal government to the individual, relying instead on voluntary measures of business. As the depression deepened, Ford Company agreed to increase the pay of its workers to encourage more spending. To the extent that government was needed, it should emanate from state and local sources and not the federal government. There is no indication that he ever wavered from the fundamental belief that too much government kills self-reliance and individuality. However as we moved into the thirties, Hoover found ways to expand the role of government.

He brought into being the Reconstruction Finance Corporation. This made money available for public works projects and unemployment relief, as well as loans to railroads and bankers for agricultural projects.

To ease unemployment, he authorized what is known as the Mexican repatriation of one to two million people of Spanish heritage living in certain states, even though 60 percent of them were American citizens. It is an historical fact that in 2005 the state of California passed an official "Apology Act" to those forced to relocate to Mexico.

To pay for these programs, he signed the 1932 Revenue Act raising taxes on the highest earners from 25 percent to 63 percent. In addition, he doubled the estate tax and raised corporate taxes by 15 percent.

Though he had vast international experience and certainly an understanding of the importance of trade, he signed the Smoot-Hawley legislation, which at the outset raised tariffs on 20,000 goods, most tied to agriculture.

In sum, both government and business were spending more, but the consumer wasn't spending. The consumer didn't spend because he didn't have the money. Fear, bank failures, and a prolonged drought contributed to the disorderly conditions, but in the end, the real problem was the absence of cold hard cash, particularly as unemployment rose. The earlier madness of Strong in keeping gold out of the hands of the consumer served to increase the debt burden, which combined with market speculation, left the nation with nothing but debt and little money to invest.

War-driven overbuilding, excess inventories, ignorance in money matters, and declining trade combined to produce an economic implosion.

Then was the depression inevitable? Nothing is inevitable. For reasons that never made sense then nor today, no one in office ever saw the necessity of eliminating the world's debt load. Debt was the cancer, and it had to be excised. No proposal was ever made to seriously tackle that issue or suggest such an operation.

With debt abounding, nations and people simply cannot make progress. They will not be able to make serious advances in living standards today as long as the world and particularly the United States endeavors to pursue world leadership carrying over $13 trillion of debt, to the interest on which we currently devote 7 percent of our national budget.

Let's return to Hoover, who for the rest of his term never saw the absolute necessity of a global effort to extinguish debt. Irrespective of the prevailing philosophy of the time and his personal views with respect to government's role in the affairs of its citizens, he should have known that the debt problem was paramount. Is it logical or even rational to suggest that people should starve and nations go bankrupt to preserve the sanctity of debt?

At the very least, Hoover should have taken steps to cancel the foreign sovereign debt owed by our allies to us, thus lifting a great burden off the shoulders of Europe. He did not.

Given the gravity of the situation, it is startling that Hoover was able to summon the courage to campaign for reelection in 1932. It certainly took courage, as he was assaulted and threatened during the campaign. Though the economic picture was bleak, with no real signs of recovery on the horizon, Hoover nevertheless began the campaign as the favorite. His earlier record of competence and achievement, combined with a formidable intellect, led many to conclude that the condition of the country necessitated the election of a man with proven ability.

His Democratic opponent in the race was Franklin D. Roosevelt, FDR for short, who went on to trounce Hoover in the election and became a glittering political star and beacon of hope for the American people and the world.

He went on to be reelected three times, and in all likelihood, would have remained president perhaps for life if it had not been for the massive stroke he suffered, bringing with it death as the Second World War was coming to its conclusion in 1945.

### The Farmers—A Struggling Political Force

It is important not to lose sight of the fact that in the decade of the twenties, America was a nation of farmers. Of course it was also a nation of inventors, but farming at this stage was critical. During the First World War, more than 50 percent of the nation's exports were in farm products.

From the end of the war until 1930, US farm exports declined significantly as global competition returned. Prices on basic commodities declined, yet the number of people employed in the industry remained stable. Farmers were hurting and the nation's banking system was weakened as the farm industry stagnated and declined.

As the fortune of the farmers continued to deteriorate, in 1930 Congress passed and Hoover signed the notorious Smoot-Hawley Tariff Act, which contrary to popular belief was a farm bill, not an industrial Act.

Though it is a fact that Europe responded by raising tariffs, they did so not out of spite but to be certain they had the dollars to pay their debt to America.

Industrial production in America at the time was almost entirely for domestic use. Export of domestically manufactured goods other than farm products constituted only 5 percent of total exports.

The farm industry was in trouble, and thus so was the banking industry. Cautious men began to withdraw currency from the banks, sensing failure. Gold was largely unavailable. Banks failed.

In 1931 with the onset of the crisis in Germany and then London with devaluation of the pound, it was profitable for investors to return to the European money markets. Within a matter of days, $725 million in gold left the United States for European shores.

By 1931 the new leadership of the Fed, in recognition of the errors in Strong's policy, was understandably hesitant and uncertain. Seemingly oblivious to the banking crisis now in full swing across the land with the stock market crash, the Fed moved to slow the outflow of gold by raising the discount rate to 2 ½ percent on October 9 and to 3 ½ percent on October 16, the largest percentage increase before or since.

The money supply went into free fall, with M1, the basic measure of money growth, dropping by 12 percent in 1931. From the economic peak in 1929 to the trough in March 1933, the stock of money dropped by one third, collapsing American business. The world needed liquidity, and the Federal Reserve did not respond.

The stock market, which was visited with its first major setback in October 1929, declined from September 1930 to June 1932 by 80 percent.

Confidence in America was shattered.

## The Prelude to the 1932 Election, the Road to the New Deal

The failure of Hoover to respond adequately to the crisis left a lasting impression across the social and political spectrum that the Republican Party had no interest in the common man but only in business interests. This was not a fair assessment. Hoover and his successors had a very real interest in the common man, but they had readily accepted the conventional economic wisdom that downturns were in the natural order of things and could not be avoided.

For government to intervene would, according to this philosophy, undercut the free enterprise system or capitalism. Government intervention was "socialist" in its orientation. It was thought that free men would become less free and in time be subject to the whims of some distant bureaucracy that was not only impersonal but would steal from the hardworking and successful men the rewards that they justly deserved.

Hoover was a contemplative, quiet, and determined man. His air of confidence was well-founded. An engineer by training, he had succeeded in business as a mine expert and owner. He had played an important role in the recovery of Europe after World War I. He was highly admired. No potential candidate in the Democratic Party had anything like his experience.

He resolutely believed that recovery was preordained. He accepted the prevailing philosophy that any man with sufficient gumption, determination, hard work, and perseverance could succeed in America. That was America. The independent, rugged individualist was the backbone of this republic. It was what differentiated America from other nations.

Yes, the economy was in bad shape, the market had failed, the banking system had failed, farmers and homeowners were losing their homes at an alarming rate, and unemployment was skyrocketing, but all of this was in the natural order of things. As his secretary of the Treasury, Ogden Mills, argued, this was essential to clean out and correct the abuses that had worked their way into business and finance during the period of expansion, which ran from the First World War up to the time of the market crash. This was the necessary castor oil, which, though very unpleasant, was essential to recovery. As a nation we simply had to tighten our belt and move on. This too would pass. Patience was a virtue.

Since this process was in the natural order of things, it was important not to interfere. Government interference should be discouraged. It would at best provide marginal assistance to few and create a dependence on government that was unhealthy. Such interference reduced man's self-esteem and sapped his determination to overcome his difficulties. Many First World War veterans were unfortunate examples of this incipient dependence. Under the banner "Bonus Marchers," they descended on Washington in large numbers, pleading and campaigning for Congress to pay the bonus they were due earlier than scheduled. They were living in unsanitary shacks in Washington, and the threat of civil disturbance hung over the city.

Hoover, apparently ignorant of the extent of their despair, ordered General MacArthur to tear down their ramshackle huts and oust them from the city in order to restore and assure civil order.

Though there were no reliable polls at the time, it was widely believed that Hoover was ahead in the race for president until he took this action. Across the nation, as the homeless population grew in size and cardboard shacks could be seen in towns and cities across the country, the Roosevelt campaign and the press coined the name Hooverville. The depression and Hoover became synonymous in the mind of the electorate. Without any sign of recovery, Hoover's reelection chances were doomed, whether the economic downturn was in the natural order of things or not.

To be fair to Hoover, he sensed the situation was deteriorating. His call for patience, combined with his assurances that time would heal all, began to run headlong into the facts.

The market crash and the resulting slowdown had an immediate impact on the gross national product. Nevertheless, Hoover remained steadfast.

He continued to promote his policy of voluntarism, neighbor helping neighbor. Within a year he clearly had misgivings about this policy. He turned to Congress, asking them to approve a $150 million public works project, multibillions by today's standards.

By 1930 the nation's gross national product had fallen by more than 9 percent, and the unemployment rate had risen to 8 percent. He and his advisors, particularly the secretary of the Treasury, Ogden Mills, remained convinced that the economy would ultimately right itself and further intervention would be a mistake.

Helen Thomas, author and Washington reporter, who covered the presidency for many years observed that "consistency is the best evidence of small minds."[cix]

Ogden Mills had been successful in business and Hoover had demonstrated executive talent, but both men were completely lacking when it came to vision.

The dynamic of innovation, invention, experimentation, and dreaming the impossible dream were the furthest things from their mind. They embraced the status quo and wrapped themselves in fear of the unknown. Years of experience somehow turned them into quintessential pessimists. Hunker down and drive all those calling for change, including the bonus marchers, out of Washington and wait.

As they sat waiting, a new but related crisis was simmering. This crisis was far worse than anything that had taken place. The so-called banking crisis of 1931 came as an immense shock to Hoover.

The failure of Kreditanstalt Bank, a highly respected and important Austrian bank, in May 1931 had a domino effect on other European banks.

Hoover's confidence once again was shaken. He was assured by the US regulators, including the comptroller of the currency, that the problem was a European problem, closely tied to reparations payments. In effect he was told that the American money center banks were immunized. Hoover was no one's fool, and such assurances left him uncomfortable. On his own initiative, he began to inquire through his private contacts on the condition of the New York banks, which continued to be the principal source of finance for Europe.

What he learned from this investigation put him into something close to a catatonic state. The banks had been using so-called "bankers acceptances," which were supposed to be self-liquidating instruments, in their European dealings.

In practice, though goods were sold and delivered, the buyer simply hadn't paid. Thus these contracts turned out to be uncollateralized long-term loans. By identifying the loans as acceptances, the banks had disguised the true nature of the agreements and their exposure.

Hoover was so stunned he was unable to sleep. He walked the floor at night contemplating the implications. Worse still, he could not confide in anyone for fear that if it became public, it would set off a second financial panic.

Clearly the debt problem was more than a European problem. Should the European banks fail, as they were then doing in increasing numbers, the US banks could not be far behind. Debt had already engulfed and destroyed millions, and it was now poised to destroy millions more through the eradication of their savings as banks across the country began to fail.

Hoover was standing on the *Titanic* without a lifeboat. Whether he truly appreciated the extent of the calamity remains an open question.

In the face of this, in 1932 he began his campaign for reelection. That took a measure of courage in itself. All indications were that he believed he would be reelected. He was hounded throughout the campaign with people yelling epithets, throwing garbage, and screaming, "We want bread."

By the time of the election in 1932, ten thousand banks had failed. The economy plummeted. Farm prices dropped by 53 percent. The American farmer was ruined; his income disappeared. International trade declined by 66 percent. Capital investment dropped from $16.2 billion annually to $750 million. Tariffs on imports further diminished world trade; the increase in the top tax rate further demonstrated confusion.

The American people, if not in total despair, were certainly filled with anxiety and real fear, fear of starvation. The year 1932 turned out to be the worst year of the depression. Gross national product in 1932 dropped 13.4 percent, and unemployment reached 23.4 percent.

Into this maelstrom stepped Franklin Delano Roosevelt. Thus the stage was set: Hoover versus Roosevelt.

Two men could not have been more opposite as the campaign progressed. Roosevelt, exuding confidence from literally every pore and taking political advantage of the deteriorating condition with superb timing and subtlety, convinced the American people of the need for change and was elected overwhelmingly.

Contrary to popular opinion, he came into office without a well-conceived plan. He was neither prophet, political scientist, nor economist. He knew the nation was in a state of dangerous despair. Fearing revolution, he was willing to try anything. Fascism and communism were on the march, and there was no law of nature that would prevent them from marching here.

His response was that he had served in government as assistant secretary of the navy, as state senator, and as governor of New York, and he knew firsthand how wrong the experts were. Roosevelt told his closest advisors to go out in the countryside and solicit new ideas. Listen to everyone and anyone. Of course he had a few ideas of his own. He loved experimentation. If something didn't work, try something else. Move on.

Franklin Roosevelt was neither a socialist nor quasi socialist. His economic philosophy, if he had one at all, was that of a reformer. That duty fell to a royal such as him in the same way a drowning man depends on a stranger to throw him a life preserver. A drowning man does not seek out a certain color of life preserver. His views could be challenged and denigrated. He simply didn't care. What mattered to him was that they worked.

Besides ambition, the driving force in his political life was the beatitudes. Though he didn't wear it on his sleeve, FDR took his Christian faith seriously. He had a duty to help others, particularly the underdog, the poor, the orphan, and the widow. The notion that he was a socialist sprang from the fact that he despised ungainly wealth. There was no reason that a few should have so much and so many go hungry. His consistency on this subject erased any doubt about his commitment to equity. What drove that commitment still remains an open question. Any show of wealth was repugnant to him, Eleanor, and his mother. In their world, there was no place for the nouveau riche.

People who went about advertising their wealth were hardly Christian and certainly not democratic. Both he and his family were paternalistic, snobbish, and pompous, yet his modus operandi and core beliefs never changed.

Though he set himself apart, he believed his views were Jeffersonian and Christian, and that is what truly counted. All men were created equal, and each of us had a duty to our neighbor.

FDR thought himself to be a man of action. Words without accompanying action were a recipe for failure. He was a consummate politician, who understood that the public had to be brought along. Thus, timing was key. He was a man of limitless hope, to the point of arrogance. Though a cripple, he truly believed he would walk again. From a medical standpoint, that was virtually impossible.

In his 1932 inaugural address, he wrote in his own hand, "This Nation asks for action, and action now." He would call the Congress into a special session and propose sweeping legislation that would give rise to what has subsequently become a benchmark for leadership, "the first hundred days."

CHAPTER 23

# The Roosevelt Era—A Lifeline Stretching to Modernity

## Franklin D. Roosevelt

In a word, the twentieth century was oxymoronic, conjoining unprecedented advances in knowledge and human endeavor with unprecedented horrors, including two world wars, the destruction of nations and peoples, and a global economic collapse.

Into this black hole stepped a politician from New York whose optimism was legendary. He would find a way to get this country and the world back on track, believing as did his counterpart and partner in this effort from Great Britain, Winston Churchill, that failure spelled the end of civilization.

Failure was never an option. He demonstrated during his twelve years in office serving as the thirty-second president of the United States, having been first elected in 1932, that he was the right man for the job and, in point of fact, perhaps the only man.

Compounding the challenge he faced, Franklin Roosevelt was an invalid, having suffered an attack of poliomyelitis in August 1921. He was permanently paralyzed, a fact that he refused to accept, going to great lengths to find a cure, which escaped him.

How does one adequately describe the critical men of the age? Where does one begin? What are the factors, personal and historical, that allow one to be considered extraordinary? Clearly, prevailing conditions or extraordinary opportunity, measured in terms of urgency, must be present.

Periods of peace and prosperity or general stability do not create the conditions essential for a dynamic leader to come to the fore. That man has to arrive at the right time and place.

Leadership demands men of principle willing to sacrifice, if need be, themselves for a cause. Principle, determination, and perseverance rather than personal gain guide their compass. Few ever get the chance for leadership, for lesser men stand in their way.

Such men or women typically are imperfect. Saintliness is seldom a qualification. Quite frequently they are people who have in their lives suffered greatly. The suffering may have been due to earlier failure. Many have suffered estrangement and have found themselves alone, no one willing to give them a helping hand. They share one overriding gift. They are men and women of faith. They believe in their destiny.

There is no word less understood than the word *faith*. Faith is invariably confused with belief. They are not synonymous. Belief is a subjective judgment concerning some external fact or event. The meaning encompasses opinion. People choose to believe due to the evidence or the testimony of others. Belief allows for differences unless it is imposed. It is frequently said that we are all entitled to our beliefs. Not so with faith.

Faith sears the soul. For faith to enter the psyche, the recipient must be fully prepared. That faith invariably involves, as noted, great suffering, suffering that invites despair. It is long-lasting, the soul being constantly tested. Such a test is typically not administered to the average man, for its force would soon envelop and overwhelm him. For the few chosen, it allows for the full development of their character, their soul.

Through perseverance, they ultimately arrive. To them, success is measured by a different standard. Their confidence cannot be shaken. They understand, though it may entail greater suffering, that they will prevail in the end. They conquer through perseverance. They overcome. Such a man was Franklin Delano Roosevelt.

He was certainly not a saint. He was cunning, untrustworthy, evasive, vengeful, and a snob.

Caught in adultery he became estranged from his wife, Eleanor, and to some degree from his children, at a time in history when such behavior invited banishment from society. He was forced to live a life of marital separation, pretending at all times that all was well.

Known universally by his initials, FDR, he suffered from a debilitating disease, poliomyelitis, which was generally associated with children, though when he contracted the disease he was a man in his thirties. He was a scion of a wealthy family, distant cousin of a former president, and by any measure a man of privilege.

He had been successful in politics, earlier having served as assistant secretary of the navy and was seen as a political comer with a powerful surname. Though his marriage had broken down, it was not widely known and did not appear to be an impediment to his future. As a distant cousin to a former president, his political future appeared to be assured. Then disaster struck.

His mother, the most important influence in his life, wanted him to retire from public life. Without the use of his legs, his mobility was severely restricted. He was not notably successful in business and law and was now disabled. His political future appeared to be at an end. Those who would write him off clearly underestimated the man. What was it that kept him going?

In the end he would not only succeed but would succeed brilliantly. I would argue that no other man given his handicap could have overcome the trials he was forced by circumstances to endure.

He was irreplaceable during a time when the people were seriously questioning the future of the nation. He met with implacable opposition both within and outside the Democratic Party. The New York Democratic leaders who ran the national party never trusted him. He was not one of them. The opposition within the Republican Party bordered on the maniacal. They argued that he had sold out his class.

In the four presidential elections that he participated in, he never carried the political district in which he lived, which was heavily Republican.

Roosevelt supposedly bristled at Republican opposition, pointing out that his actions had stayed the real possibility of revolution, in which case those who had been his most outspoken opponents would have been the first to have been "hung from the lamppost."

Though privileged and seemingly unaware of the plight of the poor as a young man, his disability and the suffering he witnessed as he traveled the nation brought forth a streak of compassion that was further awakened and fostered by his wife, Eleanor. Though separated in marital terms, she remained his closest confidante when it came to the common man, spending her life fighting for social justice and convincing him of the need for structural change.

Through all the trials, he persevered. That alone distinguished him from the many.

At various times during his presidency, particularly during the darkest times of the depression and war, he carried the world on his shoulders. He never complained of the burden. An abiding faith in a just Creator and extraordinary self-confidence carried him through. He was a man apart.

Four American presidents have succeeded in setting themselves apart.

Who were the four? Washington, whose majesty, leadership, willpower, and perseverance provided us with our independence.

Jackson, whose courage, compassion for the settlers, and determination assured the survival of the nation.

Lincoln, whose grasp of the evil of separation and slavery assured the continuation of the union.

Roosevelt, whose personal example, true compassion, and dedication prevented the disintegration of the republic and the end of civilization as we had come to know it.

There continues to be widespread disagreement over many of the policies he pursued. Those who abhor government intervention believe he was precisely the wrong man with the wrong answers to the Great Depression.

When he entered office, he had no firm economic principles to guide him. Maynard Keynes found him charming but an economic illiterate.

Contrary to popular belief, he was a strong advocate of private property. His views on government spending were decidedly conservative. A religious man and perhaps because of his disability and the paternalistic inclinations of the privileged class, he had strong empathy for the common man. In that sense, unlike his immediate predecessors, he was quite Jacksonian.

He was by any measure a fiscal conservative, insisting that the nation pursue a balanced budget regimen, which he referred to in his inaugural address in 1932.

He heralded self-reliance, believing strongly in the principle "A penny saved is a penny earned." He opposed the Federal Deposit Insurance Corporation, arguing that people—not the government—should be responsible for their own choices. He accepted Andrew Mellon's argument that government guarantee encouraged speculation.

He was appalled by the prospect of an imbalanced federal budget, and then faced with such a prospect, he had no hesitation in supporting efforts to raise taxes.

He believed that the wealthy should pay more in taxes even if they did not owe more. He was willing to have his Attorney General initiate legal proceedings against well-known public figures that he suspected were not paying their fair share. He viewed deficit spending as harmful, potentially worsening the economic condition that beset the country when he took office. When it came to money, he was a man of that age, tight-fisted. His first budget called for a cut in spending of more than 30 percent, a call made during the darkest days of the depression.

By nature he was an innovator, strongly influenced by the economic crisis of the time, and was willing to try anything. He distrusted the so-called experts, insisting they knew nothing, as he had learned earlier in his career when he served as assistant secretary of the navy.

Though he was not an advocate of government intervention, he felt that government had a role to play in putting the country back on its feet. Only in later years was he willing to accept the designation of "liberal." The war, of course, necessitated a complete change in attitude and approach to government intervention.

He was a man of deep compassion for those whom he referred to in his second inaugural address as that "one third of the Nation ill housed, ill clad and ill fed." By 1936 he had come to believe deeply in the need for government intervention, state, local, and federal, and this was as he said a moral responsibility, as opposed to the self-seeking dishonesty that was the accepted norm in business presumably until his arrival in Washington.

Sharing the ignorance of his time, he knew virtually nothing about money. In fact his mother, who held the purse strings in the family, his father having passed away many years before, handled his household accounts and paid his bills. He was a mama's boy through and through, which helped to create the famous friction that existed within the family triumvirate. His upbringing and the absence of a strong political philosophy, his personal inclinations, and the critical need to perform resulted in a willingness to listen to all suggestions, no matter how farfetched.

There is little debate as to his importance, as the one man who managed to stand in the breach to prevent the conquest of Hitlerism and a return to the dark ages.

In his heart he knew the money problem was one that had to be fixed but would never have supported socialist programs precisely because they flew in the face of self-reliance, which was both politically and personally untenable.

He was in many ways an odd duck, yet politically astute. It was widely believed among politicians that he was never to be trusted, for he had a way of telling everyone one thing and then doing another.

However, no one would question his commitment of freeing the nation from the Great Depression using whatever means necessary, including the taking of broad executive powers to force policy change and doing whatever was necessary to meet the challenge. It was in this setting that the world was introduced to the New Deal.

In a sentence, Roosevelt, with the country strongly behind him, made all the difference.

## Roosevelt—And the Others

To be sure, Churchill and Stalin, the tyrant and warrior, played critical roles. Churchill had the courage to stand alone with the British people in the early days of the Second World War and then rally the allied cause together with Roosevelt to triumph over the threat to civilized peoples.

Stalin was a barbarian of the first order who was willing to sacrifice his people and Russia by building a massive and formidable military to destroy fascism.

Without Roosevelt, however, they would have failed. His very persona was the linchpin. Roosevelt was the indisputable leader. It is not an exaggeration to say that he saved civilization. Was this simply a matter of being in the right place at the right time? I think not. Some will call it destiny, which sheds little light on the subject.

Roosevelt was chosen, in the same way Washington, Lincoln, and Jackson were chosen, through a democratic election by a free people.

Like the other three, there were no indications beforehand that he was destined to achieve such preeminence. He was the man for that critical hour, if not for all seasons.

He was cunning but a genius politician, with no equal in his time. He was also a man with deep character and emotional flaws. He was generally regarded as having a second-rate intellect.

He became governor of New York, the springboard for his run for the presidency in 1932, succeeding the most popular and some still argue the most able of politicians and leaders, the famed Al Smith. He was treated by the Democratic leadership throughout his career as a man "out of place."

The best description of Franklin Roosevelt that most would agree with, including those who knew him well, who were few, and those who knew him from afar, who constituted a multitude extending from the far reaches of Siberia to the bush in Africa, from the jungles of Burma and Malaya to the working men and women of America, was that he was a beacon of hope, whom they trusted and in many cases truly loved.

For them, he could do no wrong. His picture was often found in the rundown homes of coal miners, in the shacks of the rural poor, and in the city tenements by the thousands, if not the millions. By most Republicans he was feared; by many he was distrusted, and by some even detested.

## ROOSEVELT ELECTED AND INAUGURATED

Franklin Delano Roosevelt was elected president of the United States in 1932, amid the economic shambles that we characterize today as the Great Depression.

The name Roosevelt rang bells in political circles. He gained the Democratic nomination at the expense of more popular men within the party, such as Al Smith, because the power brokers centered in New York City believed he could win.

Unlike beloved Al Smith, he was not a big-city politician. He was by any measure an upstate New York aristocrat. At the same time, his ability to communicate, particularly with the common folk, in a voice made for radio was exceptional.

Early in life he had married a distant cousin, another Roosevelt, and was living the charmed life of a patrician until he was struck down with poliomyelitis, which came very close to ending his political career, if not his life.

FDR was different in almost every way. He was an enigma. It would be more accurate to say he was a chameleon. FDR appeared to be out of place in the Democratic Party. Here was a man posing as spokesman for the underprivileged, who never considered himself as one of them.

He was privileged and brought up that way. His sense of privilege carried royal manifestations. Looking after the people was a duty of a king. His kingdom was the nation.

His wealthy father had died when he was young. His mother, a very strong, domineering, and insistent person, doted on him for the rest of her life. Mama held the purse strings. She paid his bills. Mama was always number one. Eleanor, his wife, was at best number two, which as one might imagine, she sorely resented.

Roosevelt was manipulative and enormously ambitious. As president his words, though they carried the weight of edict, never appeared to dictate his actions. He could turn on a dime on matters of policy and friendship. He came into the office of president without a clear philosophy. In point of fact, the New Deal happened over time. It was never comprehensively planned.

Years earlier, he and Herbert Hoover had cordial relations. They might well have been in the same political party.

In 1932 the difference between the two men was attitude. Hoover was dour, uncertain, perplexed. Roosevelt, who never underestimated the depth of the problem, was a profound optimist. His optimism was contagious, and his can-do spirit was appealing. It was something the public could latch on to. Latch on they did, and they followed him, though his policies at times were contradictory, even bewildering, leaving many in the know confused.

In political circles his unpredictability was feared. Most believed that ice water ran through his veins.

The two powers that retained dominance over him were his mother and the bosses of the Democratic Party. He was cowed by both and would never buck either. He kept his distance from Tammany Hall.

Confined to a wheelchair, we know his mother wanted him to retire from public life, which he never seriously considered, reminding her with some regularity that his cousin Teddy had been president. Neither he nor his mother was willing to take a backseat to the Long Island Roosevelts.

He never doubted that the party leaders, if challenged, would turn their back on him. They too had ice water running through their veins.

Henry Wallace, his vice president, was dropped from the ticket in 1944, though Roosevelt wanted him to stay on, because Ed Flynn, the leader of the Bronx, New York, Democrats insisted, fearing a Republican victory in New York. The bosses had the last word.

## Economic Disaster

By the time Roosevelt was sworn in, March 1933, the destructive force of the depression had overwhelmed the United States and the world.

More than ten thousand banks would ultimately fail; 40 percent failed in 1929 alone. With these failures and with the Fed endeavoring to offset the excesses of Ben Strong and remaining fearful of inflation, the money supply contracted by approximately 30 percent. Post-World War I decline in commodity prices would further erode farm income. Well before the stock market crash, the purchasing power of most Americans had been in serious decline.

During the height of the go-go twenties, one half of all Americans were living below subsistence. In 1929 the average yearly income for Americans was $750, but for farmers it was $273.[cx]

Corporate profits and productivity surged during the twenties, but the worker did not participate. Business inventories began to grow, and by late August 1929, two months before the crash, inventories were running three times consumption. Production suffered a double-digit decline, and incomes decreased by 5 percent. The market crash occurred on October 24, 1929. Between the twenty-eighth and twenty-ninth of October, 1929, the market surrendered 25 percent of its value.

The historic fact is that the global economic decline following World War I, with the loss of income and buildup in debt, caused the stock market to crash and the world to go into tailspin, not vice versa.

The crash was a direct result of the global distortion and imbalance that was the disequilibrium that followed on the heels of global conflagration. In a real sense, given the war, global policies, most notably an inept monetary policy, inertia, and general confusion, made the depression both predictable and inevitable.

That is not the same as saying it was unavoidable. It might well have been averted with a far greater understanding of the fundamental nature of money, debt, and the need for global balance.

At any rate the global economic ship, that is, the world, was foundering.

The best minds were searching for a magic wand, the solution to steer the nation and the world to at the very least a modicum of stability, which was not to be found. Despair settled as a great black blanket over the civilized world.

Humanity turned to the political extremes to the right and left in desperation.

Germany and Italy adopted Fascism, and Russia tyrannical Communism. Extreme voices were increasingly heard in England and the United States.

Revolution was in the air. Desperation bred madness.

## Roosevelt Inaugurated—Congress Buys the Whole Deal

The Roosevelt inauguration brought to the nation a renewed sense of hope. However, the measures he undertook beginning in 1933 were miniscule in relation to the dimension of the problem. No one at the time fully understood that the world was bankrupt.

Given the state of affairs, he began his service as chief executive in 1933 endorsing at least implicitly the prevailing philosophy, the thinking of the classical economists, which today would be labeled laissez-faire capitalism.

The First World War had destroyed the underpinnings of society. There was simply no place to turn. Debt had overwhelmed all levels of commerce. I suppose if a president is seeking Congressional support, the surest way of getting it is to win an election in a landslide by seven million votes during a time of crisis. FDR arrived at such a time. The first issue to be tackled was the banking crisis.

The American banking system was collapsing. As farm prices had fallen during the twenties, in increasing numbers farmers went bankrupt. The farmers were not able to make good on money borrowed and the banks in rural America were forced to shut their doors. During the decade an average of six hundred banks failed each year as land values plummeted some 30 percent.

Depositors, wary of banks, withdrew gold and currency, "before the bank shut down." The effect of this had a serious negative impact on the money supply. The Federal Reserve might have responded but did not. "From the cyclical peak of activity in August 1929 to the cyclical trough in March 1933, the stock of money fell by over a third."[cxi]

FDR was sworn in as the thirty-second president on March 3, 1933. As the first order of business, he proclaimed a nationwide banking holiday, beginning after midnight on March 6 and lasting until March 13, 14, or 15, depending on the location of the bank.

Only solvent banks were allowed to reopen after the holiday. They had the imprimatur of the United States government, and depositors began to take money from under their mattresses and redeposit it in banks. This fostered an immediate turnaround in the money supply.

In addition Congress passed the Banking Act of 1933. This legislation created the FDIC, the Federal Deposit Insurance Corporation, which insured bank deposits beginning in 1934. Roosevelt was at first dubious about insurance, believing that depositors had a responsibility to know who their banker was. However, he signed the legislation, and it remains an important cornerstone of banking today.

## "The Country Was Dying by Inches"[CXII]

Moving on from the banking crisis, Roosevelt began the arduous task of turning the economy around. To accomplish that he must get Americans employed.

The debate, then as now, was not about the gross domestic product or the preparedness of the United States for conflict, but about the one necessity of life itself, to be able to work or have a satisfactory proxy.

The role of government had never been defined. The great majority of Americans appeared to accept the orthodox view, that government had no role in the private affairs of men. Economic downturns were considered as one of the unfortunate accidents of life, even by the common man.

FDR believed that the private and public sectors had to work together. He deplored those whose fortunes were gained by feeding on the little man. He was adamant that government control public utilities in order to make energy affordable.

A very American caricature of this age was the image of the rugged individualist. FDR's distant cousin Theodore Roosevelt thrived on this image. Most Americans did as well. The idea that some might need outside assistance violated their manhood. In such a society, government had no role to play.

If extreme circumstances, meaning abject poverty, required some form of welfare, it was to be kept to an absolute minimum. To do otherwise would make people dependent, the antithesis of self-sufficiency.

Those who preached government aid and support violated this premise. They were detested and outcasts among the political elite. They were socialists, anarchists, and communists. They threatened to destroy civilization. God help the man who was tagged a "red."

As he increasingly brought government into the picture, the political class became increasingly convinced that FDR had inclinations in this direction. His recognition of communist Russia, his meetings and flirtation with Stalin, and his willingness to send large amounts of arms to the Russians to fend off the Germans contributed to this suspicion. His support of a true socialist for the office of vice president, namely, Henry Wallace, appeared to validate this suspicion.

Later accusations that he brought communists into government, the famous case of Alger Hiss, the Rosenbergs, the theft of atomic secrets, and even later suspicions surrounding his principal aid Harry Hopkins helped to create a political divide that remains with us today.

Recessions cleansed the system was the philosophy of the day. To be unemployed was unfortunate, but it helped build character through belt-tightening. It closed businesses that were superfluous. It resulted in people working harder and smarter and more efficiently. With businesses closing, there was an excess of labor, and thus wages began to fall. This was viewed as a positive development. Labor was the key item in the cost of doing business. If an owner could reduce the cost of doing business, the prices of his goods would fall and demand would increase, which in turn would lead to recovery.

Work may be a necessity of life, but so was the business cycle. Economic cycles were an unfortunate but essential aspect of life, as was unemployment, which was certain to follow. This reasoning went completely unchallenged. It was so ingrained in the minds of the world's leaders that when labor revolted against the planned wage cuts in the coal mines of England, government called out the militia.

Any concerted act of labor, even after the rise of unions, was seen as a threat to private property and thus anarchist.

It was this ingrained cultural thinking that Roosevelt successfully broke during his years in office, even if that had not been his original intention.

The banking crisis completely immobilized Hoover. Prior to FDR's inauguration, Hoover wanted Roosevelt to join with him in taking steps to relieve the crisis. Roosevelt said, "No; you are the president; the decisions are yours."

As conditions worsened, Hoover had taken important steps, the most noteworthy being the Glass-Steagall Act, an important banking reform measure. He created the Reconstruction Finance Corporation to keep people in their homes and the farmers on their farms, which Roosevelt continued.

However this was not nearly enough. In his 1932 inaugural address, with the now famous line "We have nothing to fear but fear itself," Roosevelt appeared to sense both the despair of the nation and the smell of revolution.

He was not afraid to take chances. If fear had been a dominant trait of his, he would never have run for governor of New York and the presidency, given his disability. Roosevelt's optimism came from the soul of the man; fear never entered his psyche.

He grasped the most important lesson for nation-states: that no people, even under tyranny, will long starve for the benefit of the political or ruling class. "Try anything" was his motto and an imperative of the time, a fact that Hoover did not grasp and we do not grasp today.

It was never a matter of Roosevelt embracing government. He was a pragmatist, a political pragmatist of the first order, who understood that if he was ever to accomplish anything, he would first have to survive politically.

If Roosevelt was to succeed, he had to provide the Americans with answers to their pressing needs. If by embracing government he could be assured that we would get there, he was open to the embrace.

Roosevelt may not have had a firm political or economic philosophy, but he knew the nation was in deep trouble and something had to be done quickly.

Government might not be the ideal answer to all questions, but it defended the common man, and FDR was their spokesman, their watchdog.

Above all he believed that a way could be found, using the expression of today, to jump-start the economy. Jobs were essential, and prices must remain reasonably firm so that industry could afford to hire personnel.

Programs large and small were started to create jobs. The CCC, the Civilian Conservation Corps, a work relief program for unmarried young men, arguably the most successful of his many programs, succeeded in reforesting broad regions of America, preventing dust-bowl conditions. He increased regulation, creating new agencies such as the Securities and Exchange Commission, appointing Joseph Kennedy, father of a future president, as the first commission chairman.

His hope took the form of programs. The fact that this involved the government in ways unheard-of in America's past did not bother him at all.

Clearly his administration was characteristic of those who argued for activist government. His inaugural address in 1932 stated plainly that the American people wanted action, "action now." He meant, and they understood he meant, action by government.

Those who opposed him did not understand that he did not consider wealth as the measure of class. He and his extended family were members of a very special class that sprang from his heritage, not his money. Roosevelt's money at any rate was controlled not by him but by his mother and was largely taken for granted by him.

CHAPTER 24

# A New World

### INTELLIGENT GOALS ARE A PREREQUISITE FOR SUCCESS
The programs FDR initiated had goals in addition to employing able-bodied men. They reversed the decline in prices—otherwise known as deflation—which he saw as the principal cause of unemployment.

Of course he needed the support of Congress, who controlled the purse strings. Worse still he needed the support of the Supreme Court, which was wedded to the past and would, as he was about to learn, declare unconstitutional any law that constituted any interference with private property.

FDR implicitly understood that capital or savings could not distinguish private from public spending. Which sector was spending the money was not critical. What was key was that money was invested, invested and not consumed. The products produced would eventually be consumed if and only if the public had the money to buy them, and that meant employment.

Circulation of capital was what mattered. The greater the circulation, the healthier business must be. The economy was like a giant dynamo or generator that gives off light. Slow down the generator or dynamo, and the lights dim and eventually go out. Declining circulation could be measured by a decline in the money supply, which meant that a decline in business activity must soon follow.

Excessive circulation meant that prices would rise faster than the capacity of business to produce, and this imbalance in time would result in higher prices, a drop in demand, and thus unemployment. Balance had to be maintained.

## A Plea for Higher Prices

On the other side of the ledger, the programs he initiated, carried to an extreme, smacked of socialism. Agriculture continued to be of overriding importance. Attempting to hold farm prices above the market level to aid the bereft farmer meant that the city dweller had to pay more with money that he did not have, and thus was further disadvantaged.

Nevertheless, Roosevelt pushed ahead in a sustained broadly based effort to raise prices.

Of course, if prices were to move higher, then the monetary standard should move higher. Initially FDR attempted to achieve this by ordering the US Treasury to enter the market and purchase gold.

The official exchange price for gold since 1834 was fixed at $20.67. This was an artificial price well below the market. Thus there were virtually no sellers.

In all cases an attempt to hold the price of an asset below the market price simply produces scarcity. In other words no one will willingly sell property at a price below its true value unless driven by extraordinary circumstances. People would rather hoard it.

Thus this gold project was doomed from the start. It is surprising that Roosevelt and his advisors understood so little about money and the laws of economics that he would attempt this in the first place.

Why didn't the Federal Reserve simply increase the amount of dollars in circulation? Wouldn't that have allowed people to buy more, thus sustaining the price level? Dollars could be freely converted into gold at the fixed exchange price. If the amount of dollars in circulation were increased, the world would rush to convert the dollars into gold, thus reducing dollars in circulation with nothing achieved.

On the other hand, if the price of gold were increased to thirty-five dollars and by law Americans were prevented from buying gold and had to turn in their gold to the Treasury, incremental dollars would stay in circulation and prices would firm. This was the avenue FDR finally chose to go down.

Foreigners could continue to convert dollars into gold, but it would cost thirty-five dollars an ounce. Gold was made more expensive. More dollars would be circulating.

## The Roosevelt Devaluation

By Executive Order 6102 signed on April 5, 1933, Roosevelt forbade the hoarding of gold in the United States. American citizens had to turn in gold to the Federal Reserve for $20.67 per troy ounce, customary use by industry excepted. The price for international transactions was raised to thirty-five dollars, the equivalent of $600 today. Roosevelt was going down the right road for the right reason, but this devaluation ultimately failed.

Devaluation means that the currency is worth less, and therefore an individual's buying power has been reduced. At first blush this would seem completely contrary to FDR's plan. Of course he did not want the consumer buying less. Quite to the contrary, his policies were designed to have the consumer ultimately buying more.

Appearances deceive, and in this case deceived completely. By raising the official price to an arbitrary fixed level, Roosevelt and his advisors were endeavoring to determine value. Price can never determine value. Value determines price. Price can only be set by the market.

Had the Treasury purchased gold at a price that the sellers were willing to accept, which given its relative scarcity (this is speculative) was probably in the sixty dollars an ounce price range, gold would have come out of the woodwork. This would have been the basis for a substantial increase in the money supply. The liquidity squeeze would have disappeared overnight.

The decision to devalue brings profit to producers. As demand is stimulated, the producer in order to meet that demand hires personnel, who then spend, resulting in an economic upturn. Devaluation brings huge bonuses on the liability side of the ledger as well. By devaluing the dollar by, say, 50 percent, the purchasing power of debt is effectively devalued by 50 percent.

The debtor has twice as many dollars as he had previously, but his debt hasn't changed. The lender continues to collect the same amount of currency, but the value of the currency is now worth half of what it used to be. The debtor wins, and the creditor loses. Through the simple act of devaluation, enormous amounts of debt have been excised.

Is this fair? Is this just sleight of hand? The answer to the question is not as obvious as it appears. To arbitrarily cut my debt to the creditor in half indeed is not fair, but not to repay him at all is far less fair. If the choice is bankruptcy or devaluation, devaluation is vastly preferable. The purpose of commerce is not to reward creditors but to increase wealth.

Given the level of our national debt, shouldn't we rush to devalue today?

All financial questions should be that simple. A nation's currency carries symbolic meaning. It tends to be treated as one might treat the flag. To suggest that a currency should be devalued is insulting, disrespectful. It calls into question the policies being pursued by the nation. It is suggestive of fundamental weakness. Devaluation interferes with trade, or so it is widely believed.

In point of fact, it serves to increase the exports of the nation devaluing, while reducing imports. This not only results in an improved balance of trade but works toward making a nation more self-sufficient, for foreign goods are no longer inexpensive in comparison to domestic manufacture or production.

Devaluation enhances domestic employment. It spurs production, since it increases the prospect of return.

On the other hand, it makes everything foreign more expensive. Planning a trip to Europe would cost a great deal more.

For a nation that has been languishing and losing its competitive edge against other nations, it revitalizes the work ethic. Once again the nation begins to move forward.

The question for the United States and the world today is "What do we devalue against?" We are no longer on the gold exchange standard. Furthermore, as the dollar is the world's reserve currency, if a way could be found to devalue, the effect would be to devalue the dollar reserves of every nation on the planet.

The purchasing power of other nations such as China would be severely reduced. International trade would be disrupted. There are no easy answers, but there are answers.

## The Solution

All that said, all currency must truly reflect asset value. If currency is misaligned, it has to be adjusted. That may be politically difficult and may cause serious problems, but there is no substitute.

FDR understood that the dollar was overvalued, as was all currency, as the world descended into depression.

He took action, and that was his strength. His devaluation against gold was insufficient given future developments. Today we are doing virtually nothing except complaining as both the nation's debt and global debt continue to climb. At some point the system will not be able to take more, and the market will collapse, currency and debt with it. This fact simply points out the importance of leadership.

FDR's aim with devaluation was to put more currency in the hands of the consumer. He had deep empathy for the working man and his plight. Labor and labor unions were a key constituency of the Democratic Party. He was a gentleman farmer, which kept him close to the plight of agriculture.

The economy did begin to show signs of improvement, rising from the abyss after bottoming in early 1933, when unemployment exceeded 30 percent. With dips along the way, the economy showed intermittent signs of recovery before turning down again in 1937.

Whereas a return to prosperity had been the goal of his presidency at the time of his election in 1932, as the decade came to a close, expectations now focused on recovery. Prosperity was presumably beyond reach.

I am convinced history will write that the failure of the New Deal did not lie in the scope of his programs or that they had a government orientation, but his inability to reestablish global equilibrium by bringing debt and disposable income into proper balance. To have accomplished this, a far deeper devaluation was called for.

There is no question such steps would have significantly altered asset values. Asset values had already suffered massive declines as a result of the now decades-old depression; further damage was likely to be minimal.

A further substantial devaluation would have neutralized the global impact of debt, giving the global consumer greater spending power, enhancing profitability.

To wrest the world from depression necessitated devaluation. The answer to the economic woe we suffer today both here and globally resides in a full recognition of decades-old excessive consumption funded by debt. Today we must work to bring currency and asset values in line, and that means devaluation. As wages and prices adjust, the consumer will have more disposable income, reentering the market for cars, trucks, appliances, and houses. Unfortunately, monetary devaluation today appears impossible as there is no longer a gold standard.

However, there is another way to accomplish the goal, which I cover in the last chapter. An expansion will begin in earnest, and we will have been freed from the economic chains that bind us all today. Without a doubt, creditors and others will lose and lose big-time, but as you will shortly see in the experience of Germany after the Second World War, solutions are there, but they take imagination and courage, particularly political courage.

## Roosevelt's Programs—How Expensive They Can Be

Roosevelt believed that stable and rising prices were key to the rejuvenation of world commerce. As he surveyed the landscape during the decade of the thirties, he was met by the constant threat of businesses closing, unemployment rising, and foreclosure of businesses, housing, and farms.

Government programs were critical, but he understood that the private sector was key to recovery. If farmers were to grow crops, at least those who had not been swept away by the aftereffects of the stock market crash, they must be assured that they would be able to sell their produce at a profit. Having to borrow in the first place to plant, irrigate, and fertilize, there appeared to be no other way for the lenders and borrowers to take the risk without assurance that they would be able to realize a return on their investment.

Thus FDR introduced agencies to provide price support, including payments to farmers not to grow crops on their land, in other words, to allow the land to remain fallow to reduce competition.

Another aspect of his many programs encouraged the establishment of cooperatives. With new irrigation techniques and new soil conservation measures, it would be far less expensive for the individual farmer to work with others. Cooperatives provided marketing capability and expertise on all aspects of modern farming by calling in experts from government and academia to lend assistance.

*Life, Liberty, and the Pursuit of Money*

Roosevelt sent to Congress during his three terms a plethora of programs designed to employ and to jump-start economic recovery, including the following: in 1933 the Civilian Conservation Corps, which would employ 300,000 for forestry and flood protection; the Homeowners Loan Corporation to refinance home mortgages in default to prevent foreclosure; the Tennessee Valley Authority, for cheap power; the National Industrial Recovery Act, covering a wide range of businesses, with codes to foster higher prices (which the Supreme Court found to be unconstitutional); the Agricultural Adjustment Administration, a program that paid farmers not to produce (found by the Court to be unconstitutional); in 1934 the Securities and Exchange Commission to regulate securities; in 1935 the Social Security Act for the elderly; in 1935 the Works Projects Administration (WPA), a program for unemployed to preserve skills and self-respect, which during its existence employed 8.5 million; the Wagner Act, broadening the rights of labor; in 1937 the Farm Security Administration to aid poor farmers; in 1937 the US Housing Authority for low-cost construction; in 1938 the Fair Labor Standards Act, dealing with hours worked and wages; in 1938 the Agricultural Adjustment Act, funded by the federal government to prevent overproduction, which replaced the 1933 Act; and others.

He never believed that these programs offered a permanent solution to the unemployment problem. FDR, like his cousin earlier in the century, was a strong advocate for reform. He was not an advocate of the welfare state.

Well before the Second World War, FDR was a busy man, as the aforementioned indicates, perhaps the busiest president in history.

Was all this legislation effective? History has been debating that ever since his passing and will continue to do so. Obviously those who benefited most directly think so. However, history is a stern master and marker, and some would say, cynical. Clearly, certain programs were far more effective than others. There is widespread agreement that Social Security was a godsend. On the other hand, observers have concluded that the NIRA, the National Industrial Recovery Act, distorted market conditions and the Supreme Court did the nation a favor by finding the legislation unconstitutional.

In agriculture was it wise to pay farmers not to plant crops when many, with little or no money, in the cities were starving?

Experimentation is wonderful, but it has its limits.

These programs and their implementation cost an immense sum of money. The money had to be obtained from somewhere. In an era when fiat money, that is, running the printing presses, would have been viewed as irresponsible, such was not possible.

The money had to be found, that is, it had to come from the savings of others, including America's corporations.

The best measure of success would be the impact of these programs on labor. During the darkest days of the depression, the unemployment rate exceeded 30 percent. That occurred in early 1933. The rate began to decline so that by 1935 it was closer to 20 percent. By 1937 it was approaching 14 percent. Beginning in 1937 unemployment ballooned, and by 1938 it was skirting 20 percent, dropping back to the high teens just prior to the war.

By any measure we have today, FDR's policies would not have been viewed as successful. Though unemployment dropped very sharply from 30 percent in 1935 and then reversed upwards in 1937, Roosevelt had neither the money nor the ideas to turn it around a second time. From his standpoint, what were the alternatives?

There were of course other critical factors in play. First, and many would argue foremost, was the money supply. The money supply, M1, grew every year from 1919 until 1929, many thanks to Ben Strong, but then entered a long period of decline until 1936.

Growth in money and Congressional legislation were at odds with each other. As uncomfortable as this might seem, the facts are what they are. FDR might have been doing his own thing, but so was the Fed. They were literally acting at cross-purposes. To explain this conflict is difficult. The Fed was always concerned with inflation, while Roosevelt's concern was deflation. It was as if the two never spoke to each other or had different constituencies.

Implicitly Roosevelt's policies required an expansion of the money supply, while the Fed was endeavoring to constrict it. It is no wonder then that everything turned out as it did. If this wasn't sorry enough, we then had the slight matter of taxation.

To Hoover and Roosevelt, the rates of taxation didn't seem to matter. Under all circumstances and conditions, what mattered most was balancing the budget. Both must be spinning in their graves as they view the spending and tax policies of Washington today.

As the depression deepened in 1931–1932, Hoover decided that the government needed additional revenue. Thus Congress passed the Revenue Act of 1932. This Act raised tax rates across the board. The top tax rate went from 25 percent to 63 percent. Two decades earlier, at the time the income tax was first introduced, it was 7 percent.

This happened under Hoover's watch. Please bear in mind that Hoover was a Republican. The corporate tax rate had a 15 percent increase to a rate of 13 ¾ percent. The estate tax was doubled. Revenue first; depression be damned.

Roosevelt, who had concluded years earlier that the wealthy were a combination of crooks, robbers, and thieves, and worse still, nouveau, and in desperate need of revenue for his programs, decided to raise rates further. Submitting to Congress the Revenue Act of 1935, known fondly as the "soak the rich tax," it raised the top tax rate to 79 percent, with a graduated corporate tax and dividend rate.

The all-time high tax rate was raised to 94 percent in 1944–1945 to cover the expenses of the war.

Budget balancing remained both a priority and a struggle for FDR.

He and Secretary of the Treasury Morgenthau recognized that the private sector at some point had to provide jobs. Government could only carry the burden for so long. The sheer expense of carrying hundreds of thousands of workers, whose work, though valuable, was not profitable, required additional revenue, which translated into more taxes. Others had to pay.

Those others were the farmers, businesses, entrepreneurs, and speculators who earned revenue, made a profit, and ultimately paid the taxes. It was the tax revenue that sustained government employment, but there were after all absolute limits.

Bear in mind that government consumes; government does not produce. However, certain programs, though they consume tax revenue, are investment-oriented and are the first critical step in the production-employment process, such as the highway program or the GI Bill. Nevertheless, it remains true that it is the private sector, not government, that provides the jobs and thus the tax revenue to sustain our standard of living and a functioning economy.

This is made possible only through profit. If there is no profit to be taxed, there is no revenue for government. If there is no revenue for government, there cannot be government employment. Without profit, commerce comes to a halt, and tax revenue nosedives.

Though Roosevelt must have understood this, his understanding was shallow. This may have been the result of his patrician upbringing. He appeared to believe that large numbers of rich Americans had money squirreled away that should flow to the government irrespective of tax liability. He never seemed to be able to tie these pieces together.

## The Economic Fundamentals—What FDR Did Not Understand

To fully grasp this critical moment in world history and the mistakes made, one must look to and review the basics. Every exchange requires both equality and proportionality for balance.

People will never freely exchange one ounce of gold for one ounce of silver because their respective values are different. The value of gold and the value of silver are not equal. In large part this is due to a fact of nature: the supply of silver greatly exceeds the supply of gold.

Currency is the mechanism we use to measure equality and proportionality. Between countries with different currencies, supply and demand are in constant flux. The relative value of one currency versus another, for example, dollar versus euro, must by definition be constantly changing. Thus fixed exchange rates distort the market.

All that is produced is useful. Its flexibility of use, its durability, its breadth, and its laborsaving potential determine its quality and utility.

If the demand for a product produced exceeds the cost of production, cost as measured by the amount invested in plant and equipment and the labor expended to produce it, the producer realizes a profit. That profit has value, which he can later expend or invest in a new plant. That value is surplus. Another word for surplus value is *savings* or *capital*.

This surplus value, savings, or capital is dormant until the producer does something with it. The producer can buy commodities or consumer products and consume them. If that is done, the producer no longer has savings. The producer cannot invest. Thus neither investment nor growth are possible at this point.

On the other hand, if the producer invests rather than consumes, the result is an increase in money circulation.

Whereas before there was only one plant, now there are two. Money begets money. Circulation begets incremental money, M-C-M1. Credit the economists Adam Smith and Malthus for this simple explanation.

It is the intensity of circulation that produces the profit and thus the savings, which gives rise to a surge in production, invention, redesign, and lower unit cost, which we know as development.

Circulation could be thought of as a gigantic dynamo; the faster it spins, the more energy it gives off. Capital and labor are the fuel for the dynamo. The dynamo won't function, won't give off energy, without both factors operating in tandem. To speed the dynamo, additional labor is needed. Translated, that means employment. To speed the dynamo, capital/savings is also needed. The end result, economic development, cannot be accomplished without those means, that is, without both capital/savings and labor or its proxy, machinery.

For any nation that consumes more than it saves or produces more than can be utilized, the growth rate will slow, and over time, if consumption is dominant, the dynamo will cease to function. We refer to such periods in a nation's history as periods of recession and depression.

Every product produced is a union of labor and capital. The union of labor and capital gives birth to the product.

The quality of every product is dependent on the quality of labor. Often missed by capitalists is the critical element of skill.

Modern-day capitalists and business owners downplay the importance of quality of labor. Quality encompasses innovation and invention. Thus the quality of product differs from country to country.

Today the money-grubbers reason that if they can get someone to work for less, then their profit will increase. This reasoning is flawed. Unskilled or less-skilled labor has a direct impact on quality. The less-skilled are less-productive. Furthermore, the entrepreneur sacrifices the prospect of innovation and invention. The more able, the more innovative, labor is the more productive. The quality of the product and thus the competitive position of the owner are advanced by virtue of labor's ability.

If an owner seeks to increase profit by reducing labor cost, for example, laying off staff, he or she sacrifices human genius and its potential. Labor is not homogenous. Globalization assumes homogeneity. The argument is that an unskilled Chinese worker will be as productive and as innovative as a skilled, experienced American worker and will work for less. This is sheer nonsense.

A good example of the absurdity of such thinking is when the Red Sox team traded Babe Ruth to the Yankees to reduce compensation expenses, with the argument that there were many right fielders in their organization who could take his place.

In American history, the South was not nearly as productive as the North due to slavery. Slave labor was inexpensive, but it was also unproductive and devoid of human genius or at least its application. In any contest, the North was sure to prevail, and as we all know, did.

## For Roosevelt Money Meant Mama

In FDR's family, money was never an issue. Patrician families never discussed money. Such matters were for the plebeians and their peers, the nouveau riche. As a businessman, Roosevelt had never made any money to speak of. Mama had the money.

On the money subject, he could be very caustic and disbelieving. He had the IRS go after Andrew Mellon, the distinguished secretary of the Treasury, whose paintings, given freely to the nation, occupy the National Gallery.

FDR thought Mellon should be paying more in taxes. When told that he had no tax liability, Roosevelt apparently responded that he should pay more taxes anyway. Liability apparently had nothing to do with the matter.

With his patrician duty in mind, Roosevelt felt a continuing obligation to help others. Government was the vehicle for getting that job done, particularly now during this period of crisis. No matter how pure the motive, how charitable and beneficial, it is important to remember that consumption erases savings, thus limiting future production. Infinite consumption brings economic potential to an end. To keep the dynamo spinning, there must be profit and thus the savings to be reinvested. This in turn gives rise to additional profit and new jobs.

Given Roosevelt's proclivities, American corporations were increasingly reluctant to invest, for the most obvious of reasons. There is no investment if there is no potential for gain. Extraordinary tax rates combined with the inherent risk of investment quashes potential.

How little Roosevelt understood commerce and the driving force behind it is borne out in a proposal later watered down by Congress, made initially by Henry Morgenthau to FDR.

In order to get savings, corporations were not reinvesting. He argued for a new tax, the undistributed profits tax, to replace the corporate income tax. "The President was also talking about using the income tax in a new way, not just as a tax for revenue, but also as a means of social reform."[cxiii]

The Undistributed Profits Tax was enacted in 1936. It turned out to be a political disaster. The justification for the tax was that wealthy taxpayers were successfully avoiding the payment of income taxes by seeing to it that the corporation, which in some cases they controlled, did not pay dividends. Dividends produced revenue, which Roosevelt was in dire need of.

The unexpected result was an increase in unemployment, which had until 1938 been falling. The tax was first reduced and then excised in 1939.

By taxing the savings of business, Roosevelt was destroying the critical potential for growth. The bizarre nature of this proposal is self-evident today, but the economic ignorance of the times, combined with his personal desire to close the gap between rich and poor, fostered this and other ideas that were fundamentally unsound. Zealotry without careful reasoning can produce greater hardship.

Rooseveltian pride would never have allowed him to admit his mistakes, but he made them. Fiorello LaGuardia, the mayor of New York during Roosevelt's reign, may have put it best when he observed, speaking about himself, that "I make very few mistakes, but when I do make a mistake, it's a beaut."[cxiv]

At the same time, the Federal Reserve, doing its thing as gold came back to the United States due to Hitler and the thirty-five dollar gold price, decided to curtail the money supply. M1, which had increased by 55 percent from 1933 to 1937, declined in 1938 by 1 percent.

One mistake FDR made repeatedly concerned the price structure. A fundamental tenet that lay at the base of all his proposals was that recovery demanded rising prices. That view was shared by virtually all economists, analysts, and advisors. Falling prices meant declining profits, and declining profits translated into declining wages and higher unemployment.

This view was at the heart of the National Industrial Recovery Act, with its codes designed to provide workers with a higher pay scale with goods produced and sold at price levels above the prevailing market. Many asked at the time, "Who could afford them?" Similarly the Agricultural Adjustment Act, where farmers were being paid not to grow crops, had as a goal higher farm prices and thus greater income for the farmers, but created a hardship for the city dweller.

FDR was under the illusion that still prevails in many quarters today, that consumption is the driving force behind economic growth rather than investment.

Investment of course is not possible without savings. Capital pays for productive labor. The Depression had wiped out a giant share of the world's savings. The private sector was out of the game.

Government participation was the only life force available in the crisis. Government intervention was the answer; history would likely say a necessity. Due to its size and economic might, government had the power to jump-start the economy as Roosevelt sought to do. This could never have been accomplished through taxation, which was self-defeating, robbing Peter to pay Paul, killing the goose if you will that laid the golden egg. For government to accomplish the goal, it had to borrow capital and then invest it strategically.

At the same time, it should have taxed consumption, that is, all consumption other than necessities, most particularly luxuries, which by definition are wasteful. Economic waste is a synonym for luxury. Luxury taxes, rather than income taxes, could have and should have been imposed. This would have steered additional capital into investment.

The average person, if given the choice, would rather invest than give money to the government in the form of taxes. The entire effort should have been pointed in the direction of investment and production. This is more than just simple theory, for this is exactly the program that Roosevelt and the nation followed after Pearl Harbor. The war years were years dominated by government investment, through borrowing, leading to production on a massive scale while denying luxury.

By 1945 the United States was building a ship a day and 16,000 planes a month, making major advances in technology, the atom bomb, and feeding the world. At the same time, consumer goods were rationed here at home, and luxuries were nonexistent.

Savings, investment, and production were American economic policies during the war, and they worked marvelously. We not only won the war, but the nation was infinitely wealthier than it was when the war began. A similar policy would work just as well today.

Such a policy is being stymied by this nation's fascination with consumption, combined with bureaucratic waste, public and private corruption, irrational tax and spending policies, and related ills, such as globalization.

## Gold and FDR—"Never the Twain Shall Meet"

Gold was the symbol of virtually everything that Roosevelt opposed. He had many an enemy during his career. Sometimes he prevailed, and sometimes he didn't. Gold was an enemy of a different sort. He described it in what became known as his bombshell message to the London Economic

Conference in 1933, a conference that had been called with the expectation that the United States and Britain would return to the gold standard in order to bring about currency stabilization. "For all practical purposes Roosevelt's angry message to the conference on July 3, the so-called 'bombshell,' terminated practicable negotiations in London. It categorized adherence of gold as a fetish of international bankers and made clear his intention to raise internal price levels."[cxv] Simply put, Roosevelt intended to inflate the United States dollar.

If Senator Sherman had seen gold a century earlier as "God's money," Roosevelt viewed it in 1933 as *the* false god.

Like the Great Roman Emperor Theodosius, he would, to the best of his ability, remove its influence from the affairs of men. In this effort he succeeded. It may well have been his greatest success.

By edict, gold could not have been simply done away with. It was the world's standard. It was the centerpiece of commerce. The Brits and the United States had watered down the standard, but not the rest of the world.

In his conscious effort to raise all prices, gold might be pivotal, he thought, and as I have recounted, he set out to raise the price by instructing the Treasury to buy gold. He reasoned that if the gold price rose, so would other prices.

On another occasion, he seriously considered raising the price by 21 cents. Asked by his advisors how he came to that number, he replied, "It was a lucky number, 3 x 7."[cxvi]

A higher gold price meant a cheaper dollar, he reasoned, and thus a positive influence on the price structure. It was his way of beating deflation. FDR's analysis was badly flawed. It was one of his "try anything" schemes.

On the other hand, a far more expansive money supply flooding the banking system with currency would raise the price of gold and other prices as well.

Adjustment in the price of gold was ultimately accomplished with passage of the Gold Resolution Act in 1933 and the Gold Reserve Act in 1934, specifying that contracts requiring payment in gold were unenforceable, while taking away the right of all Americans to hold or trade gold. Trade and possession of gold were made criminal. The dollar was formally devalued as measured in terms of gold from $20.67 to $35.00.

Though this constituted a step in the right direction, allowing for a more expansive monetary policy, it was insufficient, as I noted earlier. This legislation and his many programs did not succeed in bringing us out of depression. Where was the failure? What was missing?

CHAPTER 25

# A Standard for All Time

### Money and Value, the Twain Must Meet

Currency serves but one function: it is the tool by which to measure value, the value of product. Today and for the past three decades, the United States has run year-to-year a very substantial fiscal deficit domestically or, to put it in simple terms, the United States government is spending substantially more each year than it receives in taxes and other revenue. Joining in this spending binge is the American consumer. We are a nation going broke, albeit slowly.

Internationally the picture is very much the same.

As conceived by John Maynard Keynes and presented at the critical monetary conference held in Bretton Woods, New Hampshire, in 1945, such a development was to be rendered impossible. Any deficit in excess of 1 percent would necessitate a revision in currency value.

International deficits give rise to currency overvaluation, which in turn stokes consumption. The ratio of consumption to production shifts in favor of consumption with deficits. The country is consuming more than it is earning. In effect it is going broke, if ever so slowly.

Order, balance, and common sense require that we maintain equilibrium in our worldly dealings. We and our partners have chosen instead to ignore all of this in favor of consumption. We consume, but we do not adjust the value of the dollar to reflect the decline in wealth. This is possible because the central banks have the power to alter, control, or otherwise peg the value of currency. In other words, the value of the dollar is artificial. This distortion becomes global, as the dollar is the world's reserve currency.

The American consumption binge has now been going on for decades. As a result of this, our global trade account, known as the current account, is a scandal. Balance hasn't been achieved since the Reagan years, and we are nowhere near balance today.

Though the discipline of maintaining balance in the current account was orthodoxy for all nations up to the collapse of Bretton Woods in 1971, we choose instead to ignore this deficit. Whether we choose to ignore it or not, we must ultimately come to grips with the reality. The trade deficit is telling us that we import far more than we export. We know from the statistics that is the case. For the most part, those imports are consumed.

Yet how can this happen? If two nations are exchanging value for value, neither should be in deficit. Reason demands that some mechanism be in place to assure that this happens. Prior to the Great Depression, continuing imbalance would have triggered an outflow of gold from the importing nation. That nation would eventually have run out of gold, and this would have limited its ability to import further. However, with a printing press, we just keep printing.

Is it possible for this to go on indefinitely? What will bring this to an end? That is truly the great overriding question of the day. No nation appears ready to tackle the issue.

Balance requires that nations running continuing trade imbalances must account for them by changing the value of their currency. Otherwise the international monetary system becomes a farce. For example, in our imbalanced trade with China, the dollar value should have declined and the yuan value markedly appreciated. This would have eliminated the trade deficit. Both nations have refused to budge, and thus the deficit grows.

## Debt, Debt, Debt—Forever a Cancer

One critical failing over the centuries is that the global leaders never tackle the matter of debt directly. For example, German reparations were put on hold, and much global debt was rescheduled, but that is not excision.

The American consumer during the Depression years carried a debt burden. Roosevelt's policies helped, but they were not enough.

Irrespective of the causes of the Depression, in the end it became a debt crisis. By increasing the price of gold and the money supply in tandem, some relief was realized but not nearly enough.

To reduce the global impact of debt, FDR should have made three separate but related decisions.

First: all moneys owed by Germany and German citizens to the United States should have been forgiven, excused, excised from the books. It was very clear with Germany in turmoil and Hitler in power, England would never receive reparation payments. The Brits should have made the same decision; so should have France. The economic and psychological impact on Germany would have been incalculable.

It would have demolished the Hitler thesis and his most telling political theory, that the Allies had been unfair when they drew up the Versailles Treaty plans in 1919 and were determined to bleed the German people dry. The German people believed this.

Second: private creditors, including the banks that would sustain loan losses as a result of this decision, could have received special consideration, both in terms of taxation reimbursement and recapitalization, to minimize the impact on them for these losses. Given America's relative financial strength, this was very doable.

Third: a targeted price for gold, as opposed to a pegged price of thirty-five dollars, should have been introduced. The target should have been set at sixty to sixty-five dollars and not pegged at thirty-five dollars. To this extent we would have been following the British example, which allowed sterling to float. Let the market set the price.

Under these circumstances there would have been an international wave of gold selling, which, deposited in the banks, would have driven the money multiplier. There would have been an abundance of currency and gold to spend and invest.

The justification for taking such an approach is that it would constitute a full recognition of the cost of war. We in effect would be saying that in the future, we are going to live in the real world.

The war made the world poorer, a lot poorer. The debtor-creditor contracts thus had to adjust, as did the value accorded debt. Global debt had impacted us all. The war bankrupted Europe. The fact that the United States was the world's creditor did not change that.

A bank with loans that are not paid will go bankrupt, though failure to pay is not the fault of the bank. Devaluation is simply recognition of reality. It is not intended to be a statement about a people or nation.

Such devaluation would have set off an investment boom. Abundant liquidity would mean that everyone, domestic and foreign, could afford to buy the products rolling out of the mills. Stock prices would have surged. Higher nominal prices would have encouraged inventory liquidation, followed by restocking.

America would have been back in business—and the world with it.

## What about Inflation? What Inflation?

Contrary to monetarist thinking and prevailing economic doctrine, including economists such as Milton Freidman, who might have argued that such a program would have been inflationary, that is not so.

Price inflation only occurs when one endeavors to hold the value of currency to a level below its true value. On the other end of the spectrum, people will spend and consume an overvalued currency for the same reason they sell overvalued equities.

The critical factor is not, as Freidman argued, that the rate of growth of the money supply determines inflation. Rather, it is artificially priced currency in relation to the value of goods and services which gives rise to a rapid rate of growth in the money supply that produces price inflation.

Thus the exchange rate must always be the critical point of focus. It was not made the point of focus then, and is not now. Today, as in the thirties, monetary policy is failing due to a lack of understanding of currency.

## For Lack of Boldness, Opportunity Is Lost

The conversion price for gold remained fixed at thirty-five dollars until August 15, 1971, when Richard Nixon announced that the United States would no longer sell Treasury gold for dollars. It was only then that the artificiality of the price became apparent. Gold subsequently moved above $800 by the late seventies.

Since August 1971 the United States has been on a strict fiat money system, that is, the ultimate standard or measure is trust and trust alone, trust in the people and in the government. As one might surmise, the result has been wholesale abuse.

By 1938, with unemployment again on the rise and with budget deficits in prospect, the New Deal came under fire. The Roosevelt promises of final recovery and prosperity were being called into question across the political spectrum. The domestic economy was deteriorating, which could not be denied.

In the mid-thirties, due to the yeoman work of men such as Secretary of State Hull, international trade experienced a rebirth as revisions were made in Smoot-Hawley. The Reciprocal Tariff Treaty Act was passed in 1934, giving the president power to negotiate bilateral trade agreements around the globe, with emphasis on reciprocity. This Act fostered cooperation and reopened trade. International trade increased and assisted in the recovery.

However, great uncertainty persisted. Adding to the uncertainty was the matter of peace or war in Europe. Isolationism dominated the American political scene. The American military had been dismantled after the Great War. FDR was in a policy box with no apparent exit. Serious consideration was never given to what had become a Washington standard, deficit spending.

The nation had little choice but to borrow to meet major certain crises, such as the First World War and Depression. However, government borrowing in peacetime to meet current operating expenses was another matter entirely, imprudent at best and a step in the direction of bankruptcy at worst.

There was no Congressional support for such a policy, and the public would have reacted with dismay. By this time there was general agreement that debt had played a key role in the global collapse. Debt was the continuing problem, not a solution. With thinking more deserving of oxen than of men, most believed that we had no choice other than to pay down debt, period. More taxes perhaps?

Roosevelt was by nature austere. His support of the Economy Act in 1933, which cut government employee salaries by 15 percent, is indicative. This step was taken to assist in balancing the budget. All budgets should be balanced, and that would include his own. Roosevelt, as some have suggested in the political debates that have raged since his time, was never for giveaway programs.

He was dead set against what he called the dole. He thought every able-bodied man should work. At the same time, he believed that everyone should be given that opportunity and helped along the way. He was not under any circumstances, as countless observers have argued, for the welfare state.

On the other hand, he believed, as did many a social economist at the time, that laissez-faire capitalism was dead and buried forever. He was certainly wrong about that. He felt that a new equitable approach to commerce had to be found, and that was critical if democracy was to survive. His cause was democracy, a more democratic America.

Government had a critical role to play in leading the nation in a new direction, he believed. In time this would lead to a rebirth. He was by every measure an idealist. He should have been more of a realist. However, he believed in America and in private enterprise, though the private sector attacked him unmercifully. Exactly where all of this would eventually lead, he simply did not know.

Whether the New Deal would have subsequently taken us down the road to ruin, as his political opponents have since suggested, we will never know, for on December 7, 1941, the Japanese bombed Pearl Harbor.

CHAPTER 26

# Pearl Harbor and Beyond

---

## The End of the Beginning

Doubts concerning Roosevelt's New Deal persisted, coming under increasing scrutiny until December 7, 1941, when bombs on Pearl Harbor forever changed the nation and the world.

Pearl Harbor was cataclysmic. In a matter of hours, the past was extinguished. In monetary terms the event was not a total disaster. It meant a new beginning. The debt that the world had carried forward since the First World War through the Great Depression went up in proverbial smoke.

Nine years had passed since Roosevelt's victory over Hoover. Yet the nation continued to struggle. Though unemployment had declined from the dangerous levels of 1933, the future remained unclear and the general health and welfare of the American people uncertain. Talk of prosperity had passed from our lexicon. The Americans were more than willing to settle for a sustainable recovery.

The rise of dictatorship was the story of Europe, threatening to engulf America, even as Roosevelt promised never to involve Americans in a foreign war. In the course of one day, virtually all that had been considered gospel in economic, financial, and monetary terms was discarded.

The war had begun in earnest for the Americans and the world, and the financial system that would be put in place at war's conclusion, neither Franklin Roosevelt nor his advisors had any conception of as mobilization for war ensued. The New Deal had not achieved its goals, but war would usher in a new era, with America leading the way to prosperity.

## Germany 1940

Germany, the nation of Beethoven, Holy Roman Emperors, scientists, and artists and a history of militarism, barbarism, and strong dictatorial leaders, was on a war footing. In deep despair at the end of the First World War, Germany abandoned totally its Christian principles and turned to savagery under the leadership of Adolph Hitler.

It rearmed and conscripted vast numbers, insisting on total obedience to Hitler's will, while initiating a vast public works program. Among a great number of projects, Germany began to rebuild Berlin, with the intention that it would for a thousand years become the capital of the world. It would become the new Rome and Hitler the emperor.

His Berlin capital would have a building ten times larger than the Pantheon, the largest dome in the world for 1,600 years.

In stark contrast, the United States, a civilized Judeo-Christian nation faced with calamitous economic conditions but whose democratic traditions, faith, and able leadership retained an abiding hope in the future, turned their backs on despair. After Pearl Harbor, it rearmed, conscripted, and engaged in massive public works projects, generating output sufficient to meet all of its war needs and the needs of its allies.

## World War: 1941–1945

War meant death and destruction; it also meant full employment. With millions of able-bodied men in the service, jobs in munitions, factories, and virtually every industry were available for the taking. Women, who had never ventured far from home, were now working day and night and became producers of ships, planes, guns, and butter.

America produced in staggering amounts as no nation in history had ever come close to matching. Made in America products covered the globe. Such an effort required enormous investment. The capital for the effort was not readily available. It had to be borrowed. How much could a sovereign nation borrow?

According to the International Monetary Fund (IMF), debt levels in the advanced economies averaged 55 percent of GDP from 1880 to 2009, although episodes of much higher debt ratios were common. World War II turned out to be one of those periods. By 1945 the debt to GDP ratio approached 150 percent in the United States. Today the debt to GDP ratio in the United States is approximately 270 percent (public and private).[cxvii]

However, these statistics are terribly misleading. During the war the focus was on production. No nation before or since has been as productive. Consumption was near impossible. Consumer factories had been converted for wartime use. Everything was rationed. People saved, bought war bonds, and kept on working.

Today America borrows to consume. In 2009 capital formation, which means all that is built and improved as a percent of GDP, was approximately 15 percent; now it is closer to 20 percent. In China it is 45 percent, France 21 percent, Japan 21 percent, Korea 19 percent, and Argentina 21 percent. Since the Second World War, the capital formation percentage for the developed world has averaged something close to 22 percent. Today we are well below that level. America, breaking with its past, has become a consuming nation, not a producing one. Our gross domestic product is a testimony not to progress but to self-indulgence.

Our military remains the strongest in the world. It is the one bright spot in the picture, though annual arms expenditures appear disproportionate to the immediate threats we face.

We remain the most inventive and innovative of peoples, but the outlook is dismal. Certainly we cannot stay on the track we are on. Obesity spells death, not prosperity.

Gross domestic product statistics do not reveal the true story. The United States and its Allies won the Second World War. Seventy-five years later we are still trying to win the peace. Self-indulgence is not the road to peace and prosperity. It is the road to Rome and ruin.

## The Bretton Woods Era

Bretton Woods is a speck on the map, a small town in New Hampshire, a summer resort. Regarding Bretton Woods and its importance in global economics, one is reminded of the Biblical book Micah, concerning Bethlehem.

*Life, Liberty, and the Pursuit of Money*

"But you, Bethlehem Ephrathah, though you are small among the clans of Judah, out of you will come for me one who will be ruler over Israel, whose origins are…"[cxviii]

At Bretton Woods, forty-four nations gathered in the summer of 1944 to devise steps to bring some form of economic coherence back to a world that in the course of less than fifty years suffered through two world wars, massive destruction, the annihilation of countries of peoples, and the death of perhaps one hundred million.

The world had come a great distance from the moorings of creation. If indeed creation embodied perfection and order, the world of 1945 appeared close to dissolution.

It is virtually impossible to reconstruct conditions as they existed during the war years. If it had been a novel, reviewers would have characterized the text as a portrait of devastation, destruction, starvation, inhumanity, confusion, and despair and would have concluded that humanity was doomed.

As the ministers gathered in New Hampshire in July 1944, there were no parades, no media events, and for a world still focused on the great conflict, very little attention. There were certainly no illusions. They embarked on a huge undertaking and in all probability an impossible one.

The decisions rendered at Bretton Woods would rule the monetary affairs of men for decades, forever changing the global landscape. This conference gave rise to the creation of two institutions, the International Monetary Fund and the International Bank for Reconstruction and Development, popularly known as the World Bank.

## The Lost Opportunity—Oh, If We Had Only Understood

The expression "opportunity never knocks twice" is axiomatic. This extraordinary conference in New Hampshire unfortunately fell far short of its potential. To borrow from the popular Broadway show *Camelot*, "for one brief shining moment" the world and most certainly the United States had within its grasp the opportunity to introduce a monetary system that would have allowed for continuing worldwide recovery and reconstruction. It failed to do so.

Bretton Woods reigned for close to three decades. When that reign ended, it was not due to revolution, fatigue, or old age, but the failure of people and governments to act responsibly.

World leaders, including FDR, understood that the successful conclusion of the war would not in and of itself herald a new era of peace and prosperity. He, better than others, understood the inherent dangers of a monetary breakdown.

His first mistake, one of gargantuan proportions, was the appointment by Henry Morgenthau, secretary of the Treasury, of Harry Dexter White, an economist and senior Treasury official, as the American representative at the conference. There is no evidence that Morgenthau or Roosevelt knew that White was a member of a communist cell, the Ware Group, in Washington.

Whittaker Chambers, a senior editor of *Time* magazine, later renounced communism, testifying that he too had been a member of this Soviet espionage ring, and that it included members of the Roosevelt administration, specifically naming Alger Hiss and Harry Dexter White. His testimony was corroborated by Elizabeth Bentley, who had served as a communist spy but renounced communism and testified that White was a communist sympathizer, which White denied.

A bipartisan commission decades later, headed by Daniel Patrick Moynihan, a Democratic senator, found that Hiss and White were complicit but obtained no documentary evidence regarding White.

The basic outline for the Bretton Woods Conference had been worked out over a period of time beginning in 1942. Attending were 730 delegates from forty-four countries. The conference lasted three weeks, and the agreements reached were set to be operational in 1946, the assumption being that the war would be over by that time. Though there were forty-four nations in attendance, there were only two that were crucial. The United States and Great Britain between them controlled more than 50 percent of the world's monetary gold, which in total ran somewhat over 40 million tons.

*Life, Liberty, and the Pursuit of Money*

On the eve of the war, the United States and Great Britain controlled over 60 percent of the world's trade. The United States, with its continental size and huge resources, had before and during the conflict demonstrated its unlimited productive capability. Great Britain still had its Empire, including India and Commonwealth nations scattered throughout the Far East and the Middle East, and its close identity with Canada.

Britain in its state of financial exhaustion as the result of two wars was totally dependent on the United States. They still longed for the restoration of the Empire. Before the end of 1945, Britain requested a $3.8 billion loan and France $1 billion from the United States.

The despised and defeated enemy, the Germans, had lost virtually everything. They were forced to rely on barter and American black market cigarettes, which they used as currency immediately after the war. Given what had happened during the war, few outside Germany were concerned about their welfare.

At Bretton Woods the primary focus was the restoration of the international monetary and credit system to supply capital for recovery, and any other steps needed to restart world trade.

Though the structure of the World Bank was readily agreed to by the attendees, the design and workings of the newly created International Monetary Fund were to become the subject of intense debate.

While virtually all of the parties, Russia the exception, agreed that a comprehensive plan to deal with currency and trade among nations was essential if the many errors of the thirties were not to be repeated, the devil was in the details.

Roosevelt understood the need for a new system and had suggested to Morgenthau that an international currency might be the way to proceed. By the time of the meeting, FDR was deceased.

Britain had another resource whose value was immeasurable. He was attending the conference as their representative. The man, who was treated as an icon by government and business leaders, was the highly respected Lord John Maynard Keynes.

Keynes, an original and in-depth thinker on economic matters, was a Cambridge professor, an advisor to governments in Great Britain for decades, and an outspoken opponent to laissez-faire economics, arguing and persuading many, including Franklin Delano Roosevelt, of the wisdom of government intervention during periods of economic decline. His thinking was an influence on the New Deal.

He was the first to submit a reorganization plan to the conference.

His currency—named the bancor—plan was designed to foster balance and equilibrium. He appeared to understand, better than anyone at the conference, that imbalance in trade and commerce would result in a global state of unmanageable debt. As long as gold remained the world standard, there was no prospect of sovereign debt being paid. There were simply insufficient amounts of monetary gold available for such an effort. From a liquidity standpoint, bank failures were thus inevitable. Trade imbalances produced the illiquidity that shaped the future disaster. We suffer from that problem today, but few are willing to acknowledge it.

He intended the bancor to become a supracurrency administered by a world central bank, the object of which was not to accumulate but to measure a nation's current account or balance of payments. The world years later took a major step in this direction with the creation of special drawing rights, SDRs, in 1969.

Any nation accruing bancors would be directed to increase its imports until its debit and credit balance came back into balance. There would be no need for reserves.

Trade would be monitored by a global central bank that would have the power to modify or adjust currency exchange rates, and presumably serve as referee in international trade disputes.

Each nation would retain its own currency. Exchange rates were to be fixed but flexible, that is, they could be adjusted under certain conditions.

I expect that within this generation the world will adopt a derivation of the Keynes plan as it learns that nation-state imbalances are the root cause of global stagnation and economic failure.

An alternative to Keynes's plan was submitted by the American representative Harry Dexter White.

Maynard Keynes and Dexter White were both economists and professors. However, when it came to genius, they were not in the same league. Keynes carried with him a global perspective, while White, a bureaucrat totally dependent on Morgenthau for his position, was hobbled by other influences. Experience teaches that long-held political, social, and philosophical views, however misguided, are virtually impossible to change.

Keynes, as brilliant, perceptive, and experienced as he was, was not about to change the views of White. White was a man with an enormous ego. He was the senior Treasury figure under the secretary on all international matters. He was thoroughly caught up in himself.

The Keynes thesis was entitled "Proposals of an International Currency (Clearing) Union." One comprehensive proposal should have been sufficient to allow the delegates and key players to make adjustments as they deemed necessary. However that was unsatisfactory to White, who came forward with his own proposal.

Conceptually the Keynes and White plans were fundamentally different. In the White plan, the global entity was called the International Stabilization Fund of United and Associated Nations, now the IMF. White viewed this fund as supplementary, something of an adjunct to United States economic dominance.

It envisioned two reserve currencies, sterling and the dollar. Nations would accept in payment of international debt obligations either currency. The exchange rate of sterling would be defined by the dollar and the dollar in turn defined by the fixed price of gold. The White plan was based on the ability to exchange gold for dollars at thirty-five dollars an ounce. As had occurred during the prewar financial crises, it remained possible there would be a shortage of gold, but there never would be a shortage of dollars, since the United States government controlled the printing press.

Keynes envisioned a world bank for all nations willing to agree to the terms and adhere to its standards. The name of this bank would be the International Currency Union, or ICU.

This bank's currency, the bancor, was designed to encourage trade. Key to success was that the bank currency would not be priced. It would have neutral value. The aim was to move away from the *historical hurdle of nations with debtor or creditor status*. The long-term goal of the Keynes plan was equivalence of opportunity.

Nothing would ever stand in the way of a nation contributing to the global product. To accomplish this, it was critical that *trade of all nations remain in balance*. It is balance that maximizes the potential for production. This was Jeffersonian thinking through and through.

Imbalance inevitably allows a few to benefit at the expense of others. As a result global production must in time flatten out or decline as those not benefiting fall further behind, becoming a drag on the productive. Intuitively we accept this within the confines of a nation-state, which is the reason we focus on education and training in order that more may contribute and the nation's prosperity be enhanced.

The contest between Keynes and White unfortunately was one-sided. The United States had the money, the power, and the necessary votes in any contest. The White plan was essentially a carryover of the prewar status. A central bank could convert its holdings of dollars into gold at any time. This happened in the seventies, with Germany in the lead, which broke the back of the dollar and with it the international monetary system.

A critical difference between the two plans was that under White, debt would continue to accumulate, a fact that we are only too well aware of today.

Though Keynes took every opportunity to press home his vision and plan, White was equally determined.

In this regard we cannot ignore White's background and alleged communist leanings.

Stalin, the Russian tyrant, deeply distrusted the British. He regarded the Americans as naïve, but the British as a threat. Britain and the British secret service had endeavored to defeat the Bolsheviks during the Russian Revolution.

Consistent with this attitude, White had advised Morgenthau that the Keynes plan was simply a British ploy to regain power, to get back in the game as it were. White appeared determined to defeat this effort.

At any rate the White plan was adopted, the IMF created, and a reformulated world currency order activated in 1946.

## The Consequences of White

With the adoption of the White plan, it became apparent that certain nations would advance more rapidly than others, with the United States in the lead because of its surplus capital and virtually unlimited capacity, while those destroyed by the war would languish. As the development gap widened, the population gap would widen as well. The rate of increase in population for the second and third worlds is invariably greater than that of the first. This phenomenon is explained by the sheer need for brute labor, that is, the more hands to man the plow, the greater the product.

## The Inevitability of Failure

As they left the conference in midsummer, the delegates were understandably hopeful. This was a new beginning. If nations worked together through the newly created United Nations, they believed the prospects were bright. Unfortunately the Keynes plan, with its emphasis on production and balance without debt, was left behind.

To monitor international commerce and assure a level playing field, it was essential that the world have a global bank. A global bank would stand as referee, guaranteeing that no trade disparity persisted and every nation adhered to the terms of membership.

With Keynes global trade and growth would constantly increase, and the relative standard of living and hence wealth of productive nations would advance. No limits were placed on the potential for growth.

In a world with 50 percent living below the poverty line, we can appreciate the immense importance of a system designed to increase exponentially the production of goods and services.

With sufficient global stress of rapidly increasing population, such a plan must see the light of day.

## The United States Monopoly
With the adoption of the White plan, the world reverted back to the narrow, unimaginative, and restrictive regimen that existed prior to World War II.

The true genius of the Keynes proposal was that it offered a realistic way and, to his credit, a simple way for all the nations of the world to work together in concert to improve the standing of living of everyone. In the global bank that he envisioned, all nations would have a line of credit extended for the intended purpose of serving world trade.

The size of a nation's line would depend on the percentage of global trade the nation had achieved prior to the war. The British-United States share exceeded 60 percent. From a credit standpoint, they had the most to gain with the implementation of Keynes's plan. Over time as the nations of Europe recovered, that percentage would decline, not because the United States and Britain were less competitive, but because the rest of the world was contributing a greater share of global production.

There was nothing about the Keynes plan that worked against the interests of the participating nations. Domestic policies and concerns would be largely unaffected. All domestic business would be carried on as before. As a nation exported and imported, the currency value in international terms would appreciate and depreciate, but then very modestly, reflecting the relative advance of a nation. A country experiencing a modest decline in currency value would experience an uptick in exports. Any nation that experienced a serious disruption in its international dealings as a result of some extraneous cause would have the option of going to the ICU, the global bank, and borrowing or, if matters were extreme, applying for a revaluation of its currency. This would be mandated if the change envisioned was greater than 10 percent.

All nations would be working constantly to see that their international trade remained balanced. No longer would "beggar thy neighbor" policies, which were so commonplace before the war during the Great Depression, be possible. Those policies included competitive devaluations, high tariffs, mercantilist favoritism, and favoring trade with one nation over another irrespective of the quality or price of the product.

Keynes at heart was an optimist, who understood that people could and would advance but only by working together. If we did so, global potential was unlimited.

The Keynes plan did not require a monetary contribution, for none was needed. A credit line would suffice, and the United States had the capital to support that need.

Europe, having lost everything during the two great conflicts, had little to contribute. Yet their potential was unlimited—potential in terms of skill, manpower, knowledge, and due to the sheer size of the population, willing consumers for all the advanced goods humans were capable of producing.

What the world needed most was opportunity. Keynes grasped the universal meaning that with people given opportunity and freedom, wealth would naturally flow.

Just such a vision prompted the development in Europe of the Common Market and more recently the European Union.

On broader issues both men were in agreement, including the need to foster international trade and fiscal cooperation. The meeting produced two international organizations: the World Bank, with the formal name the International Bank for Reconstruction and Development, and the International Monetary Fund, IMF.

The World Bank would take the lead in the reconstruction of Europe, and the IMF would promote currency stability.

Volatile foreign exchange rates, which had impeded international trade during the thirties, must be avoided, both men agreed. Keynes emphasized stable exchange rates, and White proposed fixed rates. The conference ultimately adopted fixed rates or pegged rates, which allowed currency fluctuation within a band of 1 percent.

This fixed-rate regimen was adopted not because it was the wiser choice, but because this made the dollar key to all future international decisions. All currencies were to be tied to the dollar; thus the United States, with its power position, would have the last say on all matters political and commercial of importance.

This unfortunate and shortsighted decision proved crucial to bringing about the collapse of the Bretton Woods Agreement in 1971, when the United States was forced to end the selling of gold. The final termination of the agreement was in 1976.

It is abundantly clear that the exchange rate between nations must change and literally changes, however minutely, every second of every day, as products of nations and the demands for currency change depending on the flow of goods and capital. It is clear that Keynes understood this, or at the very least, understood the need for flexibility. White did not seem to comprehend this at all.

Under the White regimen, participants would vote on measures of substance, 80 percent approval being required. The United States, with 25 percent of the vote, retained veto power. The dollar and gold were to be the centerpieces of international trade.

In the Keynes view, both importing and exporting nations had responsibility for maintaining equilibrium. In White's plan the debtor nation had the responsibility to make corrections.

This would translate into what to this day is a matter of controversy: nations with a deficit in their balance of payments must make domestic adjustments in spending and restrict credit in order to restore balance. This only serves to limit production. The world is in dire need of production.

Under Keynes the importance of gold over time would have diminished. What truly mattered was the size of the line of credit, for this would fairly measure a nation's potential and its position in the world in commerce and international trade.

The odd nation out in these discussions was Russia, whose interest was not in rehabilitation but in reparations and world domination. Russia refused to sign the Articles of Agreement, finalized on December 27, 1945. The World Bank and the IMF opened for business June 25, 1946.

With the adoption of White's proposals, American world dominance was assured in the short term. Presumably America was on top, and it was going to stay on top. The shortsightedness of this view speaks for itself.

What America needed was a healthy world, not dominance. Global dominance brought responsibilities that in the long run America could not afford.

As noted, the conference created two new global institutions. On paper, together with the United Nations, they appeared to be sufficient to move the world forward.

In point of fact, everyone, including the new American president, Truman, completely underestimated the dimension and scope of the problems that the world faced.

CHAPTER 27

# Roosevelt to Truman

---

## THE TRUMAN ERA

Franklin D. Roosevelt suffered a stroke and died at age sixty-three while vacationing in Warm Springs, Georgia, on April 12, 1945. Truman, the man Roosevelt would never have chosen as his vice presidential running mate in 1944 had he had his way, was now in full command.

Simply stated, Truman's job was to end the Second World War in the shortest time possible, secure the peace, demobilize, transition the US economy from one designed to fight global war to one designed to meet the pent-up demand of consumers, assure that jobs would be available to those who would be discharged from the military, rebuild Europe and parts of Asia, staunch the advance of communism, pacify Stalin and the Russians, pay down the government debt, and politically convince the American people and our allies that he was up to the job. No man in world history had such an assignment. Tyrants of the stripe of Napoleon would hardly have braved such a chore. Nevertheless the job was his, and few showed any sympathy.

Accustomed to the autocratic behavior of Roosevelt, particularly during the war, the people expected the job to be accomplished with sophistication and alacrity, no excuses please. Presidents, after all, had supposedly limitless power. To this day what is most startling about Truman is that he seldom complained, at least in public. His attitude was very professional. He had a job to do, and he would do it. His philosophy and early policy decisions toed the Roosevelt line that was expected.

To be taken seriously, however, particularly on matters international, meant that he had to be credible in his own right. This was going to be a major hurdle, particularly with the "man of steel," Stalin.

Roosevelt and Stalin had a very good relationship. This should not surprise. FDR was royal and powerful. Stalin, the barbarian czar, was in the Soviet Union all-powerful. The two had much in common. Roosevelt had recognized the Soviet Union and had supplied the Russians with most of the military hardware that allowed them to best Hitler in the war.

The prevailing attitude in America as war came to an end in Europe on May 8, 1945, was that we had done enough for Europe. Now it was up to Europe. This attitude was so ingrained in officialdom that Truman was advised to cut off lend-lease on VJ day. The decision was reversed and lend-lease extended due to the intervention of Eleanor Roosevelt.

No one on this side of the Atlantic had any idea what the cost of reconstruction would ultimately be, but their best guess at the time was about $9 billion. By the early fifties, total grants and loans, including the Marshall Plan, would be many times that figure, a staggering sum for the time.

Lend-lease had played a critical role during the war. America supplied Allied governments from 1941 to 1945 with $50 billion, which is close to $1 trillion today. Great Britain was the principal recipient of the lend-lease largesse, receiving over 60 percent of the aid extended, including equipment, munitions, aircraft, and food stuffs, while the Soviet Union gained over 20 percent.

These "gifts" were essential to their winning the war. No provision was made for repayment.

In September 1945, lend-lease to the Soviet Union was terminated. Excess materials were sold to the Allies at a 90 percent discount.

For postwar Europe, unfortunately, more was needed, a lot more.

Roosevelt was certainly not communist. He believed in the people and in democracy, but his experiences during the depression left him convinced that capitalism was a thing of the past and that a new order was inevitable. Government would play a significant role in the future.

He was not taken in by Stalin, as has long been suggested by his political opponents. Recently released papers reveal that Roosevelt and Churchill had issued "a joint order to their intelligence agencies saying that 'enquiries should be made regarding the activities of Professor Bohr and steps taken to ensure that he is responsible for no leakage of information, particularly to the Russians.'"[cxix]

Stalin was a tyrant. That Roosevelt understood. However he came down from a long line of tyrants and barbarians the likes of Peter and Catherine the Great. Roosevelt's vigilance and calming influence would over time calm the beast, or so he must have thought.

Releases from the Russian archives suggest that Roosevelt's closest advisors were very close to the Communist Party, and one can speculate they influenced him concerning matters pertaining to Russia.

Truman, on the other hand, was thoroughly Middle America, and he saw communism for what it was, namely a global threat to freedom and democracy. Unfortunately, Stalin and his army were now in control of most of Central and all of Eastern Europe, and thus Truman and the Allies were going to have to work with Stalin and the communists whether we liked it or not.

The only alternative was to get involved in another conflict, and no one, with a few notable exceptions such as Gen. George Patton, wanted that.

Thus Truman traveled to Potsdam, Germany, in July 1945 to meet with Churchill and Stalin to determine the steps to be taken to implement the agreements reached earlier by Roosevelt, Stalin, and Churchill at Yalta in the Crimea while the war was raging. Subsequent testimony from his advisors suggests that Stalin felt he could maneuver Roosevelt and get his way. At war's end he stood astride Europe, and America was demobilizing. A little patience and communism would rule in Europe, he might well have reasoned.

Truman, the man from Missouri, and Churchill had very different ideas.

Harry, as he was fondly known, had made it clear prior to the Potsdam meeting, with Russian Foreign Minister V. Molotov, that he expected Russia to live up to its agreements. If future peace was to be assured, trust between nations was an imperative.

Neither trust nor truthfulness was in the Russian lexicon. Russian strategy was to take advantage at every opportunity.

At their meetings Truman's attitude alone must have given pause to Stalin, who, for a number of days, failed to show for meetings, an affront to Truman, with no apology. At one point Truman told his aides that he was thinking of going home. As the meetings concluded, Stalin should have had no illusion about Truman or his intentions, and vice versa.

Though war was not on the mind of either man at the time, the Cold War had begun, and when it finally concluded, both men had long since left the public scene.

In August 1945 the Second World War finally came to an end. It did not end with a whimper but through the use of atomic weapons. Men and women were again free, but for the great bulk of humanity, though free, they remained threatened, threatened by tyranny from the east in the form of communism and by the inability to produce goods in sufficient amounts to hold body and soul of the world populace together.

The guns fell silent, but human survival would remain both uncertain and threatened unless the leading nations could put together plans for the reconstruction and the restitution of commerce.

The pervasive optimism of Roosevelt had literally carried the nation away from despair and miraculously held the union together during the dark days of the depression. Among the "Big Three"—Roosevelt, Stalin, and Churchill—Roosevelt was the most important. Without America both Russia and Britain would have fallen victim to Nazi tyranny.

Roosevelt was clearly the rock upon which a new world, one with hopefully a much brighter future, would have to be built. Where was it all to begin? He had envisioned a United Nations, an organization where disputes between nations could be resolved amicably.

Roosevelt did not live to see this organization in place, for he passed away in April 1945, before it was finally constituted and before the surrender of Germany and Japan.

Uncertainty gripped the world. Who would now lead? Would it be Churchill? God forbid, not Stalin, who was more than willing. No one appeared ready.

Though it could not have been imagined at the time of the presidential election in 1944, the man who would be asked to assume leadership would be the new vice president and former senator from Missouri, a haberdasher in his earlier days, Harry S. Truman.

Truman indeed put on the mantle of leadership, and though there was little in his early background to suggest extraordinary ability and certainly not the potential for greatness, he rose to the occasion as few men could have, and with the passage of time he was included by consensus in the pantheon of great American leaders—Washington, Jefferson, Jackson, Lincoln, Theodore and Franklin Roosevelt, and Harry S. Truman.

Roosevelt had succeeded in holding it all together, defeating the enemies of civilization, and through a massive rebuilding program brought on by the war, reemploying tens of millions of Americans, including a large number of women. It would now be his successor's job to keep it going in a time of peace.

Europe, with its competing nation-states, cultures, biases, and prejudices, simply could not be trusted to pursue peace with justice. We came home after World War I and paid an enormous price in blood and treasure beginning in 1941 for having done so.

Roosevelt and then Truman were both equally determined not to make that mistake again. We would stay engaged, and that meant international institutions. The International Monetary Fund was to be one of those institutions, the least important perhaps, but necessary nevertheless.

## INTERNATIONALISM, THE UNITED NATIONS, THE WORLD BANK, AND THE INTERNATIONAL MONETARY FUND

In retrospect what Harry Truman accomplished was truly miraculous. His first assignment as president was to end the war successfully. Japan was still fighting, and an invasion planned for late 1945 would, according to Chief of Staff George C. Marshall, result in two million casualties to American and Allied forces.

At this point any monetary conference would have been viewed as a sideshow, though it would clearly be important after the war.

Preliminary papers had been written and discussions held that called for the creation of three distinct forums. The first and, in the mind of FDR, the most important was a body that would become known as the United Nations, which would meet on a continuing basis to discuss and resolve disputes between nations before they had a chance to destroy the peace.

Truman was very public about his intention to continue the policies of Roosevelt. However, these were two very different men. The contrast between Roosevelt and Truman was stark.

Roosevelt was forever the romantic idealist and Truman the paramount realist. The two men were joined by complete accident after the leadership of the Democratic Party concluded that the then-sitting vice president, Henry Wallace with his leftist philosophy, was too great a risk to take into the presidential election of 1944.

Truman was not chosen by Roosevelt but by the leaders as a result of his strong prolabor stance as a US senator and his proven integrity as a committee chairman investigating fraud in the awarding of government contracts during the war.

Though they were to run together, they were virtual strangers. Truman was invited to the White House but once, and then only to discuss the campaign. After the election he was kept totally in the dark as the war went on. He knew nothing about atomic research or strategies that were to be pursued as the war went into its final phase.

A striking characteristic of Harry, as he was widely known, was his loyalty. He refused to criticize Tom Pendergast, the head of the Kansas City, Missouri, political machine, though there was considerable evidence of machine corruption, because he was a longtime friend. It is universally agreed that Truman was above dishonesty.

Though he must have chafed at being excluded from White House deliberations, he never voiced any complaint. Upon Roosevelt's death he pledged to continue the New Deal and the war policies of FDR. Whatever reservations he had about Roosevelt's policies, they were never voiced.

Roosevelt dreamed of a world at peace, with all people working together for the common good, alleviating poverty and pursuing policies of friendship with all, including Stalin and communist Russia, though it had become increasingly clear before his death that Stalin could not be trusted. His military would represent a serious challenge to the free world at the conclusion of the war.

Roosevelt was fascinated with the prospects for the United Nations. He would do all he could to preserve future peace, including the surrender of lands to Russian domination in Eastern Europe, while overlooking serious breaches by Russia of agreements previously reached, specifically at Yalta.

Truman, on the other hand, was a total realist, and though he fully endorsed the ideal of a United Nations, he was not about to allow himself to fall prey to Russian deception and intrigue.

It became immediately clear that Truman's principal focus was to bring a speedy end to the war and a return to normalcy. At war's end he would have to address the monumental task of taking millions of servicemen off the government payroll and seeing to it that they returned home and reentered the private sector.

Would there be enough jobs? During the war many of their jobs in the factories had been taken by women, who were now to be replaced. How would this be received? Congress reacted by passage of the GI Bill, one of the most forward-looking pieces of legislation in world history. It allowed soldiers to become educated gratis at the expense of the government, thus increasing their earning potential and job prospects for the future. At the same time, it would limit the competition for jobs while they remained in school.

Fear of a return to depression days was uppermost in Truman's mind. International trade was nonexistent. Though Europe and Japan were in desperate need of everything, they had nothing to pay with and were totally dependent on the goodwill of the Americans. Neither Truman nor anyone else had any appreciation of just how great that dependence would turn out to be.

With the surrender of Japan, Truman and his advisors moved swiftly to disengage from a war economy mind-set. Millions of servicemen would not only demand jobs but also housing, food, and consumer staples.

After years of doing without, patience for the average American would run thin, and the political fallout for failure to rise to the occasion could have devastating consequences. The attention of Washington had to be focused on the conversion from a war to a peace economy. Though America had far-reaching responsibilities in Europe and Asia, as a result of its smashing victory, the political reality was that all effort and attention would be directed to the domestic challenge.

The war had successfully brought America out from under the depression, but there were no guarantees of economic stability with peace. To the contrary, one of Truman's fears was that with all the hurdles and dislocations produced by the war, converting to a peace economy might well be impossible. In other words, a return to the depression days might well be inevitable until industry had the chance to reengage the supply chain, which would ensure jobs for the millions who were now in the service. One way to accomplish this was to demobilize slowly. It quickly became clear that this was politically impossible. Other ways must be found to relieve the pressure.

As government and its resources would be sorely taxed in this effort to meet the urgency and dislocations attendant to massive demobilization, international considerations had to be largely ignored. We had led the great battle for freedom and democracy, and now it was up to the individual countries to rebuild and revitalize their economies.

Everyone was to be on his own. America had done its share, by common consensus far more than its share, and now it was up to the likes of France and England and uncountable numbers of displaced persons who were literally roaming Western Europe in search of food and shelter to pull themselves up by their proverbial bootstraps, rise from the ashes, and rebuild their war-torn economies.

That was the American view, both in Washington and throughout the country.

Such an expectation was unrealistic. Domestic concerns were so paramount here that literally on the day Japan surrendered, Truman ordered the cessation of credits of the Export-Import Bank, which had been an important source of the funding of trade with countries such as Russia.

Russian ships were in New York Harbor waiting to be loaded when the order came. Everything came to a halt. As most of the trade was in foodstuffs, such a cancellation meant that many more would starve.

These credits were reestablished only through the intervention of Eleanor Roosevelt, who pleaded with Truman, explaining how calamitous the situation in Europe really was.

Global recovery was an imperative, but how was it to be accomplished? There was no mechanism, no agency in place, to shed light on the true state of affairs. The consensus in Washington was that the rebuilding of Western Europe would cost somewhere in the neighborhood of $9 billion. There was no serious study that would support such a conclusion. Cabinet officials talked among themselves and consulted with their friends and perhaps their counterparts in England and Europe, and that was the figure arrived at.

No one had any idea of how disastrous the true picture was, including Truman. One can speculate that the European recovery might not have happened at all, at least for decades, if it hadn't been for Secretary of State Hull, who received regular reports that conditions on the Continent were calamitous. There was no prospect of recovery.

If emergency measures were not taken, all of Western Europe would be faced with starvation.

## Germany and Secretary of the Treasury Snyder versus the Brits

It is in the giving that true wealth expands at a geometric rate. The more others participate, the more the dynamic of progress accelerates.

Today, some seventy-five years after the introduction of the Marshall Plan, government leaders, historians, economists, and learned observers marvel at the success of the plan.

Its success sprang from the fact that a few men centered in the Truman White House had the wisdom to understand that the secret to economic progress and success for the individual or nation-state lies in the giving, not in the taking.

Circumstances clearly played a role. Western Europe simply did not have the wherewithal to recover on its own. The world was staring at a new and threatening tyranny in the Soviet Union, but could the United States, with all its resources, accept the burden of carrying the entire European Continent?

The ultimate failure of modern-day materialism and laissez-faire economics is that it seeks advantage by ignoring or pushing others aside to gain advantage. Life becomes an unending process that adheres to a philosophical view that "I can aggrandize, build up, and magnify my position in society, 'my wealth,' by diminishing others."

This is the centerpiece of the political and economic philosophy that holds sway today. Though the public sector continues the tradition of foreign aid, it has largely fallen out of favor as domestic demands occupy the attention of most politicians and budget imbalances form a convenient excuse for ignoring the needs of the third world. In complete fairness, however, America still shows a willingness to help others. The Bush administration commitment of $30 billion to address the AIDS epidemic in Africa is most noteworthy.

## Where Is the Private Sector?

The issue is not unwillingness but a mind-set that appears to afflict great American corporations that somehow national or international tragedies do not involve them. Untold numbers of business corporations preach equity and fairness but readily dismiss thousands of employees, while the senior executives prosper at the smallest signs of a slowdown in business. They do not see a contradiction in this. Hurricane Katrina was a national tragedy.

The private sector could have and should have taken the lead in the recovery effort. Most of those in a position to help just stood by and expected the government to handle it.

In their failure to respond to tragedy and in their sometimes callous dismissal of thousands of hardworking and productive members of society, business is taking a philosophical stand that is a far cry from the generosity demonstrated by America after World War II.

Our leading business schools appear to preach this strange philosophy: "Get all you can." Loyalty, teamwork, experience, perseverance, and balance are outdated. The destructiveness of this reigning mentality escapes them. Of course it must all end in failure, and it most certainly will, though a few, but very few, at the top of the ladder may reap unjustifiable rewards.

Unfortunately today the spirit of the Marshall Plan appears to be moribund. Yet the wisdom of that plan will stand the test of time. Can men like Truman (Harry S. Truman, president 1945–1952), Acheson (Dean Acheson, secretary of state), Marshall (George C. Marshall, secretary of state, secretary of defense, US Army chief of staff), and Snyder (John Wesley Snyder, secretary of the Treasury) rise again to show the way? Perhaps so; never despair.

## Money and Value—The Twain Must Ultimately Meet; Otherwise, Disaster

Currency serves but one function. It is the tool by which we measure value, the value or utility of the product. Today and for the past three decades, the United States has run year-to-year a very substantial fiscal deficit domestically. In simple terms, the United States government is spending substantially more each year than it receives in taxes and other revenue. We are, as I have said earlier, a nation slowly going broke.

Under Bretton Woods as conceived by Keynes, such an event was to be rendered impossible. Any deficit in excess of 1 percent would necessitate a revision in the currency value.

Today's deficit is telling us that the measure of value has broken down; otherwise the value given versus the value received would be in balance, even though the exporting nation was to nominally sell more goods to us than we do to them.

The difference would be accounted for in a change in the exchange rate of the currency. The dollar value should have markedly declined, and the yuan in the case of China should have markedly appreciated. That hasn't happened. The yuan appreciation is managed by the Chinese government. They have taken steps to limit appreciation. As a result the exchange rate is well below the true value. They are, by definition, manipulating the currency.

## Returning to Truman and Stalin, Democrat and Tyrant

It is difficult to imagine two men constitutionally more dissimilar than Stalin, a peasant native of Georgia, a cold hostile barbarian region of Eastern Europe, and Harry Truman, a plainspoken, civilized, cultured Midwestern American, thrown together by circumstances at the conclusion of the Second World War to decide nothing less than the fate of the world.

They were to meet but once, in Potsdam, Germany, after the German surrender and before the defeat of Japan, in the vain hope of putting together a working relationship that would allow for the recovery of Europe and peace to the Continent.

Not since Attila the Hun met Pope Leo in 452 AD as the Mongol was about to sack Rome were the stakes so high for peace and for Western civilization. Winston Churchill also attended this conference, as would his successor Clement Attlee, after Churchill's defeat in the British election.

Hitler's attempt to rule the world had failed. Now it was Stalin's turn.

His army, two million strong, straddled Central Europe, and the fear of Truman and the Allied military was that without provocation, Stalin might at any time launch an assault against the West, as the great czar before him, Peter the Great, had done in an effort to expand the empire.

Truman and the Allied armies stood in his way.

The Americans had provided Stalin with key support during the conflict with Hitler. He knew, though he would never publicly acknowledge, that without that support Hitler would have conquered Russia. Stalin had a good working relationship with Roosevelt and with good reason, for it was

Roosevelt who had first recognized his government and thus gave it legitimacy at a time when the world was fearful of Bolshevism and its atheistic philosophy, together with its zeal for world revolution.

With Europe literally on its back and America demobilizing, it must have appeared to Stalin that Western Europe would soon fall into his hands without major conflict with the United States.

The threat was there before Truman came into office. Roosevelt clearly understood the threat, having been warned repeatedly by Churchill and others that the Russians could never be trusted.

The facts on the ground, however, would by necessity drive policy. The undeniable fact was that the Russian army was there and peace was at stake.

Roosevelt believed that the best way to avoid conflict was the newly created United Nations. He envisioned that the great powers would sit in a body that would be known as the Security Council, modeled after King Arthur's Court, seeing himself as King Arthur, resolving disputes that threatened world peace. It was most idealistic, and Roosevelt was an idealist of the first order. Stalin was the antithesis of an idealist. Stalin was a barbarian who believed in military power, a true Mongol.

His core philosophy was made abundantly clear on an occasion when he was told that the Catholic Church and the Pope opposed his atheism and barbarous policies, he replied simply, "How many divisions does he have?"[cxx]

Characteristic of the man, Roosevelt was confident he could control Stalin, referring to him often as "Uncle Joe."

There was an additional problem that received little attention at the time. Some of Roosevelt's closest advisors were partial to Russia. Harry Hopkins, who traveled the world including Russia on Roosevelt's behalf, was sympathetic to Russia.

Alger Hiss of the State Department, who attended the Yalta Conference with Roosevelt and was later convicted of perjury, was by the evidence presented at his trial a communist agent.

Many in the New Deal who had come through the depression had come to believe that capitalism was finished and the future lay in the adoption of quasi-socialist policies.

Whether Roosevelt saw the New Deal in these terms is not clear. However, the argument that both he and his advisers were socialists at heart continued through the years and contributed to the defeat of the Democrats at the polls in 1952.

## Potsdam, a Face-Off—Truman versus Stalin

After the defeat of Germany, the Potsdam Conference was called to implement the agreements reached earlier at Yalta. The key points were the dismantling of the German war machine, zones for Allied occupation, and reparations, particularly for Russia, which had suffered widespread destruction from the German invasion.

Germany's borders were redrawn, resulting in the loss by Germany of 25 percent of its 1937 territory. In addition, Austria was separated from Germany.

Though it was designed to dismantle the war machine of the Third Reich, the conference was also to be the forum for dividing the spoils of war. The Soviet Union used the conference to justify the ravaging of Germany. The Russians had justifiable claims given the destruction that Hitler had wrought after the invasion of Russia.

The Russians set about transferring to Russia virtually anything that could be moved from their occupation zone, including entire factories and thousands of Germans, who were forcibly removed to Russia to help in its rebuilding of Russia.

Later many Germans were never accounted for, including large numbers of prisoners of war, who were sent to the mines and other undesirable places for the sake of the Communist Empire.

There were many in the West who had grave misgivings about their treatment, but the Allies looked the other way in light of the horrors that the Germans had inflicted on the world. Since this was happening in the Russian zone of occupation, there was little they could do. Because of the

Russian penchant for absolute secrecy and the effective use of their worldwide communist propaganda machine, the true facts never came to light.

In the Western zones, the Allies were most interested in seizing intellectual rights and patents, which some estimate had value of $10 billion.

Between 1945 and 1947, Western policy focused on the dismantling of heavy German industry. In addition, Germany paid $2.4 billion a year to cover the cost of Allied occupation.

The Allies made a 180-degree turn in 1948 when it became clear that Russia's intentions were aggressive in nature. Eventually Germany became a beneficiary of the Marshall Plan as it became increasingly clear that European recovery was dependent on the revitalization of the German economy. It should be noted that of the aid given to Germany, significant amounts were later repaid.

Russia never accepted aid under the Marshall Plan, though they were offered the opportunity. Their seizure of German industry in their zone of occupation more than offset aid they might have received under the Marshall Plan.

The unstated reason for the Potsdam Conference was to give Truman and Stalin a chance to get to know each other. Stalin learned quickly that Harry was not Roosevelt. Truman detested communism. Underlying their show of unity was suspicion and distrust. The meetings took place from mid-July to early August 1945.

Among the many issues was the matter of reconstruction, which in 1947 was formalized in what became known as the Marshall Plan. Russia agreed to join the United Nations.

Though Russia was technically a member of the IMF, they did not adhere to the bylaws and regulations of the Fund and did not participate in the organization for decades.

In 1946, as Churchill said in a speech at Westminster College in Fulton, Missouri, an iron curtain had descended across Central and Eastern Europe, thus dividing the European Continent. It remained that way until the fall of Communism in 1991.

CHAPTER 28

# The Critical Year, 1948

## Division Formalized

By 1947 it became clear that Russia had no intention of pursuing peace and security through cooperation with the West. The Cold War had begun, but hope of reconcilement with Russia remained the official policy in the West.

However, two events in 1948 had far-reaching consequences that were critical in setting the course of future relations between the great adversaries in the East and West. The first was the reformation of the German currency and the second was the creation of the Federal Republic of Germany with the unification of the British, French, and American zones of occupation.

Essential to Stalin's strategy of world domination was a weak Germany. Prior to the war, Germany had become an advanced state in terms of science and commerce, with a very well-educated, disciplined populace. Russia, on the other hand, was backward. Their victory in the war had been due largely to the critical support they received from the United States, combined with brute force imposed on the military and civilian population through their secret police.

As demobilization progressed in the United States and Great Britain, the strategic position of the Soviet Union strengthened. By 1948 limited economic progress had been made in Western Europe, but the communists and their front organizations were gaining political ground in Italy and France.

A crucial national election was scheduled for Italy that year, and there was a possibility that the communists would receive sufficient support in order to form a government. If Italy went communist, it was conceivable that France would follow.

Germany was still in shambles, which was much to the liking of the Soviets. There was simply no way for the Germans to rebuild without massive aid from the United States. There was no possibility of such aid being extended to the former enemy. The outlook was grim.

Stalin reacted with an aggressive foreign policy. His first act of aggression was his failed attempt to isolate Berlin, which Truman countered with the Berlin Airlift.

A critical step in divided Europe was unquestionably the formation of the German Federal Republic, which came into being with a merger of the occupation zones of the United States, Britain, and France and the national and the Berlin occupation zones in October 1949, separating them from the Russian zone.

With the communists in control of mainland China by 1948 and with the support and cooperation of Mao, the Chinese leader, Stalin approved an attack on South Korea from North Korea under the leadership of Kim Il Sung. Truman responded by sending into battle American forces, which ended in stalemate and armistice, ratified by Truman's successor Dwight D. Eisenhower after three years of fighting in 1953.

Truman had succeeded in frustrating Stalin's goals, but at a great cost in men, material, and wealth. The Korean War stimulated worldwide demand for materials and arms. This proved to be a great boon to Japan, Taiwan, and Singapore in Asia and Germany in Europe, which was still in the early stages of recovery, as well as France and England and the Low Countries.

This war stimulated a surge in public and private expenditures further supplemented by the creation of the North Atlantic Treaty Organization by the Allies, which induced spending and the permanent placement of American forces in Europe.

As neither Japan nor the Europeans had anything like the resources necessary to pay their share of the cost of building a global military, the burden fell heavily on the United States. This burden continued through the Eisenhower presidency, and as a giant share of the expenditures were for military purposes and consumption, there began a drain on American wealth and the movement of capital to other parts of the world. In time this impacted the balance of payments of the United States and undermined the currency value, leading to a full-blown currency crisis in 1971.

The effort begun by Truman to safeguard and protect freedom-loving peoples of the world in time proved successful, but at great cost to the Americans, resulting in a decline in their relative standard of living. This trend, which continues to the present, is about to explode into a new crisis as this book is being written, centered around the cost of a critical basic commodity, namely, oil.

The allied occupation forces, working with German leaders who had not joined the Nazi Party, some of whom had spent the war in Nazi prisons, were preparing for the day when Germany would be reconstituted and the Allies return home.

Konrad Adenauer was one of those men. He assumed the leadership of one of the two principal political parties, namely, the Christian Democratic Union, and became the first chancellor of West Germany with the founding of the Federal Republic of Germany.

He served in that office until age eighty-seven. He set out to align West Germany to the West, with a free market economy and a Christian social doctrine. The opposition West German Party took the name the Social Democratic Party. Besides Adenauer, two Germans had a profound impact on the German nation, economists William Roepke and Ludwig Erhard.

During the Nazi era, these two men, as members of the Freiburg School, wrote on economic matters with a free market orientation. This was in sharp contrast to the Nazi doctrine, which was socialist. The Nazis, with their emphasis on state control, introduced strict price controls over a period of twelve years prior to and during the war. Controls were essential as massive sums were spent building the war machine. At the conclusion of the war and with allied occupation, goods remained scarce, and price controls remained in effect.

In order to assure price stability, it was essential that the amount of currency in circulation equate to the amount of goods available. If the amount was more, then presumably the average price for goods would rise, a condition of price inflation.

Note the problem isn't the price; the problem is excess currency. The price increase is the effect of the currency excess, not the cause.

On the other hand, if there is less money than goods, we have entered a period of deflation. This is the period most feared and was the repetitive nightmare the world endured, particularly after the adoption of the gold standard.

In 1947 Germany, the amount of currency in circulation was five times the 1936 level. However with price controls in effect, goods were priced only slightly higher than in 1936. The value of currency was overstated by 500 percent. Under such conditions, goods simply became unavailable. No one in his right mind would exchange a product for paper overvalued by 500 percent.

To align the currency with value, the price of goods would have had to increase fivefold. This was not possible with price controls and ruinous if the controls were lifted, for no one could then afford to buy anything. This would have returned Germany to a fate that had brought Hitler to power in the first place—runaway price inflation.

People and businesses resorted to barter. A large segment of the population traveled sometimes hundreds of miles to barter goods they owned, including used clothes, for something to eat. Germans started to grow their own food. In postwar Germany, the absentee rate from work averaged more than nine hours a week. People needed the time to travel to find essentials.

There had to be an answer, and Roepke and Erhard came up with a plan, a brilliant plan at that. It would accurately be described as a currency reform plan.

## Currency Reform—the Salvation of Germany, the Deutsche Mark

Ludwig Erhard, appointed Minister of Economic Affairs, who later succeeded Adenauer as chancellor, began working closely with the Allies. They devised a plan that would put Germany on the road to recovery and prosperity and, by 1980, make it the second most powerful economic entity in the world.

The brilliance of the plan was its simplicity. There were two critical aspects to the Erhard plan. The first was to resurrect a belief in the German people that recovery was possible.

Germany had been defeated militarily and was in ruins. Survival was a day-to-day affair.

The Germans no longer believed in themselves. The younger generation made plans to leave Germany, to become expatriates.

During the Hitler era, the German people had been forced to sacrifice. The average German under the Nazis was given employment, but there was little or nothing beyond the basics for him to buy. The drill was all work and, except for the top leadership, no play. The average German had virtually no access to consumer goods for over a decade. They had nothing and had little or nothing to look forward to.

Under postwar conditions communism held attraction.

The communists argued, "If you come with us, we will feed you; we will take care of you," while the West offered occupation.

During the first days following the German surrender, the western military were under strict orders not to fraternize with the Germans. The mark and the Reichs mark continued as the currencies of the nation with uncertain value at best, and thus were no longer used in trade.

Occupation required German labor. The West of course recognized the need to pay for their labor. The Soviets, on the other hand, treated the Germans as indentured servants and demanded their labor or they would face imprisonment. In the western sectors, a policy of denazification was adopted. Prisoners of war were set free and were expected to become productive.

For Stalin and the Russians, plunder was legitimate under the terms of the Yalta and Potsdam Agreements. With their homeland destroyed, the Russians simply took everything. Of course the economic toll that this placed on Germany, particularly East Germany, which the Russians occupied, was devastating. East Germany, which had been an economically vital part of the German nation prior to the war, never fully recovered.

## CURRENCY AND MILITARY RULE

Postwar Germany went through a number of currency iterations before the introduction of the deutsche mark.

During 1945 to 1946, the Reichs mark, the official currency, as noted, was virtually valueless. Under these circumstances a new standard was desperately needed. It became American cigarettes.

Everything from antiques to shoes was exchanged for cigarettes. The Germans had access to cigarettes via the army PXs, which were opened to serve the American soldiers during occupation. Every conceivable service was paid for or measured in terms of cigarettes.

As war ended, hunger stalked the German nation. Recognizing the problem, the military introduced a military currency for the payment of services. This might have served the immediate need of the Germans if it had not been for the skullduggery of the Russians, with the alleged help of that noted economist who represented the United States at Bretton Woods, Harry Dexter White. As a senior official in the United States Treasury, White was one of the few who had access to the currency plates. At any rate, the Soviets got hold of them and flooded Germany with military currency, thus rendering it worthless.

Stalin's territorial ambitions necessitated that Germany never recover. In his mind Germany was to share the same fate of the Russian people and simply become part of a great slave state. The Russian people, living under the yoke of terror and fearful of some future invasion by the Germans, were more than willing to have the German people share their fate.

The future for Germany, particularly in the zone of occupation administered by the Russians, was truly grim, yet in some strange way, their survival was assured, as the tyrant provided them enough food to eat. Prussian influence had taught the German people to obey and not question authority.

With the destruction wrought by the Great Depression and wars, the common man might have been willing to accept socialism and perhaps even communism as the only course to follow.

The formal name for the Nazi party was the National Socialist German Workers Party. The orientation of the Germans and their governments beginning with Prussia was socialist. The state was to rule, and property was subject to its will. For East Germans, tyrants simply wore different uniforms or spoke a different language.

In 2010, with the political and social philosophy of state-run socialism consigned to the dustbin of history, it is difficult to conceive of a time when socialism and state authority were supreme. The Western concept of individual freedom was totally foreign to a large segment of the German community. Thus they became easy prey for the propaganda emanating from Moscow.

Stalin was confident that if he could stall the recovery of Germany, the Germans in time, rather than starve, would accept the communist yoke, first the east and eventually the west.

## Where Were the Allies?

Immediately after the war, France, Great Britain, and the United States treated Germany as a defeated barbarian nation.

The level of hostility toward Germany could be readily seen in the Directive of the Joint Chiefs that established US policy in Germany from 1945 until 1947. It stated that no help was to be provided to the Germans except the bare minimum needed to avoid starvation. The individual German was expected to live on 1,500 calories a day.

France had been conquered, Britain horribly bombed, and the populace of both countries, together with the inhabitants of the Low Countries, Norway, the Balkan nations, Eastern Europe, and of course Russia, had been treated with a degree of inhumanity never before witnessed in an advanced state.

There was an understandable desire for revenge, and everyone agreed that the German populace had to be reeducated. This was essential in preventing similar horrors in the future.

The precedent for reparations had been well-established in Europe. For the Russians this translated into reducing the German people to serfdom, the taking of all the implements of war, and the transfer of plants, equipment, machinery tools, rolling stock, and needed manpower for the rebuilding of

Russia. Following the Second World War, three million German soldiers and civilians were sent east to rebuild, and as noted, many never returned and others did not return until the 1950s.

The Allies agreed at Potsdam that reparations were indeed in order—the same conclusion arrived at at the Paris Conference of 1919, when thirty countries met at Versailles and held that Germany and her allies were solely responsible for all the loss and damage caused by the war. At that conference the reparation figure arrived at was measured in gold marks.

In addition, the United States agreed to transfer to Russia 10 percent of the capital goods in the western zone, but reneged on the promise as relations deteriorated.

Reparations to the West, apart from science and technology, were principally in the form of coal, although there was some dismantling of factories. Prisoner-of-war labor was provided to Britain and France, one hundred thousand to Britain and seven hundred thousand to France.

Britain and the United States received "intellectual reparations," including patents, blueprints, and all German company assets in the United States. In addition, the United States gained access to German scientists and technicians. It is estimated that the value of these rights approximated $10 billion.

The overriding influence on US policy was the Morgenthau Plan of 1944. It called for the demilitarization of Germany, the loss of territory with the remainder divided into two autonomous states, and the stripping of the Ruhr of all industry. The potential for mining was to be destroyed, and all German assets outside Germany confiscated. Forced labor was to be implemented. Though this plan met with public opposition, it had an influence on policy during the period from 1945 until 1947.

The dismantling of factories and other harsh measures in the western zones were ended in 1950 when it became increasingly apparent that the recovery of Europe depended greatly on a revitalized Germany. The growing antagonism between the East and West, the beginnings of the Cold War, also played a critical role in this change of attitude.

The shipment of factories east from the western zones stopped abruptly as friction developed between the Western Allies and Russia over foodstuffs. East Germany had been the breadbasket of Germany, and their refusal to share food with the western zones was seen as a blatant political act. Thus the West retaliated.

## TRUMAN AND EUROPEAN RECOVERY

England had suffered from both physical damage and severe financial strain. With its far-flung Commonwealth, many expected that it would quickly regain its dominance and share in the great work of reconstruction. The fact that England was again bankrupt and totally dependent on the United States for survival during the war did not seem to impress. England went into the war as a creditor nation and came out a debtor nation. France, Belgium, and the Low Countries had been occupied, and like their British allies, were in desperate need. America had restored their freedom, and wasn't it now up to them? Political speeches were filled with optimistic rhetoric similar to what one might find in a locker room before the big game. The "we can do it" spirit prevailed. In point of fact, the problems were virtually insurmountable.

Then there was Russia, with a huge army and a backward people whose homeland had been destroyed.

Last on the list of nations to receive a helping hand was Germany. Germany was on relief, and the Germans were literally starving.

In 1946 the outlook for Germany was particularly grim. It was United States policy as set out in Directive Joint Chief of Staff (JCS1067) to the Commander in Chief of U.S. forces in Germany in April 1945 that no effort was to be made to assist Germany in rebuilding its industrial base. In fact, as recounted, manufacturing, machine tools, and the industrial base were to be seized or dismantled to serve as reparations for losses suffered during the war. Germany was to be the European basket case, presumably forever.

Though not immediately recognized, Germany was critical to European recovery. The German people were industrious, hardworking, inventive, and intelligent. Given the chance, they could out produce the rest of Europe and lead Europe, and to some measurable extent the world, in raising the standard of living for the average person. In the mid-forties, this was not even considered.

Germany had been responsible for the war, and they had to be punished as envisioned by men like Morgenthau. Perhaps in time this would rid them of their Prussian, militarist aggressive attitude. For Russia, recovery had absolutely nothing to do with the common man. The communist state was not only supreme, but its power resided in the person of the general secretary, who was the notorious Josef Stalin.

Hitler had planned to conquer the world and failed. Stalin planned to create a worldwide communist empire, with him as its head. He was to rule the world, and anyone or any nation that got in his way was to be eliminated. In a world of nuclear weapons, this was, to say the least, problematic. At the time Russia did not have the atom bomb, which they developed with the help of spies in 1948. Stalin, to achieve his goal, would work against recovery, for recovery would reduce the likelihood of people being dependent on the state, and that dependence was essential if communism was to reign supreme.

Both Britain and the United States stood in Stalin's way, but through the brutalization of the Russian worker in a command economy, it was only a matter of time, as he saw it, that Russia would become powerful militarily and economically to take on the United States and Britain.

In the meantime he would lay the groundwork in a strategy known as the "salami tactic," bringing nations one at a time under the communist yoke.

Critical to the success of this plan was keeping Germany down. A resurgent Germany was a direct threat to Russia. With or without a military, the German economy might, if allowed to recover, threaten his plans and Russia itself. Stalin and the Russian people, with good cause, had profound fear of Germany.

At the moment, though, Stalin had every reason to be sanguine about Germany. His army occupied a third of Germany, and he was in the process of transporting anything that could be moved out of Germany to Russia in payment for war losses.

A large number of German officers and men were ensconced in German prisoner-of-war camps or Siberia, and he had no intention of turning them loose. At Yalta he had suggested that the Allies shoot sixty thousand German officers at random. Barbarism, like greed, knows no limits. Churchill was so stunned when he heard this that he left the table at Yalta, and Stalin had to retrieve him and make light of the matter, prompting Roosevelt's effort to defuse the incident by jokingly suggesting thirty thousand. This incident showed the mind-set of Stalin and the barbarian he was. He would do all in his power to keep Germany down. Recovery was not on the Russian agenda.

On the other hand, recovery was Truman's agenda. His problem was just how to accomplish it. In the United States, the transition from war to peace began the moment the Japanese signed the terms of surrender in Tokyo Bay aboard the battleship *Missouri* on September 2, 1945.

The boys were coming home, and their peacetime needs had to be met. FDR, anticipating this surge in demand for education, jobs, and housing, signed into law the Servicemen's Readjustment Act of 1944, the GI Bill, on June 22, 1944. This far-reaching legislation provided every serviceman with one year of unemployment benefits to give them time to find a job. In addition, it provided for zero-down, low-interest housing loans, which stimulated a mass migration from the cities to the suburbs, where people could build and own their homes. The opportunity for higher education was extended to millions who otherwise would have never obtained a college or equivalent education, allowing them to progress in life in fields unattainable to their forebears.

The great success of this sweeping legislation is borne out in the statistics. Twenty million veterans received education aid, and fourteen million home loans were guaranteed by the US government since it was first enacted.

By the late forties, America was moving forward, but Europe remained in the doldrums. A poor harvest in 1947 in Europe created fears of famine, but this did not come to pass, in large part due to America's help.

## We Have the Goods, But Do You Have the Currency?

The knowledge base essential for recovery was there, but plant and equipment and new technology could not be purchased for the best of reasons. Europe was bereft of capital. Without these reserves, they were in no position to buy from the one country that had the capacity to produce, America.

Lend-lease had been extended three times, but that barely kept European business afloat. The European countries restricted trade with one another, fearing nonpayment. To the extent that trade was taking place, it was on a bilateral basis. There were no institutional structures in place to advance trade. International trade was on a virtual cash-and-carry basis.

Though there had been an expectation that the World Bank would become the paramount institution to bring about the reconstruction of Europe, it quickly became clear it would be used for the rebuilding of large national projects such as utilities and dams, but would not reach down to private business.

International banking was nonexistent. The American money center banks had but few branches overseas, and they were primarily centered in South America, with offices in London and Paris. They were neither equipped nor interested in extending credit on the Continent. Few bankers had international experience. The bulk of the assets of these banks consisted of public securities, that is, US government, state, and municipal securities. Commercial banking in America was a deposit-taking business. Loans were extended for receivables and little else. Credit cards were nonexistent.

There was virtually no chance of an American bank lending to a foreign entity, except the very few with whom they had had a long-term relationship.

In the late 1940s, no American banker would have given a thought to lending to the Germans, though private banking had played a key role in the excess credit that flowed to Germany and set off the financial panic in Europe in the early thirties. By the standards of 2011, one would have expected Wall Street to step in to take advantage of what might have been characterized as a long-term opportunity, but Wall Street of the 1940s bore little or no resemblance to Wall Street today. Postwar capital was scarce, and public debt crowded out the private sector. Firms were organized as partnerships, with individual partners contributing their personal capital.

Today these firms are public corporations, where "other people's" money is invested. The excess speculation we have witnessed in the last decade is due primarily to the fact that partners' capital is not at risk. It is the public who stands to lose.

The economic condition of Europe might well have remained a basketcase if it had not been for the foresight of Harry Truman and his closest advisors, among them men like George Marshall, Dean Acheson, and John W. Snyder.

CHAPTER 29

# The Marshall Plan

## A Revolutionary Break with the Past, America's Gift to Europe and the World

The Marshall Plan, which Winston Churchill characterized as the single greatest act of compassion and charity in the history of mankind, proved to be the lifesaver, the bridge that gave Europe the time to rebuild its industry and infrastructure.

There were many features to the plan that made it truly unique.

As conceived it was intended to be a gift by the American people to the Europeans. It was never thought of as a loan conferring obligation. No liability was placed on the Europeans. In all of history, there is no comparable act of charity.

Following the First World War, charity groups and quasi-governmental organizations had worked with leaders such as Hoover to allay the suffering that the war had wrought on the Continent. In addition, the United States and Canada had extended limited credits to the Allies. The banks expected to be repaid, and each nation was expected to lift itself up—aside from limited aid—by its bootstraps. The Allies naively anticipated compensation from Germany. The Marshall Plan, on the other hand, was an act of charity born of compassion.

## The Economic Salvation of Europe

The pent-up demand in Europe for consumer goods and the ever-present threat of starvation and winters without heating, lighting, and consumer goods was a life without a future, which in turn created impossible political problems.

In desperation it was possible that Western Europe might turn to the communists.

It was very unclear whether, faced with the prospect of continued suffering and shortages, countries like Germany, Italy, and perhaps even France might not elect communist governments. That prospect was real indeed in 1948. These countries had large socialist/communist parties before and during the war that were well-organized.

In addition, Greece was in the midst of a civil war, with one side sponsored by Moscow. Iran was partially occupied by the Russians, who were threatening Turkey with military intervention.

Truman took steps that were truly inspired and representative of his natural genius. Truman had never completed college, like many men of his age, but was well-educated. He had a deep understanding of history. He was not a man to dither. He addressed matters as he saw them. He was very direct, which caused him serious political problems during his tenure.

He and his advisors came forward with three programs that would change the future of Europe: the pronouncement of the Truman Doctrine, the North Atlantic Treaty Organization, and the Marshall Plan.

On March 12, 1947, Truman pronounced the Truman Doctrine, granting immediate military aid to Greece and Turkey to fend off and defeat communist aggression.

NATO was formed on April 4, 1949, a mutual defense treaty, where an outside attack on any member nation would constitute an attack on all, including the United States.

West Germany was welcomed into NATO against strong political headwinds and threats from Moscow. That decision and organization secured the peace in Europe until this very day.

It is universally agreed that the Marshall Plan was the key to the economic recovery of Europe. The thrust of the plan was reconstruction, international trade, and bank development.

The plan had many features, but the primary focus was that the United States would provide the nations of Europe with funds, equipment, raw materials, and technical assistance.

A large-scale infusion of capital was needed. The critical problem was a dollar shortage. Though hard to imagine today, dollars were so scarce that international trade, which under Bretton Woods was to be settled in dollars or sterling, could not be financed. Settlement between the various central banks of Europe rested on their ability to draw on US funds. Their agent for settlement was the Bank for International Settlements, originally created to process German reparation payments after the First World War and extensively used by the Nazis during the Second World War.

A credit mechanism was established whereby the United States financed trade in dollars between private parties who exchanged their domestic currency, and the surplus (read as profit) was paid into a European Payments Union, with the nations settling with one another at the end of each month.

The European Payments Union thus became the first credit mechanism in the effort to expand European trade. In 1948 this led to the creation of the OEEC, the Organization for European Economic Co-operation, formed to administer the Marshall Plan, which was replaced in 1961 by the OECD, the Organization for Economic Co-operation and Development, an international organization to foster free trade and development in industrialized and developing countries.[cxxi]

The expansion of trade was key to European recovery. Trade barriers had to be excised, and trust and confidence restored. Bilateral relationships would not do. A pattern where some countries were expanding while others were not would leave Europe with haves and have-nots and imbalances of the type that created national friction, hostility, and depression.

Trade must be internationalized. Trade barriers must fall. This required modernization, technical assistance, and the machinery to produce first-class goods. Europe might have the expertise but was in need of capital goods besides the reserves or capital to get back on their feet.

With a long-term perspective, the leaders of these nations recognized that European integration was the key to future prosperity. A common market, a European Union, was foreseen during the darkest days following the war as the ultimate goal.

Without the Marshall Plan, it would have been but a dream, with nothing of importance accomplished. Europe needed a large-scale program, and the Marshall Plan provided it.

Between 1945 and 1953, the United States and Canada provided $44.3 billion in loans and grants to bring Europe and, to a lesser extent, Asia back. These were 1945 dollars. Today's equivalent would translate into something close to $1 trillion. This was a bonanza for Europe. During the four years of the plan, Europe experienced its greatest economic growth in its history.

The largest beneficiaries under the plan were the United Kingdom, followed by France, Germany, and Italy.

America's unique status as the sole major producer of goods of all types meant that a significant portion of Marshall Plan support went to the purchase of American products, and the remainder to pay down debt and for stabilization.

A simple explanation of how it worked is as follows. America paid in dollars, which were credited against the plan. A European national would buy American goods. The American producer would receive dollars in payment. The European buyer would pay his government in the currency of his nation for the purchase. Thus the government was now collecting funds that it could hold in reserve and invest.

American taxpayers had actually made the payment, but the foreign government kept the proceeds, which were invested in that country or used to fund acquisitions.

Russia chose not to participate. It had its own Marshall Plan, which was the dismantling of Germany and its allies.

## Germany—We Need You After All

It is hard to imagine a nation regarded with more derision and disgust than that of Germany in 1945. This can be seen most clearly in the directive to American occupation forces known by the acronym JCS 1067. This directive stated that American forces were not to take any measures that would lead to the economic rehabilitation of Germany.

This directive of course fit nicely into Stalin's policy and was reassuring to the French and to a lesser extent the British.

One presupposes that Germany was to remain the permanent basket-case of Europe. This would have certainly been the result had the Morgenthau Plan been implemented.

Two overriding facts were working against such thinking. The first was that Russia and the communists had aims totally inconsistent with those of America and its allies. A hobbled Germany would allow for the expansion of the Russian Empire. The second, and most telling vis-à-vis the Marshall Plan, was that recovery of Europe was impossible without a vibrant Germany. Our former enemy had become the key to European recovery, like it or not.

While JCS 1067 was the official American policy in force, the western Allies dismantled some German factories, but to a far lesser extent than the Russians. Further, JCS 1067 not only forbade economic development assistance but forbade the military governor from strengthening the German financial structure.

From 1945 to 1947, each of the four occupiers printed its own military currency. As the United States was in a position to provide consumer goods, that currency had value.

Access to the plates that were used to print the currency rested with the Treasury Department. As we noted earlier, the plates were stolen and given to the Russians.

The American effort to rebuild Europe while insisting that aid be denied Germany was self-defeating. This point was clearly stated in a letter by Konrad Adenauer, the first postwar chancellor, to the Allies in 1949.[cxxii]

Truman, understanding this, had directed that JCS 1067, designed to punish Germany, be scrapped in favor of JCS 1779.

Germany was no longer the apostate state. Through this directive it was now to become our friend.

JCS 1779 provided, "an orderly and prosperous Europe requires the economic contributions of a stable and productive Germany."[cxxiii]

All restrictions on heavy industry were canceled. Germany was to become a full member of the recovery team.

The shock to Stalin can only be imagined. This was a threat to his entire scheme of world domination. In addition, the Russians feared that a resurgent Germany would be out for revenge and might again pose in time a military threat to Russia. Russia complained mightily, but their pleas were ignored. From the standpoint of Truman and the Western Allies, if there was a threat to world peace, now it was from Russia, not Germany.

The new chancellor of Germany, Konrad Adenauer, was a brilliant and forceful leader. He was not fearful of Stalin or Russia. He could not be browbeaten. As a former mayor and leader of the moribund opposition, he had been thrown in prison by Hitler during the war. He had survived Hitler, and he would survive Russia. A remarkable man, Adenauer served as chancellor of Germany from 1949 until 1963.

A democrat, through and through, Adenauer set out to change Germany. He prosecuted the former Nazis at home while heralding democratic principles and tirelessly moving Germany in the direction of a true democratic state. Germany in time recovered, becoming in less than twenty years one of the top three economic powers in the world.

Under Adenauer's leadership Germany changed, but the attitude of the German people, the way they viewed their historic role as the most innovative, dynamic, and productive people on the European Continent, did not change. The Germans were determined to rise again.

## CURRENCY IS AT THE HEART OF THE PROBLEM[CXXIV]

No explanation completely satisfies as one analyzes German behavior over the centuries. From the formation of the Union in 1870 through the period that culminates in that nation's final destruction in 1945, barbarism in a peculiar way ruled the nation. Barbarity, sophistication, and civilization coexisted—a peculiar cultural mix that defies explanation. I am inclined to think that Einstein comes closest in explaining this phenomenon. Of course, he was German. His explanation was rather simple and straightforward, that Germany was "spiritually broken." The German people had become "mechanically obedient automatons."[cxxv] Early in life, he surrendered his German citizenship and became a Swiss citizen.

There was a bitter price to pay for German barbarism. From war's end until the promulgation of JCS 1779, the German people were outcasts while their industry was pillaged. There were few tears shed, and the global consensus was that the Germans were getting what they deserved.

The Reichs mark continued as the official currency. There was a slight problem, however. It wouldn't buy anything. To be more precise, goods were not available for sale for marks. To add to the misery, dollars and other currencies were impossible to obtain. Europe had a severe dollar shortage. No one was trading with the Germans, and the Germans had nothing to trade.

By 1946 the German people, in extremis, turned to cigarettes for their currency. Cigarettes were made available by the Americans, who were pleased to pay for services with Camels and Lucky Strikes. Commerce was carried on in the black market. To participate people had to have access to hard currency, which probably meant that they were engaged in some illegal activity or had access to cigarettes. Since the average German had limited access to either, it meant that they had to barter their household goods for food. This meant that a considerable amount of their time was spent traveling to the farms of Germany carrying their meager goods on their backs or bicycles to exchange for something to eat. If Europe was to ever recover, this had to change.

The cities of Germany and infrastructure were destroyed during the war, but outside the urban centers, life went on. By 1948 German manufacturing and consumption were less than two thirds what they had been in the mid-1930s.

War debt was four times the level of 1939. Without total reform progress was impossible. A starving people understood that. They were willing to try anything, including communism, to survive. That was the bet Stalin had made.

War, death, and destruction had crippled Germany economically. The German economy in 1945 was generating slightly more than half of the 1935 gross national product. During the war Germany continued to increase liquidity so that at war's end, the money supply was many times greater than it had been ten years earlier. Price fixing and control had been staples of the Nazi regime. Controls remained in place with surrender, and thus the value of the Reich Mark was unascertainable. Without value certain, exchange became virtually impossible.

Granted, Germany was engaged in a destructive war, but the unmistakable conclusion is that liquidity alone, that is, credit supplied by the government, will not bring about economic expansion. This is what the West is endeavoring to do today, and it won't work.

Liquidity is essential to stave off a banking collapse of the type experienced in the early thirties. However to successfully grow the economy, more than liquidity is needed. The key question then is "What is the missing piece?" Liquidity may be the salvation of banking, but it will not give rise to investment.

Investment is made and goods produced only when the investor stands to make a real return—that is, he stands to gain from the investment. Though Reich Marks were plentiful in postwar Germany, their value was open to question, and thus the investor would neither sell his goods nor invest in new businesses, for he did not see the potential for gain. This is exactly where we are today. Investors have the capital, but they do not see the potential gain.

All production requires investment. One must have access to liquidity, savings, or credit to begin a business. However, one will never start a business that has limited or no profit potential.

Liquidity or access to credit alone will not assure a successful business. This is the critical first step that the monetarists don't grasp. The Federal Reserve may provide the liquidity, but only business produces and business will never produce without gain.

Investment is the critical step in the process. The economic dynamic is a turbine in action. A turbine works on the principle of circulation. Every investment without exception gives rise to immediate employment. As the investment is made, the machine starts to turn. Investment and employment are truly synonymous. One does not invest and then not labor or produce. The two unite. They are mutually dependent on each other.

The turbine produces continuous power through the stages of circulation, namely, invest/employ, produce, and spend. The process then begins again.

Investment is central to circulation. Investment fuels circulation. Without circulation there can be no growth. Without investment the turbine will not turn. Draining investment by consuming impedes circulation.

The turbine has many parts but remains a unit. It is the circulation of the unit that produces the power that translates into economic growth.

The recent US experiment with TARP, the stimulus, and the liquidity plans demonstrate this clearly.

Though government intervened by pumping into the economy massive amounts of liquidity, little circulation was forthcoming. Why did this happen? What went wrong? Where did the circulation process break down?

## Reform

There are many aspects to life that demand adjustment. We typically refer to a positive change in behavior as reform.

Reform or renewal is not always possible. The affairs of a nation can deteriorate to a point that reform becomes impossible. That is what happened to Germany. In both domestic and international affairs, no adjustment, no matter how sweeping, could restore the confidence of the world and the German people in the German currency, the Reich Mark.

That fact did not foreclose the need for a currency. Every nation requires one. Commercial dealings cannot be carried on without one. To remain a nation, Germany had to have a currency.

What were the alternatives? Barter would not do. Neither would cigarettes. There was only one answer, and that was a new currency. A new currency was essential for a return to normalcy.

A new currency also signaled something equally important: Germany had a future. To assure that future, Germany had to be democratized. The centuries-old chasm between the privileged and the common man had to be closed. Class distinctions had to go.

The industrial barons had to forsake ownership in assets, accumulated over decades. Easier said than done. Germans, like peoples the world over, did not want to surrender their wealth, their holdings, their status.

Had the German people held in their hands the final say on the matter, it is doubtful that profound change, and thus a new currency, would have ever happened. As an occupied country, they were given little choice by the Allies.

Large numbers would have voiced strenuous objection had they known about the changes that were about to be visited upon them. They would have supported the status quo, with all its hardships, a nation in dissolution. In every society, inertia inevitably rules.

Nevertheless a plan was introduced and finally adopted. It was known as the Colm-Dodge-Goldsmith Plan. It saved Germany and Europe and may well have prevented the onset of a third world war.

The Russians were told nothing about the plan in advance for the most obvious of reasons. Everyone understood that they would make every effort to sabotage this effort, as they had previously, if only they had known.

CHAPTER 30

# The Deutsche Mark

### THE PLAN, A RADICAL STEP BY ANY MEASURE

On a designated date, June 20, 1948, without warning, a new currency to be forever known as the deutsche mark became legal tender of Germany. It was the decision of the century. I would argue that global prosperity as we have come to know it, without diminishing other critical decisions, dates back to that decision.

The old currency, the Reich Mark and the Renten Mark, had to be exchanged for the new. The holders of the old marks received one new mark for every ten of the old. Thus the purchasing power of currency was reduced by 90 percent. Today such a decision would appear politically impossible. However, one has to keep in mind how impossible living conditions were for the Germans at the time. Consistent with this change, bank liabilities were reduced by 90 percent. Thus the banks and other creditors did not profit from the exchange.

The exchange rate against the US dollar, now the official world currency, technically with sterling, was made three to one. It would take three deutsche marks to obtain one dollar. The exchange rate was later set at 3.3 to 1.

All sovereign debt, including debt accumulated during the Nazi era, was canceled.

Large holders of Reich Marks were to receive sixty-five pfennigs, or sixty-five cents, for every ten Reich Marks above a prescribed amount. These and other measures had the effect of eliminating 90 percent of government and private debt and savings, while eviscerating the money supply. Wages and rents were not impacted by the exchange. There, the exchange remained at 1 RM for 1 DM.

All price and wage controls were eliminated. As a result prices increased by 25 percent. To offset this, wages were increased by 15 percent.

Income and wealth taxes were cut, to encourage investment. Payments for social programs were reduced. To pay the cost associated with social hardship, a tax on real assets was introduced.

Every household received sixty deutsche marks, paid in two installments. DM advances were made to businesses, the amount dependent on the number of employees.

Note that real assets were not touched. It was paper that was impacted. The plan's authors understood that real assets—plant, machinery, equipment, tools, buildings, and so on—were true money. Paper was simply paper, irrespective of its legal standing.

Businesses that had built up inventory and had not been willing to sell for worthless currency now had an incentive to put their goods on the market. They were going to receive value for value.

In case any business missed the point, a tax on inventory was introduced. The cumulative effect of these measures was a flood of goods coming on the market, which drove prices down. Exports soared.

In addition, the Marshall Plan put 1 billion 390 million dollars at the disposal of Germany, a staggering investment for the time.

Money, that is, real assets, were the means to all future prosperity. Paper or financial assets and debt had over a long period of time distorted reality.

The new currency, the deutsche mark, was distributed in the western zones. In addition, distribution took place in Berlin, then occupied by the four powers. That meant that DM would find its way into the eastern zone, the Russian zone, as well as the western zones.

This was clearly an in-your-face move by the West, and that was just the way Stalin read it. He responded with the Berlin blockade.

Historians and other analysts have over the years speculated as to why Stalin took such a provocative action, blockading Berlin, which could have easily precipitated a military confrontation in the heart of Europe, though neither side was prepared to go to war.

The answer is as clear as a bell. It was all about the deutsche mark. With a new currency, the burgeoning German Republic was in business, and Stalin knew it. He had to find a way to isolate East Germany from this threat to his empire. The iron curtain was not to be penetrated. He would drive the West out of Berlin by preventing entry.

Certainly Truman would not risk war to hold the Western zone in Berlin, he reasoned. He badly underestimated Truman.

## Stalin versus Truman, Round 2, Europe and Britain

After approximately a year of blockade, as it became clear that the West, by engaging an airlift to gain entry, would not be driven from Berlin, Stalin, losing face every day, threw in the towel. This was a chess game, he probably reasoned. He may have lost a rook in this round, but that he could afford.

Stalin was a descendant of Mongols and Tartars. He was undoubtedly influenced in his youth by the corrupt traditions of Byzantium. The individual meant nothing to him. Latin tradition had never penetrated the nation of his birth, Georgia. He was a barbarian through and through. Might meant right. He read the liberal thinking of the West and their willingness to compromise as indications of weakness. His successors, though not as brutal, adhered to the same philosophy.

He reasoned by the Eastern standards of the fifth century. He was patient; he would have another chance; he believed. After all, the stakes were enormous—world conquest. Peter the Great, the Russian expansionist czar, had not come close to accomplishing that. He saw himself as a great czar, his opponent, this man Truman, a peon. In support of this, he adhered to the Marxist Doctrine, which predicted the fall of capitalism and the advent of socialism prior to the inevitable victory of communism. Time was on his side.

Complicating Truman's life was the unsettled state of Asia, and to a lesser extent, the Middle East, as Britain, in recognition of the loss of its empire, withdrew its forces from the world scene.

In 1948 Truman's focus was not Asia, but to aggressively pursue measures to shore up Western Europe. The Truman Doctrine, designed to assist beleaguered Turkey and Greece, the Marshall Plan, NATO, and the formation of the Federal Republic of Germany were all critical steps in this drive for recovery.

With the communist losses in the elections in Italy and France in 1948, the picture began to brighten. A communist sweep of Europe might not be inevitable after all. Though divided between East and West, Germany was central to Western strategy. Germany was the front line. Everything now had to be done to help our former enemy.

This meant that the Germans had to be gainfully employed. They had to have markets for their goods. The new currency was the critical step forward, but it was only the beginning.

To compete on the world stage, the quality of their goods must be second to none, and most importantly, they had to be priced competitively.

Bretton Woods had established the regimen of fixed exchange rates. To export successfully, it was important that the deutsche mark exchange rate against the dollar be advantageous to the Germans.

It was immediately clear that an exchange rate of 3 Dm for one dollar—which is what the original plan called for—was an insufficient advantage. The exchange rate was then reset to 3.3DM to 1, a 10 percent change in favor of German products. That this might be putting American companies at a disadvantage was not a consideration given other concerns. Later we would find this to have been a critical mistake.

However, all of this was ignored. We were now engaged in a new war. This time the adversaries were the Russians, and the conflict became known as the Cold War. We were all in this together. The fact that others were taking advantage was ignored.

Besides, there was a persistent shortage of dollars in the world, and thus an exchange rate that favored Germany and the other European nations would have the effect of moving dollars to Europe, seen as a positive development, even as it resulted in a slowly deteriorating balance of payments for the United States.

America was called on to save the world, and we would do whatever it took, even though it would have a profound impact on the average American, and over the course of five decades, deplete the nation's wealth.

The willingness to help everyone and a newfound love affair with consumption that began in the late seventies effectively bankrupted America by the early years of the twenty-first century. With the best of intentions, future crises were set in motion in the 1940s.

There were other critical players on the European Continent besides Germany in those difficult times.

Vichy France had been occupied during the war, but Charles de Gaulle had led the Free French and was embraced by the Allies, though his countrymen were of marginal importance in the ultimate victory. However at war's end, they were determined to hold on to Indo-China and parts of North Africa. The Brits might be withdrawing from the rest of the world, but the French had no such intention.

Great Britain was and remains our closest ally. We stood together throughout the long difficult years and would continue to do so. We were partners. Though it would take time to fully grasp its implications, the British Empire was shrinking by the day. Their withdrawal was creating a global vacuum, which had to be filled by the United States, or run the risk of communist takeover and expansion.

At Bretton Woods it had been decided that the dollar and sterling were to be the reserve currencies. At a fixed rate, sterling could be converted into dollars and dollars into gold. The logic was sound, but reality was not being addressed.

The war had bankrupted Britain—again. The Brits could not provide their people with consumer goods and were forced to rely on the United States. This effectively put pressure on sterling. As people sold sterling for dollars, the pressure on sterling mounted. It became clear that the market favored dollars over sterling.

This caused great consternation in London. Immediately after the war, the British people had turned out the Conservative government of Churchill. The Labor Party, a socialist party under Clement Attlee, came into power.

The party endorsed the philosophy of socialism. Socialism was the solution to inequality. The government would nationalize industry, particularly heavy industry. Jobs would be provided to all. Health care, education, and other essentials would be free. The nation would prosper, and happiness would descend on the Empire.

If socialism was the ultimate answer, and of that the Labor Party and its acolytes had no doubt, there should be no complications, and if there were, it must be the fault of others. With its experiment with the socialist model, Britain did not prosper but suffered a marked economic setback by any and all measures.

Britain in decline translated into pressure on sterling. That pressure meant that devaluation was inevitable. Devaluation would cause the world to question the very foundation of this heralded philosophy called socialism. If socialism was the perfect solution for all the economic ills the country faced, there should be no need for devaluation. The two concepts, socialism and the need for currency devaluation, were incompatible.

Devaluation meant that there was something wrong with the policy, namely, the socialist agenda. It was not a panacea after all. Thus, the Labor government found itself politically in desperate need of locating a third party to blame for the failure of policy.

They thought they had found him in an American, the secretary of the Treasury, John W. Snyder (1946–1953).

As Stalin had underestimated Truman, the British underestimated Snyder. "The blame it all on Snyder" strategy would fail, as Snyder effectively moved to counter the libel and slander thrown at him by the British government. He was not going to be the fall guy for the failure of unwise policies founded on socialist principles.

## John W. Snyder, Secretary of the Treasury—Oh, Those Troublesome Brits

As was typical of Harry when it came to appointments and, for that matter, any matter involving politics, he invariably turned to friends from Missouri and his political cronies. One of those was John Snyder, who had been a friend of Truman's since the First World War.

John was a typical reserved, pleasant, both feet on the ground, intelligent Midwesterner. He was Harry's type of guy. John came into the administration in 1946 with a broad background in banking and business, having served in a number of offices in government, including director of war mobilization and reconversion. His role was to administer and oversee the proper functioning of the Treasury Department and to make appropriate recommendations when it came to spending, in order to see to it that the federal debt was being reduced after the explosion of borrowing necessitated by the Second World War.

One might have assumed that a cabinet officer, particularly one as prestigious as secretary of the Treasury, would have considerable clout and access to the president on many matters. It was not likely, however, that he would become involved in political and diplomatic intrigue with the most unlikely of antagonists, namely, the British government.

Considering all that the United States had done on Britain's behalf, if a foreign nation could have been identified that was certain to work hand in glove with us after the war, it would have been Britain.

Winston Churchill's devotion to Franklin Roosevelt and the British people's genuine affection for all Americans abounded. Of course we had saved the British Empire; their affection was real and unquestioned.

Thus the tussle that Mr. Snyder was about to get involved in must have come as a surprise. The British government, through their allies in the press, planted stories about how Mr. Snyder was undercutting their program to bring about devaluation of the pound. Snyder never took the bait and responded as Harry might have done. He said he couldn't care less what the British did with respect to the pound, but the facts made it abundantly clear that their policies weren't working.

Though Henry Morgenthau and Harry Dexter White had turned down Maynard Keynes's suggestions for the broad framework he proposed at Bretton Woods for the aborning International Monetary Fund, there is no evidence that this in any way contributed to the antagonism.

*Life, Liberty, and the Pursuit of Money*

It is also highly unlikely that if Winston Churchill and his Conservative government had remained in power, those communication problems would have arisen, as the British remained totally reliant for virtually everything of a commercial nature on the United States.

The basis for the misunderstanding was the very different political philosophy of the two nations. In 1945 while the Potsdam Conference was meeting, Churchill and the Conservatives were defeated in a national election, which brought to power the Labor Party of Great Britain. The Labor Party today is a far cry from Clement Attlee's party of 1945.

That was a true-blue socialist party. They bought the Marx gospel hook, line and sinker.

They accepted the argument that capitalism had been responsible for the depression. Socialism was the wave of the future, and only the most recalcitrant would not accept that. The laborites were not communist, but they accepted the dominant role of the state in the allocation of resources and the ownership of key industries.

The state would decide what was to be produced, how it was to be produced, and who would benefit. Private enterprise was passé. Private enterprise might have some small role to play in a local grocery store or in a car repair shop, but as far as industry was concerned, the state was to be the owner of the means of production.

They would speak out about the excesses in the Soviet Union if brought to their attention, but never in such a way as to suggest any criticism of socialism. As a result there was a continuing tendency to treat Stalin and the Soviet Union with kid gloves, which served to increase Stalin's territorial ambitions.

To this day we do not know to what extent this attitude served to convince Stalin, as it had a generation earlier Hitler, that the West was in decline and would not when the chips were down stand in his way.

If this was the case, Stalin most certainly misread Truman, as well as the British, when he authorized Communist forces to invade South Korea in 1950.

However in 1946 the picture was very different. The Labor government of Britain set forth a policy designed to nationalize everything in sight, including two critical industries, coal and steel. Everything of an important commercial nature was to be decided from the top down.

Overriding issues such as the nature of competition, new investment, and profitability would presumably be decided by some state-run bureaucracy. Profits and losses were terms that applied to a capitalist society. Presumably they were to be removed from the dictionary.

With the passage of time, the failure of this philosophy became apparent. It was a fairy tale. Worse still, it provided the essential underpinnings of a totalitarian state.

England and Europe had suffered through an extended era of tragedy and disparity in wealth between the fortunate and the less fortunate. This should not continue, men reasoned…The solution? Let us put the state in charge.

Man could not fend for himself. The Great Depression, the Russian Revolution, and World Wars I and II represented to many the birth pangs of a new and more equitable social structure, where the needs of the many would be satisfied. To accomplish this they must be willing to sacrifice their freedom.

It was all in the natural order of things. This was predetermined, if you will, evolutionary. Man was never in control of anything. His free will meant nothing. He had no inalienable rights. He was not responsible for his conduct, and thus was of no importance beyond his service to the community as a whole, in other words, the state.

The most evil of men read in this philosophy the opportunity for great power. Hitler, Lenin, Stalin, and Mao seized the opportunity and established totalitarian dictatorships, which resulted in poverty, persecution, and the death of millions.

To be fair, the socialists outside the Communist sphere recognized the rights of the individual and his freedoms, including the right to private property, but only to a point. In the end state power, as it represented society as a whole, should take precedence. Such socialists were referred to as social democrats.

The British Labor Party, though it had extremists in its ranks, was philosophically social democrat. Today it would be hard to distinguish the social democrats of labor from the conservatives in the political structure of Great Britain.

In 1946 this was not the case. The Labor Party of Clement Attlee believed deeply in socialism, and they set out to change the social and economic landscape of Great Britain. The socialists were never able to grasp the fact that no one would invest if there is no return.

With virtually no opportunity for profit, for return on investment, investment went into a tailspin. Worse still, wealth and money were leaving the country at an unprecedented rate. The economy went into a steep decline. This was both inevitable and predictable. This great experiment with socialism was failing right in front of their eyes.

Ultimately the British regained their sense of reason, but that took decades. In the meantime, specifically on September 18, 1948, sterling was devalued by a hefty 30 percent. Given the state of British industry and finances, this devaluation proved insufficient, and Britain was once again forced to devalue in 1967, this time by 14.3 percent.

Devaluation is not a springboard for prosperity, but an indication of internal weakness and imbalance. It is a recognition that a nation, or in many cases other nations, have carried on their affairs in a manner that has reduced the subject nation's competitiveness.

Devaluation, as unpleasant as the decision might be immediately, is the only way to restore balance when the current account of a nation results in serious imbalance.

One can immediately identify a nation whose currency is overvalued by looking at the nation's economic record. A nation consistently in deficit in its international trade balance translates into a nation that has failed to produce sufficient goods and services to meet the demands of its citizens. The difference is made up with foreign imports.

Thus it is spending more than it earns. Though it may take decades, such a nation is on the road to bankruptcy. One way to address this imbalance, to right the ship, to address reality, is to devalue the currency and alter the nation's domestic economic policies. Such changes make the subject nation's goods more competitive. They also make imports more expensive.

Most importantly, they buy time. The nation should take the opportunity to correct the internal and/or external problem. Failing that, devaluation is inevitable because the market will not accept a state of permanent imbalance. Devaluation, as it passes through revaluing assets, means simply that everything is now worth less. Everyone is poorer in that country.

In a real sense, a nation consuming more than it produces ultimately is faced with a Hobson's choice, poverty or bankruptcy.

In this regard the postwar record of the United States is horrendous. If memory serves, in all but one of the past thirty years, the United States has suffered an adverse balance of payments in its current account.

There is no doubt that our casualness, a lack of concern with respect to this issue, began when we willingly gave away our wealth to assure the freedom and well-being of the Europeans and others. Of course, we were protecting ourselves as well, but we failed to tabulate the price. We never recognized the cost of this effort. We never insisted that these nations, when they were on their feet, reward us for our charity, compassion, investments, and protection.

While it is true that we were repaid money we were owed under contract, the reality is that we gave them a great deal more than we ever received. A good example of this is India. We fed India for decades, bore the cost, and then to not embarrass India, wrote off a huge debt. We will never receive payment for the schools, hospitals, and utilities that we are constructing in Afghanistan. We accept without challenge that this is somehow our duty. It may well be our duty, but in the end, it will bankrupt us.

One only has to look at the far-flung US military in places as diverse as Bosnia, Korea, Afghanistan, Iraq, Yemen, Germany, and most recently Libya, a seemingly endless list to help others overcome tyranny and poverty.

The Americans were expected to pay, and when we finally exhausted our capacity, we simply borrowed from others, such as China and OPEC, whose foreign and domestic policies are both illegal and immoral as measured by our principles.

The Americans pay the bill, never giving it a second thought, as the standard of living of the average American is diminished. If I may editorialize, it bespeaks self-destruction. Leaders promise change, but it is never delivered. Instead, we get more of the same, as if more would somehow change the end result, poverty.

Everyone agrees that we are on the road to self-destruction. Our behavior is compulsive. The irrationality of our policies is stunning.

You will find no one in a leadership position who won't agree that drastic decisions must be made, but as Mark Twain noted about the weather, "everyone talks about it but no one does anything about it."

## The Road to Prosperity—What Does It Take to Get There?

As we noted at the very outset of this book, consumption is never the answer. The farmer who destroys, devours, or gives away his crop is never wealthier.

Taxing for the purpose of consumption further disrupts the cycle of prosperity.

Taxing assets to take care of those who cannot fend for themselves may well be a duty of society. It is the cost of citizenship. This duty, combined with the necessity of each of us to consume some but not all of our produce, is part and parcel of the circulation mechanism.

As previously discussed, global commerce is a gigantic turbine, which as it spins releases power. If one visits an electric utility, one sees giant turbines spinning, providing the energy to light and heat our homes and factories. In a similar way, global commerce, through investment/employment, production, limited consumption, and savings, provides each of us with our standard of living.

Slow the turbine, and the energy released is sharply reduced.

The turbine must be balanced. The process is both circular and repetitive. It must spin at high speed to electrify the entire community.

Four steps—investment/employment, production, consumption, and savings—are required in order to sustain prosperity or, staying with my analogy, to bring light and heat to us all. Each step is essential and interdependent. However, they must work in unison. Remove one step, and the system fails.

Clearly if I consume more energy than I produce, this short-circuits the system. The entire system is in danger of failing.

Investment is most critical. If I do not construct the turbine, then neither I nor the community will have light.

I must have the skill and the money, savings, to build the turbine. The money comes from either my or another's savings generated from prior labor.

I employ people to build and to maintain the turbine. I have a turbine that can produce energy, and they have income to buy and consume the product, electricity. The price I charge for this energy they can afford, and I realize a profit, which I put into savings that allows me to build another turbine to electrify the neighboring community.

The process is self-generating; expansion is the end result. Investment is critical, and so is labor. They are interconnected. One cannot separate labor from investment.

## War—This Time Korea

In 1947 in Germany, the Western zones were merged into a new nation, the Federal Republic of Germany.

The great dollar shortage remained a scourge to recovery. Consumer goods were again becoming plentiful in America, but the average European and certainly the average German was barely making it.

The Marshall Plan was an unqualified success. However, recovery was slow. A major segment of the German population remained unemployed or underemployed. Their standard of living was far below that of the Americans or the British, and the British standard was well below that of the Americans.

The threat of Russian domination remained. China fell under the red banner, and the Soviets in 1948 developed the A-bomb. The international outlook remained grim.

America needed strong and prospering allies. Every effort had to be made to advance that cause. No price was too great. Every advantage was to be accorded our European brothers. As late as 1950, the unemployment rate in Germany was in double digits.

Bretton Woods had promised a new era of international cooperation.

With or without Soviet participation, international trade was critical to global progress. To facilitate trade between countries, unrestricted currency convertibility was essential.

In accordance with the understanding reached in New Hampshire, exchange rates were pegged or fixed. Nations were to manage their affairs, their balance of payments, in a way that would keep the existing exchange rate regimen from having to be revised.

The British experience was viewed as aberrant. British governments had insisted prior to the depression on an exchange rate that did not reflect the underlying reality.

The official rate of exchange for the pound had resulted on a number of occasions in widespread divestiture of sterling, declining exports, and widespread commercial and trade restrictions.

Nevertheless Bretton Woods had called for the dollar and sterling to be reserve currencies. However, the commercial world immediately recognized that sterling was overpriced given the state of the British economy. This produced a widespread conversion of sterling into dollars. This was a critical moment. It meant that the nations of the world, in holding reserves, would look to the dollar exclusively. Since dollar holders—except for the Americans—had an unrestricted right to convert dollars into gold at thirty-five dollars an ounce, dollars were riskless assets, and thus the world couldn't get enough of them, or so it seemed.

Foreign aid blossomed. To limit communist influence and to raise the standard of living of peoples, massive amounts of dollars were poured into nations around the world. A healthy world economy was the best way to beat back communist influence. The American government began to approach the world of spending as if there were no limits.

Through it all our balance of payments remained positive. We exported more than we imported. It remained positive because the productive capacity of the world outside the United States remained quite limited.

The fiscal conservatives in Congress sensed danger in this entire scheme but were consistently outvoted. The big spenders were not only in power, but it became increasingly clear that to be reelected, one had to support the expansion of government.

Later presidents tried to make adjustments, most notably Eisenhower, but these changes were marginal, and the spending regimen continued unabated.

In Europe Germany continued to be essential to the promising recovery.

With a continuing dollar shortage, no one raised the slightest objection when Germany adjusted the DM exchange rate against the dollar to 4.20 on September 18, 1949. Bear in mind the original conversion schedule of 3 to 1 had been deemed sufficient for balance, that is, 3 DM for every dollar. In June 1948 when the Marshall Plan was implemented, exchange was made 3.3 to 1. With unemployment still running high in Europe, the DM conversion rate was later adjusted another 27 percent.

Some months earlier, in April 1949, on the other side of the globe, Japan had set the yen/dollar exchange at 360 to 1, 360 yen for one dollar.

The hostile climate that had pervaded international relations from 1945 now took a fateful turn. On June 25, 1950, North Korea invaded South Korea. The United States intervened to help the South, and America was at war. This fateful event changed virtually everything.

As war broke out, the dollar in relation to other currencies was a good deal more expensive as measured by the exchange rate than it had been a few years earlier. The dollar was king, but dollar-priced goods were expensive as compared to the quality goods that began to flow from Europe.

A further complication was that the United States, having demobilized, was totally unprepared for war. The United States military needed hardware and needed it quickly. In addition, the American consumer was demanding more.

Europe was now in a position to meet this demand. Dollar spending exploded, and unemployment fell. In a sense it was the best of times and the worst of times.

During the course of the three years the Korean War lasted, Europe ascended from the ashes. From a commercial standpoint, Europe was now a world player. More importantly they could compete with American companies for global business. Their products, notably of German origin in the engineering field, were of the highest quality. Given the favorable exchange rate, these products were a good deal cheaper than ours.

The favorable balance of trade that America had benefited from for most of the twentieth century was beginning to slip away.

Europe and later Japan were becoming stronger, and America, flooding the world with dollars, weaker. No one seems to have paid any notice and wouldn't for years. Inertia took hold. Irrespective of the policies or philosophies of the parties in power, when it came to spending, it was always business as usual. The continuing Soviet threat dictated this.

What was missed entirely was the vulnerability of the dollar. The exchange rate was unfavorable to the Americans, and a day of reckoning was inevitable. The exchange rate was not being set by the market but arbitrarily set by bureaucrats, whose responsibilities never included concerns such as the balance of trade.

Pegged rates meant that the trade imbalance, which now favored the Europeans, was locked in. Henceforth American products would always suffer price disadvantages in comparison to similar products manufactured in Europe and Asia.

This condition was set in stone. It would go on indefinitely. Investment capital poured into Europe. European profits soared. The dollar shortage soon became a dollar glut in Europe. Though rates were pegged, the long-term outlook for the dollar in terms of purchasing power began to be questioned.

As it became increasingly clear that America would continue to ignore budget restraints, with the introduction of the Great Society Program under Lyndon Johnson, while entering into another conflict in Asia, this time Vietnam, further dollar weakness was inevitable. For the rest of the world, the solution built into the Bretton Woods Agreement was to exchange dollars for gold, and the gold rush began in earnest.

Few in the public or private sector on this side of the Atlantic understood the intricacies of foreign exchange. Europe had lived throughout history with foreign exchange. Americans, including those involved in the money side of banking, voiced little understanding or concern. As a participant in banking during this period, I can attest to the fact that the most senior officials did not have a clue.

Men like Johnson and Nixon simply did not understand the dynamic. The dollar would always be king, or so they thought. Money difficulties could always wait until after the next election. That mind-set continues to this very day.

As America and the world continued to live high on the hog, pursuing guns and butter, the stage was being set for the bottom to fall out, and fall out it would on August 15, 1971.

## Turbulence

Lord John Maynard Keynes was right. The Bretton Woods dynamic was unsustainable. The world eventually recognized this, including the Americans. Given the option of holding dollars or gold and given the spendthrift ways of Americans, the world wanted gold.

If the dollar was just another currency, the exchange value would have had to have been adjusted. Under Bretton Woods the dollar was the reserve currency. How does one devalue the global standard? Somehow it would have to be devalued against gold. This implied that gold was the world's reserve or standard. Effectively we were moving back to the prewar gold standard, which was precisely what Bretton Woods attempted to avoid.

Conceivably this calamity might have been avoided had the International Monetary Fund been given the power to carry out its mandate, which was to maintain international balance. At any rate the opportunity was lost, and so was the monetary system. Since 1971 we have been functioning without a system, every nation and their governments and most importantly the central banks pursuing parochial interests.

## It Is about Value—It Is Always about Value

Value literally means usefulness. All "things" that advance the human condition, requiring labor and/or creativity, and that are not otherwise free, have value. Money means value. Thus virtually everything has monetary value.

Value is a concept with two characteristics. It has both an intrinsic and an extrinsic component. The intrinsic, meaning unto itself, is a real benefit, for example, the air we breathe. The extrinsic component springs from its usefulness. It is laborsaving.

The degree of usefulness is the stimulant for demand. This is reflected in a price. The price is the measure of usefulness. The price must equal the usefulness. Price is the market expression of equilibrium.

For exchange to occur, both parties give equal value. This is essential for any exchange. Simply put, the law of equilibrium rules.

Typically one of the parties will use currency in exchange. Modern-day currency, fiat currency, is a manifestation of value but is not value. Thus it is an important break with the past.

During the many centuries after barter, when gold and silver, and to a lesser degree other metals, were used as currency, they constituted the measure of value. There was a merger of currency and value. An exchange for gold was final. Neither party had any additional rights. Today the recipient of the currency, dollars, for example, has the right to buy products and services from others. There is no merger. In the truest sense, the exchange is not final, though the immediate parties are no longer obligated.

Since currency is but a manifestation of value, and not value, it can neither be strong nor weak. However, the value of currency can be over- or understated.

As demand for a product increases, if the supply does not keep pace, the value of the product will rise. Under these circumstances, in a free market the price must rise for equilibrium to be maintained.

All attempts to disguise this increase by tinkering with the currency or by placing controls on prices are fraudulent. Rome, for example, reduced the silver content of its coins. Germany, by printing massive amounts of bills, created a condition of currency overvaluation.

In time the producer recognizes this and responds by curtailing supply. Shortages ensue. In order to correct this, that is, to return to equilibrium, the currency must be revalued.

A currency can cease to represent value completely. Two examples would be Confederate currency or. in the 1930s, the paper German mark.

A country whose currency is substantially overvalued has but two choices: significant devaluation, that is reform, or the introduction of a completely new currency.

An undervalued currency gives rise to the same phenomenon, but in reverse. Under such circumstances, as the price measured in currency terms is less than the underlying value, demand is stimulated.

It appears to buyers that everything is on sale. At present, this is the issue with China. China's currency is undervalued. In order to eliminate foreign competition, China relies on currency manipulation. China is a major player on the world stage because of undervaluation. The effect of this has been to put American and other foreign producers out of business.

In addition, this manipulation results in the transfer of businesses to China, since the cost of doing business there appears to be a great deal less than the cost of doing business here. Though virtually everyone knows this is going on, nothing has been done about it, as multinational corporations and other special interests find this distortion enhances their profitability. They have succeeded through their lobbying efforts in preventing action from being taken.

As a result America and other nations have experienced a substantial increase in unemployment.

Adding to the current distress is the fact that the American dollar is substantially overvalued. Just how this predicament arose, I will get into shortly.

As I noted earlier, global expansion and advancement require sufficient balance among the four components: investment/employment, production, consumption, and savings.

What is the yardstick that will assure investment in the first place? What is the measure that every participant considers as he enters the marketplace? To put it simply, what drives the decision-making process to build or not to? It is called the real rate of return.

CHAPTER 31

# The Real Rate of Return

---

**"Now and Forever..."**
As I view a market, I see it as a place where people buy and sell goods of infinite variety. In reality, a market is an exchange. I give something to get something. If I am the holder of value, including cash or my savings, I can become a participant.

For months I have been planning to buy a new pair of shoes. On my way to the store, I see an ad in the window of the local bank offering to pay 7 percent on my savings account. I must decide between the shoes, a form of consumption and immediate gratification, or the savings account, which will allow another to use my savings and thus I will gain an additional return of 7 percent. We call the 7 percent "interest."

What will be the decision? Consume or save? This may come as a surprise to many, but the answer is predictable, very predictable. One particular individual might respond by saying, "I don't care about the interest. I need the shoes." However, he or she will be the exception, not the rule. Tested over millennia, the so-called marginal participant, the typical person, will choose the savings over the shoes. Why is this so?

The reason is rate of return. Rate of return is critical to all investment. The break point, the point at which most people choose to save rather than spend, is approximately 3 percent for a short-term investment and 6 percent for a long–term investment. No one decided this, but this is how the bulk of humanity will respond given the choice.

The higher the level of interest over and above 3 percent and 6 percent, the more people will choose to save/invest rather than consume. Never lose sight of the fact that investment is the first and most important of the four components of commerce. Without investment nothing moves forward. Without investment, commerce will in time come to a complete stop.

As the rate of return falls below 3 percent and moves in the direction of zero, or should it turn negative, then consumption will increase exponentially at the expense of investment. Return, in this context, means gain. What has the individual gained by investing/saving rather than spending/consuming?

Everything received over and above the original investment is gain. In the hypothetical example of the shoes, it appears that the answer is 7 percent. However, it isn't. In the illustration the 7 percent is taxed; thus the gain is less than 7 percent.

Most importantly, since the individual is being repaid in currency and government overspending will likely reduce the currency value or its purchasing power by 6 percent, the actual return is 1 percent. In such a case, the individual did not realize a real rate of return of at least 3 percent. In fact, he or she may have less purchasing power when the term of the deposit ends than when it started. Thus there is no incentive, no reason to save, and the individual will proceed to buy the shoes, which translates into spending rather than savings, consumption rather than investment.

When we use the term *return*, we are not referring to a described rate of interest or, as the professionals say, the nominal or advertised rate. We are speaking of the "real" rate. Though it includes the stated or advertised rate, it also measures the adjustments, including taxes and currency appreciation or depreciation. For the marginal consumer to save, he or she must have a "real" rate of return, in the short term 3 percent or greater, and at least 6 percent for the long term.

If the currency is to experience a decline in exchange value of 6 percent, the real rate of return at best is 1 percent, even though the bank pays 7 percent. Why? Because his or her purchasing power, measured in currency terms, has been reduced by 6 percent.

Wise investors know this, and for this reason they move their money out of a country experiencing depreciation in currency value to a country whose currency is appreciating. Ease of money transfer, with advances in technology and communications, facilitates the movement of capital around the world. Today one can invest anywhere.

A depreciating currency reduces the return, and an appreciating currency enhances it. Governmental policies are the prime movers driving currency fluctuation. A government engaged in excessive spending, that is, where expenditures exceed revenue, all other things being equal and they never are, must expect a depreciation of currency. It is by way of devaluation that we regain equilibrium.

Between 1945 and 1971, during the so-called Bretton Woods era, currency fluctuation was minute. It was the responsibility of each government to pursue policies that would assure the continuance of the exchange rate at the agreed "pegged" level. In point of fact, governments, most notably the United States, failed in this responsibility, which was precisely why the Bretton Woods regimen fell apart in 1971.

Through the mid sixties, though America was squandering its wealth in pursuit of global recovery, domestic and international expansion, and the Cold War, exchange rates remained fixed. That was the exchange rate agreement of 1944. The exchange rate should never have been fixed since America's wealth was declining as a result of our spending policies; we were doing precisely what Great Britain did after World War I. The result would inevitably be the same.

If currency values are in equilibrium, the nominal or stated interest rate and the real rate of return are essentially the same.

The prospect of equilibrium came to an end in 1971. Fluctuating currency rates are now accepted and are critical in determining the real rate of return. Thus the nominal and real rate might show great disparity. Under such circumstances the nominal rate might rise and the real rate fall, or vice versa.

Money will invariably flow to the country or countries that will produce the highest real rate of return. Currency expectation is the critical factor when making a decision where to invest. China, though a third-world country, has investment capital pouring into it, for virtually everyone expects major currency appreciation, which will produce the highest rates of return in the world.

China at present has the best of all worlds—an undervalued currency whose exchange rate is determined by the government and held well below its true value to erase competition when exporting, and a real rate of return higher than any Western country. This regimen has been manipulated, so they come out the winner in every transaction. Incomprehensible as it may seem, the West has allowed them to get away with this.

The United States has the worst of all worlds—an overvalued currency, much as the British in the thirties and post-World War II, combined with bizarre spending policies. This overvaluation reduces the potential for exporting and drives imports, resulting in an unfavorable balance of payments, which is not self-correcting.

If this was the nineteenth century, we would have run out of gold long ago. Under the fiat or printed money regimen we are presently using, the problem does not self-correct but invariably worsens.

Adding to the absurdity is the perversity of the market. As someone borrows internationally, the creditor country's currency is sold, and the debtor country's currency is bought. This serves to drive up the price of the debtor country's exchange rate. Realistically the incremental debt should have reduced the value of the debtor country's exchange rate. In point of fact, it has increased it. In other words, the more the United States borrows internationally, the greater the value of America's currency. The market is working in reverse. Everything becomes distorted. Welcome to the twenty-first century.

Such a condition spurs disinvestment, which, under the gold standard regimen, would have driven the value of the currency down. Instead, the value keeps rising as we continue to borrow. This further restricts exports and circulation, causing global contraction. The hole we are digging just keeps getting deeper. This dynamic is measurable in real rate of return. International commerce quickly recognizes over or under currency valuation imbalances. A company sees that it will earn more by investing overseas and thus proceeds to move plant and equipment to the new domain.

This market phenomenon takes place every day in the securities markets. An investor group will not buy a certain company stock if they perceive that it is overvalued. They may very much like the company and believe in its future but will not buy the stock above a certain level. Market participants may be willing to buy a stock at $170 a share but would never buy it at $300. This is not a commentary about the company, but about the price.

Every indicator—the amount of debt, balance of payments, cost of labor, regulatory constraints, taxes, exchange rate, to name but a few—leads the reasonable investor to conclude that the real return on a dollar-based investment will generate less return than investment in another country, and the investor goes forward and invests on that basis.

There may indeed be risk in investing in another country, but the potential gain, in other words, the perceived real rate of return, outweighs that risk. Thus money pours into China, Brazil, Vietnam, India, Cambodia—the list goes on and on.

Virtually everyone would prefer to invest in the United States but not as long as the real rate of return is barely positive, or worse, negative. We cannot change the culture and infrastructure of the United States, nor do we want to, but we can alter the prospect of return by realigning the currency.

The universal rule is a rather simple one. No one will pay more for any asset than it is worth, and no one will make a long-term investment if there is limited prospect of real return.

In plain English, the US dollar today is not worth its stated value. Pretending that it is, which is what is happening now by virtue of central bank policies, will never give rise to investment but only stagnation. That is what the market has been telling us, but to this point, we have refused to listen.

As noted earlier the level of investment to consumption in the United States is approximately 19 percent. In China it is 45 percent.

For advanced nations since the midseventies, capital accumulation has averaged more than 20 percent. In this regard we are falling behind—compared to China, far behind.

## The Regeneration of Return

For international trade to be sustained, foreigners must have the financial capability to buy our products. Thus a nation's currency cannot appreciate indefinitely versus the currency of other nations because it becomes too expensive. Therefore all currencies must undergo periodic revaluation or face the prospect of seeing their international trade disappear.

## Overvaluation of Currency and the Dollar

For any nation to accumulate massive amounts of another nation's currency and hold it as a reserve carries grave economic danger for the nation accumulating, should the value of that currency fall precipitously.

Following the First World War, as Germany fell on hard times, the paper mark, as distinguished from the gold mark, had an exchange rate of four marks to the dollar.

By 1920 the exchange rate was fifty-seven marks to the dollar; by 1922 it was 430; and by 1924 it was 433 billion, which rendered the currency worthless and forced the introduction of a new currency, the Reichs mark.[cxxvi]

A decline of 100 percent at today's exchange rate level against the euro would translate into $2.75 for one euro. Just imagine a situation that would require a holder to have $2.4 billion to exchange for one euro. We would say that is preposterous. It could never happen. That is probably true absent a major war. The Germans early on would have said that this was not possible either, yet it happened, destroying commerce in Germany, wiping out the savings of the Germans, resulting in a completely broken and destitute nation, a collapse in trade, and the rise of Hitler. Yes, it can happen. It has happened numerous times in history, though not to the degree or with the consequences of devastation that occurred in the German Reich.

The modern real (BRL) was introduced in Brazil in 1994 as part of a monetary reform to end decades of runaway inflation. In 2000 the Argentine peso collapsed. The disarray was so great that for a time the Congress could not find anyone willing to serve as president. History is strewn with currency failure.

Let us not dwell on the horrors of history, but let's look at the causes behind today's problems, which will in time result in a stunning realignment of the dollar's value against the world's currencies if major action is not taken. If and when such a realignment takes place, it will bring with it a drastic reduction in the standard of living of every American.

This was never intended; it was not the plan. None of the delegates attending Bretton Woods could have conceived of a time when nations would accumulate massive amounts of another nation's currency.

No nation and certainly not Great Britain or the United States before the war would have tolerated another nation holding vast claims against their major trading partner. This would have been seen as a threat to sovereignty.

In the past a nation might accumulate gold as a result of its superior product base and productivity of its people, but gold was neutral. Gold is a universal asset. This was the misunderstanding of Ben Strong when he isolated the gold inflow into the United States from Great Britain during the twenties, believing that it was Great Britain's gold and we were simply trustees. This belief deprived the American consumer of the money to buy British goods, was thus hurtful to Britain, and hastened the onset of the depression.

To argue that it is wise for a nation to build a reserve base over and above any reasonable need is precisely the mistake that Spain made when, after the discovery of America, it sent expeditions here to gather gold, bring it home, and not spend it. Wealth is never the metal or the paper. Wealth is in the trade that results from the interaction of peoples and nations. The world economy expands through trade, not in the finding of gold or the accumulation of paper.

During the reign of Ferdinand and Isabella, Spain was the most prosperous nation in the world. A century later, after accumulating massive amounts of metal, it was one of the poorest.

Prosperity lies in trade, not in accumulation. A country selling product for currency, which proceeds to accumulate ever more currency rather than invest or spend it domestically, is taking a calculated risk that the value of the currency will not decline. For if it does, that country has lost out completely. This in fact is what happened to Spain as the price of gold fell.

A modern example of this is China, which is accumulating massive amounts of US dollars, but the purchasing power of the dollar is falling and may fall precipitously, thus greatly diminishing Chinese reserves. Remember the German experience. China should not be building reserves over and above a prudent amount, but spending domestically to build their infrastructure. China does not grasp the meaning or purpose of currency. As a result of this, it might unintentionally play a major role in a global economic calamity.

It must always be kept in mind that gold, silver, and so on were viewed in history as a reliable measure, much the same way as a ruler is a reliable method for measuring distance. Gold was never intended to be the money, no more than a ruler is intended to be the distance. Money meant the goods exchanged, not the metal. Production makes a nation wealthy, not the accumulation of the measuring device.

On the other hand, consumption always renders a country poorer. Common sense tells us that the more we consume, the less we have. The United States refuses to acknowledge this. The United States is consumption-oriented, and our $18 trillion debt is irrefutable testimony of this.

## Currency Manipulation

Anyone familiar with markets understands that in a free market, a transaction takes place when the price the buyer is willing to pay and the seller is willing to divest at are aligned. Shouldn't the currency exchange markets work the same way? Isn't that market a free market? The answer is "No!" with an exclamation point.

Since the introduction of Bretton Woods, currency exchange markets have never been free. When the expression "freely convertible" is used, doesn't that mean without restriction or market-driven? Again the answer is no, for the central banks of the world pursue policies for domestic political reasons that have the effect of moving the exchange rate away from its true market level. This is precisely the intervention that Jefferson, Madison, and Jackson feared.

One might argue that many currencies are freely convertible, isn't that so? The answer is yes, but that does not mean that the market sets the price. The reason for this is that government policy and government agents, particularly the Treasury or the Exchequer, and the central banks are pursuing policies that impact the price of the currency. These banks work in concert. Working in concert and due to their size and market power, they set the tone and direction of currency exchange and, through their action, the price.

## Currency Exchange Post-World War II

Following the war, there was dollar shortage. Trade among the European nations was de minimus. Pegged or fixed exchange under Bretton Woods with dollar convertibility into gold was the regimen.

As tariff barriers in Europe began to fall, their economies experienced modest recovery, with Germany in the lead after the introduction of the deutsche mark in 1948. The economic picture in Great Britain began to brighten following the devaluation of sterling by 30.5 percent.

In 1951 the Treaty of Rome signaled the beginning of the development of the European Economic Community. In Europe unemployment remained high, too high given the stakes of the Cold War. In 1950, in order to tackle unemployment, the deutsche mark was set at 4.1950 to the dollar. This exchange rate, as I have recounted, greatly favored Germany in a way quite similar to our current experience with China.

The Germans have always had a marvelous work ethic. They had been deprived prewar by the depression, during the war due to military expenditures, and postwar due to destruction and reparations.

The Germans then went to work and for five years experienced double-digit growth rates, which became known as the "German miracle."

No one questioned the German work ethic, but their exports soared in large part due to the deutsche mark valuation of 4.1950 to the dollar and pricing German goods cheaply.

They held a huge market advantage and would continue to hold that advantage indefinitely. There was virtually no official recognition of this fact, though it was having a measurable impact on the exports of other nations, including the United States.

Businesses may have complained and economists may have speculated about it, but no action was taken. With the Cold War raging, a healthy Germany was viewed as a major plus.

The Germans chalked it all up to their work ethic, which we now know was not the case. Without question the favorable exchange rate gave them an enormous and unfair advantage.

Prior to 1955 the United States and Britain, as occupiers, might have tamed this burgeoning German tiger. In 1955 occupation ended. The Germans were now on their own, and the world was about to pay dearly for this.

In 1958 the European currencies become fully convertible. The payment union was dissolved, and America began to experience a decline in its gold reserves. The Americans were beginning to reap what they had sowed.

In a world where if you have an advantage you might as well press it, the Europeans, with Germany in the lead, developed a customs union. Outsiders paid a trade tariff. In the nineteenth century, this was the key strategy of Prussia.

The European Community was about to become a powerful economic force. Global pressures finally emerged beginning in 1958, and the deutsche mark began a very modest annual appreciation of 2 to 3 percent through 1968.

By 1969 capital inflows were sufficient to force major currency realignment, with the deutsche mark appreciating 63 percent through 1995. Capital outflow from the United States during this period accelerated. America's gold reserves dwindled.

Bretton Woods collapsed under these pressures in August 1971.

To make up for this loss in capital, the Federal Reserve began to inflate the money supply. Aided by OPEC, inflation began to take hold in America.

Before this bout with self-destruction finally ran its course with the election of Ronald Reagan in 1980, the international monetary system was severely tested.

## Global Distortion

Post-World War II, every nation outside the communist sphere was in one way or another dependent on America.

We had to save Korea and Vietnam by force, Europe with troops and military hardware, and every friendly and on occasion unfriendly nation directly or indirectly with financial support.

As a result of this monumental effort, the world recovered from World War II, Communism and the Socialist Republics were swept into the dustbin of history, new wars to counter terrorism were fought, and America slowly but surely went broke. The world balance and currency equilibrium that were expected with the adoption of Bretton Woods proved ephemeral, just as Keynes had predicted.

Debtor-creditor relations among nations gave rise to fundamental disequilibrium, which broke the system. We are living with the broken system today, and the fractures are of such magnitude that global implosion is possible.

This outcome would have been different had the International Monetary Fund exercised the powers granted to it at the time of formation, namely, taking steps to prevent currency manipulation and other discriminatory practices that impeded the free flow of capital.

Nations, working closely with the IMF and other international organizations, should have been insistent in their trade negotiations that trade be balanced, thus giving no nation unfair advantage.

In retrospect, had the United States had access to an infinite supply of gold, we could have supported the world and achieved our global aims with the policies that were pursued. That was not the case. We should have recognized that our wealth, though vast, was finite. The movement of capital could not indefinitely be in one direction.

We refuse to this day to recognize this fact. Aggravating the problem greatly is that the dollar remains the world's reserve currency. Everyone outside of America has a stake in keeping the dollar artificially high. To the mindless in the public sector and elsewhere, it appears that we could spend without limit. Many still believe this.

Virtually every policy of ours, domestic or foreign, has a substantial quotient of consumption. Defense, Social Security, Medicare, Medicaid, agricultural subsidies, foreign aid, the Great Society, education, war—the list is endless. All consume the nation's wealth. The goals may have been admirable, but the cumulative effect will ultimately break the financial back of this, or for that matter, any, nation. Spending with a high quotient of consumption, metaphysically, cannot give rise to wealth. Wealth necessitates investment, to build and construct the very antithesis of consumption.

Investment wisely made increases wealth; unrestrained consumption produces bankruptcy.

Since the Second World War, it is clear that America and the West, both public and private sectors, have not diverted a sufficient amount of their wealth to investment. We are now paying the price for that. The public sector rarely considers investment. Consumption policies translate into votes; long-term investment typically does not.

To replenish government coffers, to expand the economy, the private sector was expected to do the giant share of the investing. As long as that investment was made, as long as the American economy was expanding, tax revenues were sufficient to cover excessive, immoderate, and duplicative spending.

By the early sixties as it became clear that tax revenue was clearly not going to keep pace with the expansion in public spending, a philosophical dichotomy developed in the West between those who advocated strict controls on government spending, the conservatives, and those who saw no limit on the role of government, the liberals.

That battle continues to be waged in the United States, and the political outcome remains uncertain.

As one ponders the past and the decisions made, one fact is indisputable. Our present plight was not entirely due to American mistakes. In a world of tyrants, we were never the aggressor, though our most recent actions in the Middle East raise some questions on that score. To the contrary, where we intervened, we were either late in coming, tepid, or timid, though there were notable exceptions.

As the global protector of freedom, we could have and should have insisted that the expensive burdens of the Cold War be shared more equitably by our Allies. A revitalized Germany, France, and Britain could have and should have been handed the responsibility of maintaining the peace and security of Europe. We should have insisted as part of our commitment to their freedom and security that they expend a higher percentage of their GDP on defense. We could also have insisted that they pay the costs associated with the maintenance of a standing American army on their territory. They did pay a portion of the cost but not the entire expense, for example, missile defense. We should have made it clear that we were the backup and they the front line.

We could have requested partial repayment for the billions, perhaps by today's measure trillions, we gave to Europe and Asia virtually scot-free in every realm of human endeavor before the end of occupation in 1955. They might have resisted, but equity demanded nothing less. In a very real sense, their freedom was maintained and their economies grew for decades at the American taxpayer's expense.

And lastly, though the world will always require a reserve currency, it should never have been the American domestic dollar. That was not the intent of Bretton Woods. Those delegates never foresaw a time when the dollar linkage to gold would be permanently severed. They would have scrapped the agreement had they thought that would happen.

The global demands on America, on top of its domestic needs, were well beyond the capacity of any great nation. America was the most productive of nations, but that potential had limitations. Our population in relation to that of mega countries was not large.

The national economy with all guns blazing could not have been expected to grow for any sustained period at a rate in excess of 4 percent, which was essential if we were to continue to do everything for everybody.

Budget restraint was exercised in varying degrees until the 1960s. Vietnam, the Great Society under Johnson, and the Nixon and Reagan years with their commitment to rebuilding the United States military clearly set us on the present path to insolvency.

Further, a global dollar-based reserve system, where no nation was required to spend the accumulated dollars in America and where there were no limits placed on the amount of dollar reserves, inhibited monetary circulation worldwide.

China, Japan, and Germany, among others, were guilty of this. Until China appeared on the world scene, the Federal Republic of Germany was the most egregious violator of the spirit of Bretton Woods. The Federal Republic maintained a tight monetary policy, relying on the inflow of dollars for its expansion. The deutsche mark was quietly becoming the global currency of choice. In recognition of this, changes in international monetary policies, when they were finally made, were made grudgingly, and then after tedious negotiation.

Changes made were limited in scope and were never sufficient to bring about equilibrium. America was bled until the arrival of Reagan to enhance the standard of living of the Europeans. The principal beneficiaries were Germany, Russia, and Eastern Europe, and to a lesser extent, Japan.

It was during this era that the artificial dollar exchange rate developed. As Reagan turned his sights on foreign capital to finance the rebuilding of the American military, the balance of payments turned decidedly against America. Imports surged as the dollar strengthened. The world was becoming wealthier, but American debt surged. Americans appeared to be living well, and they were, at least up to the recent financial crisis, but it was illusory. It was accomplished with smoke and mirrors, or a four-letter word called debt.

From the debacle one lesson is clear: a global reserve currency and a domestic currency should never be the same, for under those circumstances, every conceivable type of manipulation is possible.

The solution lies in a supracurrency, which in fact was created in 1969 as a reserve asset to supplement member nation reserves. This asset is named SDR or special drawing right. It is a potential claim on the freely usable currencies of IMF members. Thus it is a claim against a basket of currencies, and this basket determines its value.[cxxvii]

Debits and credits offset; it can't be manipulated. John Maynard Keynes and his monetary program would be finally resurrected and adopted.

Full adoption of this or some similar scheme is inevitable. It would be the critical step in preventing future currency manipulation. Currency practices would be monitored by the IMF, which would use its power to adjust trade imbalances by altering SDR balances, leaving no incentive for any nation to pursue a favorable trade regimen.

## The German Challenge Revisited

Until the collapse of the Soviet Union in 1991, the world was quick to ascribe all problems to the Cold War. The consensus was that without this conflict, all would be well.

It most certainly has not turned out that way. Terrorism is new to the world stage, but nationalism and "beggar thy neighbor" trade policy is not. It was precisely global acceptance of said policies that brought about the two world wars.

Germany was defeated in both. But the German desire to dominate Europe, at least by economic means, was never surrendered. Postwar Germany planned to lead. The key to leadership was domestic economic strength. America would do the heavy lifting, with the dollar serving as the world reserve currency. In addition, it would provide for the defense of Europe and the world while fighting local wars with American treasure and personnel. For the Germans, this was a marvelous arrangement. The French were no longer an enemy, and the Russians after Stalin, though a continuing problem, were a problem the Americans could handle.

As capital poured into Germany and as it became clear that the deutsche mark was undervalued, Germany did nothing to help in rebalancing global commerce. Pegged rates assured Germany of its international power position.

A small revaluation was made in 1961 and a larger one in 1969. In the interim they accumulated reserves and began buying large amounts of gold, which hindered circulation by sterilizing the dollars. This served to push the price of gold and other commodities sharply higher. In turn, this fed a global inflation scare, as governments and their central banks increased the money supply in the vain hope that this would ease the price surge. We now know that they had it backward. At any rate, the beneficiary was Germany and, to a large extent, the rest of Europe.

The Christian Democratic Party, the conservative party of Germany, together with its coalition partners, remained in power from 1948 until 1969. In 1969 the Social Democrats replaced the Conservatives as the governing party of Germany. This had important global consequences.

On the critical matter involving war and peace, the Christian Democrats and the Social Democrats, as members of NATO, stood foursquare with the United States.

When it came to matters of commerce, the Americans assumed that Germany and the United States were pursuing identical goals. That was never the case. Germany had been since 1945 an erstwhile ally. However, throughout its turbulent history, it never became anyone's partner. It most certainly never intended to be a partner of the United States. It planned to achieve European hegemony, which had been the goal of Germany since its inception. The European Union, as envisioned by their leaders, would have Germany as the lead nation in full competition with the United States.

It was their intent to become a friendly competitor, not an enemy, but with very different goals and aspirations than the United States. Further, within Germany the political goals of the Christian Democrats, a conservative party, and the Social Democrat Party were starkly different.

The Christian Democrats were nationalists, supported by industrialists and the business interests.

The Social Democrat Party was a socialist party. It was the inheritor of the philosophic views of Marx and Engel. It was not a liberal party of the type we have become accustomed to in the United States, with its government-program orientation. These socialists were not fearful of the Russians. They believed that the best way to peace and security was to reconcile with the Russian bear.

They sympathized with the core social philosophy promulgated from Moscow. The militarist attitude of the Russians and the limits imposed on individual freedom were in their mind a passing phase in development that would pass with economic support, particularly financial support. The best way to secure this was to provide them with the resources to build up their infrastructure. Hostile actions taken by the Russians were to be ignored and/or excused.

They were more fearful of the Americans, whom they liked and who provided the security blanket for them and for Europe, but who they felt aggravated Russian paranoia. Further, the Americans were God-fearing people who respected the inalienable rights of the individual. For the most part, European socialists were atheists, who saw religion, as Marx once said, as the opiate of the people.

Their concern was society, not the individual, which among other failings allowed them to ignore the tragedy of the Russian Gulag.

Their socialist philosophy and American democratic principles were in conflict. Since both nations needed each other, these philosophical differences were largely ignored, at least during moments of crisis. Nevertheless both the Social Democrats and the Conservatives shared one very important goal: German hegemony.

The conservative focus was westward. They envisioned a strong Germany, leading Europe eventually to political union, competing on the world stage with the United States for supremacy.

The Social Democrats, recognizing that the traditional German sphere of influence was Central and Eastern Europe, with its huge population in need of virtually everything, offered to Germany the potential of becoming the commercial wonder of the world. They were convinced that Russia, whose socialist philosophy they identified with, could be treated like a wayward son and persuaded with money to alter their extreme behavior. In other words, the Soviet Union could be bought.

The strategy called for making a huge investment with products, accompanied by large loans, making Russia increasingly dependent on Germany. This would transform Russia, with its historical tyrannical structure in many ways like their own, advance German interests, and secure world peace.

When the Social Democrats came to power in 1969, Germany's attention began to be focused eastward. Capital coming into Germany from a variety of sources, including the Middle East and of course the United States, began accelerating. The German banks, and their neighbors the Swiss, became important international lenders and currency and money market speculators. Deutsche Bank was becoming a household name, even in America.

What the Americans—including the leaders, at least prior to Reagan—never understood was that the German bankers and government were working hand in hand to advance the goal of a greater Germany. On the world stage, Germany was to be number one.

German bankers were given hints of coming changes in the direction of monetary policy by the Bundesbank, the central bank of Germany. They were encouraged to extend credit to their eastern brothers. In the money markets, this was widely known and commented on. There was an insider's game that went on in Europe, which at that time would never have occurred in the United States.

By 1971 the dollar was under the most intense pressure, being sold short by the German banks for deutsche marks. The deutsche marks were in turn loaned to the Russians at attractive rates of interest, and they in turn bought German goods. The Russians repaid the loans, and the German banks exchanged the marks, covering their dollar shorts with cheaper dollars as the dollar fell in value. As long as the dollar remained under pressure, which was inevitable with American public sector spending, this was a win-win strategy for Germany and Russia and, for that matter, Europe. The loser, of course, was the United States.

The money received by the Russians did not go to buy harmless consumer goods but was used to build up their military. To the extent that the dollars were coming in from the West, the Germans and Swiss in particular, the Russians could have guns and butter too.

In effect the Germans and Swiss, with financial help from the Americans, built the Soviet military. Unintentionally America played the key supporting role through an expansive fiscal policy and an easy monetary policy, which made it possible for capital to flow to Western Europe and then on to Russia.

When time came for repayment, the process was reversed. Since the dollar was weak and was expected to remain so, this was a bonanza for the Germans and Swiss. They profited from the loans and from the dollar short, and their businesses profited from the sale of goods.

Thus it was only a matter of time before Germany would overtake the United States as the leading commercial power.

Since the dollar short went unhedged, it was important to European bankers that they have advance notice of any fundamental monetary change in the United States.

Under such circumstances, the Russian credits were virtually riskless. Money lost on certain Russian, Polish, and Czech credits was made up with the dollar short. The more, the merrier. Of course this meshed nicely with the political goals of the Social Democrats in Germany and elsewhere.

Meanwhile, across the ocean, the effect of this policy was having a profound impact on the American economy. Recognizing the dollar weakness, the world, except for the Americans, was converting dollars into gold, and the price of everything began to skyrocket. Dollar weakness was wreaking havoc on the American price structure.

## The Eurodollar Phenomenon

The rise and fall of empires is coincident with the flow of investment capital. That was true of Rome, Great Britain, France, and now the United States.

If Bretton Woods had worked as envisioned, the international transfer of capital would have been held to a minimum. The primary purpose of pegged rates was precisely to limit the flow of capital from one nation to another. It was universally accepted that the capital generated through production in one country should stay in that country to benefit its citizens. The workers would reap the benefit, not the speculators.

The postwar investment by the United States in Europe and Asia was an extraordinary act of compassion and charity. However, without some form of repayment, it ultimately produced harmful and unintended consequences, many of which I have already described.

From a regulatory and business standpoint, neither America nor the world was prepared to make the adjustments required for what would in time become a titanic transfer of wealth, the greatest in world history, from America to other nations. Dollars flowed into the coffers of foreigners to such an extent that a new market was created by the early 1960s.

Dollars owned by foreigners on deposit outside the United States in foreign banks or foreign branches of American banks became known as Eurodollars. At the outset, Eurodollars were totally unregulated. The charter and oversight regimens of the central banks did not address this uninvited currency.

Central banks, as a matter of course, insisted that banking institutions maintain reserves against the deposits made in their domestic bank branches. Such deposits were always designated in the currency of the nation of the banks in which they were made. In other words one could not walk into a bank in New York and deposit Swiss francs or German marks. If you were to make a deposit in New York, it had to be in dollars. The Federal Reserve manages the money supply in the United States in dollars.

The Fed has no authority over marks or yen or any other currency. They also have no authority over foreign banks operating outside of the United States. Foreign banks work the same way.

Thus as Eurodollars arrived on the scene and foreigners as well as American international corporations found that they were the beneficiaries of this novel currency, banks were forced into creating a new ledger, which they designated as offshore to account for these deposits.

These dollars were unregulated, which meant no reserve requirement and no regulatory limits. This was an entirely free market. Some banks, because of their size and location, the so-called money center banks, began to take in enormous amounts of Eurodollars.

Beginning in 1976, the year OPEC quadrupled the price of oil, which to this day is priced in dollars. The effect was to create a flood of dollars, which over time would become tidal in proportion.

Banks can't simply sit with these deposits; since they are earning interest, they must lend them, and lend they do, to the third world, to consumers, to other banks, to anyone who needs a buck.

No reserve requirement assured continued growth in the Eurodollar pie. With so much currency floating around the world, borrowers had a field day. Banks pushed or arranged credit for those who could least afford debt: South American Republics, Eastern Europe, the Middle East.

With credit readily available, asset prices spiked. Demand created more demand. With so many dollars in circulation, the value of the dollar, aided by our friends, the European bankers, went into free fall and interest rates hit record highs.

A lesson never learned and not understood today is that as the price of a currency falls, there must be a market offset. That offset takes place in the rate structure. It is a universal law that as currency falls, rates rise to assure the continuation of equilibrium. Will someone please explain this to the Federal Reserve? I have tried, but they won't listen. About this time, along came Ronald Reagan and Mr. Paul Volcker, who decided to pull the plug, and the money game of the forties through the late seventies came crashing down.

## Concentration of Capital

The previous financial crisis, the one that occurred beginning in the early eighties under Reagan, had a profound impact, most notably on third-world countries, the Soviet Union, Eastern Europe, and last but by no means least, the European bankers. The Soviet Union and Eastern Europe and their socialist ideology never recovered.

The global bankers were forced to write off billions in loans extended throughout the third world. Nations, the likes of Brazil, were forced to adopt a new currency.

American savings banks and savings and loan institutions were extinguished as the federal government was forced to step in, creating the Resolution Trust Corporation (RTC), which closed or otherwise resolved 747 thrifts with total assets of $394 billion.

We have come to refer to these boom-bust cycles with their debilitating global impact as bubbles. It is an apt description. We live an illusion springing perhaps from the stars. But as Shakespeare said to Brutus, "the fault dear Brutus is not in our stars but in ourselves."[cxxviii]

Bubbles do not simply occur; they are caused. As George Santayana, the philosopher, observed, "Those who cannot remember the past are condemned to repeat it."[cxxix]

Boom-bust cycles have occurred with such frequency in history that a reasonable person might begin to believe that they are inevitable. They are not. Every bubble has two characteristics. The first, and most important, is the divergence of price and value.

Value is the objective reality. It goes to the very essence of the object. The value is unto itself. One can assess that value and through reasoning compare it to other objects. We are able to understand the value of an object in that comparison. The price, as measured in currency, should reflect that, if currency is doing its designated job.

Pricing any object above its value is simply an attempt to get something for nothing. It is fraudulent. Price and value will naturally equate in the marketplace. We refer to this as the law of supply and demand.

This equation, however, can be disturbed. Disturbance produces imbalance. Price can no longer be relied upon as an accurate reflection of value.

For this to happen, one must create the impression that demand is inexhaustible and will be sustained irrespective of supply or price. The current price is rendered irrelevant. The nominal price can move in only one direction. Thus all purchases are riskless. For such a condition to arise, the world must believe that it has access to unlimited resources.

This gives rise to a second requirement, the need for the massive concentration of capital. Nations and very large institutions have the wherewithal to concentrate resources, becoming the demons of concentration.

Governmental and other large institutions are not an obstacle or threat to progress because they are large, but because they concentrate their resources and disturb the balance required in the world of commerce. I repeat, bubbles do not occur in the absence of concentration.

The concentration of capital is inherently discriminatory. However, it is obvious that some concentration is necessary in an advanced society. A city could not build a highway or bridge, an army could not be fielded, and a factory could not be built without the capital savings of many being brought together for the project. That is the purpose of banking. However, to build that bridge means that spending elsewhere must be denied. The true misfortune of debt lies in the belief that nothing should be denied.

Banking, like all human endeavor, is subject to corruption. Citizens depositing money into local banks expects those banks to lend the money in a way that will better their community, their state, their nation. Balance and reason are expected to prevail.

They do not expect the bank to gamble or to transfer money without their permission to other lands to benefit other nations at their nation's expense simply because it is profitable.

They do not expect the bank to borrow or leverage its capital to a point that their savings as well as the bank's capital is at risk.

Banks must be managed in such a way as to limit the likelihood of failure. This requires executives of character and integrity who will exercise restraint.

Bankers did not undergo a marked change in character as the guidelines of good banking began to erode. Clearly, access to enormous sums of capital helped create a mentality of invincibility in the banking field that became evident in the attitude and behavior of bankers. They no longer focused on the community or state. They were above such mundane concerns.

However, there were innumerable culprits in this era of decline. Self-interest began to dominate judgment. The character of those who landed on the beaches of Normandy or fought on Iwo Jima no longer represented the ideal to be emulated.

This new generation was going to get all that it could for itself. Fairness and equity were no longer the measurements for reward. Political influence, deception, selling out for personal gain at the expense of others became the modus operandi. There were to be no rules of behavior. Only the fittest deserved to survive. If one must break the law, have capable lawyers standing by; better still, don't get caught.

The business schools turning out future leaders preached a core philosophy of greed as the key to success. As I write this condemnation, I sense that attitudes are changing for the better. Pray that they will.

As the crisis of 2008 demonstrated clearly, all restraint was set aside by those who should have known better. Profit and greed ruled totally. They continue to rule, as the current and past executive compensation statistics indicate.

Concentration lay at the heart of the disaster. Government borrowing set the precedent, and banking debt and leverage followed.

The regulators, including the Federal Reserve, chose to ignore the developing debacle.

By bringing together the rich and powerful—Washington, Wall Street, and government agencies—the insiders managed by the passage of laws to bypass oversight and regulation, putting Main Street at risk for self-gain, political influence, and power. It will stand as one of the most disgraceful episodes in American history. Though many of the insiders fed at the trough, few have been held responsible, and many an American has suffered unnecessarily. Claims to the contrary aside, they all knew what they were doing. All that can be said at this juncture is that they have it on their conscience, if they have a conscience.

## Back to 1971

Richard Nixon, in an effort to tame inflation and largely unaware of the games being played on the other side of the pond, on August 15, 1971, instituted price and wage controls, while at the same time ending convertibility of dollars into gold. The freeze on wages and prices was intended to last ninety days. It lasted close to a thousand.

These controls were mostly dismantled by April 1974. They did not succeed in ending inflation. On the contrary, inflation at an annual rate was running at double-digit levels when they were finally canceled. It was an experience born out of ignorance and political necessity, which may be synonymous.

As a result of this misguided effort, it became abundantly clear that controls were not the answer. Reining in spending and reducing the growth in the money supply while forcing Europe and OPEC to come to grips with reality were. Politically, however, this was very difficult.

The Federal Reserve moved cautiously, not wanting to bring about recession as the war in Vietnam continued.

Caution was not the answer. Unfortunately, the Nixon, Ford, and Carter administrations were all about caution.

Meanwhile, scapegoats had to be found for the dreadful condition that was playing havoc with the American economy.

They were aplenty—the Vietnam War, the Russians, the bankers, Nixon, Congress, the Federal Reserve, the protesting students, everyone but our Western allies, who, while proclaiming their undying friendship, continued to pursue monetary and trade policies that seriously undermined American interests.

Nixon left office and the Vietnam war ended, but the Cold War continued. American policy under Ford and Carter remained static and unimaginative.

America's strategic position weakened, in the mind of many, dangerously. Russia, Germany, and Japan's accrete global power and their influence grew as capital left America for European shores and Middle Eastern oil, creating Eurodollars.

The Federal Reserve under G. William Miller, beginning in 1978, whose job it was to stabilize the international position of the United States through a coherent monetary policy, instead pursued a policy to reelect Jimmy Carter. This was accomplished by maintaining low rates and expanding the money supply, which further dangerously undercut the dollar's value.

As it became clear that this policy would have disastrous consequences, and under pressure from American bankers, Carter replaced Miller with Paul Volcker.

Volcker moved immediately to shore up the dollar by introducing an aggressive monetary policy, but by the fall of 1979, the future of the dollar remained in serious doubt as the deteriorating international position of the United States suggested fundamental weakness.

The European central bankers advised Volcker that they no longer would supply unlimited support for the dollar. The dollar, for the first time in history, was in danger of being cast adrift.

The Russians took advantage of this historic moment by invading Afghanistan. Their intention was to ultimately flank the West strategically by first gaining a foothold close to the oil reserves of the Middle East.

The Germans stood to gain politically and economically as America was forced to retrench. The Social Democrat strategy under Herr Helmut Schmidt was working very well. From the German perspective, the outlook for further gains appeared to be unlimited.

Then the most unexpected of events occurred. Ronald Reagan was elected president of the United States.

CHAPTER 32

# Andrew Jackson Incarnate, Ronald Reagan (1980–1988)

## AMERICA IS BACK

The prevailing world opinion at the time of Reagan's election was that any changes that he was likely to make would be uneventful.

Opinion pieces in leading newspapers such as the *New York Times* suggested that there was little difference between men like Carter and Reagan. The future was baked in the cake. This turned out not to be the case. In fact, the world was in for a shock.

The cognoscenti knew very little about the Yankee Doodle Dandy spirit and, though he had been governor of California for two terms, little about president-elect Ronald Reagan and virtually nothing about Andrew Jackson. European, Asian, and some American pundits had long since concluded that the American view of the world was outdated. They failed to understand the American temperament and, most importantly, its soul.

Reagan understood both very well. America was, he profoundly believed, "the last best hope of mankind." Without America, without American leadership, humanity he believed was doomed.

Sharing the same philosophy as the seventh president of the United States, Reagan was a Jeffersonian through and through.

His campaigns, first for governor of California and then president, rang with the cheers of his followers, who were many, as he proclaimed, "Government can't solve the problem; government is the problem."

From time in memoriam, Europeans and Asians had suffered under the rule of tyrants of every stripe. They did not fully grasp the American concept of freedom. It was quaint. It had a certain charm, but it wasn't real. Most certainly it had no application to the twentieth century.

The same seemed to believe that the future lay somewhere in the east or south, with men like Mao, Che Guevara, Brezhnev, or Indira Gandhi, or in organizations that exercised global government, such as the United Nations.

The people were to be ruled by their betters, who knew what was best.

The orientation was socialist. Capitalism was dead or dying, and goodbye to bad rubbish.

Reagan and his followers not only did not believe this, but were determined to turn the world upside down and completely change the course of history as few men had before them.

Reagan believed that communism and socialism disemboweled free men, taking from them the capacity to pursue truth, each in his own way with individual talent.

The prevailing world philosophy, if allowed to flourish, would turn all men into robots where a select few would pull the strings. This philosophy was not only destructive, he said, but evil incarnate.

To save humanity from a new dark age, communism, socialism, and everything associated with them had to go. America and American ideals were in peril, and he was called upon to deliver the nation and the world. He pursued that task.

Though some of his closest advisors, including his beloved wife, Nancy, were inclined to downplay some of the rhetoric, Reagan meant what he said. He was certain of himself and his convictions.

A clear indication of just where he was headed occurred a few days before his inauguration, when in his pleasant but direct fashion he referred to the Iranians who were holding the Americans hostage as barbarians. The Iranians were the first to get the Reagan treatment and message, and they released the hostages as he was being sworn in.

Reagan understood from the start that the Russian communist jugular lay in the world of finance. A nation that could not feed itself could not possibly pose a military threat unless it was being given access to immense amounts of Western capital.

They were building their military with American dollars and had achieved strategic parity in that sphere.

He took the steps necessary to deny them access and, at the same time, begin a major program to rebuild American military capability. To accomplish this he needed the support of our European allies.

Reagan met with Helmut Schmidt twice before his inauguration and had an extended meeting with him the morning of the day he was shot to discuss matters of mutual interest.

America and Europe had very different interests and perspectives on all issues pertaining to capital and finance. Schmidt and other European leaders had been suggesting for some time that America should get its house in order but were very short on specifics.

Schmidt well understood that the flow of capital from America to Germany had provided Germany with the wherewithal to build their economy and develop their export markets, notably with Russia and its satellites. There the Germans had a free hand, with little competition.

Reagan, in consultation with Paul Volcker, chairman of the Federal Reserve Board, agreed that the best way to kill inflationary expectations in this country was to shut off the monetary spigot. This would cause a recession, but it was the price that had to be paid.

Schmidt and others were alarmed by this. They understood that this would mean that capital movement from America to Europe was endangered. If this were to happen, their long-term strategy was at risk. Schmidt did his best to get Reagan to soften his stance, but Reagan would have none of it.

Reagan was not only determined to stop the outflow of dollars, which through German and Swiss intermediaries ended up in the hands of the Russian military, but to reverse the flow, with foreign capital flowing into the United States.

To accomplish this he was determined to keep the real rate of return, interest plus currency appreciation, higher in America than Europe. Real interest rates would remain high indefinitely, as growth in the money supply was completely shut down.

America would henceforth rely on foreign capital to advance the economy and its myriad of programs. The message was a simple one. Investors would have far more to gain by investing in America than in Europe.

This put the Swiss and German bankers in a bind. They would no longer be in a position to lend to Russia, which raised the prospect of Russia defaulting on the debt it had accumulated. The dollar, which they had shorted for deutsche marks, was not going to decline further but would begin a major advance. The German and Swiss bankers faced staggering losses.

The Reagan plan ultimately achieved all its aims. It did so but only at an enormous cost. The ocean of international capital, which had been flowing from the United States since the war, Eurodollars, now returned.

The government portion of this inflow was borrowed. Government borrowing and debt increased in tandem, skewing America's balance of payments.

America did not have to produce its way to prosperity. It did not have to tax the private sector or markedly increase the money supply to rebuild the military and expand the welfare state. It simply had to borrow. Congress quickly realized that it could spend with impunity, and spend it did.

The Eurodollar pool was expanding daily. Without reserve requirements and control, the expansion might well prove infinite. OPEC alone could provide all the dollars America needed, as it continued to increase oil prices to meet ever-increasing demand.

As long as the dollar remained strong, the real rate of return would be higher here than any place on the globe. That could be assured by continuing a policy of zero growth in the domestic money supply.

The international conversion of currency into dollars in America was now viewed as the ideal place for investment. Buying dollars to pay for oil and other commodities, combined with a declining rate structure and government borrowing without domestic money growth, meant that dollars were in great demand. This served to push the dollar exchange rate higher and higher.

Foreign capital or Eurodollars took care of all of America's needs, and there were plenty of those.

The dollar appreciated by 62 percent from 1980 through 1985. The American military was reborn.

Russia, without foreign capital, fell into decline and ultimately dissolution in 1989. American business and the stock market heralded in the best of times, and Reagan joined the seventh president of the United States as a generational folk hero, who singlehandedly saved America.

And what became of poor Helmut Schmidt? Both he and the Social Democrats were soon out of office, replaced by a pro-Western nationalist Christian Democrat, Helmut Kohl.

No one of note, except for themselves, ever showed any sympathy for the predicament of the German and Swiss bankers who lost millions due to Reagan's policies.

Eurodollar funding of America, as successful as it appeared to be at the time, came at a huge price. Here I must ask you for your indulgence to explain.

As I noted from the very outset of this book, order and balance are synonymous. Disorder invites destruction, and before ultimate destruction, decline. This invariably occurs with imbalance. It is an implacable law of life itself.

From 1945 to 1971, the outpouring of dollars, though sorely needed in the early postwar years, had to have an offset. No offset was made in the world of currency.

Business accounting, codified in the fifteenth century, is based on what is referred to as the double entry system. Without dwelling on the details, suffice it to say it is founded on an equation. The word *equation* means equal. For every debit there must be an offsetting credit.[cxxx]

Record keeping would be impossible without such a system. When I write a check payable to you, the bank credits your account and debits mine.

I have less and you have more, but the sum total remains the same. Balance is maintained.

The United States exported billions and then trillions of dollars in this twenty-six-year period from 1945 to 1971, and uncountable dollars since, without sufficient offset. The books were never brought into balance.

They are not in balance today. They are not close to being in balance. This could happen because the Bretton Woods system envisioned an indirect offset, namely gold, and then only if the holders of dollars chose to exercise it.

As a result, though transfer of dollars into other currencies to foreign holders was expanding exponentially, the dollar exchange rate remained essentially the same for two and one half decades after the war. In a banking example, this would be the same as if I wrote a check payable to you and you received the credit, but my account was never charged.

Under the gold standard regimen, this could never have happened. If nation A paid nation B in gold, nation A would have less gold and nation B more. Nation A could continue to buy from nation B until it ran out of gold. Then it would be forced to stop.

In 1971 under the pressure of this imbalance, the system broke down. The fundamental equilibrium of the universe took hold, and the dollar collapsed. Equilibrium was restored the hard way, that is, by market forces beyond anyone's control.

However, the damage had been done. With the waves of dollars sloshing around the world, Eurodollars were beyond the control of any nation or all nations combined and were being loaned. There was no built-in limit to credit.

Foreigners took advantage of this in the way I previously described. It appeared that the dollar was in free fall and there was no bottom. Asset purchasers and investors rushed to buy everything. At some point the dollar might not be worth anything. It was at this point that the Federal Reserve shut down the money supply.

Though six months earlier no one wanted dollars, shutting down the domestic money supply had the effect of creating huge demand for these very same dollars. Why? The offset to zero money growth was a higher real rate of return. If there is to be no more of something, then what is outstanding must be worth more. Real return rises.

However, these dollars did not come back to the United States free of charge; they had to be borrowed, which meant at some point they would have to be repaid.

Public and private borrowing and spending soared.

Government programs, including the military, were not going to be paid for with taxes; the money would be borrowed. The currency was there for the taking, that is, simply borrow as much as you can. This became the new standard. Forget about savings. Most certainly forget about gold. It was only a matter of time before the consumer adopted this attitude, and adopt it they did.

Treasury debt, which approximated $370 billion in 1970 and $900 billion in 1980, jumped to $3.2 trillion in 1990, a 233 percent increase from 1980.[cxxxi]

With the demand for dollars soaring, the dollar exchange rate soared with it, driving imports and retarding exports, with the result that the nation's balance of payments, which during the 1970s had an accumulated deficit of $76 billion, jumped during the Reagan years to $1.06 trillion.

By all reasons the dollar should have fallen during these years, but as I noted earlier, it appreciated greatly. This is a currency bubble of the first order or, as I prefer, monetary madness.

The fiat money system, unlike the gold standard, is perverse. It works in reverse. The more we borrowed, the greater was the appreciation of the dollar. In accounting terms it was the equivalent of believing that the more I borrow, the greater my net worth. Borrowing invited more borrowing, as the cost of imported goods fell in the face of dollar appreciation.

With the retirement of Mr. Volcker and Mr. Reagan, this destructive policy should have been canceled. However, Mr. Volker's successor, Mr. Alan Greenspan, President Clinton, and the Bushes, father and son, saw the marvelous political advantages in this policy and continued it to the point of absurdity and eventual collapse.

We borrowed to fight two wars while adding trillions to domestic spending. Debt became the eighth wonder of the world. It was so easy and a political godsend. Of course this gravy train had to stop at some point, but no one in official or banking circles ever seemed to have figured that out.

After the financial crisis in 2008, the people reacted, and the spending politicians were tossed unceremoniously out of office. However, it is difficult to break bad habits, and public sector borrowing is one. There is some indication that the American people may be coming to grips with the scam. At the very least, there is the desire to bring it to an end. That is progress of sorts.

CHAPTER 33

# OPEC and China

---

## OPEC, THE ORGANIZATION OF THE PETROLEUM EXPORTING COUNTRIES, AN ILLEGAL MONOPOLY, THE DESTRUCTOR OF WORLD COMMERCE

Make no mistake about it: OPEC, the Middle Eastern-dominated oil monopoly, is an illegal entity under American law. It has grossly distorted international trade and commerce.

It is the scandal of the postwar era. This nation has tolerated this most egregious violation of law since our founding without a coherent explanation. Though it has virtually everything to do with politics, there is no evidence that the violation is a preserve of either political party. They are both guilty, and ignorance is not even a plausible defense.

As coal was in the nineteenth century, oil is the critical commodity for the maintenance of a modern society. We all recognize that if the oil supply was cut off, the economy would quickly shrivel up and literally die.

Given its importance, the oil barons have wielded great influence. As a segment, America's oil producers are the wealthiest corporations in America. Their Washington lobbyists, together with those representing the financial community, have as a result of this wealth, unlimited power.

Few American representatives are willing to take action against this interest, even as they, for domestic political consumption, occasionally express dismay at the price of oil or the profitability of these companies. That is done strictly for show.

In my banking days, though I was directly confronted by one of these huge corporations on an important banking matter, I stood my ground and won with the support of the presiding CEO. I understood from a career standpoint that this was not a wise thing to do. Then again, I had my conscience to live with.

At any rate, it is hard to speak of big oil and the oil producers' destructive habits without first mentioning OPEC.

OPEC is a cartel, an illegal cartel, per se, meaning that the only purpose for its existence is to fix the price of oil and to limit competition. From its founding it set out to be an oligarchy and has largely succeeded.

It is estimated that the twelve countries that are members control over 80 percent of the world's oil supply and are responsible for over 40 percent of world oil output.

It has done everything in its power to destroy the free market. It sets quotas for its members, whose leaders are some of the most undemocratic and greed-filled persons on the planet.

It doesn't hesitate to raise prices to achieve political goals, as it did in 1973 during the Yom Kippur War, the Six-Day War with Israel, when it raised prices fourfold.

As is the case with any foreign entity, if it is engaged in commerce in the United States, it is subject to the laws of the United States. The applicable law is the Sherman Anti-Trust Act, which forbade commercial collusion, including price fixing and the formation of cartels, and which became the law of the land in 1890.

Under the standards set for violation by the US Supreme Court, OPEC violates the law per se. As noted, the organization was formed for the purpose of fixing prices by limiting supply. This is accomplished through a quota system.

However, from administration to administration, no effective action has been taken, though everyone recognizes the harm being caused. One has to ask, "Why?" The only conceivable answer is power and influence. There is no one with a straight face who would argue that the oil market is not rigged, as companies and foreign nations and their political representatives stand to earn enormous sums. It is all about money and is corrupt to the core.

Oil traded in 2014 globally at just over one hundred dollars a barrel. It is estimated that the operating cost to extract and deliver a barrel of Saudi Arabian crude is approximately two to four dollars a barrel. At the high-end cost of extraction, which is Canadian shale, the cost may be upward of sixty dollars, but nowhere in the world does the cost of production approach one hundred dollars.

The one hundred dollars price would not be possible without the price fixing and manipulation of the trading markets. In a free market, the supply-demand ratio would in all likelihood have caused the price to fall or at the very least encourage new production. This picture may have started to change as new finds of oil and gas in the United States and modern drilling techniques offer the Americans the prospect of energy independence.

Presently, if the price shows any sign of weakness, OPEC simply cuts production. Market speculators have little or no risk, and the industry can't help but be very profitable. This cost is borne by the consumer and business, with the result that monies that might be invested end up in the pockets of the bandits. Money circulation is retarded.

The history of cartels is that they ultimately fall apart. However, that has not happened yet in the case of OPEC. I have no doubt someday it will. However, it will take determined leadership, with a strong commitment to the people rather than money interests, to make certain it happens.

The opportunity for big profit has other distressing ramifications. Since it is not the subject of this book, I will not delve into it. A former US senator from Connecticut, Thomas J. Dodd, summed it up well when he noted that the United States would never have sent troops into Iraq if they were growing carrots there instead of producing oil.

# China

We frequently use the phrase that we are trading with China. In this context the word *trade* is a misnomer. A synonym for trade is exchange. Goods are not being exchanged with China, and this can be seen most clearly in the international trading account, for there an enormous imbalance exists.

An imbalance between nations occurs when one nation's purchases greatly exceed its sales to the nation from which it is buying. In the broadest sense, it might be said that these nations were trading with one another. However, in terms of economic doctrine, trade with such a state, where the government controls foreign trade to ensure the prosperity and military security of the state, is not trade but economic mercantilism.

The purpose of colonies, colonialism, is to pursue mercantilism. The colony serves the interests of the mother country. The colony supplies the raw materials, and the mother country produces the goods, which the colony buys at retail prices.

It was just such a condition that gave rise to the American Revolution. Americans were denied the right to manufacture and produce goods. Everything went through London. The colony is the vassal state of the mother country. Its very existence is but to serve. This is the relationship we have today with China.

In 2011 we purchased from China $400 billion in goods, while China purchased $103 billion from us. China imposes restrictions on trade with the mother country. An American is not free to market domestic US goods in China.

Prior to the American Revolution, Britain had restrictions on any trade with another country such as France. We were their colony, their vassal state. Our present China relationship is not far distant from that concept. China will never accept a relationship where the United States has a favorable balance of trade. They would view this as a threat to the power of the state.

This may well be the most serious international problem the United States faces. We cannot long continue trade on this basis, as it creates an extraordinary creditor-debtor relationship, where America owes not millions or billions but trillions. This relationship alone could bankrupt us.

## Who Is Responsible for the China Problem?

When we first entered into trading arrangements with China during the Clinton administration, we justified the imbalance by arguing that China, a large isolated communist nation, was opening itself to the West and it would ultimately profit us to accept discriminatory trade terms until such time as they found their footing.

The administration apparently believed implicit Chinese assurances that once China became a member of the World Trade Organization, which has clear and unmistakable trade guidelines to protect its members, these imbalances would fade. In fact, since membership was granted to China, these imbalances have increased.

The counterargument used by that government and its defenders is that the beneficiaries of these policies are the Chinese citizens as the infrastructure of the nation is developed, which is a major plus for the world long-term.

They argue the Chinese will have more money to spend, and this will benefit one and all, particularly those trading with China.

However, Chinese citizens are not benefiting from this imbalance to the degree they should. The Chinese government manipulates its currency so that their goods are priced below market and then takes our dollars, which they then loan back to the United States government to cover our deficit. The money is never circulated. The result is high American unemployment and economic depression. In a sense this is a return to the Ben Strong era.

While it appears that everyone knows this, as certainly they do, as in the case of OPEC, nothing has been done about it. Our leaders just keep smiling.

## Modernity: A Warning

The Switzerland-based Bank for International Settlements reported earlier this year that global debt has increased more than 40 percent. to $100 trillion, since the onset of the financial crisis, as borrowers, public and private, took advantage of low interest rates. This $30 trillion increase was accompanied by a $3.86 trillion decrease in equity values during the same period. Governments, national and local, have been the major borrowers.

Marketable United States government debt went from $4.5 trillion at the end of 2007 to $12 trillion.[cxxxii]

Though individual states over the centuries have periodically been afflicted with the debt disease, as I have recounted, there is nothing in all of history comparable to today's condition. Since the onset of modernity, global bankruptcy has never been a realistic possibility. The United States dollar, the domestic currency of America, virtually by default became the world's reserve currency. Should the dollar suffer a sharp reversal, the world will suffer a drastic decline in wealth.

Interest rates today are at their lowest levels in history. One can only imagine the havoc that would ensue should rates rise sharply. Who will come to the rescue, the world's central banks? Is gold and perhaps silver again destined to become the global currency of choice?

Today's imbalances have many of the characteristics of a tsunami, where everything is quiet and peaceful before the event, and then comes the flood, the crashing, the destruction.

Global leaders and renowned international institutions express grave concern, but there is no plan of action. Certainly they care but realistically what action can be taken in a world divided between the haves and the have-nots, where 35 percent of humanity is surviving on less than two dollars a day?

Not willing to address reality, they avoid the subject entirely. Quietly they express the hope that the central banks will come up with a strategy, which means turning to the printing press as Germany did in 1921. Maybe it will work better this time? No serious person can believe that.

Is this a call for despair? No, absolutely not. It is a call for reason. The world must take stock and look carefully at what it is doing. Leading nations must be prepared to take decisive action. Solutions are there. Disaster is never inevitable.

## A Plea for Reason: Ending Central Bank Currency Manipulation, Ending Policy Favoritism

We live in an era of takers, a far cry from the generosity that pervaded this nation at the conclusion of the Second World War, best illustrated by the Marshall Plan. At the very least, everyone seems determined to get his or her share—and perhaps some of yours. This is inevitable if you are one of many who can't afford to send lobbyists to plead for your cause to Washington and other centers of power. That of course means most of us. They arrive in Washington with plenty of money to spend. They buy influence. Corrupt, you say. Of course, but the public is passive. Things will not change until the public insists on it.

The grab for money and power is certainly not universal but is abhorrent, and everyone wants to see it ended, or at least so they say. Is regulation the answer? Those with money and imagination simply work around the regs. The answer of course is integrity and responsibility. Like most people I am amazed at how often those testifying before Congress are willing to lie rather than answer truthfully. They assume that there will not be consequences. Their motto is money and power before all. Delusion comes easy. Their defense is, "Everyone else is doing it."

No question that money and power are formidable attractions. Willpower is required to handle them, which take us back to integrity.

It has been my experience in banking and business that long-term consequences are seldom considered in the great rush for more. That is what I most fear today. There will be consequences for our inaction, for our negligence, for our collective greed, for our lack of responsibility, and for our stupidity. One hundred trillion dollars is monster debt. Of course it is not all ours. Yet the consequences will affect us all. We simply don't know how or when.

## Unexpected Consequences

"It seemed like a good idea at the time" is the refrain often heard when the result of our actions is far different from what we expected. As no one has a clue how to address the global debt problem, leaders and citizens alike have chosen to simply ignore it. Perhaps it will just disappear. Not likely. The $100 trillion is not simply sitting out there in splendid isolation. It is owed to others, and it is growing exponentially. Within a matter of a few years, it will be $125 trillion and then $150 trillion. As Americans we should have learned the lesson from our financial crisis that debt will bury us all.

Prior to the crisis, as a result of decades of appreciation, we became convinced that housing prices could move in only one direction. We found out the hard way that was not the case. Trees never grow to the sky—never. Balance will be restored; that is a fundamental law of nature and commerce. There is no global authority that can simply blow a whistle and say, "That's it." We have reached the debt limit. Most likely we will just continue along, waiting, it seems, absentmindedly for the inevitable.

The inevitable will someday come, and when it does, it will come as a very unpleasant surprise. When the bubble bursts, it always is a surprise. Sometimes we are very fortunate: the right people are in the right place at the right time to stave off potential disaster, but sometimes they are not. A classic example of both was the bankruptcy of the Penn Central in 1970. Unable to obtain additional commercial paper credit lines to fund maturing commercial paper amounting to some $80 million, the railroad filed for court protection in June 1970.

The commercial paper market, viewed by many, including conglomerates, as an inexpensive way to finance operating cash needs, had grown during a five-year period (1965 to 1970) from approximately $10 billion to $40 billion, a fourfold increase. That alone was a warning sign of overdependence. The railroad's failure, at least for a time, brought the issuance of commercial paper to a halt. Virtually all debtors, public and private and lastly consumers, paid higher prices. The bankruptcy may have come as a surprise, but the warning signs were there and ignored.

Sometime later a great financial institution located in New York, operating on the principle that memories are short and seeing the enhanced profitability that could be realized by funding bank assets with short-term commercial paper, decided to go for it. Unfortunately it was a time when the Federal Reserve, as a result of Vietnam and the oil shock, was focusing on inflation, which demanded tighter credit conditions. That didn't impress this group of bankers. They were aggressive; after all a buck is a buck. The downside was never considered or was simply turned aside in favor of profitability.

Then the day of reckoning came. The bank holding company had a billion dollars of maturing commercial paper, with no lines of bank credit to support this debt. As it was near year-end and perhaps sensing problems, the so-called aggressive types went on vacation. After all, it wasn't their problem. By good fortune a thirtyish senior officer did not go on vacation and was asked by his superior to mind the store.

He was to learn for the first time how serious the situation was. He made a number of attempts to reach the most senior executive in the organization, who was not on vacation, but was unable to get through. He had no intention of it becoming his problem.

What to do? Call the Federal Reserve? The Federal Reserve did not have jurisdiction over bank holding companies. In addition, the financial press would have certainly gotten wind of the problem, and that fact alone would have rocked the financial markets.

Knowing he was on his own and acting on his own authority, he got in touch with one of the largest nonbank, nonpublic financial institutions and in complete confidence arranged a swap of assets, where the firm would enter into a repurchase agreement with the holding company, buying $1 billion of commercial paper in exchange for $1 billion of the firm's assets. The agreement was to last as long as it took for the holding company to place its paper.

The agreement was made over the phone with nothing in writing and held as planned, never becoming public.

The courageous officer in question never received as much as a thank you from the board or the CEO, and the institution went on as if nothing had happened. Arrogance is never cured quickly. I suppose this is why we need regulation—lobbyists to plead for your cause.

With the global debt situation of today, when the moment of truth arrives, and it certainly will, let us hope and pray the courageous are there, or better still, a plan of action is in place.

CHAPTER 34

# Reform

---

**MONEY, CURRENCY, DEBT, AND GOD BE PRAISED, A SOLUTION**
The critical decision made at Bretton Woods in 1944 was to establish a paper money system, the dollar and sterling serving as the anchors backed by gold. The gold backing, at least for US citizens, was theoretical, since at the time no American could hold gold without violation of FDR's executive order.

No Americans could convert their dollars into gold. For the rest of the world, the gold window was left open. This was seen to be essential if trust in the new monetary system was to be assured.

With America holding most of the world's monetary gold, combined with the industrial capacity to reconstruct a broken world, no nation or individual, except perhaps John Maynard Keynes, was in a position to seriously debate the pros and cons of this system.

The new system made the dollar king. King dollar remained unchallenged for twenty-five years. For most of the first decade, international commerce was totally dependent on the dollar. Sterling remained alive but not well, and was used primarily within the British Commonwealth.

For the rest of the world, access to dollars was essential. Every dollar printed represented a call on American productive capacity.

No one seriously questioned the dollar's value. In fact, the demand for dollars was so great, as I have recounted, that the world actually suffered through a dollar shortage until the early 1950s.

The dollar was treated with the same trust and respect that gold had been treated for most of the seventeenth through nineteenth centuries, and before that, silver and gold. To maintain that status, it was critical that the dollar's value never be questioned.

It was in many ways the perfect reserve currency, as it was acceptable in every conceivable commercial transaction.

The flaw in this reasoning was that the dollar was an IOU and did not constitute final payment. An IOU and final payment are not synonymous. The dollar was simply an IOU, and the amount outstanding lay with the government of the United States, which could print as many dollars as it saw fit. The political pressure to print more was constant.

In order to maintain value, no domestic currency can serve as a reserve currency, at least not the world's reserve. Since the Americans had an unlimited call on dollars that no other nation had, doubt about its purchasing power was bound to arise.

As people have learned over time and I have addressed in this book, an object or thing can never be a universal monetary standard. Gold and silver worked well for centuries, but so did trinkets and beads. China tried paper and found for centuries that it served commerce well, until its overexpansion led to monetary collapse.

Virtually everything has been tried, but value cannot be transferred to a third object in such a way as to assure merger with value. Value remains in the object or product and in its accumulation. We may be willing to accept paper in a transaction for an item of value, but the value is never in the paper or metal or whatever.

With Bretton Woods, the dollar could be made the world standard, but it could never be made the value standard. Value is in the product, in its utility, and that alone. The attempt to change that continues to this day. Fail it must, and fail it will.

The standard and product must be in balance. One must equal the other. Once that balance is disturbed, economic disequilibrium ensues. This of course is what has happened, and it was quite predictable, as Maynard Keynes said.

The fundamental problem isn't the paper, but rather who controls the presses. In 1944–1945 the dollar was a perfectly logical standard for a new monetary system, but for it to be the world standard, it would have had to cease being the domestic standard or the currency of the United States of America.

Thus there must always be two standards, the universal and the national. Periodic adjustment must be made in the national to maintain equilibrium with the universal.

## Debt—The Problem for All Ages

One of the three or four important messages that any student of economy can possibly gain from historical study is the significance of debt. Debt is a decisive factor in the way people and nations engage one another.

People will not willingly go into debt unless they feel that they have something to gain. Debt has negative connotations since it represents a continuing call on the labor of another. Underlying every major economic setback in history is the specter of debt. Debt will put you into bankruptcy.

Two centuries ago debt would not only have put you in bankruptcy, but it would also have put you in jail. Debtors' prisons constituted a significant portion of the criminal population in Europe and in America. The influx of people from Great Britain in the eighteenth century to our shores was from the debtors' prisons in and around London.

This raises a curious question, which is "How does one find himself or herself getting into debt in the first place?" Debt is invariably a substitute for income. When my needs or my perception of need exceeds my income, I am forced to borrow.

I allow my desires to outweigh my capacity to produce through my labor. A few observations about the meaning of debt are in order, which is helpful in a study of the subject. Debt for the purpose of consumption has no redeeming value except under the most unusual circumstances. If it is literally a matter of life or death for a nation, individual, or family, then clearly going into debt is prudent.

Great Britain, faced with the Napoleonic invasion and the prospect of losing its freedom and independence, borrowed huge sums from the world. Parents wishing to give their child a higher education may borrow money for that purpose. This is clearly an investment, a wise investment. Why is it investment, and why is it wise?

The word *investment* carries within its meaning the concept of return. Since I do not have the financial resources available to me now, I will borrow the money, certain that in time I will receive back a sufficient amount to repay the amount borrowed. In addition, I will receive an incremental amount that can be measured as a percentage of the amount invested, popularly referred to as return on investment.

Statistically a high school graduate can expect to earn $1.2 million during his or her life, whereas a college graduate can expect to earn $2.1 million. The difference, $900,000, is the return on the investment to send someone to college.

If it costs $100,000 to send a child to college, this would constitute a 900 percent return on investment.

In addition, the educated one lives a more productive life, contributing to the country and the community.

## Debt—The Conundrum

Business debt may well be essential to modernity. Without debt there is no mechanism—other than the transfer of equity—to concentrate capital for the purpose of building plants and equipment.

Inability to repay debt cripples both the borrower and the lender. The potential for economic advance is terminated.

War, particularly in this regard, is crippling. It assured the bankruptcy of the European powers after the First and Second World Wars and bankrupted Rome, England, France, and Spain in earlier centuries.

Debt was the primary cause of the Great Depression. The Great Depression cannot be defined without use of the words *debt* and *bankruptcy*. On the other hand, the United States waged the greatest of wars, the Second World War, with larger amounts of debt, and we came through unscathed.

Why the great difference in result? Conceptually when I speak of debt, I am reminded of the medical discussion regarding cholesterol. Some cholesterol is essential for the body to function properly. The same can be said of debt. If debt is properly used, it can have a positive economic effect. If not, it can be totally destructive. Critical at all times is the capacity of the borrower to repay.

Irrespective of that capacity, debt for the sole purpose of consumption is without value and thus destructive. In its many disguises, it is frequently a thief in the night.

When it comes to discerning the economic impact, it is a stimulant. Why is this so? Commerce cannot and does not distinguish debt from equity.

The seller of a home or a dealer selling a car does not care if the money in payment is borrowed or comes from savings. From labor springs demand, and the ability to meet that demand is totally dependent on the productivity of labor. In a perfect world, production and demand equate. However, under those circumstances, it is important that we do not consume all that we produce. Otherwise there is nothing left for future investment.

Again, the world we live in has been shaped by three major wars, the First, the Second, and the Cold War. War, and the military machine required, has been the culprit when it comes to public debt. Wars give rise to the extravagant use of debt. Wars end, but the debt remains. The United States is wrestling with that burden today.

Wars and consumerism will effectively bankrupt any nation.

## GLOBAL CURRENCY REFORM—THE ANSWER, THE ONLY ANSWER

"What is past is prologue" was the apt phrase used by William Shakespeare in his play *The Tempest*.

There have been so many mistakes in the past, many of which might well have been avoided if only we had known. Perhaps, but I fear it is far more accurate in describing the present global turmoil to borrow from Shakespeare again, this time from Julius Caesar, when the nobleman Cassius said to Brutus, "The fault, dear Brutus, is not in our stars, But in ourselves, that we are underlings."[cxxxiii]

The financial condition the advanced nations find themselves in today is truly our fault, ours collectively. Certainly no one country or one leader is responsible. All of us played a part, and each of us could have done something about it. We chose not to for a variety of reasons. There was treachery, and greed and ignorance. Yet we chose to ignore the telltale signs.

"Certainly the present darkness cannot last," we tell one another. "Experience proves that all recessions are temporary. Of course tomorrow will be better. It must be better because we will it so."

I refer to this naïve but hopeful philosophy as the elevator thesis. The fact that we are alive and well assures us that tomorrow we will prosper. It is in the stars. We need do nothing. We need not change our behavior, though others should change theirs. The concept of cause and effect is outmoded, no longer applicable.

Government should spend more or less. Government should tax more or less. We should elect new leaders or keep those in office. Above all, nothing truly fundamental should change. For in such an event, I might have to alter my lifestyle. That is impossible since I am interested in myself, myself alone. The purpose of intelligent life is to pursue self-satisfaction. Isn't that what we all believe? At least that is what we are being told.

Like the drunks in Eugene O'Neill's *The Iceman Cometh* standing around the bar, living their pipe dreams, reality that is truth is simply passing us by. We do not want to hear it. God forbid that we address reality.

If we choose for very much longer to ignore reality, then reality, in its often crude and cruel way, will address us. Indeed the past is prologue, but the glory days gone by are not returning. That is the point that is being missed.

The social and economic predicament—this tidal wave of uncertainty, broken homes, unemployment, food stamps, homelessness, war, and despair that surrounds us today—was caused by the actions of men and women. We created the jam, and we will now have to work our way out of it. There is no magic cure. No one will arrive in Washington, Frankfurt, London, or Tokyo with a wand.

It will be hard work, and it will require fundamental change with global implications. From an economic standpoint, almost everything of importance will have to change.

From a philosophical standpoint, in a world of 6.95 billion people, a number of widely held convictions must be discarded. This is a critical step. It could be argued this is the most critical step. Alien philosophies have frequently in the past impeded progress.

Modern humans are not, as is being widely preached today, enemies of the environment. The world and everything in it is here to serve humanity and the thousands of species that occupy the planet. Humans and the other animals have stewardship and have to act responsibly for the sake of all. It is estimated that 3.25 billion people are living on less than two dollars per day. Denying them the resources to survive is wrong. Land worship is an absurdity. Idolatry has no place in the affairs of rational people.

Globalization is a fad that has been tried many times in the past, as this book makes clear. Globalization is a modern form of colonialism, where certain peoples benefit at the expense of others. The United States and the Western world generally have suffered greatly as the globalization cure-all has been evangelized across the world. The poor have suffered most of all. The movement of businesses to other nations to avoid paying just wages has no moral basis and runs counter to the principles of fairness that underlie the Constitution.

The beneficiaries are institutions and individuals that have access to capital, the senior executives and large stockholders of the multinational corporations and their cronies in government who advance their cause and are paid with political contributions.

Globalization works against global society. Homogeneity restricts progress. Diversity gives rise to advancement. If every person did nothing but harvest wheat for a living, no advance would be possible. We move forward because we are different and have different needs and different skills.

Further, on the matter of debt, the third world is not responsible for the global debt problem. Global debt is concentrated in the advanced nations. The sovereign debt of the United States exceeds 100 percent of the annual

GDP. The European Union's is over 80 percent. Japan is 200 percent. China, which is typical of the third world, is 25 percent.

The Western world has been on a tear borrowing and consuming, led by their various governments. Government alone has been responsible for over 80 percent of the growth in outstanding debt.

Debt and consumption are joined at the hip. The United Nations estimates that the wealthiest 20 percent of the world population account for over 75 percent of private consumption.

The United States experienced its most spectacular economic growth during three crises: the Civil War, World War I, and World War II.

Growth was not due to war, but during a national emergency, all consumption is severely restricted in favor of production. Guns and less butter are produced in enormous amounts sufficient to meet the crisis.

Though there has been no declaration, we are in crisis today; it is as severe as earlier crises. We have a number of enemies, but the one that could do us in, break us financially, is consumption. It is clear that consumption is the greatest enemy this and other nations face.

To address this problem requires two important changes. Internally the thrust of our domestic policies must be to achieve the goal of every human being a producer. Everyone who wishes to produce must be given the opportunity. A person's talent, educational experience, and commitment will determine his or her income.

This approach is Rooseveltian, but it is not the same as every person having a job, for many jobs, as a result of their bureaucratic nature, add to the expense of production.

Government programs must be ruthlessly scrutinized to see to it that they are investment- and production-oriented. That does not mean that government must compete with the private sector. Government should be striving to make the private sector more successful. Government should not be viewed as the enemy of business, but its partner in this national effort.

The policies of the public sector—federal, state, and local—must be devoted to this goal. Those who do not have the skills and are not disabled must be offered the opportunity for schooling and training. They have a duty to act responsibly as citizens of this great country. No excuses, please. Unemployment should be viewed as it truly is, a threat to society.

All tax policy should support this effort. Consumption of extravagant imports should bear the greatest tax burden.

Accelerating production will put downward pressure on prices, facilitate exports, and raise the standard of living. American invention and innovation should be encouraged at all stages of the production cycle.

Backsliders, and those who choose not to participate in this great effort, should not be favored over those most committed. If you do not want to do your share, you—not the community—will pay the price.

Except for the necessities, taxation and consumption will henceforth go hand in hand.

## The International Monetary System

During the course of the next decade, we will be witness to profound change in the world of money and currency. The past will not be prologue. Those who have spent their life chasing financial instruments will find it has been an unworthy endeavor indeed. Leverage, which has fed speculative greed and consumerism, will no longer be readily available. Debt ratios will be strictly enforced.

The world will be on the lookout for breakthrough technology. Inventors and innovators will be favored in the marketplace.

The world population will continue to grow exponentially, demanding that giant strides be made in the realm of productivity.

Capital-saving advances in medicine, biology, chemistry, and many diverse fields in the world of science will do their part to hold the standard of living among advanced nations.

The motto of the next decade will not be "Shop until you drop" and "Borrow to your limit" but "Every person a producer."

The world will finally come to accept after millennia that the perception of shortage of money was illusory. The fault lay not in the stars but truly in our ignorance.

People have been doing their best to reach the ends of the earth, believing everything was linear, only to find out that they have been on an impossible journey, a journey to nowhere. For the world is round, balanced, and in order. Disorder did not flow from acts of the Creator, creation, nature, or the stars, but from ignorant, overzealous, mistaken, and greedy humans.

The recognition of this fact will shine through most clearly in the global world of finance.

As we have explained, since money is product and all product flows from labor, we will undoubtedly see more of global labor and not less.

To produce more, people will put the ax to the great shibboleths of the past that carry the appellation currency. As the currency trees fall, falling with them will be those diseases associated with them—manipulation, fraud, concentrated power, greed, leverage, inflation, deflation, perhaps even extreme poverty, although this may be a stretch in the next fifty years with the seemingly inexorable expansion of the global population.

The new standard of commerce will no longer carry the imprimatur of a dollar, euro, sterling, or yen, but will reside in concept, lodged in a neutral body that does not favor one nation or class, that favors nondiscriminatory global production with enforceable guidelines that eschew debt and nation-state advantage.

The world will not have to look far for the one body that could carry out this assigned task, and that is the International Monetary Fund, which was created for this purpose in the first place.

To achieve both balance and rapid expansion of production, the world must share a common standard, and that standard is already in place. It is the SDR, special drawing rights.

Every member nation of the IMF has an SDR quota, which is not a currency or claim on the IMF. It serves the purpose of an account to balance international trade, a means to exchange or pay other nations by claim on their currency.

In the very same way that business and labor work today, wealth measured in SDRs increases as a nation produces and sells more internationally. Underpricing and dumping are discouraged by the fact that the benefiting nation will be forced to increase imports to remain in balance.

Neither the dollar, nor gold, nor any other currency will serve as a reserve currency. SDR will be the global reserve currency.

No member nation will in the future be able to run a global trade surplus or deficit. At fiscal year-end, international trade of every nation must be in balance. Failure to balance will result in fines that will be collected by the IMF through a sequestration from the erring nation's SDR account. For any nation to run a trade imbalance will prove costly.

The dollar will return to what it was originally intended to be, the domestic currency of the United States. This should prove to be a great boon to Americans as the most productive of peoples, who have seen their wealth dissipated by governmental extravagance, corporate and military excess, and global manipulation.

The nations of the world will work together because it is to the advantage of all to do so, and the IMF will be the referee to assure compliance.

Globalization will go on, but the expansion will occur in diversity, not as is the case today, by reducing every nation to the lowest common denominator, with competition designed to beggar thy neighbor.

What steps must be taken to resolve the global debt problem?

People created the problem, and people can solve it. Sovereign debt under this plan will be transferred to the IMF and through sequester paid down over a term of many decades. The longer the term, the better, for this will ease the immediate burden on debtor nations, facilitating SDR account buildup and encouraging investment.

Of course the details in this plan will have to be worked out, and the devil is certainly in the details—and that, folks, is putting it mildly. One can only imagine the debates that will ensue with China.

However, this is the general direction we must travel—indeed a road less traveled. It is the answer for certain. I suspect it may well be the only answer.

**David Barrett**

ADDENDUM:

# A View of the Concepts

### THE UNIVERSALITY OF ORDER

We accept order as a given in our own lives. Every step we take, every decision we make is viewed through the prism of order. What is order? What are its dimensions? A disordered universe would mean chaos. A little disorder cannot coexist with order. A disordered system cannot merge with an ordered one without annihilation. Matter and antimatter can never be brought together harmoniously.

Order gives structure to reality. Order embraces the dynamic of change. Without change, finite deterioration, called entropy, ensues.

The essence of creation is synonymous with order and perfection. From this, one could conclude that life itself can never be spontaneous, for spontaneity negates the need for renewal, making the cause of existence, in the first instance, undeterminable.

Einstein put it well when commenting on faith and the orderliness of the universe…"The highest satisfaction of a scientific person…that God Himself could not have arranged these connections any other way than that which does exist, any more than it would have been in His power to make four a prime number."[cxxxiv]

Thus, it is not possible to distinguish creation from order. Creation, order, and perfection are interchangeable terms. Without order, the totality of the universe would be both irrational and unknowable, in chaos and confusion, a state that humans appear at times determined to establish.

There would be no relationship between cause and effect. Reality would be in a permanent state of unimaginable bedlam.

Progress of any sort would be rendered impossible since all progress requires order. Dynamic change lies at the heart of order. Order requires change.

This must occur in such a way so that the balance that exists throughout the universe is not disturbed by that change. The dynamic of change is essential to all that is created, to all that is finite.

A basic tenet of theology is that the Creator's being begets order. Where life is concerned, His chosen instrument is nature. Nature serves as a controller. As the universe is finite, it tends inexorably toward fragmentation and dissolution in the same way that the most beautiful of roses must inevitably decay, irrespective of the present state of beauty. Nature assures universal balance. However, the maintenance of perfection requires constructive and continuing intervention and renewal. In other words, existence requires superiority of being that is all-embracing. Such a being must be intelligent, for he must have the capacity to decide when and how to intervene.

That intervention is expressed most clearly in the dynamic of change. The act of creation, some 14.5 billion years ago, produced a perfect universe. Finite perfection and creation are identical. Creation springs from perfection. The universe is a visible expression of perfection.

In a finite universe, it is self-evident that the dynamic of change is essential to the maintenance of that perfection.

Over the ages, philosophers and thinkers involved in a range of disciplines essential to knowledge have come to understand and largely agree on the one word that best describes this phenomenon. That word is *order*.

Everything we have come to know, fundamental to all progress, advancing understanding and knowledge, is order. The sine qua non of the existence of this universe is order, and order is not possible without intelligence. Disorder may be possible in a universe where chaos reigns, but for an ordered universe, that is impossible.

Life is an imperative for order, and only intelligent life can bring order.

I do not mean to imply that life is possible only on this planet. All species will pass after their time, that is, they will become extinct. That is planetary history. However, life itself in a perfect universe will never become extinct.

As I noted in another part of this book, no species survives its epoch, yet life always survives. Creation without life would be imperfect. Life survives all. Life must survive all. Life goes to the very heart of creation.

However, life is not spontaneous. If life were spontaneous, then extinct species would reappear. In over four billion years, this has never occurred. Spontaneity would give rise to redundancy. The balance of nature would be permanently disturbed and made subject to an uncertain and unpredictable force.

If not spontaneous, then it is quite possible, though not essential, that life's domicile rests on this planet alone. Those who would argue to the contrary suggest that planetary conditions determine the origin of life, that life can arise naturally from inanimate objects. If this is so, what has prevented extinct species over the eons of time from rejoining the living on this planet?

As the black holes in the center of galaxies assure order and balance of entities made up of uncountable independent bodies, the role of nature is to see to it that order and balance are maintained on this planet. Thus, no species will succeed in achieving planetary control in such a way as to exclude all others, for to do so would be a threat to all life.

"It is clear that nature is a cause, a cause that operates for a purpose."[cxxxv]

Nature is the designated mechanism for order on this planet. In the pursuit of this assignment, it plays no favorites. Nature is the regulator but not the Creator of life, in much the same way and according to the same primordial laws that attach to gravity, the regulator of matter.

All species eventually meet with extinction, but life continues. Since order embraces change, the modification of species is essential to order to maintain universal equilibrium and preserve life. Modification of species continues in the constant pursuit of equilibrium within the full meaning of order.

An intelligent being, endowed with a free will, is the culmination of creation. The distinguishing characteristic of an intelligent being is that only he or she has the power independent of nature to establish order or to inflict disorder at his or her choosing.

However, he or she can never be victorious over nature itself. He or she remains a critical part of creation but will remain subordinate to nature. His or her destiny, like the billions of species that have gone before and those that inhabit the globe today, is extinction.

Nature's power and consequent wrath knows no limits when the totality of life is threatened. Nature has demonstrated the capability to call on all facets of the universe and has done so in the past in order to preserve life. Thus, nature's reach extends into space.

Order will allow no species over the course of millions of generations to fully occupy the polity. As noted, to do so would threaten all other species and perhaps life itself. In a flash it has destroyed the most numerous and powerful of species; the dinosaurs stand as a vivid example. All of the foregoing simply describes the imperative of order. Nothing in the universe could be defined or explained in rational terms absent the imperative of order.

It was the iconic American genius Thomas Jefferson who recognized the eternal symbiosis essential to the creation of order when he wrote in the Declaration of Independence, "the Laws of Nature and Nature's God."

As I endeavored to show throughout this work, order is essential in the commercial affairs of people. Failure to approach matters in such a way, even if carried on broadly by large numbers, secure in the knowledge that others are following, will not produce a positive result. At the very least, failure must ultimately overwhelm the effort. At the worst, humans face calamity.

## Equilibrium, a Synonym for Order and Perfection

As gravity is to space-time, equilibrium is to order.

To approach fundamental questions pertaining to commerce, we must ascertain the underlying purpose for dealings among people. As has been written, no man is an island.

We are put on this planet as participants in an enigmatic, mysterious, most would argue eternal, and most certainly singular event in the totality of time, which we call our creation.

The most striking aspect of this is that we have no choice, none whatsoever, even though as participants we pursue freedom of choice to the extent that our physical and mental powers will allow.

The riddle was marvelously addressed by Shakespeare when he wrote of man, "a poor player who struts and frets his hour on the stage and then is heard no more. It is a tale told by an idiot full of sound and fury and signifying nothing."

Many would disagree with the totality of his analysis, particularly those with a strong theological footing and foundation, but even in their assessment, they are left with the mystery "Why me? Why now?"

There remain two incontrovertible facts: we are here only for a time, and we are a single participant among many. The grand show is not about us but the totality. Yes, we have a part, but a very small part in this extravaganza. It is this role, of being a very small cog in the wheel of life, that humans find so disconcerting and for many unacceptable. From dictators to movie actors, from business barons to politicians, and the great multitude in between, we exert our influence and power in an effort to change this reality, yet we remain destined to fail.

We come to share this planet with uncountable numbers of other beings, some whose essence is but a single cell to the most complex, man himself.

The critical fact is that each of us is a participant; "A participant in what?" one might reasonably ask. In creation of course, but what does that mean? Creation is an event that does not provide insight as to purpose. As we do not have it in our power to create from nothing, we can only speculate as to the purposes of the Creator, or the "First Mover" as Aristotle referred to Him.

Yet of everything in our being, our rational intellect demands that there be purpose. This purpose, though beyond our human capacity to express in terms of language, results in our acting in concert with all participants in the pursuit of perfection. This requires harmony and symmetry.

No living being will set out if rational in the pursuit of disorder. To do so would result in destruction and perhaps the destruction of others. In the depth of our being that is in conscience, we understand that we have a duty to ourselves and to our Creator or, if you prefer, nature to act constructively. Failing this we become separated. We are outside.

If we step back, we can see the magnificence of creation through a lens of order, balance, and equilibrium. This is our era, and we will adhere to the dictates of creation or simply cease to exist.

Our intellect, our free will, does not confer upon us the right to choose but only the power of choice within the context of truth. Over the millennia it is only the human, of his or her own free will, who has the power to disobey these dictates. The consequences for him or her, both here and beyond, as his or her spirit is held to account, is total. It is life or death.

From the foregoing one might conclude that this treatise is taking a philosophical bent. That is not the case. However, to deal with questions of commerce, which is the interaction of humans with their fellows and with nature, requires that we grasp our role.

As we see throughout this book, modern man in great numbers refuses to adhere to these dictates. His justification is that this is the lifestyle that he has chosen. He does not see himself as a participant in this majestic work called creation; rather, he has come to see himself as the center of the universe. It is all about him. Everything is about him.

Thus, all things created are his for the taking. He has a Ptolemaic view of life. His appetite knows no limit. Why should it? Life is all about him.

This perverse view of life might well be described as "eat, drink, and be merry," for tomorrow we will certainly die. Such people have lost all sense of personal worth and purpose for being. To survive, they must rediscover equilibrium or reap the consequences.

## The Definition of Money—Now and Forevermore

**Money: A concept that measures product and/or the capacity to produce something of value through the efficient application of labor or its proxy.[1]**

The above definition is complete. Please note that money is first a concept. It is an idea that is made into things. There can be no "things," that is, the taking from nature, without an idea. For example, it may take discovery, invention, or genius to transform wood into a chair after gazing at a tree. This transformation gives rise to money, namely, the chair. The chair is the money; the tree is a natural resource. Yet before the chair came into being, the idea had value. Value and money are distinct concepts. Chairs have value, and so do ideas.

Money can never come into existence independent of human creativity.

Money springs from nature. Nature transcends and is all-encompassing. It lies in the realm of creation and its author, the Creator.

## Value, Value, Value—Always Value, the Key to Progress

The world's struggle to understand money is a direct result of our inability to understand value. No matter how much we desire a trinket, any trinket from automobiles to shoelaces, we can never be quite certain of the value.

This dilemma results from the fact that the value of everything is in constant fluctuation. The factors responsible for the change are too numerous to enumerate. The most obvious is supply, matched against the level of demand.

We know from experience that price settles at the point that supply and demand meet. However, it does not follow that this translates into the point of value. Price is an objective reality, but value is subjective. It is not about the worth of an article, but how much it is worth to me. As price and value digress, exchange will slow. This slowing results in a decline in price in most instances. The value to me is meaningless unless I have the wherewithal to make the exchange. Exchange is dependent on one's income, savings, or capacity to borrow. Debt serves to maintain the price level. Thus, absent debt and savings, exchange must slow. This slowing of exchange puts downward pressure on the price, which will continue to decline until there is sufficient capacity in terms of income and savings to absorb the supply. Credit thus serves to hold the price level above the equilibrium level of supply. The universal availability of credit across the world has given rise to an artificial price structure.

Since the credit implosion beginning in 2007, credit has become less available. With savings at a marginal level, income becomes essential to buttress demand. In recent years real income, adjusted for inflation, has shown little gain, resulting in price stagnation or decline.

This serves to reduce profitability, requiring business to cut expenses. Since upward of 75 percent of all business expenses are employee-related, this necessitates a reduction in staff, which in turn reduces income, which serves to put further downward pressure on price. Business gasping for relief increasingly turns to improvement in productivity to reduce expenses. Use of robotics and advanced computer and electronic systems are increasingly turned to in order to increase supply and thus hold the line on profitability.

## Value Is an Objective Concept

Value is an objective concept, a reality unto itself. How is inherent value expressed? It is always expressed in the marketplace in the same way, that is, by the setting of a price.

## Price Is the Final Determinant of Equivalency

How is price determined? The market price is the highest level one is willing and able to pay for a product, such as wheat, at this place and at this time.

Thus all efforts made to fix prices, that is, to conform to some other standard, will fail since they introduce artificiality in the setting of price. They destroy the concept of equivalency.

Intervention will set the price too high, in which case no one buys the wheat, or too low, in which case the seller of wheat refuses to sell and puts the wheat in his or her barn.

Over thousands of years with myriad, countless experiments, humans have endeavored to evade this reality. The Romans, when their mines reached the point of exhaustion and they were bereft of the metal needed to sustain their Empire, resorted to edicts and taxation to force the populace to disgorge their goods in exchange for worthless "plated coin." Goods simply vanished from the marketplace.

The merchant class, which arose from the sixteenth century and grew stronger, refused to allow the royals to steal their valuables or to buy them at artificial price levels and resorted to all sorts of gimmicks to hide them.

It was these same merchants who found a haven in a "trust" in London, where they could keep their valuables stored and not fear royal sequestration. That in time became the Bank of England.

Every "ism" known to humankind has attempted to fix prices, including the socialists, communists, fascists, and Maoists, and in America, price controls and farm quotas to drive prices higher, and the Nixon experiment with price and wage controls to hold prices down. All have failed and have had to be abandoned due simply to the fact that they result in shortages, and with shortages comes a decline in living standards.

The market price cannot be controlled, since it would disturb or misallocate resources. Humans will freely buy and sell at equivalent value at a market price. Any attempt to force an artificial regimen undercuts commerce.

## Currency

No matter how often repeated, citizens, bankers, government officials, historians, economists, and just your average Joe have never over the long difficult course of history been able to rationalize or grasp the notion that currency and money are completely different concepts.

Though related, money and currency are not the same.

Currency is always and everywhere a proxy for payment. It may also constitute money, should it have intrinsic value.

Beginning with the goldsmiths and then the bankers, notes, bills, checks, or dollars were issued, allowing the holder to go to the drawer of the instrument and collect in silver or gold the amount stated. At that moment the holder was paid since he or she was the recipient of money.

Today if I enter into a contract to buy a car, I obtain the car. What does the seller receive? He receives currency paper called dollars. What promise is the car buyer making?

The buyer, in fact, is not making a promise. All the seller has are green pieces of paper with a picture of a president on the front, which suggest that at some future time he will be paid, meaning that he will be able to use that paper to purchase goods and services.

It is legal tender. What does that mean? It means that as long as the United States government is in place, the recipient must accept it in payment of debt.

The creditor cannot say to the debtor, "Keep your paper. I want gold instead." Thus for all past obligations, and the word *past* is key here, the creditor is obligated to accept the paper.

The merchant is not obligated to accept the paper. I may build up a huge store of paper, but if I go to the store and I attempt to buy an item and hand the clerk a five-dollar bill, he may, if he chooses, say, "What is this? To which I might respond, "This is five dollars of value," leading him to say, "No, it is not; it is a piece of paper."

The paper has no intrinsic value. It does have extrinsic value; the good faith of the United States stands behind it. I do not intend to minimize the importance of this; the value depends fully on the credibility of the United States and not on the currency.

This caveat is important. After the First World War, in Germany, the Weimar Republic issued mountains of paper to forestall the ill effects of the war and the Great Depression. The good faith of that government stood behind the paper. However, we learned that wasn't enough. Shopkeepers refused to accept the paper.

In the South as the Civil War was coming to its conclusion, merchants and traders refused to accept Confederate dollars, though the good faith of the Confederacy stood behind them. There are hundreds, perhaps thousands, of other examples throughout history.

The fundamental problem is not in the guarantee but in the promise. The guarantees will last, stand the test of time, if you will, but the promise may not. No government can force others to sell the product of their labor for a promise.

Currency, with its extrinsic guarantee alone, is only a step toward payment. It isn't payment. Some will accept this external guarantee as sufficient since they have an abiding interest in selling goods, but others may not.

To assure the former, it is imperative that the credibility of the guarantor never be called into question. That is of course what happened to Rome, the Confederacy, and the Weimar Republic, among many others.

## Currency Value Must Equal Asset Value to Retain Economic Equilibrium

As wealth is measured in terms of value and value is measured in terms of the application of labor, then by logical extension, the value of all currency, which under all circumstances is but a proxy, must move in tandem with change in value. Thus as the wealth of a nation increases, the currency value should appreciate. As the wealth of a nation decreases, the currency value should fall. A classic example was the Confederacy. When it was no longer a nation, the currency became valueless.

Similarly a country beset with debt and declining fortunes will see the value of its currency fall in the marketplace to the extent of that decline.

Analogous in concept is the stock market, and for that matter, all markets where the fortunes of the company determine the price of the stock. A company experiencing a declining customer and revenue base and thus lower earnings must expect the price of the stock to decline.

The tools that analysts use to gauge the direction of stocks rely heavily on ratios such as the price/earnings ratio to estimate the true value of the stock. A decision to buy or sell will result from this analysis.

The stock analogy to currency is somewhat imperfect, as a stock certificate connotes ownership and currency an obligation. Ages past, when the holder had the right to convert the currency into metal when and if he or she chose to do so, the analogy was close to perfect, as both were assets. One might choose to hold stock; another might choose to hold silver, the currency proxy for the stock.

Today, of course, it is very different. The holder of the currency has but a promise, while the holder of the stock is a true owner. I should add here that a distinction should be made between currency and Treasury obligations; both are promises of future payment. Treasury obligations pay interest, and currency does not. Both constitute debt. All debt translates into a reduction in wealth.

It is clear then that those nations that have amassed extraordinary amounts of debt should expect their currency to be reflective of that reality.

The amount of debt, however, is not a fair measure. The United States has $18 trillion in debt outstanding, but it also has the largest economy in the world, constituting some 22 percent of world commerce.

Debt that is used to create jobs and produce return, in other words, investment, is a far cry from the debt, however satisfying, entered into for the purpose of consumption.

For example, the government through all of its agencies hires enormous numbers of people. Presumably they are engaged in very important work. However, in terms of production, they contribute very little. These expenditures are consumption expenditures.

On the other hand, an investment in an automobile plant produces jobs at the plant and trucks, which can then be carried to market.

The latter constitutes an investment, while the former is debt for the purpose of consumption.

Today both the amount of debt and the misdistribution or misallocation of the capital that flows from that debt are a principal cause of the world's current economic difficulties.

Cholesterol is a primary cause of heart disease. Yet the chemical itself in the body performs an important function. Debt in and of itself will not harm the economy, but rather, how the capital is then used is what determines whether the economic impact is positive or negative.

For any nation, if the amount of debt is increasing faster than gross domestic product, the totality of production, then clearly debt is being misused. A case in point today is Greece.

In the United States over the course of the past fifteen years, debt has been growing at an annual rate 3 percent faster than the nation's gross domestic product.

## The Problem Is In the Promise

All governments, provided they are legitimate, have the inherent power to make laws. They have the power to tax and to determine legal tender. No government has the inherent power to force labor. To labor is a matter of choice.

## Life, Liberty, and the Pursuit of Money

A government may decide that its bills are legal tender, but it has no power to insist that other entities, domestic or foreign, accept those bills at stated value in return for labor.

Taxation gives government the capacity to transfer the product of labor from one group to another. The government itself is not the laborer or producer.

The failure of currency inevitably arises when government attempts to achieve more than it has the capacity to deliver. At the onset of civilization, the farmer exchanged corn for wheat. At the time of the exchange, payment was complete. Today we exchange goods for a paper promise, guaranteed by the government for sure, but a promise nevertheless. The promise is implicit that the holder will receive on demand labor, be it in the form of product or service, for the amount stated on the bill.

Until the holder receives that product or labor, the contractual agreement has not been fulfilled. In reality the holder of the bill has a guaranteed promise from the government, which said government lacks the capacity to fulfill. The promise of government is beyond the reach of government.

The experience of the Weimar Republic and the Confederacy inform today.

Most citizens will accept government paper with its implicit promise in an exchange as long as the guarantor remains credible.

In a world of paper, credibility is the key. When it became clear that the South would lose the war, virtually no one would accept Confederate dollars. The guarantee of future payment was worthless.

Note here that had the South exchanged guns for butter, payment would have been complete. The matter of guarantee would never have arisen. Similarly had the bills allowed the holder to go to the Southern treasury and exchange those bills for gold, payment would have been complete, even if the holder chose not to immediately go to the treasury.

As long as the amount of paper bills and gold in the vault were equivalent, the two, bills and gold, merged, and payment was executed though the holder chose not to pick up the gold. That choice was the holder's.

In the case of paper currency, the holder accepts the risk. I should point out that the examples of the Weimar Republic and the Confederacy are clearly extreme. A far more likely scenario, and the one that gives rise to crisis, is the slow but certain decline in the credibility of government, all government, as it insists on promising far more than it can possibly deliver.

It is true today that a large number of governments are failing. Their failure is not apparent. Though elections are held, the need to promise is an imperative in order to get elected, or at least it is thought to be. All excesses will be addressed in the future. Hope springs eternal.

Of course, that future with the promise of peace and stability never arrives, and thus the erosion of credibility continues. Disequilibrium and imbalance, measured in terms of production versus consumption, debt versus equity, increasingly threaten the standing order. Both individuals and government ultimately find themselves trapped.

Like every trapped animal, they strike out. Since the fault can never be theirs, it must lie elsewhere. We must take action to eliminate that threat.

The German people, with their superior Prussian heritage, could never have lost the First World War, bringing the depression to Germany that followed. The fault must lie elsewhere—the Jews; the creditors, of course; the Allies with their insatiable reparations demands; the Slavs, the Poles, the French, the English.

In a real sense, Germany was endeavoring to regain balance and equilibrium at the expense of others. They felt trapped.

Global disequilibrium and imbalance are not merely periods of discomfit. They have the most dire and far-reaching consequences, as nation after nation moves to defend its interests.

The United States dependence on foreign oil, a strategic commodity, played a key role in the invasion of Iraq. Nations quickly find justification under such circumstances for their actions.

The greater the global disequilibrium, the more threatening the situation becomes.

Promises made today in the form of currency and other debt instruments far exceed the capacity of people to deliver. The cry goes out for rebalancing. One can only hope and pray that is accomplished through rational means.

## What Are the Implications of Excessive Debt?

Since debt in all forms constitutes an immediate reduction in wealth and as the gross domestic product is the measure, though I would argue a poor one, of the incremental wealth of a nation, then clearly, if the debt exceeds the product, then the wealth of the nation is in decline.

An important caveat here is that before drawing a final conclusion, debt figures must be dissected, much like cholesterol, to determine whether the debt incurred is producing wealth, such as with a new plant and equipment, or is destroying wealth, as the farmer does when he devours his crops.

There is a third category of debt, which is debt that is a mix of consumption and investment.

Education and all forms of professional training provide substantial returns on the investment made. It is obvious that without sufficient education, the productivity of a nation would be greatly retarded.

There are many other categories of spending that have a consumption orientation, yet generate returns over an extended period of time.

That being said, the fact remains that if the debt of a nation is increasing faster than the product of a nation, the wealth of that nation is in decline.

The American experience and the experience of other empires in history is that once this downslide begins, inertia and dependence, particularly the growing dependence on government, make it virtually impossible for fundamental change to be ushered in without some major intervening event such as a great war.

Rational people see war as failure of humankind to satisfactorily address conflict in some other acceptable way. Strangely, war, though destructive, has a most peculiar liberating effect. It serves to redirect the course of nations and peoples.

## Economic Collapse, the Ultimate Destruction of Debt

After seventy-five years of economic expansion, with a few setbacks along the way, the global economy as of this writing is in decline, though statistically the domestic economy of many nations continues advancing.

What is truly advancing is fear, fear of global calamity. This palpable fear was a critical element in my decision to write this book.

To overcome this fear, we must, that is, all of us, address reality. That is the real challenge.

The underlying difficulty is not that humanity has misread or ignored the statistics. The reality is that we are subject to the same natural laws that apply to all species. Modern humans refuse, absolutely refuse, to address reality, the reality of life itself.

A chasm exists between perceptions and reality.

Western humans look about their world as if they and the rest of humanity were riding a gigantic elevator. Everyone is interested in reaching the top floor. No one knows, or for that matter pretends, to know where the top floor is or what lies at the top, but we want to get to the top nevertheless.

As we ascend in this elevator, we accept the argument that we should continue on the present path with perhaps a few minor modifications, such as addressing environmental concerns; otherwise, it's steady as you go. We blindly pursue this path, doing whatever we please, denying truth or rationalizing it in order to get our way. Since truth might interrupt this quest, we push it aside and have adopted in its place the "elevator thesis," my description of this errant way. This thesis recognizes the modern contradiction that it doesn't matter what we do, what course we follow, we are destined to get to the top. We philosophically have adopted determinism, a quasi form of evolution. The syllogism is quite simple. We are better off today than we were in the past. Ignore completely the critical factors that produced this advance and simply conclude from this past experience that we will be better off in the future. This syllogism, though not logical, goes unchallenged.

Yet isn't this a sign of hope? No, it is a sign of sophomoric reasoning. It has nothing to do with hope; rather, it has more to do with self-centered expectation.

In the field of economics, it is an iron-clad law that no species can consume more than is available. For humans this translates into production. To consume, we must produce.

Debt in the modern world plays an integral role in the production process. By concentrating borrowed capital, we are able to produce more for a growing world population. In a real sense, debt is essential.

However, the imaginary elevator we believe we are on can only take so much weight, measured in terms of population and debt. Savings and investment offset this weight through production. As the ratio of saving and investment to debt shifts in favor of debt as the population increases, the elevator can no longer take the weight.

When the limit is reached, the laws of gravity step in. Gravity is the rebalancing mechanism. To prevent collapse, something has to give. The population must be reduced or the debt extinguished.

We can be certain today that debt usage and the population of the world make it impossible to continue on the path we are on. Something will have to give.

## The Elevator Is Descending—But It Is Not in Free Fall, at least Not Yet

Calamity is not inevitable. However to prevent calamity, we must address reality. Is the world of today up to doing that?

A first good dose of reality is to recognize that the modern-day world is fundamentally dissimilar from earlier periods. The idea that we are in this elevator that inevitably must rise to new heights is a fiction.

Following the Great Depression and the Second World War, the global economy, with the important exception of the United States, was in a virtual state of total collapse. Europe had been destroyed physically and financially.

Only the good offices of the United States and the goodwill of the American people stood in the way of worldwide famine.

Note the collapse was total; there was no prospect that any nation apart from the United States would repay its debt at any time in the foreseeable future. There was simply no way to get blood out of stone. The world was broke. Past debt was thus effectively extinguished. Debt, dating back many decades, was null and void.

Nations did not renounce their debt, but it was understood by all, including our former enemies, that debt payment was no longer on the agenda. Perhaps some time in the future, when all was well, debt would be renegotiated, as indeed in many cases it was.

A broken world does not think in terms of repaying debt. In 1945 the old world was swept away. There was no other choice. However, the money borrowed from American savers could not be ignored. Their labor had won the Second World War, and they expected to be paid in goods and services.

Our national debt was considerable; it constituted more than 100 percent of the war economy. That had to be paid.

However, this debt was more than offset by the capital, plant, equipment, and product built up during the Second World War when workers were denied access to consumer goods such as homes and cars as factories built tanks and planes.

Americans were holding billions in their savings accounts. Governmental debt was great, but Americans had great savings.

This debt was to be paid with revenue raised from taxation. Taxes in comparison to today were high. The top income tax rate was over 90 percent. The tax rates were progressive in nature. A progressive income tax structure levels the playing field.

The wealth gap between the very wealthy and the average citizen was relatively narrow in comparison with today. The CEO of a corporation might earn forty times the pay of the lowest-paid employee in the company. Today that figure is four hundred times. Tax rates have been squeezed so that the wealthy keep a far larger portion of their income than was the case in the decades of the forties through the seventies.

The rich have indeed gotten richer, and the poor have gone into debt, by way of the credit card. In a sense the poor are subsidizing the rich. Please accept my assurance that this is not intended to be a political statement. It is simply a fact.

Is this condition sustainable? The answer is obviously not. The point has been reached, however, where the less wealthy, and in the case of the United States, this means the large middle class, no longer has the financial capability to support government-driven spending and consumption-oriented domestic and internationalist policies, public and private.

Government derives most of its revenue through taxation. The public creates the money, and the government takes it. Without taxation, government spending would not be possible. All government would be powerless without the public's purse.

Public bodies have spent huge amounts for so long that we now take their trillions of dollars of cumulative spending for granted. Debt became a way of life.

Not only are the numbers staggering and incomprehensible, but the legislative bodies that authorize the spending have little or no grasp of the effectiveness of the programs they have authorized. It is as if a great monster has taken control of our destiny. No serious effort is being made collectively to address this monster.

### Key Currencies, the Destruction of Asset Values

As we approached the end of 2007, the nation became justifiably disturbed by the growing fiscal crises in credit and housing. Neither crisis, or to be more precise, neither bubble, would have been possible without the perverse influence of debt. Debt was responsible for the 1929 crash, the collapse of the German economy, and the global economic implosion that followed. Debt again is working to bring down the economy of the United States and, by extension, the world.

In the current crisis, and the word *crisis* is not too strong a word, the question is, "Does the United States have the will and capacity to change its spending habits and/or to excise its obligations?"

Circumstances have changed totally from the days of the Great Depression. Then we were the world's greatest creditor; now our position is reversed.

In important ways the situation today is dissimilar to conditions that existed in the thirties. Without question the most critical difference is that we have a completely different wealth transfer system, facilitated by the extraordinary invention and development of advanced communications. Further, global default is no longer possible because paper can be printed indefinitely by the world's governments. Of course, paper feeds extravagance and consumption.

We will never run out of paper as long as government stands behind the printworks. Thus we are in no danger of repeating the Great Depression precisely.

As debt continues to build, the response is to print more paper. The central banks exercise their power and did this most recently with abandon. One can only imagine that the next step will be their setting up kiosks at important intersections so that one and all can stop by and withdraw whatever one needs. However Europe, with the onset of the Greek, Spanish, and Italian sovereign crises, is having second thoughts. Official thinking in America has yet to be moved.

Instinctively we know that there is something terribly wrong with this, and indeed there is. The solution is not at hand. Allowing for mass default would precipitate another great depression, and that is totally unacceptable.

What to do?

Money must top the agenda. Money is the cumulative savings resulting from labor or the capacity to bring into being an instrument or thing that has intrinsic value or utility. Again to put it simply, money is production or the capacity to produce.

The central banks, in their effort to prevent widespread default, are not increasing the world's money supply, that is, capital and savings, but are introducing something called liquidity. As the central banks, including the Federal Reserve, open the liquidity spigot, they are making it possible for one and all to borrow to pay off debt, to consume, and to produce. Borrowing to produce is fine, but debt for the purpose of consumption or to reduce other debt may worsen the situation. It won't solve the problem.

Clearly liquidity is not money, but a stopgap measure to prevent crisis. However, a future crisis is inevitable if the liquidity/credit advanced is used for anything but to further production.

Increase in supply of any utility results in a decline in value, irrespective of the immediate impact on price. Increasing supply always reduces value. Decreasing supply always increases value. Governments and cartels may take steps to alter the price. However, they cannot alter value without altering supply.

## Ascertaining Value and the Prostitution Thereof

How is value arrived at? There is no force that can dictate value. Value incorporates the notions of balance and utility. Value has two characteristics. The first is subjective. This "thing," this widget, has value to me though it may not have value to anyone else. In order to obtain it, I must be willing to surrender something of mine. Advanced societies transact the exchange in legal tender, which we call currency.

The second characteristic is objective. Sufficient numbers of people desire this "thing." Price is simply the expression of this. Needless to say, as the ratio of supply to demand changes, the price must change. If the supply is diminishing and demand remains the same, the price will escalate until such time as the product or commodity loses its subjective value.

All commodities will ultimately lose value as the world finds more efficient substitutes. This shift is understood most clearly in the expression that "necessity is the mother of invention."

We will continue to use a commodity so long as the cost/price dynamic, measured in terms of utility, is proportionate. We can safely conclude from this that long before the world runs out of oil, for example, people will have ceased to use it, having found a substitute. Thus the fear of running out of oil is misplaced.

The effect of an escalating price structure is to advance the time for substitution. With remarkable consistency and reliability, such transformation, as history instructs, occurs in a timely manner, invariably bringing with it a more efficient, less costly alternative. Not only are we not doomed, as some of the naysayers might suggest, but we can be most optimistic that as the need becomes critical, the solution will be at our doorstep.

A synonym for value is the word *utility*. Everything, to be of value, must have utility. Utility, simply defined, means usefulness. Without utility an item is valueless. It is hard to conceive of a thing that satisfies as an antonym of value, which is worthlessness or perhaps triviality.

Everything we come across has value to someone. If we look at value in terms of exchange, however, and endeavor to measure it, we see great differences depending on such things as supply and demand, the availability of a ready alternative, the contribution it makes in building wealth, and personal preference.

Endeavoring to assign a value to a thing becomes a perilous journey since the variables that could impact the value are virtually infinite. Value, like the concept of money, is largely an abstraction. Nothing in life can have a truly fixed value, with the possible exception of life itself.

Value is exclusively in the eye of the beholder. No two people will truly value anything identically. Given the supply/demand dynamic, however, I may have to pay a stated price even though I value the item less than my neighbor.

This reality creates the dynamic we call business or commerce. Anything for sale or exchange must be assigned a value by the seller and buyer. In most cases the seller and buyer have a ready alternative. The seller may withdraw the item, hopeful of getting a better price; the buyer may seek out the alternative.

In all economic systems, and most certainly in the free enterprise system, value is constantly changing. When we speak of value in business, we mean exchange. If I own an heirloom, it certainly would have great meaning to me, and as a consequence, I think of it in terms of value, but until I come to sell it, it has no commercial value. It is something I hold precious, period.

Commercial value requires at a minimum two parties who are prepared to enter into an exchange.

Thus in the case of a real estate appraisal, the appraiser estimates but does not determine value. That can only occur when a willing buyer and seller agree on the terms. Value is determined at the moment of exchange but changes after the exchange has been made. Value is never permanent; it is a variable whose behavior is reminiscent of the electrons moving around the nucleus of an atom—unpredictable.

Thus everything I own may well have a value, but it can never be said with absolute certainty what it is at any moment in time.

We see this at work in the stock and bond market. We may buy a stock, expecting it to go higher in price, but we can never be certain. If certitude were possible, there would be no buyer or seller, for who would sell if it was known that the value of these shares must go higher? While value is uncertain, we are able to identify certain factors that will influence value.

## The Housing Bubble, a Critical Look at Appraisals

Greed is at the very heart of the imbalance that exists between nominal and real value. Yet greed would never have been allowed to raise its ugly head had it not been for the ready availability of credit. One is forced to ask the question "What would be the price of a particular home if the buyer had to pay from his accumulated savings?" Obviously the price would drop substantially.

Thus credit must always be part of the problem. Such an answer is both glib and simplistic. For certain, there are at least three occasions when the introduction of debt is justified.

The first circumstance is by acting one can realize a net increase in real wealth by increasing production.

The second is where debt is most efficient. For example, one has a breakthrough invention that can be readily marketed. The individual has to build the plant now or forfeit the opportunity.

The last occasion is when the survival of the nation or the state is at stake. In each of these cases, a lender is taking the risk. It is the job of the credit officer to measure risk. Banking is a risk business.

To the extent the lender is unfamiliar with the borrower, the business, or the property, the lender relies on third parties to provide critical analysis.

This happens most often in the world of residential and commercial real estate. The lender depends on the third-party licensed appraiser to provide him or her with information to assess the risk.

There are three basic approaches to value. They are the sales comparison approach, the cost approach, and the income approach.[cxxxvi]

A brief explanation of the three follows. The sales comparison approach is "especially applicable in appraising vacant land and single family residences."[cxxxvii] "This approach is based on the principle of substitution."[cxxxviii] No one will pay more for property x than for property y if they are equally desirable. "This principle holds that the maximum value of a property is significantly determined by the cost of the timely acquisition of a substitute property."[cxxxix]

The cost approach estimates the "replacement or reproduction cost of building and improvements"[cxl] together with an estimate of "the value of the land."[cxli]

The income approach determines value by estimating the potential income that can be derived from the property. It works out to be a ratio (gross rent multiplier) "determined by dividing the selling price of the recently sold comparable properties by the monthly rent"[cxlii] and comparing that ratio to the property at hand.

Commercial properties are typically valued by determining the capitalization rate, which is a process whereby a future net income stream is converted into an estimate of present value.

On the surface these three approaches may appear to be reasonable in determining value. Under normal or typical market conditions, this may be the case.

However rational the approach, it is always conditional. Judgment must be exercised. Common sense must be dominant if an intelligent decision is to be made.

Credit officers should never lose sight of the fact that the purpose of an appraisal is not to justify the purchase price but to determine value.

The perceived value and the purchase price may conveniently coincide, but they are not synonymous. Clearly it is in the parties' interest that they accord.

If they do agree, then the seller will get his or her selling price. The buyer will get the house of his or her dreams. The lender will get the mortgage and related business, and the appraiser will be regarded favorably. No one stands to gain if the value and purchase price do not agree.

The appraisal process itself has a built-in incentive that can be summarized by simply asking the question, "Can the sales price be justified?"

Everyone desires the same result. That desire, that bias, should never drive the decision-making process. If it does, it stands to reason that higher prices will result.

This has clearly been the case in the United States. The bias, absent sound judgment, produced the bubble.

What is the solution?

## Bubble Solutions

Over time the banking world developed a uniform process, which is both regulated and efficient. However, the process was dependent on a full understanding of macroeconomic conditions, including the possibility of a major downturn.

Experienced credit officers must have realized that housing prices, like trees, cannot grow to the sky. The culprits in this national tragedy were governments that preached home ownership with a promise of capital to all comers, the lender who out of ignorance or greed put all vestiges of common sense aside, and the buyers and sellers who refused to consider seriously their personal risk.

If we are to learn from this experience, important questions need to be answered.

The most important such question is, "Was value there in the first place?" The mortgage application process was there, but was the value there at the time the loan was made?

At the time of contract, if the value and the loan, sufficiently discounted, coincided, then it cannot be said that the lender made a bad loan simply because the value at some future time declines. Lenders are not seers. An appraisal is an estimate of present value and not a guarantee of future value.

Lending will always entail some risk. Risk has to be measured and diversified in such a way as to not put the lender or the institution at serious risk.

Experienced lenders understand this; the money-grubbers do not. What to do with government interference? We can assume they will always preach Utopia, as long as they are in need of votes.

## Critical Factors in Determining Value

Though there are an unlimited number of influences that come into play when we approach the issue of value, there are certain factors that are truly fundamental. These fundamentals always serve to influence in a meaningful way value under every set of circumstances.

## Appreciation and Depreciation

Virtually everything on the shelf everywhere is depreciating in appearance, if not in substance. The depreciation may be imperceptibly slow, but it is ongoing.

A general proposition, with few exceptions, namely, those centered in the world of art and literature, is that aging will ultimately reduce value. Factors such as changes in fashion may accelerate the deterioration or decelerate it, but change will occur nevertheless.

Let us recall that a synonym for value is utility. Utility and depreciation are in constant struggle.

Utility in the end will lose the battle. Utility value declines over time, and therefore the relative value of the asset also declines over time. There can never be real appreciation without external change.

## Value and Wealth Are Synonymous

In accordance with the definition of money, a forest neither owned nor touched by humans will ever be considered money. Yet we understand that it has value. In splendid isolation, its value rests in the realm of the potential. An asset has value and thus is money when it has been purchased, given ownership, or converted, or its usage transformed; for example, the wood being made into a ship, chair, table, and so on. We have a valuable asset that is money. The asset and the money are the same, that is, they are synonymous.

Progress is affirmed when I add incremental utility. A classic example is a worker in a factory capable of performing a single function who is replaced by a machine capable of performing two functions. This transition constitutes real progress even though the worker has been displaced. In theory this worker is now free to contribute his or her skill to another avenue of endeavor. Thus from a macro or global standpoint there is a net benefit. Progress has been realized.

During a period of high unemployment, anxiety spreads. Have we exhausted "money"? Is there a future? Of course, but it requires the willingness to change, to seek out new worlds. The infinite dimensions of space beckon. Value is there, measured by potential only. To translate it into wealth, the potential must be seized. The world awaits the explorer, the inventor.

Though the words *wealth*, *value*, and *money* are frequently used interchangeably, the word *money* is a universal. It serves as a standard by which to measure and compare anything against the totality of value extant. This standard measures the inherent value or utility of all that is produced arising from human ingenuity and labor.

Of critical importance, this measure provides us with the capacity to discern a point of equilibrium or balance in all transactions and exchanges.

Equilibrium in exchange assures fairness, and without fairness, there can be no sustainable progress. Humans thus had to create a standard. We call that universal standard money.

Money as a measure must, by definition, be a variable. Variables are abstract in conception. As for the Aristotelian view regarding that which is finite, he concluded that everything in the universe joins form with matter.

Matter alone, without form, is a metaphysical impossibility. All matter must have form. We visualize a tree. We visualize a chair. A tree and a chair are not the same. It requires imagination and invention to take the wood and reshape it into a chair.

Only intelligent beings are able to do this through the generation of an idea, the making of a chair, or in the broadest of terms, the production of goods. With this miraculous change, we have a product, and that product or products constitute money.

The money standard takes another abstract concept, equality, and gives it form to serve as a balancing mechanism to equate different substances, for example, corn versus wheat. This abstraction is actualized in the exchange of one good for another. Money, in a practical sense, should always be thought of in terms of output or production and as a standard to measure both.

The Pilgrims as they landed at Plymouth were without money. But in the landscape and in their soul lay the potential. Through the labor of centuries, that potential was converted into what we know today as the United States of America.

*David Barrett*

## Currency Is Not Money, Though the World Believes It Is

Currency is something tangible and stands as a representation, but only a representation, a stand-in, for money. Thus it can take any form.

Currency and money are not the same. It would be correct to say that money taken as a universal is the totality of output, the totality of value. Currency extant should represent this output.

Currency that is not representative is without value except to the extent that it has intrinsic value, much as gold has. Currency misused, such as counterfeit bills, have no value de jure. Currency issued that is no longer representative of value, even if issued by and under legal authority and given the stamp of legal tender, is without value.

## Currency Is Representative; Therefore, It Can Take Any Form

Indeed currency can take any form whatsoever and has throughout history, many truly bizarre.

The Canadian garrisons in the eighteenth century, unable to be resupplied on a regular basis and thus denied access to British sterling, resorted to the use of playing cards for currency. The practice was so successful that when the European wars ended, the Canadians insisted on continuing the use of cards. It took an act of the legislature to bring the practice to an end.

Currency, standing alone, will never serve to increase wealth. Neither a nation, nor individual, nor other entity can be made wealthier by simply printing or otherwise increasing the amount of currency outstanding. Wealth is increased only by increasing production and/or the capacity to produce.

Currency may represent wealth, but it never constitutes wealth. Currency can never become the ultimate standard. It serves as a visible and thus convenient stand-in, or representation, but the true standard of money is production.

The extraordinary and continuing misconception in history is that metal, particularly gold and silver, constitute real money, from which all things of value flow. Metal has intrinsic value as a metal, but in monetary terms, it is simply metal that we choose to use as currency. Gold through history has been used as currency. However, over and above its intrinsic value, gold has no special place.

Money that is production flows from savings. Savings takes many forms. Savings in a bank is the most obvious. Savings used in the production process is similar to yeast in a cake. Without the introduction of the yeast, the potential for a cake in terms of the ingredients may well be there, but without the yeast, there is no cake.

Savings flow from an earlier cycle of production. Savings I have accumulated from earlier effort involving my labors allows me to buy the materials to build a new plant.

Money and currency are joined only when the parties exchange goods produced. As humans moved beyond barter, currency was introduced as a liability, an IOU, giving the holder a claim on money, that is, future production.

The value of currency may be stable, overvalued, or undervalued. Overvalued and undervalued currencies revolve around a point of equilibrium. Equilibrium is achieved when capital flows equalize. Undervalued currency enhances real return, and overvalued currency reduces real return.

## The IOU Seekers—Fraud at Work

People spend their lives attempting to amass currency in whatever form. Frequently the seeker is attempting to benefit from the labor of others without making a commensurate contribution of labor.

Such efforts result in a transfer of wealth but never increase wealth. Wealth is increased only through an incremental increase in labor.

## Currency and Government

Currency is but a representation. It is government that gives currency legal standing, providing for its use in all domestic transactions, including the payment of debt.

For centuries the good faith and credit of the government guaranteed the conversion at a stated price into a money standard, which was for the most part metal. In this case the one exchanging did not get goods but received metal. He or she could do whatever he or she wanted with the metal; the government had lived up to its guarantee. In such a case, the representation held true, and the currency holder was paid.

A currency that does not have the right of conversion, such as today's dollar, is referred to as fiat money. Most currencies today are fiat currencies, which mean that should the state be dissolved, the paper is worthless. Since the currency extant greatly exceeds the totality of production, this currency is suspect.

Why should gold and silver constitute payment? Because that is what is clearly stated on the paper that serves as the representation. That is the contract. The price of gold and silver might move higher or lower. That has no relevancy. The contract calls for the exchange in gold or silver irrespective of price. The currency contract has been fulfilled. In the case of fiat currency, the government promises that you can exchange the paper for goods and services from some third party. The government unfortunately has no way to enforce this.

The downside to fiat currency is the day you walk into a store to buy bread and hand the clerk a ten-dollar bill that he will not accept, claiming that it is just a piece of paper. No one, not even the government, can force the clerk to sell you the bread.

A fiat money system is at its core a system of trust, and trust alone. It cannot be described as a system calling for final payment.

## Credit May Take the Form of Currency

Credit is debt, the antithesis of savings. As we enter into a credit arrangement, we borrow another's savings. All debt, to have legitimacy, must have as its backstop savings, dollar for dollar.

Failure to back debt with savings is casino speculation. If a bank were to make a loan without deposits or savings to support it, it is risking its capital and the solvency of the bank. This has occurred throughout history and is the base cause of the financial crisis that began most recently in 2007.

The primary cause of the Great Depression of the thirties was the extent to which the debt of the world exceeded savings, savings as measured by gold. Loans could not be repaid for there was insufficient gold to repay them.

## International Trade

The savings generated from the net savings of a nation provide the basis for the next round of expansion. As a nation produces more, it will find that production of certain products exceeds that required for domestic consumption. At the same time, it is in need of other products that may not be obtained domestically, such as raw materials, which will then be bought from other nations. This is the beginning of international trade. Before engaging in such trade, a nation must first meet the needs of its own citizens. International trade is a process where the excess of one nation is exchanged for the excess of another. The currencies of both nations assure equality of trade. The market value of currency makes the exchange possible. Any manipulation of that value, by definition, means that resulting trade will be imbalanced.

Currency exchanges in international trade result in change of ownership, but the amounts of currency outstanding should remain the same. In the case where one party sells goods outright to another country and is paid in that nation's currency, it must be able to convert the currency and be free to do so. Freedom of convertibility is essential in international trade. Restrictions on convertibility will have the most deleterious effect on the volume of international trade.

## The Meaning of Interest

With his memorable quips and aphorisms, Mark Twain stands with Benjamin Franklin as one of the two greatest contributors to the world of truisms. One of this author's favorites is "Everyone talks about the weather but no one does anything about it." One cannot turn on the news today without hearing at times an exhaustive discussion of interest rates and forecasts as to their direction, with accompanying comments about the Federal

Reserve, which it is believed is responsible for rates being too high or too low, depending on whether you are a lender, investor, or borrower. At any rate, it is all the fault of the Federal Reserve, we are led to believe. Like most truisms, this too is simply false. In point of fact, the Federal Reserve does not control interest rates simply because interest rates do not have an independent existence.

As many times as you and I have visited a bank or other financial institution, we have never been taken to the interest rate department. It will never happen, because the term *interest rate* is simply a description of the return on money. Money and interest rates are equivalent concepts. Money that is not invested produces a zero rate of interest. The investment of money produces a return to the investor, and we refer to that as interest. However, without the money there can be no return. Interest and money are the same. Interest is money.

Federal Reserve policy will influence both the level and direction of interest rates by increasing or decreasing bank reserves. However, the Fed does not set rates, a widely held misconception.

## INVESTMENTS

Irrespective of the type of investment, that is, stocks or bonds or debt instruments or real estate and so on, the investor is always implicitly measuring return versus risk. It is clear that when I am earning a stated rate of return, such as the rate of interest on a bond, I can easily compare it to other investments that carry a similar rate of return.

It is far more difficult when I endeavor to compare instruments with a stated or nominal return versus those without a given return, such as a traded stock. Many stocks of course have dividends, which may or may not be paid depending on the earnings of the corporation. Thus I have to compare that which is more or less certain with uncertainty of return. Of course to determine return, one has to consider every factor, including the tax consequences, in order to measure total return.

Real estate investment is not different. If I buy a home that I plan to occupy, my return is measured in terms of enjoyment and my expectation of price appreciation. While at first glance, enjoyment would appear not to be quantifiable in terms of return, in point of fact we do measure it when we purchase our domicile by comparing the expense of ownership versus the expense of rental. If the differential is great enough, I will choose one over the other. What has distorted the picture since the Second World War is that real estate values have appreciated constantly. All other things being equal, I could expect the highest return by owning real estate.

History is strewn with status symbols indicative of importance and wealth. For the Native Americans it was beads, silver, and gold. For the Romans it was silk and spices, particularly pepper. For the English it was to be a part of royalty. For the Dutch, at one point, it was the tulip flower. For Middle Easterners, it was the size of their harem; and for many a barbaric tribe, it was the number of skulls a warrior could amass.

## Symbols of Wealth Are in Constant Flux

Like fashions in dress, symbols of wealth come and go. In sufficient time, home ownership will cease to be such a symbol. Irrespective of the symbol, the moment everyone has one, it loses its majestic status. A home, though essential for providing shelter, is empty space surrounded by plastic and wood and other relatively inexpensive and readily available materials. The fascination of the past seven decades won't last forever.

While the fascination is in play, irrational behavior rules. Value has literally been turned on its head. Though the buyer bears a great deal of the responsibility for getting caught up in this madness, the fault is widely shared.

At the bottom of it all is greed. Yet none of this distortion would have been possible without credit being made widely available. Had the millions of buyers in the past six decades been forced to pay with their savings, which of course is real money, for shelter rather than rely on mortgage debt, there would today be far more rental units in place and far fewer attractive but overpriced homes dotting the landscape.

Financial institutions, banks, and others should have been focusing their effort on lending to corporations, companies, businesses, and individuals that were productive, producing goods and services that would provide employment and benefit to others. Instead, they saw the quick buck in the mortgage business and jumped on board. This was greatly facilitated by a bundling process known as securitization, where mortgages could be sold en masse like so many loaves of bread, leaving the seller free of liability after he or she had taken his or her fee.

This lucrative business was also furthered by the widespread distribution of credit cards, which gave access to credit to everyone so that credit became virtually infinite in availability. In order to own a multithousand-dollar home, all that was required was the ability to sign a contract.

Debt, the disease of the ages, became fashionable. It was to be spread across continents. Debt under such circumstances allowed for fictitious indicators or signs of wealth to develop. Frequently one would hear it said that Mr. Smith or Mr. Brown must be very wealthy, as they had a very large home with a swimming pool and a vacation home to boot. No one seemed interested in the debt that lay behind the edifices.

Government did its share in fostering the disease by passing legislation creating a number of quasi-governmental organizations designed to provide funds for borrowers to purchase homes. The best known of these are FNMA, Freddie Mac, and the FHA. The management of these organizations was compensated in accordance with their profitability. Thus they had a built-in incentive to advance the credit bubble.

This so-called wealth effect is being created from whole cloth through the misuse and flawed application of debt. With access to unlimited credit, nominal as opposed to real values persistently rise. Credit, not value, is the driving force. Values have not changed. In fact, they may actually have diminished as a direct result of the increase in supply of homes, but prices rose nevertheless.

The buyers accept this debt burden with the identical mind-set that drove their forebears to invest on margin in the stock market during the late twenties. They see gold at the end of the rainbow and forget risk.

In the interim they can live in the house, and appearances will lead one and all to conclude that they are successful. This will enhance their image and that of their family in the community. To quote the Book of Ecclesiastes, "The words of the Preacher, the son of David, king in Jerusalem. Vanity of vanities; all *is* vanity."[cxliii]

## THE DYNAMIC OF CHANGE, A PREREQUISITE FOR ECONOMIC PROGRESS

As stated above, *order, equilibrium,* and *perfection* have the same meaning. In the finite world, to maintain a perfect state requires renewal. All that is static and unchanging is undergoing some form of deterioration. For the artist, the tint of color fades. A star exhausts its fuel and in time collapses. Farming the same crop over time will drain the soil of nutrients. All species age.

A perfect state, to the extent it is realizable, requires change, orderly change. For humans to survive, they must be adept at meeting the needs of their time. The alternative is extinction. We should never fear change, for it is change that will help to sustain us.

Species fail not because there were too many or too few, but because they were unable to alter a lifestyle that they had come to know, perhaps over generations, and with which they were comfortable.

They chose to stay in the present or the past, while the universe, that is, "nature and nature's God," as Thomas Jefferson put it, demands a never-ending pursuit of perfection.

## NATIONAL DEBT

In every instance, as a person, company, or government borrows money, irrespective of the term of the borrowing, it reduces the net worth of the borrower. If I add up all my assets and assign a value to those assets, I arrive at a figure; but to determine my net worth, I must first deduct what I owe. Companies large and small must do the same, and so must government, as well as the individual.

Though it sounds politically incorrect, the fact is that governments go broke just as people and companies do. And this happens with surprising frequency. It is difficult to contemplate a country in bankruptcy, for countries, unlike businesses, don't disappear. Third-world defaults, which broke the major money center banks in Europe and the United States in the eighties, were saved from extinction by the generosity of the Federal Reserve and other central banks and governments. The culprits, that is the debtor nations themselves, such as Argentina, remain intact, their sovereignty never challenged.

They survived and, within a surprisingly short period of time, prospered, only to renew their spendthrift ways, which means that they will go broke again. These experiences seriously retard global growth and progress.

## Capital Movement Around the World

There are a number of factors that give rise to the movement of capital from nation to nation. Three have overriding significance.

First, the prospect of currency appreciation encourages investment in a country. Since the currency is appreciating, all things being equal, everything purchased there, from stocks to the manufacture of shoes, has a greater chance of being profitable than if I were to buy assets in a country where the currency is depreciating.

Second, the country so benefiting must have a stable history, society, and government, with favorable prospects to stay that way. It must be democratic. The government must represent the will of the people and provide wide-ranging freedom of choice to its citizenry. It must encourage development and an improving standard of living, and it must adhere to the rule of law and contract. It must have the necessary standing in the world to exert sufficient influence and power that its sovereignty is not threatened. It must have a freely convertible and stable currency and be creditworthy.

Thirdly, the prospect or profit must exceed prospects elsewhere. Simply put, money will seek the highest and safest return. Throughout its history the United States has been regarded as a nation with the highest credit and commercial dynamic to provide the maximum potential return. Thus we have been the beneficiary of massive capital flows, which have been in turn invested here, contributing to the wealth and the standard of living that we enjoy today.

How did this impact the nation transferring capital? In the case of Great Britain after our Civil War, Britain poured its wealth into American railroads. Before these transfers began, Britain was far and away the leading industrial power in the world. As this transfer continued over a century, Britain no longer held that title, and by the beginning of the First World War found itself sharing world power with the United States and, to a lesser extent, France.

This capital shift renders the nation from which the capital is moving the poorer in relation to the recipient. In effect one nation is relying on another to build its infrastructure. While the transferring nation may retain ownership, the capital recipient builds railroads, dams, buildings, and factories. The investors from the transferring nation may earn a high rate of return, but the recipient is blessed with real assets, that is, money.

## Foreign Exchange Risk

Currency value is ultimately determined by the real rate of return. The expectation of currency appreciation or depreciation has a profound impact on the level of interest rates. In the past, many nations have had to live with extraordinary rates. Brazil, for instance, has had rates well above 50 percent on occasion. Factored in is the expectation of a substantial decline in currency value.

Currency movement has been the bane of existence of all nation-states since nations were first incorporated. It is the policies of nations that will determine how great a swing is in store.

A nation threatened with internal strife or war, or one whose governmental policies are activist in orientation and spendthrift or control-oriented, will likely have a weaker currency than one whose policies are noninterventionist and who is politically and financially stable.

In the end it is the policies of nations that determine the level of interest and exchange rates of a nation. The market will, in its inevitable way, sort out strengths and weaknesses and arrive at an exchange rate that satisfies buyer and seller.

The universal investor will always seek out the highest return with the least amount of risk. If hypothetically market and exchange risk could be minimized, what rate of interest over a span of centuries would satisfy the typical investor?

Those who have researched the matter have concluded that an investor will invest short-term, out to one year, versus spending if the rate is 2¾ percent and for longer terms, say, ten years, 5 ¾ percent. This was the opinion of John Maynard Keynes and others who have explored the matter. My personal opinion is today's universal rate is 3 percent and 6 percent.

To expect the populace to save, it must be able to receive in real terms those percentages; otherwise there is no reason to surrender the present gratification of wants and needs to invest. Again, as we speak of return, we mean the real return. Thus all nominal rates must be adjusted by appreciation or depreciation of currency and other factors.

## Is Progress Inevitable?

Advance or progress, as we define it, is dependent entirely on constant accretion or increase in capital. There are many ways this can be accomplished; the most obvious is through labor and the savings that result. However, invention and innovation are critical as well. As the world population increases, it is imperative that the global capital pool increase at the very least in tandem, or the standard of living for humanity must falter. That of course is not happening today, as the increasing debt load of the world bears stark testimony to.

The world's economic problem in a word is consumption. Though the economic growth rate statistics in recent decades have been impressive, so has the growth in world population, which today stands at approximately seven billion. In 1950 that figure was two billion.

Clearly the United States and the other industrial nations have been depleting the capital pool, consuming capital at an unprecedented rate.

## Consumption Extinguishes Money (Capital), Destroying Wealth and Limiting the Potential for Growth

Nothing could be more self-evident than the fact that consumption destroys wealth. Debt will never cure the disease. Debt invites consumption.

## Life, Liberty, and the Pursuit of Money

Debt does have a place. Noted in this book earlier, if one borrows to facilitate production, that may indeed be a wise decision. It is patently unwise to borrow to stimulate consumption. Nothing is gained through consumption.

One has to distinguish between consumption essential for future production, such as the laborers' food and housing, the raw materials essential for making products, and infrastructure, such as roads and bridges, which allow for the timely movement of products to market, versus consumption that only serves the purpose of self-gratification, such as a luxury home or car.

Public and private-sector programs and policies rarely make such a distinction. Yet the distinction is critical and will markedly impact a nation's productivity, growth, and wealth.

This distinction appears to have been lost in the modern world. Consumerism is the ruler of our behavior. The marked change that has taken place in recent decades is the credit card, which offers unlimited credit irrespective of the purpose of the borrowing. Consumption is simply self-gratification. It is a destructive habit and eventually it must be broken, or we will self-destruct.

There is another twist to consumption that is terribly problematic and poses a threat to the stability of society. This consumption gives rise to the illusion of wealth. This illusion finds its most common expression in the sophomoric drive to impress others. We want to be with it, to be fashionable. It becomes our lifestyle.

Consumption of good food and drink makes life a joy. Attractive clothes mark the woman or man. This is not the consumption I am speaking of; rather, I am speaking of excess. Excess is a form of hypocrisy, a craving for luxury. It results in economic waste.

A society that engages broadly in this type of behavior—widespread self-indulgence—is corrupting itself in the same way as the alcoholic. We lose our sense of balance. The true fruits of our labor are destroyed by this misuse of resources.

Is all luxury wasteful? The answer is yes. The resources so dedicated cannot be used to create incremental wealth. A wasteful society is in the process of destroying its wealth. A wasteful society is in decline. One certain way to embrace decline is to pursue luxury.

## A Conundrum Called Productivity

Economic theory is built around a concept known as productivity. All production requires the input of energy. The ability to produce more with the same amount of energy, that is, labor or its proxy, measures gains in productivity. Productivity is a form of efficiency.

Over the span of time, this has been accomplished in a variety of ways, many the subject of justifiable condemnation. The introduction of slaves into an assembly line will clearly enhance productivity, but only at a huge human cost.

The thrust of Karl Marx's *Das Kapital* addressed the misuse of labor by threat, intimidation, and deceit, resulting in greater profitability for the capitalists at the expense of the laborers. The compensation that labor received for the product produced greatly underestimated the value of the contribution, he argued.

We recognize that advances in science, invention, and machinery have greatly increased the global product, particularly since the beginning of the industrial revolution. Labor with the assistance of modern tools is light-years more productive than in centuries past. That fact is not in dispute. However, major breakthroughs that enhance productivity, such as the invention of electricity, the internal combustion engine, and computers, come at a price. That price is the displacement of labor. Put simply, one needs fewer workers to achieve the same production goals. Hence labor is devalued.

No one decries advances in technology, but all advances in technology, almost by definition, serve to reduce the value of labor. Labor must now work longer hours or seek alternative employment to receive the same income.

Technological advancement squeezes labor. However, there is an offset. Labor stands to gain as the unit price of goods falls. As the laborer's cost of living falls, his or her standard of living rises, but only if he or she is able to find alternative work to match his or her skills in order to produce the same income.

Failing this, his or her standard of living falls as his or her capacity to purchase falls. The Achilles heel of modern-day globalization rests here. Technological advance and the transfer of production to low-cost states mean that the labor of the advanced states is no longer in demand. Thus their gross product and wealth decline.

A considerable effort has been made to disguise this. Labor has been given the opportunity, through intermediaries, including governmental policy, of taking on debt as a substitute for loss of income.

China, the principal beneficiary of the transfer of production, has seen to it that American citizens have this debt funded. However in the long run, the consumer and his or her proxy, the government, will not be able to pay down the debt, due to declining revenue.

## Currency and Consumption

As the gross debt of a nation rises relative to the gross product, what is the impact on the value of currency?

The value of currency must reflect this decline; otherwise the currency is no longer a representation of value.

This adjustment has yet to take place in the United States and other nations. It is simply a matter of time before it does. When that day comes, barring some global transformative invention or dramatic decline in the cost of energy, the world's standard of living will markedly change for the worse.

Where does the blame lie? There are many candidates, including irresponsible trade policies, the breakdown in fiscal restraint, the encouragement of leverage, the ease with which consumers are able to obtain credit, consumption for the sake of consumption, governmental failure, and war, to name but a few. In one way or another, all deny the need for balance.

Much of the progress we believe we have made in recent decades is unfortunately illusory.

# SELECTED BIBLIOGRAPHY

Acton, John E. Letter from John Emerich Edward Dalberg Acton, First Baron Acton, to Bishop Mandell Creighton. 1887. Available at www.phrases.org.uk, n.p.

Adenauer, Konrad. Letter from Konrad Adenauer to Robert Schuman, dated July 26, 1949). Available at www.cvce.eu/content/publication/1999/2/2/.../publishable_en.pdf, n.p.

Allied Plans for Germany After World War II

Angell, Norman. *The Story of Money*. New York: Frederick A. Stokes, 1929.

Barnes, Donald G. *A History of English Corn Laws from 1660–1846*. Oxon: Routledge, 2006.

Barrett, David. *Life, Liberty, and the Pursuit of Money*.

Brands, H. W. *Andrew Jackson, His Life and Times*. New York: Doubleday, 2005.

Bryan, William J. 1896 Address to Democratic Convention, Chicago Coliseum, July 9, 1896.

Challis, Christopher Edgar. *A New History of the Royal Mint*. Cambridge: Cambridge UP, 1992.

Clampitt, Cynthia. *Sailing for India*. Glenview, IL: Pearson/Scott Foresman, 2005.

Edie, Lionel Danforth, *Principles of the New Economics*, Ulan Press, 1922

Encyclopaedia Britannica, *Bank War, United States History*

Englund, Steven. *Napoleon: A Political Life*. New York: Scribner, 2004.

Goodwin, Doris Kearns. *Team of Rivals: The Political Genius of Abraham Lincoln*. New York: Simon & Schuster, 2005.

Gove, Philip Babcock. "Mercantilism.", 1961.

Holmes, George. *The Oxford History of Medieval Europe*. Oxford: Oxford UP, 1992.

*The Holy Bible. Revised Standard Version Containing the Old and New Testaments,*. Book of Micah 5:2. New York: T. Nelson, 1952.

Isaacson, Walter. *Benjamin Franklin: An American Life*. New York: Simon & Schuster, 2003.

Isaacson, Walter. *Einstein: His Life and Universe*. New York: Simon & Schuster, 2007.

Jefferson, Thomas. First Inaugural Address, at 1801 Presidential Inauguration, Washington, D. C., Mar. 4, 1801.

Kagan, Frederick W. *The End of the Old Order: Napoleon and Europe, 1801–1805*. Cambridge, MA: Da Capo, 2006.

Ketcham, Ralph. *James Madison: A Biography*. Charlottesville [v.a.: University of Virginia, 1990.

Newton, Isaac. "Representations on the Subject of Money." Blackmask.com. *Blackmask Online*, 2002. <http://www.blackmask.com>.

Newton, Isaac. "State of the Gold and Silver Coin, 25 September, 1717, Sir Isaac Newton." *Pierre-marteau.com/...25.../report*. Augustus Kelley Publishers, 1967. <www.pierre-marteau.com>.Parks, Tim. *Medici*

*Money: Banking, Metaphysics, and Art in Fifteenth-century Florence.* New York: W. W. Norton & Company, 2005.

Peragallo, Edward. *Origin and Evolution of Double Entry Bookkeeping; A Study of Italian Practice from the Fourteenth Century.* New York: American Institute Pub., 1938.

Randall, Willard Sterne. *Thomas Jefferson: A Life.* New York: H. Holt, 1993.

Roosevelt, Franklin D. Fireside Chat, WGBH American Experience/ PBS, May 7, 1933

Roosevelt, Franklin D. Inaugural Address, Washington, D.C., Mar. 4, 1933.

Rosen, Elliot A. *Roosevelt, the Great Depression, and the Economics of Recovery.* Charlottesville, VA: University of Virginia, 2005.

Saint-Etienne, Christian. *The Great Depression, 1929–1938: Lessons for the 1980s.* Stanford, CA: Hoover Institution, 1984.

Santayana, George, *Reason in Common Sense,* Prometheus Books, Amherst, New York, 1998

Shakespeare, William. *Julius Caesar.* Act 1 Scene 2 Line 135. New York: E. P. Dutton &, 1935.

Shaw, Wm. A. *Money, Currency Question.* London, 1950

Shaw, Wm. A. *Select Tracts and Documents Illustrative of English Monetary History: 1626–1730.* London: Frank Cass, 1967.

Shlaes, Amity. *The Forgotten Man: A New History of the Great Depression.* New York: HarperCollins, 2007.

Thomas, Helen. *Front Row at the White House: My Life and Times*. New York: Simon & Schuster, 2000.

Ward, Barbara, The Rich Nations and the Poor Nations, Canadian Broadcasting Corporation, 1961.

Watkins, T.H., *The Great Depression: America in the 1930's*, New York: Little, Brown and Company, 1993.

Weir, Alison. *Henry VIII: The King and His Court*. New York: Ballantine, 2001.

Wells, H. G., Raymond Postgate, and G. P. Wells. *The Outline of History, Being a Plain History of Life and Mankind,*. Garden City, NY: Doubleday, 1971.

# NOTES

i Clampitt, *Sailing for India*, 2.

ii Ibid., 3.

iii Wells, Postgate, and Wells, *The Outline of History*, 97.

iv Angell, *The Story of Money*, 36.

v Holmes, *Oxford History*, 6.

vi Ibid.

vii Ibid.

viii Ibid., 7.

ix Ibid.

x Ibid., 11.

xi Ibid.

xii Ibid.

xiii Ibid., 97.

xiv Ibid., 60.

xv Ibid.

xvi Ibid., 104.

xvii    Ibid., 108.

xviii   Ibid., 107.

xix     Ibid., 67.

xx      Ibid., 124.

xxi     Ibid., 115.

xxii    Ibid., 119.

xxiii   Ibid., 120–121.

xxiv    Ibid., 121.

xxv     Ibid., 122–123.

xxvi    Holmes, *The Oxford History of Medieval Europe*

xxvii   Parks, *Medici Money*, 10.

xxviii  Ibid., 124–125.

xxix    Ibid., 132.

xxx     Ibid., 133.

xxxi    Ibid., 135.

xxxii   Ibid., 136.

xxxiii  Ibid., 160.

xxxiv   Weir, *Henry VIII*, 384.

xxxv    Ibid., 385.

xxxvi   Parks, *Medici Money*, 5.

xxxvii  Angell, *The Story of Money*, 179.

xxxviii Roosevelt, Inaugural Address.

xxxix   Challis, *New History*, 66.

xl      Ibid., 93.

xli     Ibid., 99.

xlii    Ibid., 84.

xliii   Ibid., 148.

xliv    Ibid., 92.

xlv     Ibid.

xlvi    Ibid., 93.

xlvii   Newton, "Representations on the Subject of Money."

xlviii  Newton, "State of the Gold and Silver Coin."

xlix    Ibid.

l       Shaw, Preface.

li    Randall, *Thomas Jefferson*, 68, 69.

lii   Ibid., 69–70.

liii  Ibid., 343.

liv   Isaacson, *Benjamin Franklin*, 415.

lv    Ibid.

lvi   Ibid.

lvii  Ibid.

lviii Kagan, *End of the Old Order*, 225.

lix   Englund, *Napoleon*, 323.

lx    Ibid.

lxi   Bamber Gascoigne, "History of Money," *HistoryWorld—History and Timelines*, N.p., 2001, Aug. 4, 2012, <http://www.historyworld.net/>.

lxii  Barnes, *History of English Corn Laws*, 164.

lxiii Ibid., 203.

lxiv  Angell, *The Story of Money*, 76, 77.

lxv   Barnes, *History of English Corn Laws*, 251.

lxvi  Ibid.

lxvii    Ibid., 252.

lxviii   Ibid., 253.

lxix     Ibid., 254.

lxx      Ibid.

lxxi     Ibid., 257.

lxxii    Ketcham, *James Madison*, 116.

lxxiii   Ibid., 131.

lxxiv    Angell, *The Story of Money*, 275.

lxxv     Ibid., 276.

lxxvi    Ibid., 107.

lxxvii   Randall, *Thomas Jefferson*, 361.

lxxviii  Ibid., 301.

lxxix    Ibid., 385.

lxxx     Ibid., 500.

lxxxi    Ibid., 504.

lxxxii   Jefferson, First Inaugural Address.

lxxxiii  Ketcham, *James Madison*, 319–320.

lxxxiv   Ibid., 322.

lxxxv   Ibid., 350.

lxxxvi   Ibid., 358.

lxxxvii   Ibid., 635.

lxxxviii   Brands, *Andrew Jackson*, 29.

lxxxix   Ibid., 97.

xc   Ibid., 465.

xci   Ibid., 554.

xcii   Angell, *The Story of Money*, 286.

xciii   Ibid., 286–287.

xciv   Ibid., 287.

xcv   Ibid., 291.

xcvi   Goodwin, *Team of Rivals*, 402.

xcvii   Ibid., 403.

xcviii   Angell, *The Story of Money*, 293.

xcix   Ibid., 293, 294.

c   Ibid., 294.

ci    Ibid.

cii   Ibid., 295.

ciii  Bryan, "1896 Address."

civ   Angell, *The Story of Money*, 348.

cv    Ibid.

cvi   Saint-Etienne, *The Great Depression*, 6.

cvii  Ibid., 7.

cviii Acton, "Letter from John Emerich."

cix   Thomas, *Front Row at the White House: My Life and Times*

cx    Watkins, *The Great Depression: America in the 1930's*, 44

cxi   Saint-Etienne, *The Great Depression*, 36.

cxii  Roosevelt Fireside Chat, May 7, 1933

cxiii Shlaes, *The Forgotten Man*, 270.

cxiv  Ward, The Rich Nations and the Poor Nations

cxv   Rosen, *Roosevelt, the Great Depression*, 37.

cxvi  Shlaes, *The Forgotten Man*, 148.

cxvii data.worldbank.org, *IMF Data*

cxviii   Micah, *The Holy Bible*, 5:2.

cxix   Isaacson, Einstein, 483.

cxx   02varvara.wordpress.com, *Voices from Russia*

cxxi   Organisation for Economic Co-operation and Development, N.p., n.d, Accessed Aug. 8, 2012, <http://www.oecd.org/>.

cxxii   Adenauer, "Letter from Konrad Adenauer."

cxxiii   Allied Plans for Germany After World War II This entry isn't in the bibliography; full details need to be put there, and corrections made here to reflect the proper author/shortened title info.

cxxiv   Barrett, *Life, Liberty, and the Pursuit of Money*, 257.

cxxv   Isaacson, 24.

cxxvi   Officer, Lawrence H., "Exchange Rates Between the United States Dollar and Forty-one currencies," MeasuringWorth, 2015, URL: http://www.measuringworth.com/exchangeglobal/ This entry isn't in the bibliography; full details need to be put there, and corrections made here to reflect the proper author/shortened title info.

cxxvii   International Monetary Fund, "Fact Sheet—Special Drawing Rights (SDRs)," International Monetary Fund Home Page, Mar. 30, 2012, Aug. 5, 2012, <http://www.imf.org/external/index.htm>. Per *CMoS* 14.245, since this is original content on the Internet, the details should appear here in the notes rather than in the bibliography. I tried to provide the information requested in CMoS (as I quoted to you in the comments for Notes), but I can't tell the difference between the two dates you listed. Please identify the dates and list only the appropriate one.

cxxviii   Shakespeare, *Julius Caesar*, Volume 1, Act 2, Scene135. Please put the proper citation in terms of Act x, Scene x.

cxxix   Santayana, Reason in Common Sense, 284, Volume 1 of The Life of Reason.

cxxx   Peragallo, *Origin and Evolution*, 1, 54 144. How do these page numbers relate to the source? Are they separate page numbers and should therefore have spaces after each comma?

cxxxi   TreasuryDirect, U. S. Department of the Treasury Bureau of the Public Debt, n.d., Accessed Aug. 5, 2012, <http: www.treasurydirect.gov/>.

cxxxii   Isaacson, 385

cxxxiii   Shakespeare, William. *Julius Caesar*. Vol. 1, Scene 2. Act 140

Addendum Notes
cxxxiv   Wyatt and O'Donnell, Aware in South Carolina, 208

cxxxv   Wyatt and O'Donnell, Aware in South Carolina, 209, 215, 216, 219

cxxxvi   Wyatt and O'Donnell, Aware in South Carolina, 215

cxxxvii   Ibid

cxxxviii   Ibid 212

cxxxix    Ibid 216

cxl    Ibid

cxli    Ibid 217

cxlii    Ibid 219

cxliii    The Book of Ecclesiastes, 1.1,1.2

# INDEX

## A

Abraham, 1
acceptances, global, 185, 357
accumulating bancors, 288
Acheson, 303
Acheson, Dean, 303
Act, Sherman, 200
Act of Dissolution, 38
Acton, 428
Adams, John, 122, 143
Adenauer, 309, 428
Adenauer's leadership Germany, 323
Afghanistan, invading, 366
Africa, 79, 252, 302
African Americans, 117
Agricultural Adjustment Act, 265, 271
Agricultural Adjustment Administration, 265
Agricultural Subsidies, 354
aide Harry Hopkins, 257
AIG Insurance, 163
Alaric, 5
alchemy, 59
Aldrich Commission, 201
Alger Hiss, 257, 305
allied forces, 298
allied occupation forces, 309
Allies, victorious, 189
allies colonial, 81
Ambassador Benjamin Franklin, 86

America, 1, 21, 34, 38, 58–60, 63, 72, 78–79, 85–86, 105, 107, 110, 112–13, 119–20, 122–28, 130, 132, 134, 136–37, 139–40, 144, 146–48, 157, 165, 167–68, 175, 191, 195–96, 198–99, 201, 208, 213, 222–24, 241–42, 252, 259, 276, 278–80, 294–95, 297, 300–303, 314, 316, 321–22, 331, 338–42, 346, 350, 352–57, 359–61, 366–67, 369–70, 373, 376–77, 379, 394
America and American ideals, 368
America demobilizing, 305
America independence, 133
American bankers, 217, 318, 366
American cigarettes, 311
American colonies, 81, 130
American debt surges, 356
American independence, 86, 139–40
American Indian, 11
American Institute Pub, 430
American money center banks, 244, 317
American naïveté, 186
American neutral trading rights, 130
American occupation forces, 321
American Relief Administration, 213
American representative Harry Dexter White, 284

*495*

American Revolution, 79, 81,
    83–84, 86, 91, 101, 107–8,
    124, 139–40, 376
America's gold reserves dwindle, 353
Andrew Jackson Incarnate, 367
Andrew Mellon's argument, 250
Angell
Anglican Church, 114, 121
Anglican religion, 115
Anglophile, 219, 229
anschulss, 182
anti-Semitism, 31, 52
Antoinette, Marie, 84
appraisal process, 408
Aquitaine, 70
Arab forces, 25
Arabian desert, 42
Arabian Peninsula, 25
Arab Muslims, 28
Arabs, 3, 5, 48
Arab traders, 5
Aragon, 34, 36
Argentina, 94, 280, 417
Argentine peso, 349
Aristotle, 391
Aristotle Onassis, late, 146
Armistice, 213, 308
Army PX, 311
Arthur, King, 305
Articles of Agreement, 294
Asia, 29, 33, 76, 158, 206, 236, 289,
    295, 300, 330, 341, 355, 361
Asia Minor, 23

Asians, 367
Asia silks, 91
assets, riskless, 340
assurances, implicit Chinese, 376
atom bomb, 272, 315
atomic secrets, 257
atomic weapons, 297
Attila, 304
Attlee, Clement, 335
Augustus, 14
Austria, 87, 104–5, 176–79, 191, 217
Austrian, 87, 177, 179
Austrian bank, largest, 221
Austrian Emperor, 177, 179
Austrian interests, 179
Austrian wife, despised, 125
Austro-Hungarian Empire, 209
Austro-Prussian war, 179
awaited Jackson, 148

**B**

balance of payments, 19, 106, 284,
    293, 309, 330, 336, 339–40,
    348, 356
Balance of Payments and
    Repercussions, 72
balance of payments problem, 19, 65,
    68, 72, 166
Baldwin, Stanley, 224
bancor, 284–85, 287, 293
Bancors, 284, 287
Bank Act, 111
Bank Charter Act and Germany, 20

bankers acceptances, 28, 244
bankers panic, 201
Banking Act, 256
Bank of England, 103, 228
Bank of England bills, 93
Bank of England notes, 103
Bank Restriction Act, 90–91
bank's charter expires, 138
barbarian czar, 295
Barrett, 428
barter, 6, 12–13, 283, 310, 324, 326
Bastille, 79
Battle of Hastings, 69
Battle of New Orleans, 140
Battle of Trafalgar, 88
Bavaria, 180, 184
BC Rome, 14
Beethoven, 279
beggar thy neighbor policies, 101, 290
Beleaguered Jewish Community, 51
Belgium, 105, 211, 213, 217, 314
Belisarius, 23
Bentley, Elizabeth, 282
Benton, Thomas, 152
Berlin, 102, 308, 328–29
blockading, 329
Berlin Airlift, 308
Berlin blockade, 328
Berlin occupation zones, 308
Bethlehem Ephrathah, 281
Bible, 121
Biddle, 144, 147, 150–56, 161, 168, 203

Biddle, Francis, 144, 147, 209
Biddle-Jackson, 144
Biddle legislation renewing, 227
Biddle's bank, 155, 163–64
Big-City Politician, 252
bills
notorious Smoot-Hawley tariff, 241
silver certificate, 235
bimetallic, 191–92
Bishop of Rome, 24
Bismarck, 4, 179–81, 183–86
convulsed, 182
Bismarck's intention, 181
Black Death, 33
Bland-Allison Act, 200
blockade, 211, 329
Bolsheviks, 177, 212, 286
Bolshevism, 304
Boulder Dam, 239
Bretton Woods, 274, 281–82, 303, 312, 317, 320, 330–31, 333, 339, 342, 346, 350–51, 353, 355, 361, 377–78
Bretton Woods Agreement, 292, 342
Bretton Woods Conference, 227, 283
Bretton Woods Era, 281
Bretton Woods system, 371
Brezhnev, 367
Britain, 81, 84, 87–88, 90–91, 93–95, 99, 101, 113, 115, 118–19, 123, 126–27, 133–35, 139–41, 143, 148, 167, 181–82, 186, 190, 213, 215, 220–21, 224–26, 229–32,

*497*

237, 283, 286, 289–90, 297, 308, 313, 315, 329–30, 332–33, 335, 350, 355, 376, 418
Britain's imposition of taxes, 167
Britain's primacy, 229
British, 85–86, 88, 100, 106, 108–9, 115, 117–19, 122–23, 126, 128, 130, 133, 136, 139–40, 142–44, 181, 224, 226, 228, 230, 276, 286, 289, 292, 321, 333–35, 339, 344, 347
British and French fleets, 81
British Commonwealth, 177, 377
British Dragoons, 142
British embargo, 90
British Empire, great, 184
British financial crisis, 148
British General Cornwallis, 85
British in New Orleans, 157
British king, 122
British Labor Party, 335
British mercantile system, 85
British merchant rights, 133
British mint, 101
British Monarchy, 133
British naval blockade, 213
British paper, 92
British Parliament, 81, 93, 108
British philosopher, 227
British population, 225
British prime minister, 186
British prisoners, 142
British production, 89

British products, 229
British rule, 82
British secret service, 286
British supremacy, 181
British taxes, 122
British trade, 82, 123, 130
British treasury, 99
British underestimated Snyder, 332
British war debt, 225
Brits, 88, 93, 97, 99, 116, 119, 134, 186, 219, 221, 273, 302, 331
Bryan, 200, 428
bubbles, 159, 218, 230, 362–63, 403, 408
Bubble Solutions, 408
bullion, 65, 68, 72, 75, 93, 106–7, 200, 204
bullion content, 65, 67–68
Bundesbank, 359
Bush, 118, 127, 373
Bush, George W., 118
Bush administration, 302
Bushes administrations, 189
business accounting, 371
business cycle, 257
business schools, 364
Byzantine emperors, 23
Byzantine Empire, 20, 29, 34
Byzantine Orthodox Church, 28
Byzantine power, 29
Byzantine Venice, 25
Byzantium, 3, 23, 25, 29, 33, 329
Byzantium Empire, 28

## C

Caesar, 14
Caesar, Julius, 14–15, 21
Calhoun, 141
Calhoun, John C., 148
Canada, 86, 283
Canadian garrisons, 411
capital
capital flow, 288
capital flows, massive, 418
capital flows equalize, 412
capital inflows, 353
Capital Movement Round, 417
capital pool, 419
capital recipient, 418
Capitol of India, 78
Carnegie, Andrew, 207
Carolingian Empire, 26
Carolingian Renaissance, 25
Carter, 366–67
Carter administrations, 365
case Madison, 137
Catholic, 35, 178, 184, 238
Catholic Church, 25, 36, 305
Catholicity, 19, 35, 38
Catholic king, 73
Catholic theology, 36
CCC, 259
central bank, 138, 284
Centralized power, 227
centuries barter, 343
Chancellor Bismarck, 183, 186
Chancellor of Germany, 323

change France, 87
change Germany, 323
Charlemagne, 25–26
Charlemagne's kingdom, 26
Charles de Gaulle, 331
Charles the Hammer, 24
Chase, 167, 169–70, 174
chief delegate Harry Dexter White, 291
Chief Justice John Marshall, 119
China, 5–6, 25, 33, 42, 48, 50, 58, 60, 62, 68, 71, 76, 90–91, 106, 118, 130, 136, 146, 190, 235, 263, 275, 280, 288, 304, 337, 339, 344, 347–52, 373, 375–78, 383, 386, 421
China paper, 48
China relationship, 376
China's currency, 344
China silk, 24
Chinese, 58–60, 90, 96, 165, 377
Chinese goods, 136
Chinese government, 236, 304, 377
Chinese monetary system, 235
Chinese stock of silver, 235
Christian, 3, 26, 31, 53, 112, 246, 430
Christian civilization, 24
Christian Democratic Party, 323, 357
Christianity, 22–24, 26–27, 35, 38, 52–53, 80
Christian philosophy, 41
Christian principles, 279
Christian prohibition, 30, 69

Christians, 26, 28
Churchill, 219–20, 222, 224–25, 228, 251, 296–98, 305, 307, 315, 333
Churchill, Winston, 193, 215, 219, 224, 232, 247, 257, 304, 318, 321, 333
Churchill's defeat, 304
Church land and valuables, 39
Church of England, 35, 38–39
Church property of England, 2
Cicero, 53
circulation
Circulation of capital, 260
City of Antwerp, 52
Civilian Conservation Corps, 259, 265
civilization, Western, 22, 38, 112, 304
Clay, 137, 151, 154, 161
Clay, Henry, 151, 154
Clemenceau, 186
Clement Attlee's party, 333
Clinton, 118, 127, 189, 373
Clinton administration, 376
clipping, 65, 71
coin
Coinage Act, 112, 198
Coin makers, 65
Colm-Dodge-Goldsmith Plan, 326
colonialism, 376, 382
Colonial secession, 107
Colonial trade, 81
Columbus, 188
Commonwealth Nations, 283

communism, 39, 245, 295–97, 307, 315, 329, 353, 368
Communist Empire, 306
Communist forces, authorized, 334
communist goal, 294
communist leanings, 286
communist losses, 330
communist spy, 282
competition, 31, 41, 49, 89, 137, 185, 189, 191, 210, 222, 264, 300, 334, 374, 386
competitive devaluations, 290
complication, 43, 53, 69, 214, 341
Concentration of capital, 362
conditions Germany, 212
Confederacy, 395–96, 398
Confederate currency, 343
Confederate dollars, 395, 398
confederation, 177–80
Confederation of States, 178
Conference
Conference, Paris, 313
conflagration, global, 236, 254
confusion, gold silver, 104
Congress of Vienna, 101, 176–79
Conservative government of Churchill, 331
Constantinople, 3, 20, 23, 28–29, 33–34, 49, 52, 186
crowned jewel, 23
Constitution, 109, 115–18, 123, 131, 134, 144–45, 148, 161, 166, 227, 382

Constitutional Convention, 125
Constitutional Monarchy, 73
consumption curve, 21
consumption expenditures, 397
Consumption extinguishes money, 419
consumption habits, 19
consumption policies, 354
Continental Congress, 109, 124, 126
Continental paper, 110
control, denied Byzantium, 25
control Stalin, 305
conversion schedule, 340
convertibility
Cooke, 169
Cooke, Jay, 169
Coolidge, Calvin, 233, 235
Coolidge administration, 237
Cornwallis, surrounded, 85
corporate tax rate, 267
Cost approach, 407
Cost approach estimates, 407
country
Creator, 1, 39, 56, 114, 131, 193, 208, 226, 236, 249, 388, 391–92
Creditanstalt, 221
credit card mania, 232
Crimea, 52, 296
Critical factors in determining value, 409
Cromwell's control, 40
currency
Currency Act, 119
Currency and military rule, 311

currency bubble, 45, 372
currency expectation, 347, 418
currency failure, 47, 349, 397
currency famine, 41
currency manipulation, 137, 344, 351, 354, 356
currency overvaluation, 274, 343, 349
currency value, 19, 43, 45–46, 77, 95, 99, 222, 274, 276, 288, 290, 303, 309–10, 343, 346–47, 395–96, 412, 418, 422
Czar, great, 304, 329
Czar of Russia and Talleyrand of England, 179

## D

daisy chain, 159, 169, 207
dangerous man, 144
*Das Kapital*, 421
Death struggle, 149
Debasement of currency, 64
debt
debt FDR, 275
debt figures, 399
debt funding, 129
debt instruments, 60–61, 399, 414
Debtor-creditor relations, 353
debt problem, 240, 244
debt ratios, 384
Declaration of Independence, 114, 124, 390
defeating Henry Clay, 156
deficit, fiscal, 274, 303

Definition of money, 392
deflation, 192, 225, 259, 266, 273, 310, 385
demilitarization, 314
de minimis payments, 288
Democrat, Christian, 370
Democratic Convention, 200, 428
Democratic National Convention, 426
Democratic Party, 117, 200, 242, 248, 253, 263, 299
Democratic Senator Daniel Patrick Moynihan, 282
Democrats, 162, 305
Democrats, Christian, 358
Demonetization of silver, 198
denarii, 14–15
denazification, 311
Depreciating currency value, 44
depreciation of currency, 126, 346, 419
depression, 18, 46, 82, 105, 159–61, 171, 197, 199, 208, 223, 227, 235–37, 239, 243, 245, 249–50, 254, 263–64, 266–67, 269, 271, 273, 275, 277, 296–97, 300, 305, 320, 334, 350, 352, 399
depression conditions, 36
depression era, 232, 235
Depression overwhelms, 223
depriving, colonial investments, 212
determined president Francis Biddle, 150
Determining value, 409
Deutsche Bank, 359

Deutsche mark, 327, 352-53, 357, 369
Deutschland Uber Alles, 186
Deutsche mark exchange rate, 330
Deutsche marks, 310–11, 327–29, 351, 359
Deutsche mark valuation, 352
devaluation, 19, 57–58, 67, 71, 100, 214–15, 221, 241, 261–64, 276, 288, 332–33, 335–36, 343–44, 346, 352
devalue, 215, 220, 223, 261–63, 335–36, 342
Dewey, 164
Dickenson, 140
disequilibrium, 45, 99, 254, 398
distant cousin Theodore Roosevelt, 256
District of Columbia, 153
Divine right of kings, 176
Dm, 328, 330, 340
DM conversion rate, 340
DM exchange rate, 340
Doctrine, Monroe, 157, 206
Doctrine, Truman, 319, 330
Domestic exchange rates, 287
Dutch East India Company, 78

**E**

Earlier Truman, 322
East Byzantium, 20
Easter, 51
Easterners, 20
East Germans, 312

East Germany, 311, 314, 329
East India Company, 182
East Indies, 76
easy money policy, 217, 219, 231, 233
Ecclesiastes, 416, 427–28
Economic collapse, 400
Economic cooperation, 320, 427
Economic cycles, 257
economic disequilibrium, 201
Economic downturns, 193, 243, 256
economic implosion, 239
Economics of recovery, 430
Economic theory, 421
economists, classical, 193, 255
economist Adam Smith, 268
economist William Roepke, 309
Economy Act, 278
Edgar, Christopher, 428
Edict of Expulsion, 51–52
Edward, 51–52, 430
Edward I, 51
Einstein, 74, 323, 387, 429
Einstein, Albert, 74
Eisenhower, 340
Eisenhower, Truman's successor Dwight D., 308
Eisenhower presidency, 309
Eleanor, 246, 253
electoral votes, 133
Emperors of Rome, 14
employment, 64, 111, 165, 195, 234, 260, 269, 311, 325, 338, 344, 393, 416

Engel, 358
England, 2, 20, 27, 35–36, 38, 40, 42–43, 49, 51–52, 65, 67–70, 72–79, 81–82, 87–88, 90–91, 96–104, 106–7, 123, 128, 130, 133, 169, 183, 190, 213, 217, 219–20, 228, 255, 257, 301, 308, 314, 334, 380
England bills, 91, 93–94
England's land, 36
England victorious, 81
English Corn Laws, 428
English East India Company, 78
English goods, 90
English monarchs, 73
English moneyers, 65
English philosopher John Locke, 114
Enlightenment philosophy, 79
equilibrium, 20, 31, 44, 47, 96, 137, 228, 274, 284, 343, 347, 362, 371, 379, 389–91, 399, 410, 412, 416
Era, Truman, 294
Erhard plan, 310
Estates General, 83
Eurodollar funding of America, 371
Eurodollar phenomenon, 360
Eurodollar pool, 370
Eurodollars, 361–62, 366, 369–71
Europe
European Crusades, 28
European currencies, 352
European Payments Union, 320
European Recovery Program, 237, 430

Europeans, 79, 113, 151, 309, 314, 318, 336, 338, 341, 353, 356, 367
Europe hyperinflation, 216
exchange, medium of, 9–11, 13, 91, 106–7, 188
exchange rate, 58, 137, 212, 235–36, 277, 284, 288, 292–93, 304, 327, 330, 339–41, 346–49, 351–52, 419, 427
exchange value, 8, 217, 288, 342
excommunication, 2, 24, 32, 40
expansion, economic, 44, 79, 193, 324, 400
Export-Import Bank, 301
Extended depression, 197
extinct species, 388
Extraordinary tax rates, 270

**F**
facilities, productive, 14, 95, 384
factories east, 314
Fair Labor Standards Act, 265
Falkland Islands, 82, 119
famed Herbert Hoover, 235
famed Robert Morris, 124
famed Teddy Roosevelt, 238
Far East, 33, 59, 78, 111, 283
farmers
farms, 1, 9, 107, 142, 216, 258, 264, 324
Farm Security Administration, 265
Fascism and Russia tyrannical communism, 255

FDIC, 256
FDR, 48, 240, 246, 248, 253, 255–57, 259–60, 263–68, 270–72, 277, 281, 289, 295, 299, 316, 377
FDR's analysis, 273
FDR's family, 270
FDR's inauguration Hoover, 258
FDR's mother, 246
FDR's plan, 261
FDR's policies, 266
federal budget, imbalanced, 250
Federal Debt, 97, 138, 333
Federal Deposit Insurance Corporation, 64, 256
Federalist bastion, 156
Federalist merchants, 134
Federalist power, 156
Federalists, 115–18, 130, 133, 135, 143, 147, 202
Federal Republic of Germany, 309, 330, 338
Federal Reserve, 44, 50, 156, 202, 204, 209, 214, 218, 220, 226, 230, 233, 241, 255, 260–61, 271, 325, 353, 361–62, 365–66, 372, 404, 414, 417
Federal Reserve Act, 203, 209
Federal Reserve and Treasury, 317
Federal Reserve Bank, 220
Federal Reserve Bank of New York, 213, 218, 224
Federal Reserve Board, 203, 214, 369

Federal Reserve Board in
    Washington, 227
Federal Reserve Note, 204
Federal Reserve policy, 414
Federal Reserve System, 150
Federal treasury, 165
fiat, 11, 19, 35, 44, 50, 90, 94, 96,
    103, 111, 277, 347
fiat currency world, 92
fiat money system, 372, 413
Final determinant of equivalency, 393
final payment, constituted, 195
final recovery, 277
Finland, 105, 177
Fiorello LaGuardia, 271
First and Second Banks, 149, 153
First Bank, 111, 116, 135, 138,
    143–44, 147
First Baron Acton, 428
First Chancellor of West Germany,
    309
First Inaugural Address, 425, 429
First Duke of Marlborough, 224
First World War, 51, 118, 185–86,
    188–89, 224, 242, 279, 319, 332,
    395, 399, 418
Flynn, 254
FNMA, 416
Ford, 365–66
foreclosure, 51, 264–65
foreign creditors, 43
foreign exchange, generated, 212
Foreign exchange risk, 418

France, 24, 29–30, 34, 68, 72, 79–91,
    93, 101–2, 104, 110, 115, 118–19,
    123–25, 134, 140–41, 143,
    145, 161, 176–77, 179–81, 186,
    190–91, 205–6, 210–11, 217–18,
    221–22, 232, 275, 280, 283, 301,
    308, 313–14, 321, 330, 355, 360,
    376, 380
France devalues, 223
France's defeat, 222
francs, 180, 223
Frankish Empire, 24
Franklin, 86–87, 122, 125, 430
Franklin, Benjamin, 124, 139, 167,
    414, 424–25, 429
Franklin Delano Roosevelt, 81, 118,
    139, 199, 248, 252
Franklin Roosevelt's decision, 63
fraudulent banking practices, 172
freedom-loving peoples, 309
freedom of choice, 63, 390
free market orientation, 309
Freidman, Milton, 276
French, 83, 85–87, 109–10, 125,
    133–34, 139, 144, 181, 186, 212,
    222, 321, 331, 357, 399
French and Indian War, 81, 109, 119
French Assembly, 176
French industrial production, 223
French Parliament, 83
French people, 79, 83, 85, 87, 177, 180
French representative Talleyrand, 177
French Revolution, 125, 175–76, 181

French society, 176
friend Ben Strong, 229
friend Montagu Norman, 229
Fundamental imbalance, 62

G
game, insider's, 359
Gandhi, Indira, 367
GDP, 280, 355
GDP ratio, 280
General Staff George Catlett Marshall, 318
George, Lloyd, 186
George C. Marshall, 303
German and Swiss bankers, 369–70
German and Swiss intermediaries, 369
German assets, 314
German bankers, 359
German banks, 359–60
German banks for deutsche marks, 359
German barbarism, 323
German challenge revisited, 357
German communists, 212
German Confederation, 177–78
German delegation, 210
German Empire, 179, 181–82
German Federal Republic, 308
German financial structure, 322
German hegemony, 359
German industry, heavy, 306
German marks, 361
German miracle, 352

German nation, 175–76, 309, 311
German people, 211–12, 222, 275, 310–13, 315, 323–24, 326, 399
German perspective, 366
German Reich, 349
German reparation payments, 320
German reparations, 275
German Republic, 329
Germans, 29, 183, 192, 209–12, 214, 217–19, 222, 234, 257, 283, 306, 308–14, 318, 323–24, 326–27, 330, 338, 349, 352, 357, 360, 366, 369
German States, 87, 175, 179, 181–83, 198
German surrender, 304, 311
German unification, 198
German Union, true, 183
Germany, 46, 72, 105, 123, 177, 181–87, 189–91, 195, 205–6, 209–14, 216–18, 221–22, 234, 237, 241, 255, 264, 275, 279, 283, 286, 296, 298, 302, 304, 306, 308–16, 318–19, 321–24, 326–28, 330–31, 337–40, 343, 349, 351, 353, 356–60, 366, 369, 395, 399, 427
Germany and German citizens, 275
Germany post World War II, 46
Germany's borders, 306
Germany was spiritually broken, 323
GI Bill, 300
Glass-Steagall Act, 258

Global currency reform, 381
Global economic expansionism, 206
Glorious Revolution, 73
God
    nature and nature, 22, 114, 232
    nature and natures, 390, 417
gold bullion, 188, 196
gold coins, 1, 6, 97, 119–20, 211
golden calf, 17, 105, 112, 199
gold exchange, 44, 170, 262
gold-greenback, 198
gold market, 197
goldmarks, 210, 212, 313, 349
gold monometallism, 77
gold ratio, 77, 192
Gold Reserve ct, 273
gold reserves, 93, 204, 215, 221, 352
Gold Resolution Act, 273
goldsmiths, 41, 47–49, 61, 65, 394
Gold Standard Act, 209
Gold Standard for Europe and America, 183
goodness Jefferson, 1
goods
Gould, Jay, 197
government, federal, 61, 116, 129, 134, 150, 161, 165, 180, 239, 265, 362
Governor of New York, 237, 245, 252, 258
Great Britain, 84, 86–88, 91, 94, 99–100, 103, 106, 113, 115, 136, 143, 181, 184–86, 211, 214–15, 219–21, 224, 228–29, 231, 234, 247, 283, 291, 295, 313, 331, 335, 350, 352, 360, 379, 418
Great Britain and France, 86
Great Depression, 75, 193, 196, 209, 212, 222, 225, 229, 235, 249, 251, 275, 279, 282, 290, 292, 312, 335, 380, 395, 402–4, 413, 430
Great Newton, 74
Great Society, 354, 356
Greece, 52, 94, 319, 330, 397
Greek state Sparta, 182
greenbacks, 171, 192, 196–98
Greenspan, Alan, 373
Gregory VII, 28
Gresham's law, 2, 12, 15, 19, 164
gross domestic product, 256, 280, 397, 399
Gross domestic product statistics, 281
gross national product, 68, 232, 243, 245, 262, 324
gross product, 44–45, 421–22

# H

Hague, Frank, 37
Hamilton, 110–11, 113, 115–16, 118, 125, 127–31, 135, 143, 147, 149, 203
Hamilton, Alexander, 113, 191, 198
Hamilton America, 128
Hamilton Plan, 111, 126, 198
Hamilton's Federalist, 129
Hamilton's proposal, 129

happiness, 112, 114, 120–21, 124, 131, 332
Harbor, Pearl, 58, 64, 272, 278–79
Harry, 297, 299, 307, 332–33
Harry Dexter White, 282, 312, 333
Harry S. Truman, 298, 303
Hawley Smoot Tariff Act, 232
Helmut Kohl, 370
Helmut Schmidt, 368
Henry, 2, 35–40, 42, 66, 70, 73, 137
Henry I, 66
Henry II, 70
Henry II consolidates, 70
Henry's treachery, 40
Henry VIII, 2–3, 35–36, 73, 78, 80–81, 101, 430
heritage, superior Prussian, 399
Herr Helmut Schmidt, 366
Hiss, 282
history, the most unsordid act in, 321
History of English Corn Laws, 428
History of gold, 47
Hitler, 51, 58, 88, 211, 217, 234, 271, 275, 279, 304, 306, 310, 315, 323, 335, 349
Hitler, Adolph, 279
Hitler era in Germany, 51
Holy Land, 30, 53
Holy Roman Empire, 175–76
Hoover, 193, 231, 237–38, 240, 242–45, 253, 258, 266–67, 279, 319, 430

Hoover, Herbert, 48, 213, 231, 236, 253
Hoover's confidence, 244
Hoover signs, 241
Hopkins, Harry, 305
House of Burgesses, 122
House of Plantagenet, 70
Hurricane Katrina, 302
hyperinflation, 212, 216–17

I
ICU, 285, 287, 290
illiquidity, 204, 284
illusion, 14, 45, 59, 215, 271, 281, 297, 420
IMF, 280, 283, 285–86, 292, 294, 307, 354, 357, 385–86, 428
IMF members, 356
Inaugural address, 246, 250, 258–59, 424, 430
inauguration, 368
including Franklin Delano Roosevelt, 283
including Henry Clay, 150
including Jackson, 117
including Madison, 129
including Truman, 294, 301
income, disposable, 214, 234, 263–64
income taxes, corporate, 270
independence, 8, 86, 100, 110, 114–15, 124, 135–36, 139, 249, 379, 390
India, 21, 24–25, 55, 78, 91, 181, 186–87, 191, 336–37, 348, 428

Indian trade, 106
Indo-China, 331
industry, insulated fledgling France, 89
Infinite consumption, 270
influence, balance Strong's, 233
influence Jackson, 153
institutions, owed American, 213
interest rate department, 414
interests
interference, resented British, 122
Internal economic weakness, 20
International Bank for Reconstruction and Development, 281, 292
internationalist, 118, 136
International Monetary Fund, 281, 283, 292, 298, 342, 353, 385, 428
International settlements, 320
International Stabilization Fund, 285
intrinsic value, 16, 67, 159–60, 395, 404, 411–12
invade South Korea, 334
invention, 21, 41, 43, 45, 56, 65, 84, 101, 135, 145–46, 172, 191, 209, 243, 268–69, 288, 392, 405, 407, 419, 421
IOUs security, 60
Iran, 319
Iranians, 368
Iraq, 186, 337, 375, 399
IRS, 270
Islam, 24–25
Italian bankers, 41, 49

Italian city-states, 28
Italians, 28–29, 49
Italian states, 3, 24, 33–34, 42, 49, 78
Italy, 25, 28–29, 34, 87, 176, 217, 255, 308, 319, 321, 330
Italy, Switzerland, and France, 105
Iwo Jima, 318, 364

## J

Jackson, 117–18, 139–42, 144–45, 147–51, 153–59, 200, 203, 227, 249, 252, 298, 351
Jackson, Andrew, 117, 138–39, 144, 153, 156, 199, 227, 367, 428
Jackson bête noir, 202
Jackson era, 127, 139, 156
Jackson-era notes, 159
Jacksonian, 250
Jacksonian policies, 158
Jackson legacy, 161
Jackson orders, 156
Jackson's America, 152
Jackson's legacy, 158
Jackson's time, 158
Jackson's vice president, 141
Jackson's victory, 140
Jackson veto, 154
Jackson victory, 157
Japan, 60, 68, 76, 105, 280, 298, 300–301, 304, 308–9, 340–41, 356, 366, 383
Japanese bombed Pearl Harbor, 278
JCS, 314, 322–23

Jefferson, 22, 85, 111, 113–18, 121–36, 139, 141, 144, 147, 149, 200, 203, 298, 351, 429
Jefferson, Thomas, 22, 113, 131, 390, 417, 429–30
Jefferson, William, 118
Jefferson era, 137
Jefferson Hamilton Divide, 127
Jeffersonian freedom, 132
Jeffersonian idealist, 147
Jeffersonian internationalist, 118
Jeffersonian policies, 118
Jeffersonians, 111, 117–18, 132, 141, 143–47, 246, 367
Jeffersonian tendencies, 118
Jeffersonian thinking, 285
Jefferson's job, 129
Jefferson's philosophy, 120, 124
Jerusalem, 28, 416
Jewish bankers, 49, 53
Jewish community, 31, 50–51, 53, 69
Jewish participation, 53
Jews, 3, 30, 34, 51–52, 212, 399
John C. Calhoun, 141, 147
John Maynard Keynes, 170, 193, 274, 284, 377, 419
John Quincy Adams, 141
Johnson, Lyndon, 341
John Wesley Snyder, 303
J. P. Morgan, 201, 219
Junkers, 178–79
Justinian, 23

**K**

Keynes, 193–94, 214, 223, 237, 283–86, 288, 290–94, 303, 353
Keynes, Maynard, 237, 250, 284, 378
Keynes and White plans, 285
Keynes Plan, 284–87, 289–92
Kim II Sung, 308
King George III, 121, 124
King of England, 49, 123
King of England and Ireland, 35
King of France, 125
King of Prussia, 180
Knickerbocker Trust Company, 201
Konrad Adenauer, 309, 322–23, 427–28
Kreditanstalt Bank, 244
Kubla Khan in China, 50

**L**

Labor government of Britain set, 334
laborites, 334
Labor Party, 331–33, 335
Labor Party of Great Britain, 333
land boom, 156
land loans, 156
Large holders of Reichs marks, 327
Latin Monetary Union, 104
Latins, 23, 29, 52
leaders, known New York City Democratic, 237
Lenin, 237, 335
Lifeline stretching to modernity, 246
life Rachel, 142

Lincoln, 65, 117–18, 138–39, 141, 147, 162, 164, 166–67, 174, 249, 252, 298
Lincoln, Abraham, 429
Lincoln Treasury, 168
liquidity, 44, 57, 153–55, 170, 191–92, 195, 201, 204, 221, 230, 241, 276, 324–26, 404
liquidity crisis, 201
liquidity pressures, 201
liquidity spigot, 404
liquidity squeeze, 261
loans
local moneyers days, 66
Locke, 79, 83
Locke, John, 134
London, 42, 68, 74, 86, 93, 104, 106, 122–23, 128, 182, 184–86, 199, 218, 223–26, 241, 273, 317, 331, 376, 379, 382, 394, 430
London Economic Conference, 272
Lord Acton, 227
Lord John Maynard Keynes, 225, 342
Louis, 79, 81, 83–84
Louisiana Territory, 89, 133, 143
Louis XVI, 84–85, 89
Lucky Strikes, 324
Ludwig Erhard, 309–10

# M

Madison, 111, 113–16, 118, 122, 125, 129–30, 134–37, 139, 141, 143, 147, 149, 200, 351

Madison, James, 110, 113, 133, 429
Madison's attention in Philadelphia, 110
Madison's proposal, 129
Malthus, 268
Manhattan Island, 11
Mao, 308, 335, 367
communist tyrant, 91
Maoists, 394
market
market speculation, 239
market speculators, 152, 197, 202, 375
market value, 137, 414
marks, paper German, 343
Marshall, 303, 321
Marshall, John, 117
Marshall Foundation, George C., 429
Marshall Plan, 295, 302–3, 306–7, 318–22, 328, 330, 339, 429–30
Marshall support, 321
Martel, Charles, 24
Marx, 358
Marx, Karl, 421
Marxist Doctrine, 329
Massachusetts, 108, 122
Matter of nullification, 145
Mayor of New York, 271
McKinley, 202
McKinley, William, 199
M-C-M1, 268
Medicaid, 354
Medicare, 354
Medici Money, 429

Mellon, 270
Mellon, Andrew, 238, 270
mercantilism, 106, 126–27, 135,
    375–76, 427, 429
Messer's Roepke and Erhard, 310
metal, shiny, 4, 9
metal coin, 112
metal content, 67
metal scarce, 106
Metternich, 4, 177, 179
Micah, 281, 427, 429
Middle Ages, 5, 9, 22, 24, 42,
    47–48, 50, 53, 78, 205
militarism, 82, 182, 279
military
military currency, 312, 322
Military rule, 311
military threat, 323, 368
Miller, William, 366
Million-dollar wedding, 227
mines, 14–16, 41, 68, 89, 306, 394
Mint and Coinage Act, 112
mint coin, 67
minters, 67, 74
minting, 65, 91, 112
Mint rates, 75
misguided monetary policies, 189
misread Truman, 334
moderate tariff Madison, 137
Molotov, 297
Moltke, 181
Moltke, Von, 179
monasteries, 26–27, 32, 36, 38

Mondale, Walter, 168
monetary gold, world's, 282, 377
monetary gold reserves, 223
monetary system, international, 188,
    275, 286, 353, 384
monetary terms, 103, 279, 411
money
money changers, 48, 66, 71
moneyers, 65–67, 70–71
money-grubbers, 409
money-grubbers' reason, 269
money supply, 19, 41, 44, 46, 57,
    63–64, 69, 71, 77–78, 93, 98, 103,
    105, 158, 160, 188, 192, 198–200,
    205, 207, 215–16, 222, 224–25,
    233, 241, 254–56, 260–61, 266,
    271, 275, 277, 324, 327, 353, 357,
    361, 365–66, 369–70, 372
Money usage in Rome, 14
Mongols, 3, 29, 50, 304, 329
Monsieur Poincaré, 222
Montagu, Charles, 75, 222, 225-26
Montagu Norman, 218, 219, 224-25
Montesquieu, 166
Morgenthau, 315
Morgenthau, 283–84, 286
Morgenthau, Henry, 267, 270,
    282, 333
Morgenthau Plan, 314, 322
Morris, Robert, 110–11
Moscow, 78, 90, 312, 319–20, 358
Moses, 1, 189
Muslim invaders, 28

Muslim invasion, 33
Muslims, 24, 28, 34
Muslim's expansionist goals, 24

# N
name Hooverville, 243
Napoleon, 4, 80, 82, 87–91, 93, 95, 97, 104, 133, 143, 148, 176, 185, 295, 428–29
Napoleonic crisis, 103
Napoleonic era, 90
Napoleonic invasion, 379
Napoleonic Wars, 90, 99, 169, 179, 219
Napoleon's ability, 88
Napoleon's armée, 181
Napoleon's army, 90
Napoleon's Continent, 148
Napoleon's control, 134
Napoleon's sphere of influence, 89
Napoleon's tenure, 87
Napoleon's victories, 90
national bank, 116, 125, 131, 133–35, 146, 152, 161, 174–75, 204
National Bank Act, 174
National bankruptcy, 82
national debt, 84, 128–29, 262, 402, 417
National Industrial Recovery Act, 265
nationalism, 39, 80, 90, 290, 357
National Industrial Recovery Act, 271
National Socialist German Workers Party, 312

nations
Native Americans, 415
NATO, 319–20, 330, 358
Nazi doctrine, 309
Nazi era, 309, 327
Nazi Party, 309, 312
Nazi prisons, 309
Nazi regime, 324
Nazis, 177, 309, 311, 320, 323
Nazi tyranny, 297
Nelson, 428–29
New banks aplenty, 155
New Deal, 48, 241, 251, 253, 263, 277–79, 283, 299, 305
New England states, 108, 156
New Germany, 182–83
New Hampshire, 274, 281–82, 339
New Orleans, 139–40
Newton, 74–77, 184, 221, 424, 429
Newton, Isaac, 78, 101
Newton solution, 77
New York and London, 207
New York banks, 213
New York Democrats, 254
New York Stock Exchange, 348
Nixon, 342, 356, 365–66
Nixon, Richard, 277, 365
Nixon experiment, 394
Norris LaGuardia Act, 238
North Atlantic Treaty Organization, 308, 319

North German Confederation, 179–80
North Korea, 308, 340
notes, goldsmith, 48
notorious Josef Stalin, 315
NRA, 265
Nullification, 145
nullifiers, 156

**O**

occupation, 9, 122, 181, 306–7, 311–12, 352, 355
occupation zones, 306–8, 312
Occupying France, 210
O'Donnell, 427, 430
OECD, 320
OEEC, 320
Ogden Mills, 238, 243
Ohio icicle, 18
oil prices, 370
oil supply, world's, 374
Onassis, 146, 317
OPEC, 118, 337, 353, 365, 370, 373–75, 377
orders General MacArthur, 243
Organisation for Economic Co-operation and Development, 429–30
Organization for Economic Co-operation and Development, 320, 427
Origin and Evolution of Double Entry Bookkeeping, 430
Oswald, 86

**P**

papacy, 24, 28–29, 32, 35, 38, 40, 42, 78, 80
paper bills, 92, 98–99, 170, 398
paper emissions, 111
paper IOU, 394
paper money, 44, 48, 50, 57, 91–92, 103, 108–11, 119, 124–26, 169–70, 196–97, 209
Paper negates payment, 61
Paris, 17, 30, 33, 79, 104–5, 115, 133, 139, 180, 185–87, 191, 210, 222, 317
Paris Peace Conference, 186, 189
Parliament, 36, 73, 79, 85, 96–98, 119, 122–24, 128, 167, 224–25
parties
Patton, George, 296
payments, suspended specie, 168
payments problem, massive balance of, 3, 90
payment union, 352
peace accord, 87
Peels Bill, 97
Pendergast, Tom, 299
pepper, black, 5
Peter, chair of, 40
Petroleum exporting countries, 373
Philadelphia, 129, 143, 152
Philosophie Naturalis Principia Mathematica, 74
philosophy, 3, 79, 84, 106–7, 112, 114–15, 120, 129, 193, 235,

237–40, 242, 255, 257, 295,
  303, 329, 332, 334–35, 341,
  367–68, 381
Picasso, 160
plague, 19, 33–34, 68, 79, 82
plague England, 73
Poincaré, 222–23
Poincaré France, 223
Poland, 176–77
policies
policy China, 188
Pope Leo, 304
popes, 28, 35, 305
Popes Urban II, 32
population, global, 385
population gap widens, 286
Portugal, 78
Post Civil War America, 175
Post Jackson, 158–59
post Napoleonic era, 105
Postwar Germany, 310–11, 325, 357
postwar investment, 361
Post World War II, 347, 353
Post WWI, 254
Potsdam, 296, 304–5, 313
Potsdam Conference, 306–7, 333
Potsdam meeting, 297
pound, 5, 14, 93, 184, 220, 241,
  333, 339
pound sterling, 99, 108, 184–85, 219
power
powerful American Senator
  Sherman, 105

Presidency, Jefferson, 134
Presidency, Madison, 137
President, Anglophile, 220
President Cleveland, 200
Presidential contender, 105
Presidential inauguration, 429
President Jackson, 148
President Madison, 144
presidents, 114, 117–18, 144, 151, 167,
  199, 255, 270, 295, 340, 395
President Tyler, 161
President Wilson, 218
President Woodrow Wilson signs, 203
price controls, 309–10, 394
Price of currency, 45, 217
printing IOU, 173–74
Prisoner of war labor, 313
Proclamation of Empire, 181
producers, 61, 152, 220, 261, 268,
  343, 383, 397
Progressive Era, 238
Progressivism, 238
property, church, 32
prophet Muhammad, 25
Protestant, 178, 184
Prussia, 102, 104, 176–82, 190,
  206, 210, 312, 353
Prussia mobilizes, 179
Prussian and Russian armies, 87
Prussian dominance, 181
Prussian influence, 312
Prussian king, 181
Prussian leadership, 104, 184

Prussian mentality, 183
Prussian militarist tendencies, 104
Prussian military, 180
Prussian power, 182
Prussians, 81, 104, 175, 178–79, 181, 315
Prussian terms, 180
Prussian territory, 177
Prussian war machine, 179
purchase silver, 235

## Q
Quebec, 82
Queen Elizabeth I, 110

## R
Rachel, 142
rate of return, 53, 344–46, 414
Rate of return, 54, 345
rate of return, real, 344, 346–48, 369–70, 418
rates
Reagan, 127, 274, 356, 359, 367–70, 372
Reagan, Ronald, 118, 168, 353, 362, 366–67
Reagan plan, 369
Reagan's policies, 370
real estate appraisal, 406
Real interest rates, 369
real rate, 346–48, 369–70, 418
recoinage, 67–68, 70–71, 77, 261
recoinage effort, 76

Reconstruction Finance Corporation, 239, 258
redemption value, 60
Regeneration of return, 349
Reich Bank, 182–83, 211
Reichsmark, 183–85, 187, 190, 217, 311, 324
Reichsmark, backed, 184
Reichsmarks, 185, 217, 311, 324–27, 349
relativism, 37
reminting, 66–67
Rentenmark, 217, 327
reparation payments, 222, 275, 319
reparations, 210, 214, 222, 294, 306, 313–14, 352
Reparations Commission, 212, 217
reparations payments, 244
expected, 213
reparations revenue, 222
repay, 43, 46–47, 49, 58, 60, 207, 218, 262, 360, 380, 402, 413
replacing Henry Harrison, 138
Republic, new, 129, 131, 143
Republican Party, 116–17, 242, 248
Republicans, 115, 130, 133–34, 237, 249, 267
Republicans, Jefferson, 149
reserve currencies, 20, 263, 285, 331, 339, 342, 355, 378, 386
Resolution Trust Corporation (RTC), 362

Resumption of cash payments, 97, 103
Resumption of convertibility, 93
return
Revenue Act, 266–67
Revenue Act raising taxes, 239
Revolutionary America, 107
Revolutionary America and Americans, 107
Revolutionary break, 318
Revolutionary War, 86
Rhineland, 211
Rhineland cities, 30
Ricardo, 237
Roaring Twenties, 221, 231
Robber Barons, 150
Rockefeller, John D., 207
Roman coinage, 13
Roman currency, 19
Roman Empire, 19, 112
Roman law, 28
Romans, 2, 6, 13–14, 16, 19–20, 22, 25, 31, 59, 65, 72, 111, 394, 415
Rome, 2, 5–6, 9, 13–16, 18–22, 24–25, 42, 52, 59, 63, 65, 72, 78, 90, 101–2, 112, 175–76, 279, 281, 343, 360, 395
Rome's coinage, 15
Roosevelt, 209, 245, 249, 251–54, 256, 258, 260–61, 264–67, 270–73, 278–79, 283, 294–99, 304–5, 307, 430
Roosevelt, Eleanor, 295, 301
Roosevelt, Elliot A., 430

Roosevelt, Franklin, 78, 160, 245, 247, 252, 279, 298, 333
Roosevelt, Franklin D., 229, 240, 246, 294, 430
Roosevelt, Teddy, 193, 206, 238
Roosevelt, Theodore, 118
Roosevelt administration, 282
Roosevelt devaluation, 261
Roosevelt elected and inaugurated, 252
Roosevelt embracing government, 258
Roosevelt Era, 246
Roosevelt forbade, 261
Rooseveltian pride, 271
Roosevelt inaugurated, 255
Roosevelt inauguration, 255
Roosevelt money, 270
Roosevelt policies, 266, 299
Roosevelt promises of final recovery, 277
Roosevelt's death, 299
Roosevelt's policies, 275, 299
Roosevelt's programs, 264
Roosevelt's reign, 271
Rosenberg, 257
Rough Rider personality, 206
Rough Rider Roosevelt, 209
Royal Mint, 428
RTC (Resolution Trust Corporation), 362
Ruhr, 212, 314
Russia, 26, 29, 81, 87, 90, 105, 161, 176–77, 181, 186, 190–91, 237, 251, 283, 294, 296–97, 301,

*517*

305–7, 313–15, 321–23,
  359–60, 366, 369–70
Russia and Eastern Europe, 356
Russia defaulting, 369
Russia military, 369
Russian communist jugular, 368
Russian domination, 299, 339
Russian Empire, 322
Russian expansionist czar, 329
Russian foreign minister, 297
Russian gulag, 358
Russian people, 312, 315
Russian Revolution, 286, 335
Russians, 257, 294–96, 305–6,
  311–13, 319, 322–24, 327, 330,
  357–58, 360, 366
Russian ships, 301
Russian tyrant, 286
Russian winter, cold, 90
Russian zone, 308, 328
Russian zone of occupation, 306
Russia of agreements, 300
Russia tyrannical communism, 255

## S

Sales comparison approach, 407
Salvation of Germany, 310
Santayana, George, 363
Sardis, 6
savings, accumulated, 56–57, 213, 406
Scandinavia, 27–28, 105, 217
Scandinavia and Eastern Europe, 27
Scandinavian economies, 26

Scandinavian merchants, 26
scarcity gold, 41
Scarcity of currency, 143
Schmidt, 369
Schuman, Robert, 427–28
SDR account, 386
SDR balances, 357
SDR quota, 385
SDRs (special drawing rights), 284,
  356, 385–86, 427–28
secession, threatened, 141
Second Bank, 118, 135, 138, 144, 147,
  150, 153–54, 164–65, 204, 227
Second Bank president, 147
Second World War, 64, 194, 224,
  229, 236, 240, 264–65, 280, 295,
  297, 303–4, 333, 344, 354, 380,
  402, 415
Secretary of Commerce, 237
Secretary of Treasury, 224
Securities and Exchange
  Commission, 259, 265
Security Council, 305
Senator John Sherman, 18
Servicemen's Readjustment
  Act, 316
Seville, 77–78
Seward, William H., 167
Shakespeare, 363, 390, 430
Sherman Anti-Trust Act, 374
ships, global economic, 255
Shortage of currency, 45
Shortage of money, 201

Silk Road, 5
Silk Road to China, 6
silver, 2, 8–9, 13–16, 18, 20, 23, 26, 29, 41–47, 49–50, 52, 59, 63, 68–69, 75–78, 91, 101, 103–5, 107, 109–10, 155–56, 159–60, 183, 187–88, 191–92, 195–96, 198, 200–201, 206–7, 211, 235–36, 268, 343, 351, 378, 394, 396, 411, 413, 415
Silver Act, 236
Silver Certificate, 50
silver mines, 2, 14, 119
silver ore, 78
silver price fluctuations, 69
Silver Purchase Act, 235
silver ratio, 76, 78
silver trade, 26
Sir Isaac Newton, 74, 429
sixteenth century, 24, 37, 40, 42, 78, 394
slavery, 4, 114, 117, 124, 141, 145, 249, 270
slaves, 2, 14, 24, 29, 41, 59, 72, 112, 118, 130, 141, 174, 421
slowdown, 79, 84, 157, 166, 302
Smith, 237–38, 252, 416
Smoot-Hawley, 277
Smoot Hawley legislation, 239
Smoot-Hawley legislation raising tariffs, 245
Snyder, 303, 332–33
Snyder, John, 332

Snyder, John W., 332
Snyder, Treasury John W., 318
Social Democrat Party, 358
Social Democrats, 335, 357–59, 366, 370
Social Democrats in Germany, 360
socialism, 90, 192, 205, 229, 260, 312, 329, 332, 334–35, 368
socialist agenda, 332
Socialist philosophy and American democratic principles, 359
socialists, 199, 242, 245, 257, 305, 309, 312, 335, 358, 368, 394
Social Security, 265, 354
Social Security Act, 265
South American Republics, 362
Southern delegates, 129
Southern treasury, 398
South Korea, 308
sovereign debt, foreign, 240
sovereign debt doubles, 222
Soviet espionage, 282
Soviet military, 360
Soviet participation, 339
Soviets, 308, 311–12, 339
Soviet Union, 295–96, 302, 306, 308, 334, 357, 359, 362
Soviet Union and Eastern Europe, 362
Spain, 24, 28–30, 34, 52, 76, 78, 105, 107, 123, 188–89, 191, 350, 380
Spanish milled dollar, 112
Spanish silver, 79

Special Drawing Rights. *See* SDRs
specie circular, 156–57, 159
species, 55, 90, 110, 119, 124, 126,
　143, 149–50, 155, 159–66, 168,
　170, 196, 382, 388–89,
　400–401, 417
spices, world's, 5
Spice trade, 5
Staff George C. Marshall, 298
Stalin, 237, 251, 257, 286, 295–99,
　304–5, 307–8, 311–12, 315–16,
　323, 328–29, 332, 334–35, 357
Stalin's goals, 308
Stalin's policy, 321
Stalin's strategy of world domination, 307
Stamp Act, 109, 119–20
Stanton, Edwin M., 167
star, yellow, 51
starvation, 3, 19, 22–23, 36, 80, 161,
　180, 189, 193, 195, 208, 213,
　216, 222, 229, 235, 237, 245,
　281, 302, 313, 319
State Cordell Hull, 277, 301
State Dean Acheson, 318
state debt, paying, 132
State Department, 305
states
State Senator, 245
Statute of Jewry, 51
Statute of Merchants, 52
sterling, 184–85, 214–16, 225–26,
　228–31, 276, 285, 292, 320, 327,
　331–32, 335, 339, 352, 377, 385

sterling bills, 100, 214
sterling exchange rate, 228, 285, 292
stock market bubble, 218
stock market crash, 231, 241, 254, 264
Strong, 216, 218–21, 224, 226–27,
　230–31, 239
Strong, Ben, 209, 213, 216, 218, 220,
　224, 226, 229, 231, 233, 254,
　266, 350, 377
Strong's death, 233
Strong's policies, 219, 241
succeed Jefferson, 134, 143
support Hamilton, 129
support Hitler, 304
Swiss, 359–60
Swiss and German bankers, 369
Swiss citizen, 323
syllogism, 401
Symbols of wealth, 415
system

**T**

Taiwan, 308
Taiwan and Singapore in Asia and
　Germany, 308
Tammany Hall, 253
tariff arrangements, special, 72
tariff revenue, 141
TARP, 325
taxes
Tennessee Valley Authority, 265
term circulation, 338
Thatcher, Margaret, 100

Theodosius, 19, 273
Third Central Bank, 150
Third Reich, 306
Third-world defaults, 417
Tocqueville, 151
Toryism, 108
Tours, 24
Tower of London, 51
Tower of London and Windsor, 69
trade
trade deficit, 275
trade disparity, 288
trade imbalances, 127, 215, 284, 341, 357, 386
trade policies, beggar thy neighbor, 357
trade routes, 5–6
trade surplus, 288
treasuries, empty, 91
Treasury Department, 291, 333
Treasury Department, 322
Treasury holdings of gold, 200
Treasury notes, 161, 169, 200
Treasury Ogden Mills, 242–43
Treasury securities, 96, 203, 317
Treasury Snyder, 302
Treaty, Jay, 133
Treaty of Ghent, 140
Treaty of Rome signals, 352
Truman, 294–301, 303–5, 307–9, 314, 319, 323, 329, 332
Truman, Harry, 118, 298, 304, 318
Truman's agenda, 316
Truman's attitude, 297

Truman's fears, 300
Truman's focus, 330
Truman's job, 295
Truman's mind, 300
Truman's principle, 300
Truman tradition, 118
Truman White House, 302
Turkey, 319

**U**

Ultimate destruction of debt, 400
Uncle Joe, 305
underestimated Truman, 329, 332
unemployment
unemployment rate, 199, 229, 243, 266, 339
unemployment relief, 239
United States, 18, 20, 45, 57–58, 64, 68–69, 71–72, 84, 86, 89, 94, 97, 100, 103, 105, 111, 116, 118, 125, 127, 130, 133–36, 138, 143–44, 146–51, 155–58, 160, 169–71, 173, 175, 178, 183–84, 186–88, 191–94, 202, 205–6, 209–11, 213–16, 218, 220, 223–27, 229–32, 234–37, 247, 252, 254–56, 261–62, 271–77, 279–83, 285–86, 288–91, 293, 302–3, 305, 308–9, 312–13, 315–16, 319–20, 322, 331, 333, 336, 341, 346–56, 358–61, 366–67, 369–72, 374–76, 378, 380–83, 386, 395–97, 399, 402–3, 408, 417–19, 427

United States and Britain, 229, 272, 352
United States and Canada, 319, 321
United States and Great Britain, 282–83, 308
United States of America, 105, 379, 411
United States Treasury, 197, 312
Universality of order, 387
US policy in Germany, 313
US Supreme Court, 374

**V**
value, dollar's, 350, 366, 378
value of money, 43, 103
Value, value, value—always value, 392
Van Buren, 157, 161
Vanderbilts, 246
venerable John Lord Maynard Keynes, 237
Venice, 5
Vergennes, 86–87
Versailles, 79, 84, 86, 214, 234, 313
Versailles Agreement, 319
Versailles Treaty plans, 275
Vice president, 157, 254, 257, 299
Vice President Van Buren, 154
Vichy France, 331
Vienna balance of power, 181
Vietnam, 356
Vietnam War, 366
Vikings, invading, 27
Virginia, 85, 106, 111, 113, 120–22, 138, 141, 143, 429–30
Virginians, 143–44

Vladimir Lenin, 190
Volcker, 366, 373
Volcker, Paul, 362, 366, 369

**W**
Wagner Act, 265
Wallace, Henry, 254, 257, 299
Wall Street, 132, 146, 150, 197, 204, 209, 218, 230–31, 318
wampum, 106
Ware Group, 282
War Germany, 211, 307, 324
War mobilization, 332
Warm Springs, 294
Washington, state banks, 168
Washington, George, 50
Washington bureaucrat, 151
Washington lobbyists, 373
Washington's cabinet, 115, 127
weak leader Napoleon III, 180
wealth, 2–6, 17, 19, 21, 23, 25–32, 37, 40, 42, 44–45, 49–51, 53–56, 58, 68, 72, 76, 78, 83–84, 88, 103, 105–7, 112, 118, 128, 131, 143, 145, 152, 167, 172, 185, 188–91, 205–6, 219, 230, 246, 259, 289–90, 292, 308, 317, 326, 334–36, 346, 350, 354, 361, 374, 385–86, 396, 399–400, 409–12, 415–16, 418, 420–21
wealth gap, 46, 402
wealth taxes, 328
wealthy family, 248

wealthy father, 253
Webster, Daniel, 150–51
wed Jacqueline Kennedy, 317
Weimar Republic, 395, 398
West and Austria Hungary, 181
Western Allies and Russia, 314
Western and Central European Empire, 25
western border, 182
Western Empire, 102
Western Hemisphere, 112, 206
Western Pacific, 206
Western world, 48, 175, 187, 195, 210, 382–83
West Germany, 309, 320
West Indies, 76, 130
Westminster College in Fulton, 307
Whigs, 117, 161
White, 282, 284–86, 291–94, 312
White, Dexter, 284
White Plan, 285–86, 289, 291, 293–94
White regimen, 293
White's background, 286
White's Plan, 286, 293
Whittaker Chambers, 282
wife Eleanor, 248–49
Wildcat Banking, 157
Wilhelm, 181
William I, 69, 102
William Jennings Bryan, 18, 105, 108, 199
Wilson, 186, 430
Wilson, Woodrow, 185

Wilson Administration, 209
workers, unskilled Chinese, 269
Works Projects Administration, 265
World Bank, 281, 283, 285, 292, 294, 317
World Bank and International Monetary Fund, 298
world population, growing, 401
world trade, 41, 53, 62, 77, 127, 187, 220, 245, 289
World Trade Organization, 376
World War, 39, 58, 181, 189, 192, 209, 228, 242, 254, 280, 292, 298, 326, 335, 383
WPA, 265

## Y

Yalta, 296, 300, 306, 315–16
Yalta and Potsdam Agreements, 311
Yalta Conference, 305
Yankee Doodle, 367
Yankee Doodle Dandy, 139
year OPEC, 362
Years War, 81, 84, 91
yen, 340, 361, 385
Yom Kippur War, 374
Yorktown, 85, 139
Yuan, 304
Yuan value, 275

## Z

zone

Made in the USA
Lexington, KY
27 March 2016